de Gruyter Studies in Organization 2

Wilson: Political Management

de Gruyter Studies in Organization

An international series by internationally known authors presenting current fields of research in organization.

Organizing and organizations are substantial pre-requisites for the viability and future developments of society. Their study and comprehension are indispensable to the quality of human life. Therefore, the series aims to:

- offer to the specialist work material in form of the most important and current problems, methods and results;
- give interested readers access to different subject areas;
- provide aids for decisions on contemporary problems and stimulate ideas.

The series will include monographs collections of contributed papers, and handbooks.

H. T. Wilson

Political Management

Redefining the Public Sphere

Walter de Gruyter · Berlin · New York 1985

H. T. Wilson
Professor of Public Policy and Law at York University Toronto, Ontario.

For Lyle

Library of Congress Cataloging in Publication Data

Wilson, H. T.
  Political management.

  (De Gruyter studies in organization ; 3)
  Bibliography: p.
  Includes index.
  1. Representative government and representation.
  2. Political participation.   3. Legitimacy of governments.
  I. Title.   II. Series.
  JF1051.W55   1984   320.2   84-17608
  ISBN 3-11-009902-0

CIP-Kurztitelaufnahme der Deutschen Bibliothek

Wilson, Hall T.:
Political management : redefining the public
sphere / H. T. Wilson. – Berlin ; New York :
de Gruyter, 1984.
  (De Gruyter studies in organization ; 2)
  ISBN 3-11-009902-0
NE: GT

Preface

This book began as an effort to write an essay on the possibility and desirability of a practical science of politics. This essay eventually became chapter seven. Thereafter, I decided to try to bring together some additional themes which I had worked on relatively independently of one another. I now began to realize the reason why I was carrying on researches in areas and disciplines which seemed so diverse. The unifying element was the gap between political reality and political possibility, and the poor use that was being made of that resource for which politics and government exists and from which it acquires its legitimation – the people.

Aiding and abetting this gap, oddly enough, was political science itself, with its apparently unbridgeable divide separating political thought on the one hand from political and governmental institutions on the other. As an established part of the academic division of labour, American political science had made a decision to dissolve its close relation to politics and government as early as World War I. This was the only way it could acquire the status of a profession and a value-free science. The final stage to date of this apolitical line of development came with the rise of behaviouralism. This event was important because it now became clear that the apolitical nature of behavioural political science was largely a result of the impact of the social sciences, particularly sociology.

It is no exaggeration to call sociology the science of Society, because its mission is to extend and complete Society by assisting in the normalization of its division of labour. In pursuit of this, it must co-opt and absorb citizenship by reformulating its active orientation so that it now appears to constitute one among many passively ascribed role options available to everyone who works, consumes and spectates in advanced industrial societies. Citizenship as active display *must* be pacified in order to avoid the circumstance in which people can temporarily rise above Society through the experience of politics and the political. This would make it possible for them to see that Society is really only one culturally and historically specific *form* of collective life rather than a synonym for it.

The main theme is the urgent need for political management and the unsatisfactory, even dangerous, consequences of allowing Society, with its *organizational* approach to collective problem-solving, an undisputed mandate. To this end, I have tried to locate the origin of the problem in the work of Aristotle, responding as he was to the demise of the Greek city-state and the rise of imperium. Aristotle knew that a dynamic equipoise was needed between politics as active citizenly display and political institutions, but could not, for understandable reasons, put the *polis* behind him. His proposed political science sought to reconcile these concerns by combining theoretical analysis with the rigorous comparative study of political institutions and practices.

Political Management seeks to justify a renewed interest in the public sphere on the part of agents and members alike. It argues that our legal and representative institutions were *never* intended to carry the present load on them. The quality of public policies and deliberative processes bears all too eloquent testimony to this fact. Agents are first and foremost members, and do not lose this status as a result of becoming elected, appointed or scheduled officials in government. Furthermore, agents cannot automatically be presumed to be superior citizens just because they monopolize positions in the governmental and political system. Citizenship as active display builds upon the passive and ascribed status of citizen but is certainly not synonymous with it. Similarly, agents may or may not be better citizens than (other) members.

Today we are seeing the full-scale emergence of new public spaces alongside those places in the societal division of labour where the formally established processes, structures and mechanisms of representative government and politics are to be found. Examples would include the work place, neighbourhood and local affairs, single issue concerns of publics, whether organized or spontaneous, the disciplines of political science and the social sciences, and the university and higher education generally. While these new spaces are no substitute for established processes and mechanisms, and must not be allowed to supplant them, they do point to possible spaces for political display that deserve serious study, particularly in light of the increasing role of the mass media, polling, and direct democratic techniques.

Few things emerge more clearly from the analysis offered here than the fact that we have expected for too much from societal and organizational techniques as devices for dealing with political problems in non-political ways. The organizational principle in practice is the leading edge of the apolitical, or even anti-political, bias of *Society* as a culturally and historically specific *form* of collective life that wants its members to believe it is the best, or only, one available. This explains Society's preference for a notion of citizenship which views it as a passively ascribed status, and one among many passively ascribed role options, rather than the kind of active display which allows people to rise above it, however temporarily, and see it for what it really is.

A final point relates to the supremacy of process just cited. The superiority of political activity, including not only display but participation, reflection, and deliberation by the people, is not something that can ever be adequately demonstrated so long as we remain tied to a frame of reference in which we simply acknowledge that it is, after all, the moral or ethical thing to do and then go on and do just the opposite. Ethics and morals reference *membership,* and it is often precisely these concerns that allow reality to exist at such substantial variance with some "ideal." Politics, through its various modes of political activity, must be defended on the objective ground of the superiority of the *outcomes* as well as by reference to the ethical norm of process for its own sake.

Downsview and Richmond Hill,
Ontario, August 1984   H. T. Wilson

Acknowledgments

I am grateful to the Faculty of Administrative Studies of York University for the opportunity to pursue and complete these researches with the assistance of an adjusted teaching load and the use of Faculty facilities. It is difficult to express my gratitude to McLaughlin College, for it has provided me with an environment thoroughly conducive to scholarly work for many years. Not only have I been able to make use of a spacious and pleasant office in the College, but I have been blessed since joining it with excellent secretarial assistance. I particularly want to thank Mrs. Donna Armborst for her willingness to type this manuscript for more hours than I would care to remember. Thanks also go to Mrs. Kirsten Semple and Mrs. Sally Marshall for assisting her in this endeavour, often on an "overload" basis. Graduate students, both professional and academic, have been members of numberless captive audiences that I have employed while working through these ideas, and I am very appreciative of their patience and interest. Naturally, I embrace without hesitation full responsibility for all the ideas and views put forward in *Political Management*.

Contents

What first undermines and then kills political communities is loss of power and final impotence; and power cannot be stored up and kept in reserve for emergencies, like the instruments of violence, but exists only in its actualization. When power is not actualized, it passes away, and history is full of examples that the greatest material riches cannot compensate for this loss. Power is actualized only where word and deed have not parted company, where words are not empty and deeds not brutal, where words are not used to veil intentions but to disclose realities, and deeds are not used to violate and destroy but to establish relations and create new realities.

Hannah Arendt, The Human Condition. Chicago: 1958, p. 200.

We need a revolution in democratic consciousness if we are to avoid being caught up ourselves in the backwash of the revolutions in the rest of the world. We need to give up the myth of maximization. We need to imagine soberly whether competitive, maximizing behaviour is any longer rational for us, in any ethical or expedient sense, or whether the very high level of material productivity that we now command can be made to subserve the original liberal-democratic vision.

C. B. Macpherson, Democratic Theory. London: 1973, p. 184.

Political science is suffering from a difficulty that originates in its very nature as a science of man in historical existence. For man does not wait for science to have his life explained to him, and when the theorist approaches social reality he finds the field pre-empted by what may be called the self-interpretation of society. Human society is not merely a fact, or an event, in the external world to be studied by an observer like a natural phenomenon.

Eric Voegelin, The New Science of Politics. Chicago: 1952, p. 27.

We seem to have reached the end of our confrontation of reason and its claim of a right to plan human societies. Every aspect of this claim seems subject to the most severe criticism. All of us cannot help feeling the danger that underlies the attempts of certain of our fellow men to set forth rational plans for the design of human systems. We seem to have no rational basis for accepting our leaders or their experts.

C. West Churchman, Challenge to Reason. New York: 1968, p. 79.

Leaving things to the Government, like leaving them to Providence, is synonymous with caring nothing about them, accepting their results, when disagreeable, as visitations of Nature. With the exception, therefore, of a few studious men who take an intellectual interest in speculation for its own sake, the intelligence and sentiments of a whole people are given up to the material interests, and, when these are provided for, to the amusement and ornamentation of private life.

John Stuart Mill, Representative Government. New York: 1953, p. 205.

Chapter 1
What is Political Management?

Political management is an attempt to merge representative and democratic processes with effective government in the public interest. It assumes the priority of politics over economics, and refuses to equate politics with the state and government. It believes that mechanisms of articulation between citizens, publics, and leaders can and should be improved, and that it is useful in pursuit of this objective to reconceptualize the idea of care for "public things" as the problem of political management. Management is understood to be an approach to problems soluble only provisionally, and only by citizens and publics *along with* their politically elected representatives and those in appointed or tenured positions of public trust. Reciprocity is thus both an ideal and a goal of political management. There are no "final solutions" in the public sphere, nor should we wish there to be. Process is often its own justification in democratic politics, even if we have to pretend otherwise when we attempt to formulate, carry out and evaluate public policies.

Too much emphasis has been placed on the difficulty of reconciling public opinion and consensus with "rational" decision-making for this writer. I am going to argue that this view equates rationality with expert knowledge and advice to leaders and governors and all too often *stands in the way* of intelligent public policy formulation, implementation and evaluation. Contrary to prevailing notions, it is rarely a question of maintaining a delicate equipoise in these matters lest the democratic moment lead us astray from rational decisions. Indeed there is something seriously wrong with mechanisms of representation, participation and access when such a view can be accepted without cavil by citizens and publics no less than by those who allegedly represent them. I am convinced that present devices for distending the activities of citizens and publics from the activities of states and governments *accentuate* an already embarassing disparity between public policy-making on the one hand and public understanding and support on the other.

Political management points to the very existence of citizens and publics as grounds for mobilizing their needs, interests, and capabilities in pursuit of *intelligent* public policies. The problem of consensus is false inasmuch as it presupposes that the possibility of sensible public policies is the prerogative of states and governments. Only the latter, it is argued, can bring together the relevant expertise with an eye to rational decisions. This fragments politics and reason by setting them up as two tasks which are presumed to be at the very least difficult to reconcile, if not thoroughly antithetical to one another. What is reasonable to the experts and to those whom they advise is presumed to pose a problem for public officials in representative democracies operating under the rule of law. The solution for this problem – consensus management – takes for granted the essential rationality of "top down" policy-making by officials and experts and the essential irrationality of "bottom up" interest and support by citizens and publics. It also assumes that any equipoise realized between the two, however temporary, necessitates legerdemain of one sort or another.

All of this has serious consequences for the theory and practice of *representation*. Instead of being understood as a dynamic attempt to deal constructively with the contrasting imperatives of leadership and participation, the theory of representation is seen as a major vehicle for *unhinging* leadership from the *constraints* of public participation. The major means for achieving this goal in parliamentary systems has been the political party and the doctrine of "responsible government." In fact, governments and leaders are increasingly responsible for the sorry state of public knowledge and understanding, aided and abetted, it must be said, by commercial and/or political constraints and the sensationalist nature of mass media. Public enlightenment and understanding is not some spurious after-effect to be governmentally engineered if it is to be taken account of at all. Public policies will quite simply be *less intelligent* in the absence of the dialectic that representation alone can mediate between participation and leadership.

This does not mean that citizens and publics no longer need their elected representatives, and those appointed and tenured officials who collectively help carry out the functions of government by dint of the expert knowledge and skills they possess. It does mean that citizens and publics are no less necessary as an *ongoing part* of policy formulation, implementation, and evaluation than their leaders, governors and officials. The reason for this is very pragmatic and straightforward, not moralistic in the least. In the absence of this component public policies will simply be less intelligent, sensitive and relevant than they would be otherwise. Citizens and publics are not being "included in" in order to meet the needs of good consensus management here. On the contrary. Public officials desperately *need* citizen inputs on a continuing basis, as the present state of public policy in the advanced societies readily indicates. No public policy can be rational from the standpoint of democratic values if it is based upon the dichotomy between governmental decisions and public support save by sheer accident.

It is senseless to insist that we endorse and thereafter seek to implement a conception of reason that is hardly even appropriate any longer to the operation of business enterprises and technical processes. Yet this is precisely why reason and unreason have been bifurcated in the present unseemly way by publics and citizens no less than by their leaders and governors. What would be reasonable would be any set of activities in the public sphere that sought to redress the present imbalance between governmental initiatives and public participation in the interest of intelligent, sensitive and relevant public policy. That this will require a far more open circulation of individuals between citizen and representative roles must be clear. Yet this is not to say that only in a representative capacity can individuals have an impact on public policy making. Indeed, this assumption is precisely what accounts for the narrow circulation of elites "representing" only the best organized interests and occupations in our society at present. Movement back and forth between citizen and representative roles is essential because of the need for common sense intelligence in the public sphere. That this would have the likely effect of making the distinction between the roles and functions themselves less rigid is to be both expected and welcomed.[1]

Only through *destructuring* routes of access and influence can publics and their representatives render both participation and leadership more responsible and sensible. Political management thus endorses the metaphor of management and managing, but at the same time refuses to see management as an *organizational* function involving top-down decision-making by leaders drawn from a relatively small percentage of the many and varied populations of a complex modern society. Instead it is committed to the proposition that only through its approach to politics can the representative function itself be retrieved from the permanent control of meritocratic status groups and hierarchies in the upper reaches of the public sector. For political management, functions are understood to be rationally allocated precisely to the extent that they are open and fluid, based on as free a circulation back and forth as possible. *Political management is the collective self-care for public things,* coupled with the continuous requirement of determining just what these things are at any given time. Ideally it sees process as primary, the activity itself as problem-solving rather than decision-making, and the system as ultimately experimental, if only because in collective life there are (and can be) no final solutions. Is political management possible? Is it desirable? I would argue that it is becoming *indispensable* with the rise of the public sphere and the increasing role of government in society and in the international economic and political arena. I hope that this alone will be justification enough for the effort that follows.

References

1 See particularly *Anticipatory Democracy: People in the Politics of the Future,*
  edited by Clement Bezold with an introduction by Alvin Toffler (NY: Vintage,
  1978); and Charles Taylor, *The Pattern of Politics* (Toronto: McClelland and
  Stewart, 1970). Compare to Jeffrey Pressman and Aaron Wildavsky, *Implementation* (Berkeley: University of California Press, 1975).

Chapter 2
Politics and Polity: A Delicate Equipoise

I

It is not uncommon to hear individuals interested and knowledgeable in the subject of politics decrying the apolitical or nonpolitical character of the advanced societies while expressing gratitude for the legal and governmental structures which allegedly hold the system together in the absence of politics. Frequently this point of view is tied to the belief that politics and the political is in serious decline from some earlier state or condition of collective life. It is surprising how often this earlier condition is equated with the Athenian city-state or *polis,* more surprising still how rarely the claim of a modern equivalent is disputed, or even questioned. While there is a certain truth to the argument that legal and governmental structures are devices to make up for the *absence* of politics and the political, the present situation cannot but be considered a serious problem for advanced industrial societies. Accordingly my discussion in this chapter will centre on the analysis of this problem, and will offer some provisional solutions aimed at establishing an equipoise between politics and polity salutary for political management.

As for the prior political estate of selected human beings in earlier times, such a claim needs to be taken, at the very least, with a grain of salt. Certain properties of the Athenian polis in the fifth and fourth centuries B. C. clearly constitute ideal arrangements for political participation, but only if the environing social and economic system is set aside. Thus the limitation of political participation to individuals of leisure, and the exclusion of slaves and women from this category, can no longer be taken seriously as a model for political practice. The nature of politics and the political as a speech and deed directed to ethical and moral concerns certainly is appealing, but then this presupposes liberation from the needs and demands of daily life. It is precisely the Greek view of politics as the highest pursuit of which men were uniquely capable which led them to rigidly distinguish it from every day demands and necessities. It was the thoroughgoing belief in a hierarchy of activities based on what was uniquely human as distinct from what men shared with the rest of animate nature which led the Greeks to place politics and the political at the top and the necessities of daily living (food, shelter, sex and reproduction) at the bottom of this hierarchy.[1]

It is precisely the inevitability of institutions, whether conventional or structural in nature, which provides us with the "other side" of politics so defined
and understood. Indeed, this point is clear throughout Plato's political writings, where, if anything, the lion's share of attention goes to institutions.
Plato's concern for political order led him gradually to skepticism about the
possibility of politics as a speech and deed directed to how life *should* be
lived. In the event, he came to favour institutions which, he hoped, would
provide not only order but permanence, at least in the short (or medium)
run. Plato was no doubt reacting to the cataclysmic events of his own time,
most prominently the military defeat of Athens and the execution of Socrates. We know that he maintained a lively interest in advising the ill-fated
rulers of Syracuse, and may even have been the first governmental consultant. It is not without interest that Plato's forays into the sphere of practical
politics were notoriously unsuccessful; some of the reasons for this are important for what follows.

Plato's loss of confidence in politics and the political was closely related to
the lack of stability and permanence given in his perception of speech itself
as a deed at the time he was writing. The last thing that such a conception of
politics could guarantee was permanence. In the face of the realities of
Athenian life, Plato sought a blueprint for the ideal state, one which would
reconcile all the qualities of human being in a properly organized, benefi-
ciently directed, political and social system. In *The Republic,* this ideal state
takes shape as an organization of qualities of the soul formed into a societal
hierarchy, with the wise at the top and the courageous not far below them.
At the base, not surprisingly, were those artisans and craftsmen whose tasks
were most closely tied to every day life needs and demands. What is intrigu-
ing is that this vast majority comprehended not only those engaged in agriculture and the domestic arts, but those adept in the fabrication of useful
(and artistic) objects as well. Justice was understood to constitute the harmonious reconciliation of the temperance and moderation required of artisans and craftsmen, and the wisdom and courage required of the two "guardian" classes.[2]

This static order became more difficult for Plato to endorse as an actualizable possibility following his unsuccessful efforts on behalf of the tyrants at
Syracuse. As a consequence, he moved more and more in the direction of
what he considered to be a best practicable state. This is evident from his
last major treatise on politics in which the state's good health is more obviously the result of guardians who function as lawgivers. *The Laws* is hardly
less a denial of the desirability of the polis than *The Republic,* but does
attempt to compensate for the absence of any concern for law in the earlier
work. Laws are counterposed to personal whims in *The Laws,* a further
development out of the conception of statesmanship found in Plato's middle

political essay *The Statesman.* The statesman, we are told, must function like an artist, a weaver, and a manager. At least two of these three metaphors are related to the mundane functions carried out by artisans and craftsmen in *The Republic,* indicating some sort of acquiescence in the equation of politics with the needs and demands of everyday life.[3]

If *The Statesman* is significant for the categorization of good and bad states that would later form the basis for much of Aristotle's analysis of ideal and real political systems, *The Laws* is notable for constituting its author's effort to construct a "second-best state" which, though far from ideal, is the best practicable hope for real men. It is his equation of the central role of laws with the frailty of human nature that underscores Plato's conception of institutions and laws with the best practicable state. Still, one cannot ignore Plato's claim to have been concerned about generating useful blueprints from the very first. Nevertheless, it is clear from a careful reading just how far circumstances, and his interpretation of circumstances, have taken Plato away from the formal ideal toward the best practicable. Even at this, however, the residual ideal nature of the state depicted in *The Laws* shows itself in the treatise. The "nocturnal council", made up of the ten eldest guardians is, after all, beyond the law, a condition evident from the way Plato sees them acquiring wisdom even in his last political work – by gazing at and contemplating the stars.

The most immediate relevance of Plato's political writings to my interest in political management lies in his near-total commitment to *blueprints.* It is the formal character of Plato's approach which will prove such a significant basis for comparing his work to that of Aristotle. However influenced by experience and actual events Plato could legitimately claim to have been, it is difficult to take issue with the argument that they fell into a subsidiary position relative to Plato's intellectual commitment to an ideal. Plato is the first to distrust politics because of its contingent character and lack of permanence, as noted, but it is imperative that his response to his own distrust be understood as a wholesale endorsement of contemplation over action. For the first time the non-participant, standing above and beyond the fray, is seen to possess a wisdom in matters political not available to those immersed in the mere activity itself, however wealthy and leisured they might be. A pattern of thinking is inaugurated in which the earlier view of speech as a deed is supplanted by a conception of action as fundamentally speechless.[4]

II

It is in the context of this basic shift in thinking about politics that we must encounter Aristotle's contribution. Aristotle begins his work already aware of the need for such a shift in the light of past and present political realities. Aristotle will be almost exclusively concerned with taking account of, then superseding, the Plato of *The Statesman* and *The Laws*. In this task he will be preoccupied with the fact that he is living through the twilight of the city-state system, but will not, as a consequence, react to this reality with formal blueprints for either ideal or best practicable states. To be sure, it is all-too-easy to exaggerate the differences on these matters between Plato and Aristotle, the moreso where each is understood to represent the source of radically divergent concerns, interests and values. Aristotle does not, it turns out, ignore the question of ideal states at all. It is rather the different method of investigation to which his scientific training and animus has committed him that constitutes the basic point of difference between them.[5]

Aristotle comes to an analysis of the problems of politics already committed to a comparative science of politics. Comparative method begins with actual systems, and endeavours to scientifically analyze the strengths and weaknesses of possible alternatives based on extrapolation from the properties of real systems. Thus Aristotle's political works display a consistent and understandable absence of the sort of formalism given in a concern with blueprints and a commitment to design. His is a "systems analysis" that begins with discussion of "pre-political" institutions found in the household like slavery, property, marriage, and children. Only afterward does he turn to an analysis of ideal states in theory and practice. Plato's works figure prominently in the first part of the discussion, while actual states like Sparta, Crete and Carthage are dealt with in the second. There follows a general theory of "political constitutions" (better translated as political bodies or bodies politic), where he discusses citizenship, types and combinations of "pure" systems, their different contributions to "distributive justice", and the theory of kingship.

In the ensuing sections what is most significant is the way Aristotle focusses on his best practicable "mixed system" – polity – as a combination of oligarchy and democracy. In this he disagrees fundamentally with Plato, whose best practicable ideal in *The Laws* was a combination of monarchy and democracy. Aristotle appears to stand with *The Statesman* in viewing monarchy or kingship as so unequivocally a "pure" ideal as to be unavailable in any form or combination to a best practicable system. Note also Aristotle's combination of *oligarchy* and democracy. Plato had delineated three good systems and their perverse forms in *The Statesman*, and while democracy was the third "good" type (after monarchy and aristocracy), oligarchy was a perversion of aristocracy, as were tyranny and chirocracy of monarchy and democracy respectively. Aristotle thus formulates his best practicable state – polity – out of a combination of a "good" system – democracy – and a perverse one – oligarchy. It is this combination which underscores Aristotelian realism, for it points to the best viable state as one which must necessarily reconcile the strengths of one good system with the perversions of another. In the process, it is to be hoped that the effect of the combination will minimize the bad effects of *both*. This is clearly evident in his equation of "best practicable" with the rule of the middle classes.

This only seems contradictory so long as we ignore the fact that pure forms can never be expected to operate at their maximum in combination. Indeed Aristotle might argue that pure forms are not intended to really operate at all, whether in combination or on their own. Thus it is fruitless to begin with relatively unorganized experience, then move directly to formal ideals and blueprints as Plato did. Better to proceed scientifically, comparing various actually-existing states in operation, then seek to extrapolate the most beneficent features and thereafter combine them. Here it is institutions in the form not only of structures and processes but attitudes, values and predispositions as well which become central factors. Whereas Plato compared *two* sets of *formal types* – three good and three perverted – Aristotle insists on a method which attempts to build up real possibilities based on combining the strengths of two types of state where this combination minimizes the bad effects *found in each*.[6]

It is Plato's failure to realize the relative insignificance of the fact that one set of states is alleged to be good and the other bad, when compared to the fact that *both sets* are formal in nature, which makes Aristotle's "scientific" approach to studying and assembling best practicable states so important. Plato's perception of "best practicable" in every case takes the form of compromise, a giving in to the all-too-limited possibilities allegedly discovered in real human beings in the world. Aristotle, by contrast, comes to his types and combinations by extrapolation from actual systems in operation, without assuming that reality must of necessity be judged wanting because it is limited by the presence of the very human beings, and human nature, that one ostensibly ought to be trying to improve and render beneficent in both individual and collective senses. This is not to say that Aristotle's method does not generate types possessing formal properties and characteristics. It is rather the process by which the particular combinations in question are composed that is of importance to any comparison of Plato and Aristotle on these matters.

Even after Plato had acknowledged the importance of the rule of law as a criterion of best practicable states, he continued to contrast such lawfulness to the ideal. Aristotle, on the other hand, sees the general happiness, combined with the possibility of moral and ethical improvement, to depend on such legality as a minimal condition. For Plato legality is an acknowledgment of the *impossibility* of really having an ideal state and form of rule which might secure the general happiness. For Aristotle, it was rather the need to reconcile wealth and numbers in a single system which motivated his emphasis on lawfulness. Thus the combination of oligarchy and democracy will provide for the twin prerequisites of sound political rule – stability and representation. Justice for Aristotle means a delicate equipoise of these two properties achieved through the careful construction, and subsequent monitoring, of a constitutional system – a "body-politic" – as well as a certain measure of equality. This in contrast to Plato, particularly in *The Republic,* where justice is the harmonious operation of a highly, and quite rigidly, stratified system of orders or castes.

It is Aristotle's commitment to reconciling wealth and numbers, in the face of their clearly conflicting demands as bases of political power and influence, which was perhaps most responsible for his lifelong aversion to formal blueprints not based on considered experience and careful comparison. While the mere presence of law is no objective guarantee of a good state, Aristotle did believe that the "constitution" or construction of the body-politic could minimize the likelihood of bad laws. Legality remains a relative guarantee of goodness, promising more than personal power or force can over the long run, but the processes by which laws are made, executed and enforced depend on constitutional properties of the system prior to laws. Most significantly, it is the balance achieved between wealth and numbers, and how this balance is reflected in the activity of citizenship and the representative function, that will play a large part in determining how effective and ethical a body politic's laws will be.

It is therefore not inaccurate to say of Aristotle that he transmuted Plato's ideal forms of rule into *ideals* which real systems should seek to realize through the salutary combination of characteristics discovered by careful comparison of, and extrapolation from, actual political systems. Ideals are the values that are maximized by one type of system, so the combination of two or more types of states indicates that there are different ideals that the best practicable system should seek to harmonize and to maximize. In the case of the proposed combination of oligarchy and democracy, here we are faced with ideals which have been transformed into competing values seeking a hearing in the system. Aristotle saw goodness in such a system, for it is precisely this sort of competition that makes it constructively dynamic and promises a viable polity. Far from sharing Plato's terror of unprogrammed change, Aristotle believes that some process is absolutely essential to the long-life and ethical objectives of the best practicable state.[7]

III

This brief comparison between Plato and Aristotle on the question of ideal and best practicable states does more than remind us of the importance of method as it relates to experience and preferences. It also forces us to address again the issue of political knowledge, and the role of the theorist whose contemplations are assumed (by the theorist) to be a better basis for improving practice than that of the people being governed, wherever we find them and in whatever disposition and station. Without turning away from what might be broadly described as the intellectual task, Aristotle provides an alternative approach to and method of producing knowledge relevant to politics. As a *scientist* he builds up the notion of possibility in the political field as something which must be viewed from the perspective of experience and careful comparison, thus as an actualizable reality that it is *desirable* to actualize both from the standpoint of efficiency and from the standpoint of ethics. Plato's preference for formal blueprints attempted to generate sufficient "system rationality" in the political order to compensate not just for human limitations in general, but for the twin problems of power and participation in particular.

Knowledge is clearly offered in the form of blueprints for the ideal state by Plato as a way of *avoiding* these problems, but it is because Plato initially believed that such an approach could in fact succeed in avoiding the problem that he took this tack. The point is less why he did this in early works like *The Republic* and more his inability to fundamentally alter his point of view in *The Statesman,* but especially *The Laws,* thereafter. Nevertheless the distance travelled is considerable, and it requires us to accept in a general way the distinction between two types of mind often cited as a valid basis for contrasting Plato and Aristotle. Aristotle, as Jaeger has pointed out, lacked the theoretical and contemplative sweep of Plato's mind, but possessed instead the capacity for methodical observation and comparison of existing systems, and the careful utilization of experience.[8] If Plato was the first government consultant, Aristotle was the founder of political science as a mode of inquiry and a discipline. Aristotle's very commitment to what might in general terms be called a scientific approach to the description, analysis and evaluation of states, governments and constitutions compelled him to reconceptualize both the nature of political knowledge and the role it might play in the improvement of the system and the lives of its citizens.

In this endeavour, it was incumbent on Aristotle to deny the supremacy of the theorist and his blueprints in favour of the proximate knowledge realized through the methods of political science. This also implied a different evaluation of citizens and publics, since for Plato the purpose of the blueprint was to circumvent the need for the participation, or even the meaningful representation, of the people. Plato's fear of instability and disorder, while understandable, was no more sensible from the standpoint of his experiences than were the parallel concerns of Aristotle. It is the radically different character of Aristotle's intellectual response to the twilight of the city-state which should be underscored here, for it attempts to take account of the people *as a resource for* rather than an impediment to good government and the ethical life of all citizens, *including rulers*. At the very least, the people constitute a central political reality, and retain this centrality when observed by the political scientist. Political science can only be adequate to its tasks when it acknowledges its datum in all its dimensions, rather than attempting to circumvent it by reference to formal blueprints specifying ideal states.

This perhaps helps explain why Aristotle resisted as fundamentally inapplicable most or all of the dominant metaphors and analogies used by Plato in his political studies. Thus it is analytically unrealistic from the standpoint of any scientific approach which claims to proceed from political phenomena to conceptualize forms of political rule by analogy with the precision found in natural science, mathematics, and medicine. It is somewhat ironic that Aristotle, with his respect for natural science and his resulting commitment to experience, observation and comparative method in the study of politics, should take this sort of issue with Plato. Yet it becomes clear that the basic difference between the two lies in Aristotle's commitment to a scientific study which proceeds from the *phenomena* of politics rather than from an attempt to impose a model of good practice from more precise disciplines on politics from above (or outside) it. Aristotle is scientific by temperament, which suggests a respect for the integrity of the phenomena, and an attempt to generate methods for knowing the humanly political based on an acceptance of it *as a given*.

Plato's approach, in clear contrast, is "scientistic" to the extent that it refuses to see the phenomena of real politics as the essential stuff of political reality, and is inspired far more by the *results* of the disciplines be cites as proper models than by their methods. Aristotle pointed to the science of politics as a discipline whose methods would be determined by *its* materials rather than by formal analogies with disciplines whose methods implicitly or explicitly violated the spirit and sense of these materials. Even though the methods of the natural sciences, mathematics, and medicine may suffice in different ways for the proper performance of *their* respective activities, they cannot function as models in the study of politics whenever adherence to such models requires us to ignore the phenomena of politics. Such a tack leads invariably to an attempt to emulate the methods of the disciplines being employed in a metaphorical way, and therefore favours what Karl Popper has called a "utopian" and holistic approach to complex problems present in the constituent elements of political reality and their interaction. The danger of the theorist with formal blueprints is precisely the appeal his plan may have for any tyrant anxious to improve his hold on a system and convinced that a given blueprint will help him realize it. Aristotle's attitude toward Plato's view of political knowledge in its relation to political practice was no doubt affected significantly by the latter's efforts on behalf of the rulers of Syracuse.

This is not an argument, however, for supplanting a Platonic with an Aristotelian approach. It simply points up some of the clear limitations and possible dangers of Plato's approach when compared to that of Aristotle. In effect, we leave Aristotle's approach where we find it for now, reserving critical analysis for a later point in the book. Political knowledge for Aristotle was not only proximate, but provisional and incomplete. It therefore could achieve its highest and best purposes only in the context of a viable political system rather than constituting an alternative to such a system. Plato's conception of the ideal, and even perhaps the best practicable, state led him to an unambiguous position not only on the nature and role of political knowledge but on political rule itself. In effect, the theorist sees himself either compensating for the limits of human capacity expressed in *both citizenship and rule* with his formal blueprint, or complementing rulers by helping them make sense of it in and through successful applications and interventions.

Aristotle's understanding of politics, even in the context of the best practicable state, appears to take for granted the incompleteness of political knowledge as something intended to complement ongoing practices. In this sense political knowledge must be understood to constitute *part of the political system itself,* not something distinct from it capable of producing and sustaining a reality superior to that available to citizens and rulers alike. Aristotle's understanding of the complementary role of political knowledge provides us with the first example of an *interventionist* approach aimed at improving practice and the ethical life *of citizens and rulers alike.* The essence of this new relationship will be a piecemeal and incremental, rather than a holistic and utopian, approach to knowledge and practice.[9] It will assume that politics is an activity which should constitute man's highest function, but that this activity can only be carried out if a delicate equipoise between politics and polity, process and structure, citizenship and an environing framework is maintained. Care for public things involves all citizens, rulers and thinkers alike. Neither rulers nor thinkers are allowed to set themselves apart from politics, whether because of an unseemly love of power or as a result of construing thought as a form of contemplation divorced from practical activity in the world.

Plato's twin difficulty with the limits of practical knowledge is thus resolved, albeit in a way he would hardly find salutary. Aristotle finds himself unable to accept the possibility of absolute knowledge on the part of *either* an elite of rulers or the theorist as designer of formal blueprints. While it is probably the case that Plato saw the possibility of absolute political knowledge to lie in the *combined* abilities of rulers and theorists working together, it is his obsession with certainty, coupled with the fear of disorder and uncontrolled change, which would have led him to resist the provisional, incremental, and to some extent experimental nature of the dynamic, if delicate, equipoise between politics and polity proposed by Aristotle. Failure to see that rationality and the power to reason are a product of being human led him to construe knowledge in terms of a narrow expertness restricted to the few. Thus one could argue with merit that the case for the people lies not simply in the moral requirement that their opinions be represented, but in the foundational character of commonsense rationality and in the dependence of sound (effective and ethical) political systems on the mutual interdependence between commonsense and expert knowledge.

IV

Aristotle's discovery of political science was important for reasons not directly related to the scope and limits of political knowledge in its relation to practice. Given in the distinction between ethics and politics is the separation of society from government, the good man from the good citizen. Since it is precisely out of this separation that the possibility and sense of representation, as well as the need for it, arises, it will be necessary for me to attend to some of the issues raised by it. Plato had not felt it important to deal with this separation, or even the distinction on which it was founded, because his lifelong commitment to blueprints, and to the role of the theorist, even in later political works like *The Statesman* and *The Laws,* still took the pure ideal as its point of departure. To be sure, the *polis* or city-state, all too often in its Spartan rather than its Athenian variant, constituted his *empirical* reference point, but it was its *idealized* form to which Plato submitted his own experience.

Further, it was raw experience, rather than experience carefully scrutinized, which constituted the basis of Plato's conception of an ideal political space within which rule and governance should occur. It is probably as a consequence of this that Plato failed to attend to the fact that political and military events were rendering the unity of society and government in the idea of the state obsolete. Aristotle's view of the best practicable state, as noted, proceeded from such a radically different approach to and understanding of political knowledge that it seems inappropriate to use this term to refer to the work of both thinkers. Plato remained tied to the city-state in its ideal-ized form, albeit with an acquiescence to the need for laws, while Aristotle reacted at a somewhat later date to the reality of city-states submerged in a larger empire. This empire was the ultimate political force, while cities like Athens, Sparta, Corinth and Thebes became urban aggregations of indivi-duals who had surrendered the power to govern themselves to a larger political space. In effect, they were urban *societies* within a political space that comprehended Greek and non-Greek alike.[10]

This collapse of the state as a *polis* where society and government were indistinguishable carried with it important consequences for the idea and practice of citizenship. Denied the power to function as citizens in the way in which successful men of wealth, leisure and knowledge had become used to, these men were thrown back on the reality of the fact that theirs was no longer a *political* space at all. Aristotle, while certainly aware that the fact of Macedonian domination would have serious implications for the assumption that the city-state was a relevant political space, was no less tied to it in certain respects than Plato. Thus, it continued to constitute *the* relevant possible and desirable space, but did so only to the extent that Aristotle found the Macedonian imperium politically unsatisfying or incomplete on its own. For Aristotle the realities of empire had not so much negated the possibilities of politics and polity as it had provided a challenge to the inge-nuity of the political scientist, now faced with the fragmentation of political rule and societal life in what was once *the* unified reality – the city-state.

Aristotle's method was bound to generate an acknowledgement of the fact of plurality, and it is very important so see in his continued focus on the city-state as the relevant political space neither nostalgia nor a lack of real-ism. It was rather Aristotle's inability to conceive of an alternate *political* space in his writings, not his view that the city-state could be revived, which explains his continued reference to the polis. In effect, Aristotle, though aware in large measure that its time as a *political* space had passed, contin-ued to treat the city-state as *the collective or societal space* within which to conceptualize new ideas about citizenship, law, and representation. My own assessment of Aristotle's position on this matter would be that many of his ideas would not be compatible with the city-state even as a collective or societal, rather than a political, space. I also think Aristotle was aware of this, and believe that in those areas where his ideas seemed to be designed for this societal space as the relevant reality he had good reasons for his views, ones that are still important today.

Aristotle, after all, was dealing not only with political and military realities, but with moral and ethical considerations which clearly guided him in his concern for the relation between the good man and the good citizen. Op-

position to Plato's ideal state could not be explained strictly on the grounds
that the method was incorrect or inappropriate, or even that it generated
states or forms of political rule which did not "work". Aristotle's method of
research and comparison, and his *formal* (not normative) taxonomy of best
practicable political arrangements, was based upon a conception of practice
and the practical which had a clear ethical component. This in contrast to
our understanding, which is far closer to what Aristotle termed productive
knowledge in his tripartite distinction between practical, theoretical and
productive forms.[11] Improving political *practice* meant improving the
chances of citizens participating in the ethical life inasmuch as this could be
equated with political life. Where this became impossible, either because of
the restriction of the franchise to a select few, or as a consequence of the
impossibility of self-governance, it was imperative that political science put
its theoretical findings in the service of practical needs and concerns.

Thus the city-state posed some difficulties for Aristotle even when it was
functioning as an effective political space. Indeed, it is his distinction between the practical and productive which makes it very difficult to accept
any view of him which denies the subordination of the efficient and effective
to the practical in his work. Events thus constitute an *opportunity* for Aristotle no less than a danger, but this fact can neither be offered as evidence
that he saw the *polis* as the appropriate political space, nor pointed to in
support of the claim that the failed to disentangle the ethical from the political in his work. Aristotle was too much the political scientist for this to
happen. His method of empirical analysis and comparison, far from denying
the role of ideas and values, saw such theoretical knowledge as desirable
only to the extent that it would allow people to lead ethical lives in and
through the exercise of citizenship. This view was held in full knowledge and
understanding, I believe, of the fact that citizenship and political self-rule
had been irretrievably sundered from one another.

Practical improvement must now take a somewhat different tack, and the
question of the *difference* between the good man and the good citizen was
now effectively intersected and cross-cut by the distinction between rule and
citizenship. In the event, the actual separation of these two functions led
Aristotle to concentrate less on the extreme, yet complementary, categories
of nature and reason, and more on the constructive, albeit realistic, role of
habit and convention in molding the good citizen in and through the proposed system of formal education. Although respect for and obedience to
law is certainly to be included as a property of this curriculum, Aristotle sees
the law more in terms of the deference required to the new form of imperial
political rule than as a vehicle for the constructive exercise of citizenship. It
should be transparently clear from his reliance on the educational system
(like Plato) to inculcate good habits and attitudes (unlike Plato) that Aris-

totle has already reconceptualized citizenship in less active and individualistic terms as a social, thus an ethical, duty and necessity.

To the extent that citizenship is thus conceived and understood, habits will prove more important than commonsense reason, exercised in the form of individual display, in its exercise. Law becomes the major vehicle for framing and organizing the new "body-politic" as a *society* whose deliberations should, but may not, be tied to the exercise of political rule. The confusion in Aristotle's work on the matter of political space is therefore complemented still further by the simultaneous need for good citizens in the absence of any real possibility for the constructive exercise and display of citizenship as it had been understood and practiced earlier. It is in this sense that one may with justification argue that the key to understanding the real significance of the distinction between society and government does in fact lie in the way it points up the collapse of collective self-rule in and through the exercise of citizenship in the polis. The unity of society and government in the concept of the city-state, however idealized, presupposed a particular sort of *activity* on the part of the few who were full-fledged citizens.[12]

It is almost as if Aristotle is trying to compensate for the collapse of this unity and intensity by redefining citizenship and the citizen in a more passive way which allows the function to be "available" to a larger mass of persons. These persons are clearly denied, and may indeed be incapable of exercising, collective self-rule through the aegis of a political practice that takes its point of departure in ethics and the ethical life. What makes it both possible and necessary to reconceptualize the nature of citizenship is precisely the inability of even a small portion of the inhabitants of a city to any longer really function as citizens in the face of the separation of citizenship from political rule. In effect, by addressing the notion of citizenship as a property of habits encouraged by and inculcated through a system of formal education, Aristotle was acquiescing in citizenship as an ethical *rather than a political* function. This would account for the separation between the good man and the good citizen in his work, and would render sensible his discussion of citizenship as a property of the system produced through the authoritative medium of formal education. The good citizen disappears in favour of the good man as a passive "pseudo-citizen", one who is a product of a non-deliberative process devoted to *socializing,* literally *producing,* individuals whose habits regarding law and citizenship reflect the nature and objectives of the emerging apolitical form of collective life.

V

What has just been said bears importantly on the elemental tension between politics and polity. In order to maintain a delicate equipoise between stability and representation, Aristotle found it necessary to favour the development of institutions whose effect would be to create and sustain a realistic "body-politic" containing oligarchic and democratic properties. To this end he sponsored a notion of the "best practicable" state whose legal and educational institutions were devoted to providing both "rules of the game" and training in basic values and understandings so necessary to the perpetuation of the system. The result, admittedly, was to water down and render essentially passive the activity of citizenship by redefining it as a set of functions or roles. Still, it would appear unavoidable in the light of the eclipse of the polis and the inherent restrictions on active citizenship which it offered even when operating at its best. In any case such a compromise is always to be preferred to the fate of the tyrant's subjects, or rather, his victims.

It was Aristotle's view of political knowledge, and his commitment to a scientific approach as I have described it, which required him to address political phenomena as the incontestable basis for constructing political systems. Thus his method, with its basis in political reality and its preoccupation with comparision and extrapolation, led him to a radically different understanding of the relationship between thinkers, rulers and citizens from that developed by Plato. Knowledge was provisional and systems themselves were experimental. Nevertheless law und education were needed to guarantee system stability, particularly in the face of the redefinition of citizenship necessitated by the decline of the polis with its loss of self rule. Law and formal education are to constitute the central institutions, along with religion, for inculcating ethics and morality, now understood as a *societal,* rather than a political, set of values, beliefs and attitudes. This means that citizenship loses its political character, at least in the sense understood by citizens of the polis. It becomes *social* in response to the fate of the post-imperial polis as a societal, but no longer a political, reality.

The separation of, and resulting distinction between, the good man and the good citizen thus carries with it a particular understanding of what it means to extend the responsibility for the care of public things to a wider body of individuals. To be sure, Aristotle was to some extent responding to the realities of his own time. The fact that the polis was now little more than a city meant that it constituted a social rather than a political space in the new imperium. This fact became even more obvious under the subsequent domination of Rome. What is important about this distinction between the social and political is the role that a society without political self-rule would have to give to morality and ethics in sustaining it. In effect society becomes the custodian of the morality of a body of individuals whose very lack of the possibility of political self-rule necessitates their *production* as passive non-citizens, socialized in the correct values and appropriate behaviours, but denied the privilege of the experience of collective self governance.

That such a denial could be construed as *incapacity*, particularly when coupled with the passivity encouraged by law and formal education, is hardly surprising. In the event, the consequences for subsequent efforts at representation must be clear. Representation, particularly under the influence of modern Christian conceptions of proper rule, departed radically from Aristotelian understandings on a number of key points. Foremost among these was the Christian view of wealth as property, and its consequences for the care of public things. Christianity required the owner of property to exercise a stewardship over his possessions. Instead of wealth liberating its possessor from the cares and burdens of daily life so that he could actively participate in public affairs, its understanding as property required him to abjure the public realm in favour of the responsibilities of stewardship. Representation is favoured as a device which will allow the owner to be a steward at the same time that he delegates the good management of his interests to representatives.[13]

The deeper key to an understanding of the breakdown of possibilities for representation beyond what has already been mentioned is provided by the phenomenon of speech itself. Once speech loses its elemental aspect as a deed central to the ongoing mangement of the public realm, it becomes only superficially possible to "re-present" at all.[14] If commonsense and theoretical symbols separate and thereafter become alien to one another, the capacity for representation becomes nothing more than delegation of the sort outlined. Who, or what, after all is being represented, and what do we really mean by the term? Voegelin very wisely suggests that the concept cannot but be understood as an idea intended to realize the activity of speaking and discussing politically. The polis dies not as a result of capture and the decimation of its leaders and citizens but rather as a consequence of "the disintegration of the beliefs that make it an acting unit in history." Thus it is conceivable, as history shows us, for a society to remain a physical and organic reality but lose its political character altogether.

Plato's approach to the relationship between knowledge and practice had provided a blueprint for disaster when not functioning as legitimation for tyranny. As a formal programme put into practice in a thoroughly anti- (or a) political manner, it showed little interest in the problems of representation to which Voegelin addresses himself. Plato was virtually uninterested in the way that the mass of citizens (or subjects) understood their social and political reality, and opted for a relationship between the theorist and the ruler which rendered the issue largely moot. Aristotle's method forced him to take commonsense understandings of these matters seriously, with the result that his political science began and ended with extant political realities as the basic stuff from which to fashion recommendations for improvement. Though aware of what would need to happen if *any* notion of citizenship was to be salvaged in the shadow of imperial power, Aristotle steadfastly refused to ignore citizenship as an exercise in representation, even in the absence of any hope for the revival of the polis.

Rulers are citizens too, and it is imperative that this fact be kept firmly at the forefront when they function as governors. No less than citizens is theirs a set of functions and roles rather than an activity which overcomes the distinction between citizen and ruler. Representation in the presence of such recognition can promise remembrance, coupled with recovery of the knowledge of a set of symbols common to citizens and rulers alike. Aristotle's political science sought to reconcile the theorist's need for his own symbols with an appreciation of political phenomena. This would provide a basis for the joint exercise of citizenship, inasmuch as it was possible under the circumstances, by all citizens in the society, including rulers. It is the privilege of experience that Aristotle is after even as he attempts to maintain a constructive dynamism between oligarchic and democratic elements. Stability and representation cannot be reconciled in a way conducive to any sort of ethical life aimed at the general happiness simply in and through institutional arrangements, however.

The secret of a truly balanced polity is what brings institutions legally formed and educationally valued to life in the form of experience – common symbols between citizens and their governors which make representation possible, even likely, *because conceivable*. What makes representation conceivable is the capacity of citizens and their governors to see themselves in each other, indeed to be and share in the reality of this relationship as the essence of politics in the Aristotelian polity. This polity is no ideal, either because it is formal in character or has been imposed from above (or outside) by a theorist and/or a ruler. It is possible, and not simply because it has been conceived on the basis of an extrapolation from raw experience. What makes it possible is the fact that its composite parts have been seen to work in the best interests of citizens, whose happiness lies in the preservation of the ethical life in the face of the impossibility, perhaps even the undesirability, of the restricted norm of citizenship available in the polis.

The political scientist's expectation that discrete parts from different actually existing systems can be brought together to constitute a harmonious whole which realizes happiness in and through the ethical life is neither a vague hope nor an iron-clad guarantee. Aristotelian understandings of the nature and role of political knowledge, and humility regarding the way it is acquired and utilized, underscores the very different view of political reality and its improvement understood by him when compared to Plato. There is no vainglory in such an enterprise, either for the theorist or for the ruler, because there is no notion operative which is determined to make what is supposed to be right or correct "work", even in the face of the reluctance or refusal of the central political phenomena itself – the citizenry – to endorse the blueprint or behave in accordance with it. To say of such a collective that it is experimental is only to draw attention once again to the evanescent character of the properly political, whose permanence is to be found solely in the likelihood of its permanent re-emergence.[15]

Institutions are not then superfluous, or even optional, to the preservation of politics given polity, for the continuance of the best practicable state requires laws and formal education. But it is representation which remains at the core of this reality; it is its lifeblood. Common symbols and the capacity to mutually comprehend possibility in reality and reality in possibility make it possible for citizenship to operate as an enterprise involving *mutual* understanding. None of this is to gainsay the requirements under law of responsibility of governors to those they govern. It does suggest the limits of any notion of representation premised on concrete "interests" as a basis for the operation of a polity, however. Roles and functions may be a problem for the purist who wishes to restore some form of polis, whether in old or new guise. But it must be construed as an *opportunity* to improve the capacity and commitment to represent by the political scientist, sensitive to the need to transcend the rigid, fixed, and virtually permanent distinction between agents and members seemingly ordained by such realities, and committed to realizing the best practicable state.

References

1 This is discussed by Hannah Arendt, in *The Human Condition* (Chicago: University of Chicago Press, 1958) in particular, but also in *Between Past and Future* (NY: Viking Press, 1961). While I rely heavily on much of her reasoning in these two books, particularly her view of theorizing *vis a vis* politics understood as an *activity,* and the comparison of Plato and Aristotle which emerges from it, I differ somewhat from her in her attitude to Marx and in her refusal to bring theoretical and institutional analysis together. In effect, I believe that a restrained optimism is possible for practitioners of political science only if they honour what is in effect an Aristotelian programme. This is discussed in this and subsequent chapters.
2 Plato, *The Republic,* translated with an introduction by H. D. P. Lee Harmondsworth: Penguin, 1955); *Plato's Republic,* translated with an introduction by F. M. Cornford (London: Routledge and Kegan Paul, 1941). For an excellent commentary, J. S. Findlay, *The Discipline of the Cave* (London: Allen & Unwin, 1966); and Ernest Barker, *Greek Political Theory* (London: Methuen, 1960).

3 Plato, *The Laws,* translated with an introduction by Trevor J. Saunders (Harmondsworth: Penguin 1970); Plato, *The Statesman (Politicus)* translated by J. B. Skemp and edited and introduced by Martin Ostwald (NY: Liberal Arts Press, 1957). Also J. B. Skemp, *Plato's Statesman* (New Haven: Yale University Press, 1952).

4 See Arendt, "What is Authority?," Chapter 3 in *Between Past and Future,* pp. 91–141. Also, Arendt, *The Human Condition,* pp. 175–247.

5 Aristotle, *Politics,* translated with an introduction, notes and appendices by Ernest Barker (London: Oxford University Press, 1946); Barker , *The Political Thought of Plato and Aristotle* (London: Oxford University Press, 1906).

6 Barker, *The Political Thought of Plato and Aristotle* (passim); Aristotle, *Politics,* 1252–1253 a, 38, 1279 a 17–1297 a 7. All citations are from *The Politics of Aristotle,* 4 Volumes, translated by W. L. Newman (Oxford: Clarendon Press, 1902).

7 Aristotle, Politics, 1325 b 14 – 1329 a 39.

8 Werner Jaeger, *Aristotle: Fundamentals of the History of His Development,* translated by Richard Robinson (Oxford: Clarendon Press, 1934).

9 See my *The American Ideology* (London: Routledge, 1977) pp. 101–121, 236–241, and 248–253, where I argue that Popper's piecemeal approach is appropriate to practice, and even to its disciplined observation, so long as it is not the *sole* basis for theoretical development. In a sense this affirms Aristotle's twin concerns with both theoretical understanding and comparative institutional analysis. Also see generally James B. Rule, *Insight and Social Betterment* (NY: Oxford University Press, 1978).

10 Victor Ehrenburg, *The Greek State* (Oxford: Basil Blackwell & Mott, 1960); Alvin Gouldner, *Enter Plato: Classical Greece and the Origins of Social Theory* (NY: Basic Books, 1965).

11 Aristotle, *Prior and Posterior Analytics,* introduction, text and commentary by W. D. Ross (Oxford: Blackwell, 1949), 89 b 9; *Politics* 1261 a 31. See generally W. D. Ross, *Aristotle: A Complete Exposition of his Works & Thought* (NY: Meridian, 1959).

12 Aristotle, *Politics* 1325 b 14 – 1326 b 24. Compare to *Ibid,* 1328 b 33 – 1329 a 39. Also see Sheldon Wolin, *Politics and Vision* (Boston: Little, Brown, 1960) Chapters 1 and 2; and particularly Francis D. Wormuth, "Aristotle on Law", in *Essays in Political Theory,* edited by Milton Konvitz and Arthur Murphy (Ithaca: Cornell University Press, 1948), pp. 45–61.

13 See Arendt, *The Human Condition,* pp. 58–72, for a discussion of the development of this tension into the modern period.

14 Eric Voegelin, *The New Science of Politics* (Chicago: University of Chicago Press, 1952), pp. 27–106. Compare to Hanna Pitkin, *The Concept of Representation* (Berkeley: University of California Press, 1967).

15 Arendt, *The Human Condition,* pp. 188–207.

Chapter 3
Society, Law, and Legitimation

I

Emphasis in the foregoing on the Greek experience is less a consequence of any nostalgia for the polis and more because the work of Plato, but particularly Aristotle, constitutes something of an epitome in the general area of political theory. That so many political scientists and political theorists date the development of thought and research in their discipline from the work of one or both of these seminal thinkers must count for something. While the idea that the two dominant traditions of political thought emanate from Plato and Aristotle respectively may appear to give too little credit to the contribution of the modern, as opposed to the ancient, teaching, modern political theory is not without its debts to either or both of these men. This is particularly the case at the very highest level, where consideration of the ancient teaching almost always constituted at least the point of departure for modern political thinking, where it did not provide the basic categories of analysis to accept, contend against, or oppose with new conceptions more appropriate to the modern historical form of intellectual self understanding.

The decision to move almost directly to the analysis of modern institutions not only short circuits the contributions of political theorists from the period after the death of Aristotle down to the mid-seventeenth century, but ignores the emergence and central significance of key political *institutions* of actually existent states as well. In the first case, the weak response is to say that my own "historical" tendencies in the analysis of institutions do not dispose me to a view of thought which focusses on chronological development and serial sequencing. It is rarely the case that such an analysis of thought in political philosophy is able to capture the real inspiration and indebtedness of one thinker to others on whom he appears to depend, rarer still where the imposition of such sequencing makes any sense of the way thinkers discontinuously, and often wholly unexpectedly, have an impact on the development of real political institutions. Historical process is difficult enough to sustain without such considerations coming to notice. Taking account of the actual influences on the emergence of political institutions over time, when these influences may readily include the ideas of political theorists, makes the entire matter even more tenuous, although by this account certainly not impossible.

As for the short-circuiting of any discussion of institutional developments as they took shape in actual states, it must be admitted that the Roman political experience in particular perhaps could have been the subject of extended remarks. Here I have mainly the Roman Republic and the early Empire (to 130 A.D.) in mind, and it is perhaps significant to note that some of modernity's most "practical" political thinkers and theorists were well-schooled in the political accomplishments of Rome. Foremost among these accomplishments were the specific institutional arrangements for representing key constituent elements in the emergent body politic, even from the earliest time of the Republic. The Roman Republic was broken up from the start into plebeians and patricians, and this fundamental class distinction was reflected in political arrangements in a way which would have done justice to Aristotle's method, if not his specific suggestions for the Greek city state. This, of course, is as it should have been, a combination of oligarchy and democracy, albeit one which ceded a vast initiative to the organizing and consolidating powers of the first great families.

Perhaps even more important, at least for my purposes in this chapter, is the emergence and development of legal and juridical institutions and processes. Without in the least downgrading the importance of representative institutions, which will in any case be discussed in a subsequent chapter, it is fair so say that Rome left its unique mark more in this area of institutional polity than in any other. A second reason for this may well be the way in which the earlier-noted role of thought and theory intersected and related to these institutions over time. For example, the well-known contributions of post-Platonic and Aristotelian thought were clearly in evidence in the institutionally significant distinctions between civil law, the law of nations, and natural law. Indeed the institutional fount of the Empire itself rested on the fact that the law of nations derived its flexibility in application from a conception of natural law first enunciated by the late Hellenistic School of Stoicisim under the leadership of Panaetius. Civil law was similarly legitimated by reference to natural law, and it is well to notice in passing that Roman institutional usage of such a notion was the first of many from that day down to this.

While it is easy to denigrate Roman political thinking on grounds of its being too "practical" in our sense of the term rather than Aristotle's, its indebtedness to the Greeks on the matter of seminal ideas and legitimations is beyond cavil. From pedagogues and tutors all the way up to the leading thinkers and theorists of the period that ends with the reign of Julius Caesar, the Hellenic and Hellenistic source is always evident. Indeed this fact rarely if ever bothered the Romans, who believed themselves as early as the middle Republic to be a chosen people destined to govern the known world. Ideas and thoughts in pursuit of this goal were often tentatively accepted and evaluated, but their role in providing legitimation for Roman military and political action cannot be denied. In particular, the Romans were the first to combine reference to nature and to law as a device for sanctioning and justifying their imperial designs. Nevertheless, one cannot ignore the subsequent flexibility already mentioned which application of the idea of natural law permitted, for whatever reasons, in the form of the law of nations – *ius gentium*.

A major consideration to bear in mind is the fact that the Romans were the first of many subsequent civilizations, empires and states to make protracted use of Greek thought, at least as an intellectual sounding board and source of legitimation if not in more sustained and "practical" ways. Thus my interest in Roman institutional developments, while not solely directed to an analysis of the application of Hellenic and Hellenistic concepts and concerns, must count for less relative to the present need for political management in advanced industrial societies precisely because of my preoccupation with the Aristotelian *method* rather than one instance of its utilization in general terms. At the same time, reference to this method as an epitome is necessarily inspired by some of the very concerns of a practical nature which motivated Roman political practice, at least those institutional developments and preferences directed more concertedly to citizenship and the ethical health of the state than to power and the growth of empire.[1]

II

It will do us no harm to begin this section with a working definition of what I mean by the term institution. An institution is a pattern of behaviour which is socially approved, or at least socially tolerated. Its essence, as Max Weber pointed out, is the *expectation* that individuals will not only behave in ways that fall within the range of tolerated or approved behaviour, but will continue to behave in a more specific sense as they have done in the past. Thus it takes the form of an enactment of individually held values, beliefs and understandings in *societal and historical* space. This may happen in the context of what we call "structures" or processes, or may simply be understood as collective action pure and simple. Neither the distinction between ideas and material structures, nor that between the individual and the collective, thus have any real bearing here. Just because we think of institutions as "structures" in no way alters the fact that we do not really have in mind only the buildings or physical space where they are discovered. Indeed, such an understanding of what an institution is tells us much about the rationalistic preoccupations of our civilization as a culture.[2]

What I mean by this is apparent from the all-too-prevalent tendency nowadays to use terms like institution and organization interchangeably in advanced industrial societies. Here the non-rational and spontaneous properties of institutions and institutionalization are downplayed or ignored altogether in favour of an emphasis on contrivance and conscious design. My point is not to take an opposite tack, and declare organizations to be entities standing apart and distinct from Western institutions. On the contrary. It is precisely our rationalistic bias which must be seen to function as a continuing source of legitimation for the activities of key institutions of modern Western civilization like capitalism, science, science-based technology, the rule of law and organizational bureaucracy. Thus the tendency to equate institution and organization is not so much incorrect as incomplete. Our commitment to reason as instrumental, ends/means rationality constitutes one of the most elemental values, beliefs and attitudes functioning at the core of our collective conscience as a culture. It is therefore precisely *the way* we claim to be a civilization rather than a culture that underscores what is clearly one of our most central cultural properties.

Belief in the contrived and consciously designed character of our institutions is a part of this cultural essence, to be sure. I am certain that this resistance to the spontaneous, collective, perhaps even unconscious nature of our basic institutions is closely tied to our deification of the individual and individualism. At the same time, this enterprise has not taken place in the absence of some awareness of the significant changes in our understanding of the individual that have accompanied the emergence of advanced industrial societies out of their less formally organized, less concentrated an centralized forerunners. In effect, individualism at present is in the process of being "socialized", by which I mean rendered functional rather than dysfunctional for Society. Durkheim had promised that such a resolution would "normalize" the bad features of the division of labour at the time he wrote, and it was within the context of organized work, labour, and occupational contexts that this socialization of individualism and consequent normalization of the division of labour was supposed to take place. The individual is not just a social category from the standpoint of analysis in the new understanding; he is also seen to be the product of socialization processes which literally "produce" him in real time and space as a "person".[3]

These organizations, though providing the proximate context, do not, however, partake of the institutional fabric of advanced industrial societies because they possess physical, or even formal, structure, but rather because they *reflect* certain fundamental values, beliefs and understandings found in (and produced by) the environing society. The basic values of Society as a culturally and historically specific form of collective life, in turn, include respect: for the idea of the domination and transformation of nature secured through the aegis of instrumental rationality; for the individual as the (alleged) vehicle of this domination and transformation; and for complex formal organizations whose bureaucratic structures are treated as *subsystems* of Society. Society *means* a form of collective life which phantasizes itself as a rational social organization, a bureaucratic structure writ large. Of course such a phantasy, and even the attempts to realize it in practice, tells us far more about ourselves as cultural beings who *value* reason and rationality than it does about such values, and the structures which allegedly give material expression to them, as embodiments of unchallengeable objective properties.

Durkheim argued that Society, so understood, constituted a secular god. In this conviction he followed a long line of French social and political thinkers going back at least to Rousseau. Rousseau believed that the society as a political community needed a civil religion. From the perspective of my analysis, this entire tradition of thought, from Rousseau down to Durkheim, with the work of Bonald, Maistre, St. Simon and Comte in between, constitutes an all-too-successful acquiescence in the *impossibility* of politics. I would submit that it is in the nature of a "political" theory which had already accepted as given the priority of polity as an institional form *precluding politics* that the theory of Society first took shape.[4] Thus the problem of the urban commune or city as a social space which has lost the capacity for politics can only be addressed when a new equipoise on the order of the Aristotelian conception is advanced. This requires the introduction of concepts which have been at the centre of political thought ever since, like sovereignty, contract or compact, legitimacy and legitimation, and representation.[5] These relatively modern concerns complement those arising out of the relationship between nature, convention and law already mentioned.

To say that the social, or rather the societal, has effectively pre-empted the political is to point to the development of institutions which in the modern setting announce the rise of the nation-state, centralized rule and increased reference in this context to law and legality, coupled with urbanization, secularization, capitalism and (capitalist) industrialization. Bringing the problem of universal recognition down to earth so that it became a problem of human collective life rather than one of life after death is perhaps the most auspicious event of modernity. To be sure, only when human effort could be reconciled with the saving of one's soul, as for example in the working out in practice of the "protestant ethic" of worldly asceticism, could the conditions be right for the thoroughgoing secularization of Christian religious practice in the protestant countries. It was really only after such worldly asceticism had made it possible for these practices to be endowed with religious significance that the unfettered emergence of modern secular

institutions could take place. Both capitalism and national state centralization favoured urbanization and increased reference to law and legality as a
basis for civil and individual action.[6]

The combined effect of these practices, jointly undergirded by the new
secular spirit, contributed to the exponential growth of Society as a culturally and historically specific form of collective life. One point which should
not be downplayed in this regard arises out of the often ignored distinction
between capitalism and industrialization. In its earliest phases, capitalism
was almost exclusively a set of *commercial* practices directed to the *exchange*
of goods produced by craft and guild methods. Such practices had not yet
received the sort of legitimation that the Reformation's emphasis on
"worldly asceticism" would later provide. Nonetheless there was recognition at the level of everyday life that the new middle class bearers of these
skills and interests were increasingly important members of the late medieval estates and urban cities. Capitalism would remain solely a set of commercial practices long after its values had secured theological, and subsequently secular, legitimation – from approximately 1550 to the discovery of
steam power in the late 18th century by James Watt. It was only with the
steam engine that it became possible for capitalism to secure control of the
activities whereby the products it exchanged were produced or fabricated.
The result – industrialization – constituted capitalism's first "take-over",
and began the long decline of the arts and crafts in so many areas of collective life.

Industrialization's major effect on capitalism was to make it possible for an
economy to develop on a societal, and even a trans-societal, scale. No longer
would capitalism be restricted to exchange in a market between relatively
small sellers owning and managing individual enterprises of a commercial or
retail nature. While worldly asceticism had necessitated hard work in the
world, coupled with the savings and investment which followed from strict
religious prohibitions against conspicuous consumption, the resulting enterprises had always been restricted by the absence of efficient technologies of
production. With the discovery of steam power, the technological means
were suddenly at hand for generating an economy or economic system based
on capitalism as a set of values and attitudes *and a world-view*. The subsequent rise of Society as I have defined it must be seen in large part as a
response to this "generalization" of capitalist values outward, from the market and the individual entrepreneur and family enterprise to key secular
institutions in the civil and public sphere. Indeed it is only by reference to
the institutions already cited that one can make a case for the idea of a
capitalist *society* at all.[7]

Central to this development was the emergence of *the firm*, buttressed by
the rise of political economy (and subsequently economics) as its major

source of intellectual legitimation. Political economy did for industrial capitalism what Calvinism had done for earlier forms of commercial capitalism. The firm was by and large a concept, or rather a normative concept,
whose formal properties as discussed by political economy rarely saw the
light of day in the actual practices of the mills, mines and factories of early
industrial capitalism. The idea of the firm thus set a standard of sorts, but
mainly functioned as a source whereby capitalist practices, often of the very
worst sort, were provided with ongoing and effective legitimation. More
important, however, was the dialectic set in motion by the emerging interdependence, in spite of severe conflicts and antagonisms, between the market and the firm. Firms resulted from the decision to temporarily withdraw
from the market, capitalize one's assets, and generate a new basis whereby
the required tasks could be carried out *internally* in pursuit of economic
objectives – employment rather than exchange on the market.

Re-entry into the market on these new terms gave firms an advantage that
entrepreneurs who were less organized for production as an *internal* activity
could rarely compete against. Imitation became the sincerest form of flat-
tery in the new equation, as the major competitive units in given markets
became firms rather than entrepreneurs on their own. At the same time the
conditions were now in place for the development of Society – a form of
collective life whose formally meritocratic character belied the new stratification order standing behind it. This order consists of organizational hierarchies cross-cut by occupational structures whose purpose is nothing less
than Durkheim's dream come true – a "normal" division of labour based on
occupational individualism. In the event, success in a career has displaced
both capital accumulation and the attainment of political power as available
objectives. Particularly in the first instance, though to a lesser extent in the
second as well, the working out of "worldly asceticism" has been thoroughly
transformed, if not obliterated altogether. Success in a career is the occupational embodiment of Durkheim's conception of positive, rather than
negative, individualism.

Such individualism was intended to overcome the tension in the negative
conception between the individual and Society by making its achievement
coincident with maximal performance of an occupational function. This
implied a far greater "availability" than the earlier bourgeois notion, with its
bias toward capital accumulation, could possibly allow. In effect, its attainment increasingly came to be understood not as a result of effort energy in
the face of traditional restraints and resistance, but rather as an indicator of
successful socialization, particularly through the aegis of formal schooling
and education. It is imperative that this socialization agenda be properly
comprehended in its scope and objectives, which is to say that we cannot
ignore the role of schooling and the early educational process in favour of an

exclusive emphasis on work, labour, and occupational settings. While it is admittedly difficult to reach a decision on these matters based upon cause and effect reasoning, the function of formal education, either in positively promoting, or in not resisting, the values of occupational individualism must be counted as a central component in the emergence of Society as a culturally and historically specific form of collective life.

III

The rise of Society with the emergence of an ascending dialectic between the market and the firm necessitated a governmental response of one form or another. To be sure, many Western countries have relied on public sector institutions almost from the start of the modern economic order. Here mercantile institutions and residues of institutions continue to play a peripheral, and occasionally even a prominent, part in particular national economies. While these elements are a part of the total landscape of the public/private nexus in advanced industrial societies, they have been more than complemented in the large majority of cases by the subsequent development of structures intended as a response to the economic and social effects of capitalism, industrialization, and consequent urbanization and secularization. The extension of legal rationality from the professions, courts and legislatures to wide-ranging law enforcement and regulatory bodies is one instance of such a response. The emergence of client-centred public bureaucracies alongside the merit civil service to administer the welfare and service needs of vast populations, particularly in urban areas, is another.

What all of this implies for the citizen is a vast increase in the governmental and legal-judicial presence. Thus what would nominally be called the public sector has expanded beyond even what was required to administer an industrial society no longer able to afford the luxury of laissez-faire as an ideology of effective legitimation. Too much has become known about the dependence of economic interests themselves on viable governmental and legal-judicial protections and preferences for such thinking to be taken seriously as a rendition of reality, historical or contemporary. At the same time the social costs, euphemistically termed "side effects" by the die-hards, have necessitated an extension of bureaucratic employment far beyond what was initially believed necessary in the interests of non-partisan administration and effective law enforcement and regulation. With the growth of public sector responses aimed at the welfare and service needs of citizens, it has become possible for the first time to see government as an "us" rather than solely as a "them". A major indication of this, for better or worse, is the newfound realization that the public sector must be seen to produce, rather than simply consume, GNP.

To the argument that business and the private sector could do the job better, the response has been: "Then why doesn't business do it?" The short answer is that people require a vast number of services performed for them by governments which business simply does not want to perform. Indeed the private sector is one of the major consistent *beneficiaries* of such services, and is all-too-ready and willing to allow their provision by public authority with little (if any) thought of an alternative in mind. Business and industrial effectiveness and efficiency, it turns out, *presupposes* the performance of a taken-for-granted set of mundane functions and services, just as laissez-faire in an earlier time presupposed an environing framework guaranteeing protection of property and contract rights, backed up by traditions, conventions and habits of civility and deference. Society may have made individualism more "available" in the way indicated, but this did not have the effect of rendering collective life more potentially or actively political. On the contrary. It rather provided a new occupational basis for avoiding politics and the political in ways already sanctioned by the practice (if not the theory) of representation.

Citizens typically rationalize their passivity and deference by noting that they are, after all, consulted, and that this is really all one needs in the presence of reliable and time-tested institutions of polity like representation and the rule of law. In point of fact, the rule of law, though clearly a precondition for most of the practices we normally designate as political, is not itself "political" in the sense intended here at all. This will be clarified further on when I discuss forms of legitimacy and legitimation in the modern state and their significance for citizenship and governance. What might be properly considered political are those very institutions of polity which, I have argued, historically emerged in recognition of the *impossibility* of politics following upon the demise of the *polis*. Citizenship, as Aristotle readily realized, must in consequence become a *societal* function or role whose model and motive force is the good man rather than the good citizen. The sort of availibility realized in and through positive individualism thus restates the original effort to make politics itself available through the aegis of institutions of polity.

The good man becomes the well (or properly) socialized individual no less today than before. Among other things, socialization has come to include the assumption that the scope of state action ought to be at least as great as it is at present. This is underwritten by what Hannah Arendt has called the "socialization" of activities originally carried out in the household. In a society of job-holders, labour and the requirements of the life process displace and render meaningless the original sense of the distinction between

public and private realms. To the extent that the exponential growth in the
public sector participates in and inspires this development, it becomes even
more difficult to associate government with the political rather than the
social. Apart from the role of government as employer, however, is the
pre-eminence of the societal, underscored by the reality of organizational
hierarchies and occupational orders whose differences are often miniscule
when compared to the matters on which they agree.[8]

My point in drawing attention to the presence of a *formally* meritocratic
stratification order in advanced industrial societies is to address the fraudu-
lence of the present ideology of legitimation. I also wish to argue that this
ideology in operation is contributing to a wholesale process of societal *closure,* aided and abetted by occupational individualism with its bias toward
isolated, defamilized men and women whose self-worth is based on occupational status and position in an increasingly atomized order. The support
such a development receives from the wrongheaded notion that moral and
social enlightenment depends on the city as the harbinger of civilization
cannot easily be overstressed in its significance. The confusion of societal
roles and political display is, after all, a central property of the *depoliticized*
city as an urban social space. Why be surprised at the way in which organizationally biased conceptions of function have infiltrated institutions of
polity as they have taken shape under a regimen thoroughly favourable to
urbanity![9]

It is important when drawing attention to problems bearing on roles and
functions not to categorically indict what are in fact very real human constructs necessary for negotiating in all forms of collective life. The point is
rather the rigidity and fixity of roles and functions which arises out of continued allegiance to societal, and therefore essentially organizational, conceptions and understandings. It is precisely the organizational conception of
institution, already mentioned, which makes flexibility and change *more*
precarious because of its overly rationalistic bias. The present meritocratic
order is problematic because it relies on the sort of formalism and formality
virtually guaranteed by organizational conceptions of roles and functions
favouring hierarchical stratification and closure. This formalism and formality is the essence of a societal order which has perverted the substantive
ideals of meritocracy, with its bias toward openness and opportunity, in
favour of *castes* certified by either traditional, or newly ascendant ideological, elites and movements. A striking parallel can be observed to hold
between this development and the earlier perversion of the labour theory of
value under the rigours of capitalist industrialization.

What the societal/organizational conception of functions and roles has to do
with legitimation should be clear from the rather unique world-historical

claims of meritocracy. The argument has always been that here for the first time *objective* criteria of "performance" can be brought to bear on decisions regarding positions in the occupational order. This in place of "traditional" tendencies to make such decisions on the basis of family, class, caste, race, tribe, ethnicity or gender. To the extent that this claim was presumed to hold in appointments to and advancement within the public sector, the argument for a meritocratic civil service appeared beyond criticism. It would displace processes of decision based on "irrelevant" criteria like political partisanship and loyalty, class, family, and education, or traditional practices and preferences. Meritocracy, though originally an argument in support of performance criteria in public sector bureaucratic employment, now constitutes the ideology which is regularly convoked to justify authority in many work, labour and civil contexts in advanced industrial societies.

This is a very difficult argument for the public as citizens to get a handle on, the moreso where one senses that things are amiss but cannot (or dares not) articulate why. Apart from the now conventional, but nonethless important, attack on meritocracy in practice for its middle-class urban cultural bias, there are more subtle aspects and properties in need of careful scrutiny. A major problem with meritocracy in practice has already been alluded to, and it is a difficulty that can be seen to hold for most, if not all, efforts to implement new ideas. It is the *formalization* of meritocracy in organized bureaucratic structures, whether in the public sector or elsewhere, which effectively undercuts the egalitarian promise of the ideal, and turns it into an ideology whose main job is to legitimize the "rights" of job-holders to their positions in perpetuity. To be sure, this problem has been made even more acute by the historic tendency to equate meritorious performance in the civil service with the protection afforded to non-partisan administration by tenure and job security.[10]

It is imperative nevertheless that the phenomenon of rational domination be brought to notice as the major property of meritocracy as an ideology of legitimation. What makes it an ideology, I would argue, is precisely the fact that the values and preferences it claims to honour are no longer reflected in the structures and practices where it is said to be embedded. It legitimizes one form of hierarchial stratification order over others, and does so on grounds which are far more effective today than any argument based on ascribed characteristics can ever be. On the other hand, one is forced to ask who gains and loses, both within and outside of advanced industrial societies, as a result of the operation of this order, buttressed by an ideology proclaiming the advent of rational domination. It turns out that, in addition to the general cultural, class, and urban bias already noted, there are certain process characteristics which demonstrate the *incompleteness* of the meritocratic regimen in practice.

Foremost among these characteristics is the tendency to appoint and promote on the basis of formalized criteria of "objective" merit, coupled with
interviews where "personality" characteristics are significant bases for decision. In between, while occupying given positions, roles, or jobs, the Peter
Principle operates and holds sway. This principle underscores how we have
tended to invert the original ideal of meritocracy, *presuming* competence
because individuals occupy given positions *etc,* rather than requiring them to
demonstrate fitness on a regular basis. Of course, this latter is wildly impractical, as Michael Young pointed out forcefully over twenty years ago. In
addition, it fails to take account of the way individuals build up vested
interests in the occupancy of given positions over time, often in spite of
adversities and discomforts. To the extent that Michels' "iron law of oligarchy" can be seen to hold in all forms of organizational employment, a certain (often considerable) amount of what Merton has termed "goal displace-
ment" cannot help but take place. In the event, the original mandate of
public service is conditioned by and subordinated to perpetuation of and
advancement in one's own career. This suggests the need to try to achieve as
much harmony as possible between a high level of performance and the
occupational's own assessment of self-interest.[11]

Still, the issue is a real one. Meritocracy in practice can only claim superior
standing relative to its predecessors to the extent that it can show real routes
of mobility for those who are deserving, as well as the sort of open society
that would feature such mobility as its centrepiece. This raises the question
of social tinkering to redress imbalances in educational and related kinds of
opportunities, as well as legislating equality *by results* through quotas, affirmative action, and the like. The difficulty with meritocracy in practice
under this regimen is precisely the demand for continuous massive state
action in and through bureaucratic employment which it necessitates. In
addition, it invariably takes shape in a way which benefits the middle classes
almost exclusively, with promises of a "trickle-down" effect at best a sham.
Meritocracy in practice, to the degree it can be made to work in processual
ways which oppose the always-present tendency to structure, organization,
and order, turns out to be a co-optation of government in action by the
middle classes so total as to be beyond even Aristotle's wildest imagination
when he sponsored the "balancing" role they might usefully perform in
mediating opposed interests.[12]

IV

Max Weber was the first social and political thinker to encounter the problem of rational domination as one endemic to the key institutions of modern Western civilization. He saw the development of meritocracy, particularly as it had taken shape in its earlier bureaucratic variant, as the basis for an unavoidable conflict between reason and the process of rationalization and world de-enchantment in industrial societies. Capitalism's capacity to provide continuous formal rationality in the field of specifically economic action by dint of its supercession of feudal and mercantile modes had been largely negated. This had occurred mainly as a consequence of its very *success* in generalizing its values from the market to the firm, and thereafter to the state and to the society and culture as a whole. Weber even argued that this success would compromise fundamentally the formal rationality of both the market and the firm, because such practices could not, after all, be expected to occur in the absence of an objective need for them. Today, states and governments not only provide residual aid and comfort to business and industry, as well as being supportive in traditional ways through property, contract, tax and regulatory legislation. They often engage in economic activity directly on behalf of the so-called private sector by providing access, perquisites, and invaluable information and services like training, growth incentives and investment.

The disjunction between operative ideologies of legitimation and the socio-economic and political reality could hardly be drawn more clearly. One of the more ambiguous aspects of Weber's legacy arises not from the tension between reason and rationalization already noted. Weber had argued that in the industrial societies of his day a new form of legitimacy had entered the picture. Instead of practices and values being legitimated on the basis of traditional or charismatic authority, they now were justified increasingly on legal-rational grounds. Legal-rational authority for Weber constitutes nothing less than the prototype for meritocracy. It is a decidedly more "objective" basis for legitimizing the ascendancy of individuals, groups and classes than either resort to habit and convention on the one hand or the so-called "gift of grace" of the charismatic leader on the other. Indeed, the institutional embodiment of this more objective authority for Weber is modern "rational" bureaucracy, though here it is essential that his ambivalent attitude to bureaucracy as the leading edge of the rationalization process be remembered.

Legal-rational authority is to be discovered in precisely the sorts of objective bases for decision and action which characterize the formal ideal of bureaucratic administration rather than its actual practices. Bureaucracy is therefore rational only in the conditional sense that it favours rationalization when working under formally ideal conditions. At the same time, its *failure* to work at its best drew criticism from Weber the sociologist, who reminded his readers that, *given rationalization,* there is no alternative to bureaucracy except a return to dilettantism in the field of administration. Capitalism's success subverts the practices that made this success possible, and bureaucracy is one of the major upshots of this development in both private and public sectors. Bureaucracy at one and the same time aids and abets rationalization and world de-enchantment while helping to compromise irretrievable capitalism's capacity to engage in formally rational market, firm and accounting and control activities.[13]

From the standpoint of political and administrative institutions, legal-rational authority as a basis for legitimation means many things. First, it presupposes precisely the sort of rationalistic bias which sees institutions in strictly organizational terms, thus as structures more than processes. Second, it provides the groundwork for meritocracy by its understanding of what is meant by law and legality. In the main these terms refer less to judicial courts, particularly those in common law countries, and more to the scope of law broadly defined to mean not only legislation, but its implementation and supplementing by law enforcement, civil service administrative decisions, the rules, regulations and orders of regulatory bodies, the decisions of administrative tribunals, and more recently those clientele agencies which dispense welfare and provide services of one type or another. In all the above cases there is bureaucratic structure, broadly speaking, but also a meritocratic basis of legitimation for office holders, albeit a formal rather than a substantive one.

Even if the third characteristic of legal rational authority as a basis of legitimation – that idea that no one is above the law – were enforceable, it would still presuppose the presence of objective grounds for interpreting the meaning of given statutes, provisions, *etc.* and applying them to specific instances. The fact that this assumption is either publicly accepted, with resulting deference, or treated cynically by citizens, tells us much about the nature of the legal, juridical and administrative seen from the standpoint of the needs of *institutional* polity. When looked at from the perspective of a public need for, and interest in, politics and the political as a dynamic, and truly reciprocal, relationship between all citizens, *including elected representatives, appointees and officials,* law and legality can be seen to threaten politics with the sort of passivity that invariably follows from the legalization and judicialization of the public sphere attendant on the reduction of problems and possibilities to "rights" and "liberties". No viable politics is possible for a people that have abrogated their powers either to non-elected judicial guardians or to the palpable fiction of objective and neutral decisions by public bureaucrats and technocrats.

Legal-rational authority is the hallmark of advanced industrial societies, however compromised in practice this form of legitimation is. Weber, wiser than most of those who followed him, knew that its value was conditional upon the acceptance of certain fundamental assumptions about reason and rationality that he himself remained ambivalent about to the end of his life. He realized that this type of legitimation, while increasingly important, could never be expected to displace traditional and charismatic modes altogether. Though the occasions for charisma might change, its possibility would not, at least for the forseeable future. As for traditional authority, it was the final resting place of legal-rationalism and the "rational domination" which it and meritocracy both endorsed. Civilization shows itself to be a culture which *values* reason and rationality, and sediments conventional notions of what these terms and concepts mean in ongoing processes of socialization. Rationality becomes a "tradition" in advanced industrial societies in more than just a vague sense, a point all too readily manifested in the gap between meritocratic *practice* and the meritocratic principle.[14]

A fourth point in criticism of legal-rational authority as a basis for legitimation would underscore the demonstrably *greater* danger it poses to politics and the political than traditional (but certainly not charismatic) types. I have in mind here the idea that one should respect the office not the person. This is often extended to the view that one *must* respect the office even if one does not respect its incumbent. Admittedly this holds also in the case of traditional authority, though here the basis for the claim is far less persuasive in the contemporary setting than are the "objective" grounds of legal-rationalism. While we might tend to think first of publicly elected officials when trying to fit this claim to reality, it has been extended to comprehend a vast number of bureaucrats, technocrats, officers, officials, and just plain employees in public sector administrative settings where one or another form of meritocracy holds sway, if only as an extension of the pre-eminent form of legitimation accorded to elected officials.

In these latter instances, the reality of employment and job-holding function to pre-empt, and at the same time to encourage, a non or a political attitude or stance. These individuals partake of the protection provided by legal rational authority as an "objective" basis for legitimation, while they inhabit organizations devoted to job security and the career principle. Following a period of probation, a vast number of these persons receive effective tenure, a provision which can just as often serve to subvert as to guarantee meritocratic performance. Hegel's distinction between politics, government and the state, once the subject of mockery in British and American academic circles, becomes empirically credible as a basis for *describing* advanced industrial societies. Respect means deference and implies an objective rational character, but one which is seen to inhere in the total organized structure of job-holding rather than in particular positions on their own. Passivity is enshrined in the idea of respect for the position even in the face of the incompetence, malfeasance, or arbitrary and tyrannical qualities of its incumbent. Instead of legitimacy being conferred residually and as a function of "habits of obedience", as in the case of traditional authority, it is conferred *positively* in the form of respect for the rationality of the bureaucratic structure, the objectivity of its task allocation scheme, and the neutrality rather than capability of its occupants when in role.

MacIver treats legal-rationalism as a form of legitimation expressive of the myth of authority. By this he means to imply that traditional authority is more basic and fundamental than either charisma or legal-rationalism. He would probably agree with my assessment, following Weber, of legal-rational authority as a *subset* of traditional authority rather than a parallel type. Here charisma is understood to constitute a temporary act of *destructuring,* and therefore is the pre-eminent basis for innovation and change in all societies inasmuch as change is seen to inhere in the undermining of established structures. MacIver's reference to respect for the forms of authority one finds in one's society clearly favours both tradition and legal-rationalism over charisma.[15] While I am not suggesting that cataclysmic changes ought to engulf societies in the absence of objective conditions making such changes unavoidable, politics and the political is made virtually impossible where the requirements of social order, as well as social labour, discourage resistance to such passivity and deference. Such deference comes to constitute socially correct behaviour, as the parameters of what is acceptable in the realm of the ethical and political shrink by comparison with the stupefying range of "choices" available in the field of consumption and "lifestyle".

A popular argument intended to lull citizens into acquiesence on the matter of deference and passivity emphasizes the fact that they must *accept* as authoritative the pronouncements of given individuals if these latter are to successfully exercise authority. Not surprisingly, this argument has had a long run in organization and administrative theory, where the muddled notion of consensus is always available to complement selective socialization with aggregate passivity. Hence the absence of effective, and consistent and continuous, resistance is seen as evidence of acceptance. Resistance, when it does occur, is treated as an individual problem, and the person's specific work, family, and related problems are pinpointed in order to "explain" his inability to adjust and accommodate. This argument, though found in the main in the disciplines cited, is a logical extension of the observations of both Weber and MacIver, albeit one addressed to the need to *affirm* passivity and deference as assent through the anti-political vehicle of consensus. Consensus is a societal rather than a political mode of action or inaction, and indicates the degree to which ethical concerns, like the practical and the prudential, have been subverted by the demands of propriety and appropriateness.[16]

Legitimacy, already passive in its essence, acquires the status of a myth invested with the mantle of objectivity. Weber's original consternation, addressed to how *any* form of domination could possibly be rational, is lost or displaced by the determination to construe the absence of politics and the political as political affirmation rather than simply societally proper conduct directed to labour and consumption, behaviour and spectating, leisure and lifestyle. The idea that anyone could find solace in the discovery of similarities and affinities between legal-rational and traditional bases of legitimation, particularly where the latter is understood to mean habitual and conventional modes of behaviour absent of reason and deliberation, is perhaps the most distressing aspect of social-scientific studies of "political" phenomena. At the same time, one must never forget the origins of sociology in particular in the desire for the restoration of social order following the French Revolution and Bonapartism. The animus and motive force of the social sciences must be understood even today to favour collective order, organizational hierarchies, however legitimized, and a "positive" conception of individualism absorbed in the routines of work, labour, civility and propriety, rather than any alternative which poses challenges to this order in and through a *political* mode of action. The hostility of the social sciences to politics and the political, whether explicit or latent, can hardly be overstressed, given their increasingly central role as arbiters of "rationality" in advanced industrial societies.

V

The preceding discussion has no doubt raised at least as many questions as it has answered. This is probably as it should be. The reader may be disconcerted about the absence of a formal definition of what I have in mind when I speak of politics and the political. He may also feel that I am being uncharitable in the extreme to Society and the rule of law in my haste to make a case for political mangement. Institutions, after all, are essential, and doesn't my admission that this is the case undermine the criticisms that I offer? The short answer is that it does not. My argument is not that institutions, conventions, traditions and legitimacy are not needed, but rather that politics and citizenship *is*. While it is clear that a conventional and/or legal framework is necessary for the possibility of politics in the contemporary context of advanced industrial societies, this does not mean that institutions of polity, and the extension of the legitimacy they receive to non-elected legal, judicial and administrative personnel, should absorb and effectively displace this possibility altogether.

The source of this either/or confusion is to be discovered, as noted, in Aristotle's conception of what would constitute a viable politics in Greek cities that had lost their power of self-government with their absorption into empire. But in this case there was still a determination to preserve the good man, if not necessarily the good citizen, inasmuch as he was different from the good man. The modern effort at solidarity has gone far beyond Aristotle's concern about the need for political institutions, and has redefined the moral as the specifically societal, rather than simply the non-political. This development is a modern one, and underscores the culturally and historically specific character of Society as a *form* of collective life rather than a synonym for it. It is readily seen in the transmogrifications which terms like practice and prudence have undergone, away from their clear ethical emphasis toward instrumental rationality in the first case and propriety in the second. To the extent that the first is seen to inhere in organized structures and fixed roles rather than in individuals as acting subjects, rationality and propriety become two sides of the same coin expressive of good socialization.

A harbinger of this latest stage of thinking about the ethical and political underscores what happens when their separation, first accomplished by Aristotle, is overcome in ways that annihilate both ethics and politics. I have in mind Durkheim's discussion in *The Division of Labour in Society* concerning what holds a city together given the combination of conflicting values and the relatively close quarters of its inhabitants. Durkheim argued that a provisional solution to this difficulty had been achieved in the urban towns of the higher middle ages, but that the subsequent process of industrialization had undermined it. Faced with the problem of what he termed dynamic or moral density, only an alternative to prevailing forms of interaction could overcome it. Typically, he argued, individuals were either attracted to those whose values they shared, or repulsed by those with whom they disagreed. For Durkheim this meant that urban life would be a tenuous matter at best, given the combination of factors already mentioned. It was in a third form of interaction that Durkheim believed he had discovered the secret of collective life in an urban setting.

Here it was the discovery that some differences *complement* one another in given collective settings which formed the key insight for his "solution" to the problem of dynamic density. As such it is the basis for both a "normal" division of labour where different occupations are "solidary" with each other, and the prototype of apolitical civil behaviour based on occupational individualism in and through fixed work and labour roles. The idea that training precludes flexibility in the functions one can perform expertly is not at issue here. It is rather the notion that such requirements, however sensible in the occupational sphere, should become a model for "political" practice which concerns me. Durkheim's analysis, inspired by Smith, overcomes Smith's hesitancy about endorsing the division of labour for its progressive or civilizing properties in favour of an emphasis on the need to restore solidarity under the new modern conditions. The earlier solution, wiped out by the disorganization attendant on industrialization, can be recovered in and through the joint efforts of sociologists and occupational groups committed to maximizing those values supportive of a normal division of labour. These would include occupational individualism, as well as respect for Society as the only available form of collective life in the circumstances.[17]

What is so important about Durkheim's "solution" is its a or even anti-political character. Durkheim, in common with his students, believed politics to be divisive, and was categorically against even governmental action in the economic sphere on grounds it would impede solidarity. A normal division of labour, let it be noted, goes far beyond criticisms of conventional political institutions to endorse the joint annihilation of the ethical and political. Politics, already compromised irretrievably by the transformation of the *polis* into an urban *social* space, was now joined by ethics, no longer permitted to exist independently of specifically societal needs and demands. The social is moral, the moral social, Durkheim once said. While it is clear that he often appeared to intend this in a generic sense, whereby social was meant collective, a more specific purpose is frequently on his mind in his writings on the matter. Durkheim gives aid and comfort not only to those anxious to maintain social order at all costs, but in the process even supplants the residues of individual craftsmanship found in the concept of cooperation with the rigid structural and fixed role demands of division of labour, however normal it is claimed to be.

Nowadays, and in light of the clear contribution of Durkheim to the defense of the "normalizing" function of the social sciences in advanced industrial societies, it may seem antediluvian to once again try to address the classical question: Is man a social and/or a political animal? Nevertheless it constitutes, if anything, a more important issue today than in the past, given the pre-eminence of Society and the social. We believe, on the whole, that social order demands the restriction of politics and the political to office-holding and officialdom, coupled with occasional plebiscites where citizens affirm which of two or more teams is to govern. While matters are somewhat different in multi-party systems where coalition governments are the norm, this rarely works to the advantage of politics and citizenship. Aristotle's distinction between the social and political had arisen out of the specific circumstances of the decline of the Greek city-state. As such it addressed the issue of how many individuals in a given collective could feasibly be political animals even if man in the generic sense was alleged to be one. A parallel concern asked what preconditions were necessary in order to realize what might be construed as one's latent potential for politics.[18]

Aristotle's answer was not a clear and definitive one, and this fact has been of the greatest importance in understanding the fate of his political science. One thing I can say with confidence is that while collective life is presupposed in discussions of politics and the political, Society and the specifically social are not. This suggests the distinct possibility that they may well be mutually exclusive, such that the presence of one precludes the presence of the other. This would appear to hold when looking at individual human beings, where societal requirements militate against anything more than the mildest and most passive involvement with institutions of polity. Confusion between collective life and Society is undeniable, particularly in the writings of Locke. On the other hand, unless we want to argue that the state itself is instituted, built up and based upon force or the threat of force, there must be some notion of consent operative. Hence the myth of authority cited by MacIver makes all too much sense, so long as its presence is not presumed to preclude politics.[19]

Consent must be directed to recognition of the mutuality of roles and the plasticity of governmental structures if it is to avoid a full-scale capture by Society and the social. Collective life is indeed presupposed in this case, but neither the impossibility of politics nor the absorption of the moral and ethical into the social. Institutions, I stated at the outset, are not to be solely understood either as organized structures or as the product of conscious rational design. To admit that they are built up out of habits, traditions and conventions, as well as expressive of core values, only poses a problem for politics where such spontaneity is equated with stupefaction and sleepwalking, as in the rationalistic understanding of tradition. What makes politics incomprehensible for this latter is precisely its lack of predictibility and fixity. Theirs is an *organizational* conception indicative of the triumph of the social sciences, and Society and the social generally. Their loyalty to order is beyond cavil, and their capacity to distinguish its meritocratic properties of rationality and objectivity from mere "traditional" forms constitutes the key to the success of its ongoing project of legitimation.

Human beings are political animals, and, while this presupposes collective life, and a myth of authority based on consent, this is clearly insufficient in the absence of a better understanding of what the emergent public sphere could be. Society, being manifestly apolitical at best, prefers to point to the Durkheimian urban space as evidence of progressive and civilizing developments which it was impossible to realize under the restricted franchise of the Greek city state. But this hits on precisely the problem endemic to such an understanding. It is not that such a proposal only "works" in slave states where the few leisured can be citizens. It is rather the question of what conditions would need to be created, and which jettisoned, in order to realize our common nature as political animals which is at stake here. There is no easy answer, but this much is clear. Society says to the citizen: Why would you want to waste your time doing that when you could be relaxing or having fun? Politics is not a matter of work or duty, however, any more than it requires intellectual, or even commonsense, brilliance. Neither, incidentally, is it a matter of "symbolic reassurance" on its own.[20]

Society, in the form of bureaucratic capitalism, frustrates these developments, not so much in externally coercive ways as through its own logic, internalized in and through socialization processes like formal education and the mass media. It equates itself with collective life, and points to meritocracy and legal-rational authority as synonyms for rational domination. It argues with every fiber of its being for a conception of social order which in practice is virtually indistinguishable from the stupefaction that its social scientists so often attribute to tradition and the traditional. At the same time that it does this it accentuates the alleged differences between them by pointing to the rationality and objectivity of *our* civilization in contrast to *their* "culture". There is not only no reason for accepting such self-serving notions of legitimacy, directed as they are to the establishment of rigid stratification orders; there is no longer any sense in doing so. Political management *needs* citizen inputs, along with a concerted effort to undo the rigid distinction between citizens and rulers. Bureaucratic employment is not the way to do this, because what it achieves is all too often achieved at the cost of thoroughgoing depoliticization, as noted.

Human beings are manifestly political animals, most of whom are waiting for the right conditions in which to demonstrate this fact about their nature. Whether these conditions can be expected to emerge without assistance is a key consideration for the immediate future, given economic downturn and the poverty of governmental thinking and policy in the face of it.

References

1 For a good summary study, see F. E. Adcock, *Roman Political Ideas and Practice* (Ann Arbor: University of Michigan, 1964).

2 Max Weber, *Theory of Social & Economic Organization* (Glencoe: Free Press, 1947), pp. 87–132 at pp. 118–123. On our rationalistic preoccupations as a culture, see my *Tradition & Innovation: The Idea of Civilization as Culture and its Significance* (London: Routledge & Kegan Paul, 1984).

3 Emile Durkheim, *The Division of Labour in Society* (NY: Macmillan, 1952); and Wilson, *The American Ideology*, pp. 171–199.

4 Wolin, *op cit,* Chapters 9 and 10; Robert Nisbet, "Conservatism and Sociology," *American Journal of Sociology,* Volume 58 (1952), pp. 167–175; and Albert Salomon, *The Tyranny of Progress: Reflections on the Origins of Sociology* (NY: Noonday Press, 1955).
5 A good introductory discussion of compact or contract is found in George Sabine, *History of Political Theory* (NY: Henry Holt, 1937); of sovereignty in W. J. Stankiewicz (editor) *In Defense of Sovereignty* (London: Oxford University Press, 1969); of legitimacy in Weber, *op cit,* pp. 124–132, 324–329, and Jurgen Habermas, *Legitimation Crisis* (Boston: Beacon Press, 1975); and of representation in Voegelin, *op cit* and Pitkin, *op cit.*
6 Max Weber, *The Protestant Ethic and the Spirit of Capitalism* (NY: Charles Scribners, 1952). For extended discussion of this controversy Robert W. Green (editor), *Protestantism, Capitalism and Social Science: The Weber Thesis Controversy* (Lexington, Mass: D. C. Heath, 1959).
7 See Arendt, *The Human Condition,* pp. 126–167, and compare to Wilson, *The American Ideology,* pp. 171–181 and 62–65.
8 Arendt, *The Human Condition;* Corinne Gilb, *Hidden Hierarchies* (NY: Harper and Row, 1966); and Randall Collins, *The Credential Society* (NY: Academic Press, 1979).
9 Jane Jacobs, *The Economic of Cities* (NY: Random House, 1969).
10 Wilson, *The American Ideology,* pp. 200–230; Wilson, "Elites, Meritocracy and Technocracy: Some Implications for Political Leadership" in *Political Leadership in Canada,* edited by Hector Massey (forthcoming). Also note Arendt's remark in *Between Past and Future,* pp. 173–196 at p. 180: "Meritocracy contradicts the principle of equality, of an equalitarian democracy, no less than any other oligarchy."
11 Laurence Peter, *The Peter Principle* (NY: Morrow, 1969); Michael Young, *The Rise of the Meritocracy, 1858–2033* (Harmondsworth: Penguin, 1958); and Robert Michels, *Political Parties* (NY: Collier Books, 1961).
12 Aristotle, *Politics,* 1295 a 25 – b 39, 1296 b 15 – 1297 a 7.
13 Weber, *Theory of Social & Economic Organization* pp. 181–280, 319–341. Also Weber, *Law in Economy & Society* (Cambridge: Harvard University Press, 1954).
14 Wilson, *Tradition & Innovation.*
15 R. M. MacIver, *The Web of Government* (Glencoe: Free Press, 1947).
16 Chester Barnard, *The Functions of the Executive* (Cambridge: Harvard University Press, 1938). Compare to Herbert Marcuse, *One Dimensional Man* (Boston: Beacon, 1964), pp. 104–114 and Loren Baritz, *The Servants of Power* (NY: John Wiley, 1960). On practice and prudence Josef Pieper, *The Four Cardinal Virtues* (Indianappolis: Notre Dame Press, 1966).
17 Durkheim, *op cit,* pp. 54–63, 256–282.
18 See especially Aristotle, *Politics* 1177 a 12 – 1181 b 12–15.
19 John Locke, *Second Treatise of Government.* On consent, Hanna Pitkin, "Obligation and Consent," *American Political Science Review* Volume 59 (December, 1965), pp. 990–999 and Volume 60 (March 1966), pp. 39–52.
20 As argued by Murray Edelman in *The Symbolic Uses of Politics* (Urbana, Illinois: University of Illinois Press, 1964).

Chapter 4
Politics, Representation and Sovereignty

I

If law as a basis of legitimation frames the contours of Society as a culturally and historically unique form of collective life, it is representation that provides a basis for mediating between political leadership and public participation. If "stability" can be seen to ensue from the formal and abstract statement of individual rights and liberties, coupled with the legal basis of governments in legislation, the representative principle ought always to be available to challenge the sort of political passivity all too compatible with meritocracy's promise of "rational domination." One might reasonably contrast institutions of representation and institutions of stability in the modern polity, or even delineate these distinctive functions in the ongoing operation of one particular institution. In any case representation stands as the major barrier to bases of legitimation like "rationality" which, while no doubt generally sound in the public mind, need to be challenged in specific ways from time to time.

A major difficulty has already been alluded to in this regard however. Representation in action appears to have shoved its distinctly *political* character to the side in favour of its institutional properties. Elections, for example, become plebiscites which require the public to select individuals who all too often are not seen, and do not see themselves, as citizens first and representatives second. This is hardly surprising. After all, they are expected, after election, to inhabit relatively fixed roles and positions, and to enact legislation as a part of a government which is not really understood to be comprised of members of the public at all. Added to this is the tension between constituency and wider total system needs given in the requirement of party discipline and "responsible government," and the essentially passive nature of elections in two party systems where the party structures are evanescent and the issues rarely clear-cut. In the ongoing competition between institutions of representation and institutions of stability, the latter would appear to have clearly carried the day in two party systems, to the point where representation itself is effectively circumscribed in a vast number of its aspects by the concerns of stability, legality and resulting public passivity.

This has led many political analysts to jettison all reference to "the public" in favour of the allegedly more empirically credible notion of "publics." Here the idea is to pave the way for the legitimate recognition of interest and pressure groups by equating their concerns with those of a public and collective nature.[1] To be sure, this causes difficulties by underwriting yet another escape from *both* individual and constituency-based representation. What remains is the present tendency to confuse the legitimate right of access of these groups with the enactment of policies conducive to their best interests even when they conflict with a broader public interest. Thus we are told about the legislature's need to balance competing interests in the effort to maintain a dynamic equipoise between their respective claims. This situation becomes especially difficult to resist when it is remembered how dependent legislators, bureaucrats, and ministers frequently are on the expert knowledge possessed by these groups. Indeed it is precisely possession of such expert knowledge by these groups which often makes it possible for public bureaucracies to maintain a consistent leverage against politicians. Such groups are the key to bureaucratic power on the "input" side of the policy process, a factor generally downplayed in favour of an emphasis on bureaucracy's output functions of implementation, execution, and/or enforcement.

In common with the representatives of the people, but for very different reasons, interested persons and groups also need to remember the priority of their membership in the general public. In truth it is this general public which is more concrete and more real than any of the specific publics, roles, or functions "abstracted" out of it. This point is not simply a moral or conciliatory gesture. It is implicit in the only sensible understanding of the origin and continuing basis of reason in Society and politics. In contrast to the habit of treating rationality as a property of institutional training and certifying mechanisms and processes in the societal superstructure, I view reason first and foremost as a *substructural* characteristic whose foundation is human nature itself. Such a posture must make sense if only because it provides us with the only way of explaining the presence and functional role of the institutional mechanisms alluded to. How could these latter processes exist at all in the absence of a substructural capability which speaks not only to historic origins but to everyday embeddedness in the forms and parameters of thought, the structure of language and the core of basic, taken-for-granted, values?[2]

It is this consideration, more than any other, which leads me to address the matter of representation in the most serious possible way in what follows. Many issues cry out for attention, and do so from a vast number of disciplines and discrete areas of concern. The issue of representation involves us in historical, descriptive, moral and epistemological concerns, touching as it does virtually all facets of political life in advanced industrial societies almost without regard to ruling ideologies and doctrines. Max Weber had argued that the formal properties of all industrial societies in the West were similar in spite of political differences, but had implied that these latter differences were progressively less persuasive given the increasing dependence of all such societies on bureaucratic organization and management, and rationalization generally. I want to suggest that his definition of politics as "a slow boring of hard boards" holds for all these societies, regardless of ideology, and that it comprehends in every case a problem of representation which expresses the "other side" of the fundamental myth of authority discussed by Mac Iver. In effect, it is implicit in the very grant of legitimacy to rule or govern which the public gives to some of its members, thereby creating them as agents.[3]

Being a member means being human, while being an agent implies a position, role or function which presupposes membership. It is when agency becomes too rigidly bifurcated from membership as a result of the hierarchial, class and status biases of role structure that individuals treat agency as an alternative to membership rather than *a form of membership*.[4] This tendency was first given aid and comfort by the "rationalization" of legitimacy in and through the sort of positional incumbency found in *both* traditional and legal-rational forms of authority. More recently, it has benefitted from the fact that the established legal justification for passivity implicit in the claims to objective rationality promoted by legal and judicial mechanisms has been more than complemented by an approach to government operations heavily in the debt of organizational and administrative/managerial values. It is to the idea of Society as an historically and culturally unique form of collective life whose historic origins lay in the attempt to *replace* traditional forms with consciously contrived ones that we must turn if we are to understand the pre-eminent role accorded to organization in contemporary social structures.

Society *means* a form of collective life based on the normative ideal of rational organization, a point all too vividly brought home by careful inspection of the work of those so central to legitimizing its emergence after the French Revolution, from Bonald and Maistre, through St. Simon, Comte and Enfantin, to Durkheim.[5] This fact has important consequences for any analysis of the nature of representation. In addition to its central role in generalizing the organizational model of the bureaucracy and (later on) the firm to the total system in the ways suggested, Society also manifests a clear preference for passive legal-rational and meritocratic forms of legitimation over active representative and political ones. If representation points to the idea of the public and to automatic membership, Society reminds us that it is a goal-oriented purposive mechanism no less than bureaucracies and economic organizations. As such it is no less in need of hierarchies, roles, positions and structures than are the subsystems which it alternatively reinforces and challenges. As it happens, the truncated notion of rationality found in the strategic and instrumental concerns of bureaucracies and economic units is perfectly compatible with the model of legal-rational authority presently institutionalized throughout Society in the form of rational (meritocratic) domination.

My point is that Society is fundamentally hostile to politics, and to any thoroughgoing critique of the representative principle as it presently operates in advanced industrial societies. It is Society and meritocracy which resist the idea that reason is a basic *human* property which sustains the work, labour, civil and career sectors of the institutional superstructure, while it imposes absurd models of organizational rationality on the family to demonstrate its apparent "inefficiency."[6] This only reinforces the tendency of members to ignore the range and combination of functions undertaken by all substructural groups, the family included. Such activities are taken for granted or shunted to the side in order to make a case for occupational individualism as the other side of meritocracy and apolitical passivity. Like "informal" organization in the work setting, substructural functions all too rarely show up in Society's organization table, with its bias toward narrow and truncated conceptions of reason and rationality. To be sure, this is fully compatible with its determination to distend and distinguish itself as much as possible from what it condescendingly deigns to observe and evaluate under the label of "tradition", usually elsewhere.

One very significant upshot of Society's hostility to politics and the political is the way its notion of the whole as a rational configuration requires it to fragment the public. The public in effect is broken down and reconstituted not simply as interested publics formally and instrumentally organized for the attainment of comparative advantage, but in ways that deal with the remaining residual by equating passivity with "rights". Thus, what remains of the public after interest groups and organizations have been taken account of is reconstituted in terms of *occupation* (labour, work, career, civil society), *consumption,* and *spectating* (the market and audience modes). In the latter case we are made aware of the disjunction between the idea of observing in an unorganized way and the reality of latent socialization in occupational and consumer values carried out through the one-way initiative of broadcasting and mass media. Formal schooling, the most conscious and continuing effort at "socializing" carried on outside the family, is increasingly being viewed in occupational terms, even if those being formed and molded are not "represented" before governmental bodies in the way their parents' occupations frequently are.[7]

The claim of passivity is difficult to take issue with when the system of government is seen as a set of mechanisms which must be influenced and controlled as much as modern organization, coupled with objective specialized knowledge, will allow. Indeed, writers on the subject of the public interest in its relation to interest groups all too often assume that the only alternatives to such a conception of politics and the political involve authoritarian one-way options. Marx may well have been correct to dismiss the distinction between the general interest and particular interests on the ground that only the latter side produced the distinction, never the former. While such a distinction may possess immense normative and symbolic significance in our political culture, it can hardly be equated with particular configurations of the public and its governors, except arbitrarily. Majority rule, it turns out, can only "work" if collective decisions cut across divisions of the population so that no minority finds itself perpetually on the losing side. Legal provisions for civil rights and liberties and for the protection of minorities are attempts to take account of the possibility of precisely such an eventuality.

Nevertheless, the fact that most people interact societally in either the occupational mode, or through the "activities" of consuming and spectating, places politics in the work and labour category. It is not so much the activity involved as the *time* it takes that disposes individuals in the direction of passive non-involvement. Leisure is confused with "time off from work", and the notion of home and family from nascent capitalism continues to carry the day, albeit in substantially new guise. Strains on the family as an intergenerational network imposed first by capitalism, then by Society, create a situation in which anyone suggesting *more* time "outside" the home for political purposes looks like a home-wrecker. The problem has to do with the present decimated and enucleated nature of the family in advanced industrial societies. It can only succeed in shutting out the totality that increasingly determines it if it ignores the occupational and socializational life of its members and does not fall prey to a conception of "privacy" which is organized around television.[8]

An unexpected source of support for this argument comes from the very streamlined character of the nuclear family itself. The more Society's demand for participation and function intervenes in its affairs, the more its response segments its remaining members off into elements of the present or future work and labour force "resting up" between shifts. This in tandem with the gradual dismemberment or extinction, through mobility and/or disinclination, of the old, the retarded, the physically, emotionally and mentally ill, the *civilly* as well as the criminally "deviant", and the unborn child. What is astonishing in light of these developments is the persistence of families in *any* form. It attests clearly to the indispensable range and combination of functions performed by the family, even in its present decimated state. It continues to constitute, today no less than when Aristotle wrote, the fount of political possibility, however prepolitical in every sense it may be. Nothing could better underscore the consequences of occupational individualism, particularly now that it has been generalized to both genders, than the way its demands fragment, segment, dismember, incarcerate, terminate and abort those who cause it difficulties or inconvenience it.

II

Having introduced the issue of passivity, and contrasted its good side (legality) with its problematic one (occupational individualism, consumption and spectating as "activities"), let me try to address the issue of representation mentioned at the outset. In the first place it is tied fundamentally to the doctrine of popular sovereignty, if only because the concern to represent constitutes an unavoidable alternative to the apparent impossibility of everyone standing for or *presenting* themselves. The distinction noted earlier between representation and re-presentation suggests itself here, since to represent (re-present) must mean to present again what one stands for on a given matter but cannot himself present. It thus implies not only that what is represented has already been presented, but that representation is faithful to those who would present themselves, if only this were possible. This in turn calls attention to the notion of possibility and the possible which is given in the idea that there is something about collective life which makes self-presentation impossible and/or problematic in the public sphere.

"Representation", as Voegelin correctly points out, is a commonsense language symbol rather than a theoretical one. The fact that it has generated theoretical, as well as commonsense, disputation at least since classical times cannot gainsay the fact that it is not a theoretical concept in its own right. Voegelin puts the matter concisely when he says that "man does not wait for science to have his life explained to him." Faithful to his understanding of the Aristotelian procedure for theorizing in political science, he contrasts the symbols of everyday language with those of political science in order to underscore the limits of the latter discipline. Of considerable significance for any discussion of representation is the following remark, which both clarifies the statement cited above and goes beyond it:

Hence, when political science begins, it does not begin with a *tabula rasa* on which it can inscribe its concepts; it will inevitably start from the rich body of self-interpretation of a society and proceed by critical clarification of socially pre-existent symbols. When Aristotle wrote his *Ethics* and *Politics,* when he constructed his concepts of the polis, of the constitution, the citizen, the various forms of government, of justice, of happiness, *etc.,* he did not invent these terms and endow them with arbitrary meanings; he took rather the symbols which he found in his social environment, surveyed with care the variety of meanings which they had in common parlance, and ordered and clarified these meanings by the criteria of his theory.[9]

This distinction between the language symbols that provide self-understanding and illumination for the members of a society, and the symbols of political science, is not intended to obscure the priority of the former and the limits of the latter relative to them. While both types of symbols are related to one another, it is through the act of critical clarification that political science emerges *within* collective life. It is as a result of this activity, Voegelin argues, that the body of concepts in political science will become a basis for filtering out some symbols of everyday language that do not appear theoretically fruitful or valuable. While this is happening, political science will of course be developing new concepts intended to provide clearer and more critical descriptions of political reality. What is necessary to keep in mind, however, is the fact that the description and critical clarification of political reality, which is the function of political science, always goes on in tandem with the activity of politics itself. Since the activity of politics is, or should be, the single most important effort at self-understanding and illumination that any collective engages in, it is imperative that the difference between the symbols that result from this activity, and those of political science at any particular point in time, be taken careful account of.

In the case of representation, it is the confusion between types of symbols and the nature of disputation which needs to be kept in mind. Most important in all this is the point noted earlier. It is imperative that we not confuse the concepts of political science with those symbols central to the activity of politics itself, society's most important effort at collective self-understanding and illumination. Thus it is not that there is one term with two meanings where analysis of "representation" is concerned, but rather "two sets of symbols with a large area of overlapping phonemes."[10] This is readily understandable if only because the symbols of political science not only presume everyday efforts at collective self-clarification and illumination through language, but build upon this ongoing reality through critical clarification and description. This means that the two sets of symbols will frequently approach one another and may even be identical from time to time. But all of this is quite different from arguing that there is no valid distinction between the two types of symbols, or that they can be confused without consequence.

Voegelin is concerned to save a mode of thought and discourse from its absorption into everyday life. The claim that disciplines are reflections of social, cultural and/or economic "forces" has been popular at least since Marx, if not Harrington and Locke. Indeed, the notions of superstructure and substructure which I employ throughout this study make precisely this presumption, and have, it must be pointed out, a lineage which goes back at least to Ricardo and political economy rather than to Marx and Engels, as is often assumed. Without for a moment denying the need for a distinct clarifying activity in the intellectual sphere such as Voegelin is concerned to preserve, it must be noted that his distinction between the two types of symbols serves a purpose which is not always as central to this study as it is to his. Voegelin's concern to save political science from the situation it has fallen into by confusing the two sets of symbols extends to the practical possibilities of a science of politics itself. This issue is discussed in a separate chapter further on. Suffice it to say here that it is the unrealistic, perhaps even dangerous, expectations encouraged by such a "science" in its more interventionist moments that concerns him. They spring from the failure to adequately attend to the *limits* set for political science as an effort at critical clarification by the fact that it takes place in tandem with the ongoing act of collective self-illumination and understanding which we call politics.

Nevertheless my differences with Voegelin hinge on a different view of what precisely is at stake in critique for those engaged in political science. What I do with the fact that commonsense language symbols produced by a society are prior in every sense to their critical clarification only underscores this. Critique for me cannot be confined to simply clarifying how a symbol like representation, for example, has been altered over time both in conceptual and "practical" terms. My purpose in addressing representation as a necessary and unavoidable compromise between popular sovereignty and an exercise of power unfettered by responsibility and accountability is to make a case for improving its likelihood. To be sure, we first must appreciate how it is understood by the public, and how it has been implemented in governmental and political practice. The purpose of all this is to draw attention to precisely what is problematic about the gap between ideal and practice. It requires us, in short, to consider what goals or objectives we want to serve (and in what order) preparatory to careful scrutiny of our representative institutions and processes.

Attention to the priority of commonsense language symbols, not excluding the ongoing dependence of critical clarification on such symbols, is a way for me to address the ideal of popular sovereignty as something which representation in practice must seek to approximate as much as possible. In the event, political, technocratic and bureaucratic leadership must move away from the prevailing notion of representative institutions as devices to unhinge leadership from the constraints of responsibility and accountability toward a view of representation which attempts as much as possible to maximize participation, access and dialogue.[11] Where existing institutions are discovered incapable of promoting this latter view, it will be increasingly important to find new institutions capable of doing so. Established institutions originally brought into being to perform representative functions may never have performed them, or may no longer do so. This may be a result of their very sedimentation in the political culture under examination, or vested interests may have taken effective control of them over time.

In either case they come to function as institutions of stability rather than representative institutions, with the result that representation becomes synonymous with formal rites and rituals. It is for this reason that democratic societies under the rule of law need to be continually dynamized, infused with new ideas and processes which are to some extent (but not totally) the result of critical clarification in Voegelin's sense of the term. One upshot of such an effort at critical clarification would underscore the gravity of continuing to see rights and liberties abstractly secured through the operation of the legal and judicial system as a justification for political passivity. The purpose of such rights and liberties must be understood as a *necessary basis* for political life rather than an alternative to it. They make politics possible as an *active* pursuit of representation, understood as a working given which *presumes* the priority of member to agent.[12] This fact must be clear from the very reality of a legal system where the unevenness of access, process and justice continues to be tolerated on class and income grounds.

The irony of all this is that it is only in and through politics that the present distribution of enforcement processes and mechanisms can conceivably be improved. In contrast, the passive conception of rights and liberties as the possession of "stakeholders" combines with the view of representation as an institution of stability to brand politics and the political at one and the same time too demanding of a member's off-work time and essentially destabilizing. The Aristotelian conception of a political system as a "body-politic" is overwhelmed by the literary understanding of such a metaphor, and such usage becomes indicative of the user's intention to leave reality in favour of the dizzy heights of "normative" political theory. Similarly, representation bears within its forms of understanding and usage this distinction between the empirical and the normative. The first coincides with the real world of "concrete" individuals and/or interest groups, while the second addresses what would be an ideal arrangement if only it were possible. No one queries the stunted notion of possibility prefigured in such a rigid distinction between ideal and reality, or credits anyone who does.

In the attempt to render the "real" world concrete, in line with the instrumentalizing of the practical and prudential, the tension between the individual and interest groups as concrete reference points manifests itself. On the one hand the entire social order is supposed to exist to serve the needs of the individual. On the other, however, this individual is even more obviously a societal creation than was the case when Society was less developed as a total system of organization and socialization. Thus, to be an individual means to be a "person" with rights and liberties whose defining characteristic is his work/labour/career and the way he spends his off-work/labour/career time. Politics is definitely not a preferred way to "spend" this latter time, since it can be shown to be work and labour by the mere fact that so many people earn a living either engaging in it or carrying out its technocratic and bureaucratic "other side". It is increasingly possible to view individualism as a central value of the system *because* its needs are best "represented" through the aegis of occupation, consumption, leisure and "life-style" generally.

While an interest group system is admitted to favour those who can afford to organize and know best how to maximize the organizational principle in practice, this is not thought to oppose individualism. If it underwrites the guarantee of tangible benefits accruing to individuals represented through the operation of the interest group mechanism, this is not thought to be all that damaging to those individuals who fail to receive such representation. It is at this point that one expects to hear reference to abstract legal and juridical rights and liberties, supplemented by a constituency (or party list) based electoral system. Unorganized individuals are thus represented in the main through the mechanism of the constituency in two party systems, whether that constituency be a riding (district), a province or state, or the nation as a whole. If it is pointed out that an individual's vote is skewed and distorted even if he votes *for the winning party* (or coalition) by the presence of more than two parties running in a given constituency, a similar lack of certainty is shown to be a property of the shifting equipoise achieved between competing interest groups operating on governments and political parties.

Another matter of even greater consequence regarding the operation of plural constituencies as bases for electing political representatives arises out of the streamlining of government itself. In the first place, there is the continuing fact of party discipline as a vehicle which can frequently require a representative to vote against the best interests of his constituents. Since the argument for plural constituencies has always constituted the pre-eminent justification for the considerable discretion granted by members to their elected representatives, the gap between ideal and reality should serve to make a strong case for greater instruction from members and more consistent accountability from agents. In a multi-party system, where parties function more like interest organizations in their own right, the absence of a constituency system can frequently be justified by national characteristics like a country's size, population homogeneity, and traditions and customs. More significant is their claim to represent the interests of more individuals than can be represented through the interest group mechanism in two party systems, even at the cost of stability and the guarantee of coalition governments.

Plural constituencies lop off the defeated elements at the subsystem level both in space and time. This is even the case when it is discovered that these elements combine to make a *voting majority,* as is often the case when more than two parties run without losing their deposits. The "elements" that are lopped off must be understood to constitute individuals both as members of the polity "at large", and as actual or potential members of interest groups. By the time those who represent all constituencies have been brought together under the aegis of party discipline, the bias in favour of stability over and against representation is virtually unchallengeable in two party systems. To be sure, this fact is only aided and abetted by the nature of party structures in two party systems where a constituency basis of election sends a single member to the relevant governmental unit. Such parties are typically organized only for purposes of fighting elections, and evidence parliamentary or executive control rather than control through a central office as is the case for *both* interest groups in two party systems and parties in multi-party systems.[13]

All of this has been complemented in recent years by the fundamentally misplaced application of a model of political and governmental practice from *the theory* of business organization and management. In the first place, it is all too rare to find real business organizations employing such models in practice to any greater extent than many public sector organizations. What such models do is inspire a confidence in the public mind regarding the efficient and rational operation of the governmental system which is almost completely unjustified. It is not simply the fact that political systems cannot divest themselves of unprofitable branches, or engage in action with similar large-order consequences. Also significant is the point that even if it were possible to operate political systems, or just governments, in such a way as to maximize the desired properties of the theory of business organization and mangement, the result would be a serious distortion of both the political and legal goals of the system.

Indeed, even in its present state of discontinuous and largely symbolic application, technocratic and bureaucratic values in practice are producing such distortions. A prominent example would be the tendency of the unorganized public in particular to accept the technocratic and centralist conception of federalism in federal systems of government without cavil. Whereas federalism is properly understood to constitute a relationship between coordinate jurisdictions, where each jurisdiction has its own exclusive sphere of activities and functions, the prevailing view of Society as explicitly a business organization *writ* large has further beguiled the public into a perception of this relationship as one of *levels* rather than coordinate jurisdictions. In the event, a hierarchial and organizational model is substituted, and the provinces or states are viewed as vehicles for carrying out policies framed in the only jurisdiction that really counts. Incursions into areas of provincial or state exclusivity are more than matched by the managerial *cum* technocratic argument that only through a hierarchical understanding, one which treats the federal "level" as synonymous with policy formulation and the provinces or states with implementation of these policies, can efficient and rational organization and operation be secured. Such a model of government equates governing with "system steering".[14]

Perhaps the most insidious blow to a dynamic and manifestly political conception of representation comes from the very social, behavioural and administrative sciences whose task it is to defend Society and an apolitical ideal of societal membership. Here "research" is marshalled to demonstrate that the very weaknesses of the political system as I have just described them need not cause undue concern. The fact that individuals do not secure effective representation of their views, needs and interests in the general case where representative democracy under the rule of law is the order of the day is lessened in its significance by the fact that political, but particularly bureaucratic, party and judicial functions are often allocated or taken on by individuals who "represent" given regions, ethnic, racial and linguistic/cultural groups, classes, genders, and values, needs and interests. Hence the notion of representation is seen to be served in ways which do not necessitate formal elections, but instead point to significant societal variables in the general population, and to socialization as a process sufficient in its own right to displacing politics and the political.[15]

The major thing to be noted about such a conception of representation is its passivity. People are represented as "members" of variously defined groups in the Society because these properties of their background, socialization, and person are "reflected" in the way people distribute themselves in government employment, in political parties, in the legal and judicial system, and in appointments to executive and other bodies for individuals who may or may not have been formally elected in the ways already mentioned. The effective "method" for resolving the problems I have alluded to is thus to turn away from the effort to make the theory and norm operational in favour of passivity. Such passivity may take the form of an emphasis on abstract rights and liberties, coupled with ever-increased reliance on judicial bodies to secure and maintain political rights, or it will emphasize distinctly *societal* roles and functions like occupation (work, labour, career), consumption, spectating, leisure and lifestyle over political and public ones. The latter, to the extent they exist at all in the public mind, are seen to coincide with work and labour "beyond the call of duty" for the reasons that have already been indicated.

III

My idea of critique thus goes substantially beyond "critical clarification". While such problems and difficulties may *begin* in problems of language and communication, they have real human consequences that draw attention to the *reasons behind* the gap between rhetoric and reality in any given case. Where this gap is seen to be a central problem for political systems, as is the case where ideals are not realized in practice, the purpose of critical clarification must be to point this out, but only as a *first step* in the effort to bring it to public notice. While Voegelin may be correct to underscore the difference between the symbols of political life and those of political science, it is the failure of political science to offer assistance to attempts to realize everyday life symbols like representation in practice which perplexes this writer. It is precisely the priority of those symbols generated by collective efforts at political understanding and illumination in the general population which requires political science to see the task of critical clarification as a necessary *beginning*. No more than the public's agents in government and politics can political scientists be allowed to ignore the priority of their status as *members*.

The persuasive effect of political symbols and language has been pointed out, albeit incompletely, by Murray Edelman on at least three occasions. My complaint with his analysis, in *The Symbolic Uses of Politics* and elsewhere, is his failure to address the reasons behind particular gaps between ideal and practice, rhetoric and reality. Instead, Edelman falls into the trap of effectively fetishizing these gaps by treating them as evidence of "human nature" at work. There is no way in which to dissuade him by pointing to the very different kinds of examples he presents. Every attempt to reason along these lines only makes his argument more secure to him. Fetishism is the by now well-established intellectual and commonsense habit of treating particular realities of given cultures, collectives, or historical periods as evidence of tendencies endemic to the human condition, wherever we find it. The very variance discovered in particular instances is seen to require the reduction of these instances to a single property which all exhibit in common. While for me an appeal to "human nature" is indicative of the inability *or refusal* to address the reasons behind particular "gaps", thinkers like Edelman employ such appeals in order to discredit excessive rationalism in political science.[16]

It is my willingness to acknowledge the clear limits of political science relative to political life which, ironically enough, motivates me to press the rationalist case against both Edelman and (occasionally) Voegelin. The fact that I accept such limitation makes me want to do as much as I can in and through political science to address problems which are considered significant and pressing in political life. Admittedly, there will be in all of this a tendency to formulate new problems, or conceptualize them in ways unfamiliar to the public, but this, as one might say "goes with the territory". Nevertheless, the purpose of this is clear enough, and, so long as it does not unhinge itself too much from real political systems, can certainly be salutary and valuable in its own right. This is because public understandings and conceptions themselves change, and are no more amenable to static characterizations than appeals to human nature. Indeed, I find something bizarre about such appeals in all their many and varied forms. They at one and the same time convey omnipotence and impotence, in both cases because they claim to cover all examples offered but really cover none.

Language is a vehicle and, particularly in political science, must partake of the efforts at collective self-understanding and illumination as a dynamic and ongoing (or ideally so) activity found in everyday life. This is only endorsing the Aristotelian procedure over Plato's approach, and points to Voegelin's correct assessment of precisely what Aristotle's method constituted as a practical form of political inquiry. To acknowledge the priority of commonsense symbols in the ways indicated requires that the symbols of political science be addressed not only to clarifying what the former symbols mean then, but what significance ought to be accorded to particular discrepancies between rhetoric and reality, ideal and practice. It is not enough to simply point to the wealth of examples one can cite as evidence of the pervasiveness of human nature and the essence of the human condition itself. Such thinking ignores or fundamentally misunderstands the dynamic character of everyday life as a form of rationality in its own right. "Human nature" is often an intellectual device for claiming an exclusive property right to reason and rationality as forms of thought carried out by a small elite or caste group.

"Critical clarification" thus constitutes the first phase of critique or analysis for me. At the same time such analysis is not carried out "for its own sake". But neither does it promise the public practical results independent of their interest, concern and participation. It is only because of my acknowledgement of the priority of the symbols of everyday life, particularly as they are addressed to public matters, that I am able to press the rationalist position here while simultaneously resisting the tendency to turn away from political reality in favour of blueprints and formal ideals. To say that analysis is not carried out for its own sake is therefore not to promise "results". On the contrary. One of the major difficulties attending behaviouralism in political science as a discipline has been the truncated and excessively instrumental notion of practice and the practical which it had to point to in order to justify its attack on historical, institutional, and even anecdotal pursuits. The paradox of such a claim is the way the discipline, method, or approach in question is obliged to ignore or supplant public understandings in its effort to demonstrate practicality. Failure to acknowledge its limits relative to everyday life, and particularly political life, causes it to seek the very *theoretical* unity of theory and practice for which more contemplative and dialectical approaches have often been (wrongly) criticized.[17]

None of this is therefore to be understood as an endorsement of criticism for its own sake. Bringing to light the gaps between rhetoric and reality, ideal and practice, becomes an absolutely indispensable function of political science when these efforts take their point of departure in an analysis of central symbols of the social cosmion itself. Thus my interest in representation, the rule of law, and the tension between polity and politics. Critical clarification of the concept of representation does not content itself with restating the rhetoric promoted by those who govern, and largely accepted by non-governing members. This is the dilemma of the present legal-rational justification for Society as a form of collective life superior to politics. Institutional polity comes to stand as a necessary surrogate for politics and the political. It provides the form and rhetoric of representation, while effectively protecting meritocracy against the threat posed by its substance. Sufficiently formalized and fitted out with the necessary rhetoric, these institutional forms underwrite the notion that even citizenship itself is automatic and given. In fact this is not the case at all.

Human beings are rational, or capable of reason, by dint of being human, and they are also "social" in the sense of being members of particular cultural and historical collectives. But human beings do not automatically acquire the status of political beings because they are human, therefore rational and social. Politics is an *activity* that human beings only become a part of when they participate. Citizenship is not something automatically conferred on them, or something which they acquire by encountering or observing the activity passively. In this sense, it is even misleading to speak of status at all, for this is, not surprisingly, a static and one-dimensional concept which forms one of the cornerstones (along with role) of sociology and, to a lesser extent, other social, behavioural and administrative disciplines. In its essence it champions passivity, observation (however "disciplined"), an exclusivist conception of rationality as synonymous with institutional and professional training and certification, and a preference for form and rhetoric over content and active display. The social sciences, as noted, originate in the concern to re-establish through conscious, purposive design those effects earlier realized by pre-modern structures sundered by urbanization, industrialization, secularization, and national-state centralization.

One important consequence of this preference for order, form, status, and meritocracy has been the disrepute into which politics fell with the rise of progressivism in American social and political life. That the preference of progressives for non-political forms of representation, coupled with their general disdain for "politics", should coincide almost perfectly with the professionalizing objectives of political science, public administration, and sociology should surprise no one. Persuading the public in general of the superiority of meritocratic and manifestly anti-political forms of government should perhaps have been more difficult than it was. Even when its apparent preference for a merit civil service in state and federal jurisdictions is taken account of, it should not have been so easy to turn the public against the electoral method of representation in favour of political appointees and scheduled civil servants allegedly "above" politics. It was the association of politics with corruption and "dirty hands", particularly where it was shown to involve the profit motives of significant entrepreneurs, financiers, and corporations, that probably guaranteed that the public would turn against its own best interests.[18]

Instead of trying to improve the quality of the electoral mechanism in and through active participation in politics, the voting public endorsed a full-scale withdrawal from political governance. In addition to extensions of the merit principle, already sullied by the fact that its non-political claims could only be protected by tenure of office for incumbents, there was the increasing tendency to turn to outside experts, who might or might not be classified and scheduled after being appointed. Finally, there was the phenomenon of commission government in municipal elections, a trend which went far beyond the borders of the United States. Here the electoral method was preserved, but at the expense of explicit partisanship. The idea that parties were a corrupt basis for organizing contestants in elections has a long and distinguished pedigree in American politics, originating in Madison's attack on factions and factionalism. What makes such efforts doubly frustrating for anyone concerned about the lack of public motivation is the fact the parties are the *only* vehicle in two party systems that can at one and the same time stand apart from and aggregate private interest groups, the real reference of Madison's broadside.[19]

One could even argue that it is precisely the idea of collective life as a continuous series of gaps between ideal and reality that is partly to blame for public disdain toward politics and the political. Better to sidestep the problems raised by actual instances of political life and activity, pointing to them as evidence of human (or fallen) nature, while deluding ourselves that the real issues can be dealt with by experts, bureaucrats and technocrats. The desire to convert political issues into technical problems requiring expertise and administrative competence is not, after all, a characteristic of agents and their delegates alone. It is frequently discovered to be a central property of the socially responsible careerist, consumer, observer and spectator as well. Being a societal member in the ways indicated can frequently lead individuals to prefer problem/solution fixes which absolve them of either involvement or responsibility to ones which demand their time, effort and careful consideration. It is the paradox of representation as a formal rite and structured set of relations that it becomes the more a or anti-political the more societally responsible it becomes as a set of fixed functions or roles.

Agents cease to be members in several important senses once representation is viewed as a function delegated to others, *no matter who they are and how often they are brought to account.* I would argue that representation *in any form* is the most serious of compromises with the ideal of collective self-government through the direct "presentation" of individuals to one another. Because this is the case, every effort must be made to guarantee that it does *not* become a formal fixed series of rites and structures segmenting agents off from members, leadership from participation. It is the societal monopoly of structures and roles which persuades us of the necessity of their rigid formalization, all in the name of a meritocratic and unabashedly organizational norm of rationality. Fixed roles and hierarchical structuration based on objective claims to rationality are not necessarily legitimate characteristics of human collective life and therefore should not be fetishized in the ways already addressed. They indicate the presence of a culturally and historically specific *form* of collective life with clear a or antipolitical properties.

Destructuring the role system on which the meritocratic conception of a rational hierarchy is based only seems impossible if we maintain a view of human nature which demands its institutional repression and channelling lest we revert to the savagery of the so-called "state of nature". The price of civilization, argued Freud, is the renunciation of instinctual gratification, coupled with subordination to institutional controls. Sociology's origins and purposes echo the argument for a social and political contract derived from the fear of a return to Hobbes' state of nature, while pointing to institutions as necessary bases of repression and sublimation given the realities of human nature.[20] My problem is not with institutions, for I believe they arise out of the fact that human beings are rational and social by "nature". They therefore perform indispensable functions in any collective setting. What I am taking issue with is the claim that human beings have a political nature conferred on them automatically because it can be argued that they are, after all, political animals.

All this means is that human beings have the *potential* for being political animals, a potential that must be actualized through effort, interest and concern. Society makes it easy to be "social", almost by definition, for this is our culturally and historically specific form of collective life. To say that people are "rational" by nature is, however, a quite different matter. Here it is the disjunction between societally acceptable and politically necessary forms of reason and rationality that cannot be ignored. Forms of rationality modelled upon societally respectable types emphasizing instrumental and organizational/bureaucratic characteristics are manifestly a or anti-political because they see the problem of stability and order as one arising out of the infirmities and failings of the human condition. In the event, they always favour institutional formalism and role rigidity, the dominant characteristics of an increasingly closed, meritocratically rational society. Its preference for a or anti-political modes of interaction is reflected in the central role accorded to occupational individualism, with its long socialization and subordination to structure, as well as "off-work" functions like consuming, observing and spectating.

A most serious failing of representation in practice in advanced industrial societies arises out of this role fixity and formal institutional rigidity. There is no expectation amongst members of the public that the practice of representation will involve a *relationship* between members, some of whom *happen* to be functioning as leaders and governors. Instead, leaders and governors are not expected to act as members or really interact with members. They are expected to act quite differently from members, and to interact only (or mainly) with other leaders and governors.[21] Today it is the combination of deference to the objectively rational properties of the meritocratic caste order, coupled with disdain toward politics and politicians, and an all-pervasive sense of futility, which underwrites the prevailing "myth of authority" in advanced insturial societies. Representation, wherever it is discovered to be *necessary* rather than simply convenient, must be dynamized through the destructuring of the present repressive apparatus of institutional polity. Our cities, towns and rural areas need not surrender their power of collective self-government as the city-states of Aristotle's time were required to do. No one is really trying to take this power away from them. It is the people's for the asking.

Why don't the people know this? If they do know it why doesn't it concern them? Some tentative answers have been suggested here and in earlier chapters. Yet the point must be made that, in the present circumstances, such a question borders on the absurd. Why should anyone endorse all the activity and concern I seem to be encouraging when everything and everyone seems fine, just fine? What is wrong with careerism, occupational individualism, consumerism, and increased dependence on mass media and all-pervasive institutions of socialization? In the first place, it is precisely our severely confined range of real choices that allows us to accept, largely without cavil, the obvious superiority of Society. Second, we are so preoccupied with order and the fear of disorder that we resist treating our own form of collective life experimentally. This, we believe, will cause the breakdown of Society and the loss of what we have. Third, we point to the rest of the world, quite legitimately in many cases, and pride ourselves on the superiority of our way of life relative to any other cultures and collective forms we have examined. Finally, we presume that *all activity, including politics,* is work or labour, and that pleasure is to be discovered only in the passivity and privacy of off-work pursuits.

It is these sorts of fears and preoccupations which lead us to a fundamental lack of confidence in our own capacity for happiness. Human beings often appear to have vested interest in unhappiness, but to say this is not to argue for its permanence as an ineffable property of human nature. Our choices are much greater than we think, and the creative promises and possibilities of commonsense rationality, complemented by the institutions which are anchored in this substructure, are far more important to a human future than the formal, fixed, and hierarchical structures of our present merito- cratic caste order. After all, such structures are far more a hindrance to innovation than a guarantee of it. In fact, they are best understood as *the result of earlier innovations.*[22] Neither will what we have "fall apart" if we experiment with it. Indeed, it may fall apart if we do not. In the absence of the destructuring I have suggested, the quality of public policies is going to get worse and worse. As for comparing ourselves to others, this is far less sensible from the present vantage point than looking backward and forward and thinking about what we could do and could be. Finally, it is politics and the political, as thought and process, criticism and deliberation, which will have to become *more and more central* if we are to turn Society's (and meritocracy's) present monopoly around. While I would never argue that politics can accomplish everything, it is a necessary catalyst in the effort to open up Society and give us a confidence which we richly deserve.[23]

IV

Political management therefore need not mean the disintegration of collec- tive life, but its preservation. Dynamizing representation will allow the ex- pansion and full-scale utilization of the presently abstract rights and liberties protected by the rule of law and legal and judicial authority. At the same time it will give a new meaning to the individual and to individualism as a constructive and manifestly public and political expression of activity and function. Societal characteristics of human beings, with their preference for institutional forms, will always be a necessary part of collective life, but they can and will be put in their place relative to the care of public matters. This will improve the likelihood of a salutary competition between forms and expressions of reason and rationality in Society, in contrast to the prevailing societal monopoly. This fact will have important consequences for operative notions of function, for it will permit us to resuscitate practices more in accordance with cooperation than mere division of labour. Function has been subordinated for far too long to meritocratic and bureaucratic conceptions of "functional rationality".[24]

Function need not be predefined in hierarchial and organizational terms, with obvious consequences for individuals and individualism. The implications for reason and rationality of perpetuating the present arrangements have already been pointed to. The societal monopoly which equates reason with formal structure and meritocratic values has allowed incumbents and their supporters to point to the superior efficiency and "rationality" of the present system. Here the argument from the theory of business organization and management already cited looms large. What is largely forgotten, apart from the fact that most businesses and industries do not even approach the requirements of the theory, is the radically different purposes of government and the political system. These purposes dictate different criteria for evaluating the performance of government and politics. The fact that this obvious point, while true, has no impact on the present situation only serves to underscore the publics' lack of interest and confidence, as well as its confusion, on the matter. Not only can governments not divest themselves of unprofitable branches. Failure to recognize the urgent need for new criteria of evaluation in line with the real purposes of governments and political systems underscores the present failure to distinguish efficiency from *effectiveness*.

A final point concerns the concept of the state, which has rarely contributed as much light as it has heat to dialogue in either political science or political life. This concept's difficulties would appear to stem in large part from the fact that it originated in political science rather than political life. Marx at one and the same time upended Hegel's metaphysical notion of the state, arguing that it constituted nothing less than an "institutional incarnation of political alienation", while redefining it to mean the "executive committee of the ruling class". Hegel consistently uses "the state" as a cover concept favouring institutional structures which make politics virtually impossible. It is Hegel's equation of the state with civil bureaucracy which led Marx to his most virulent criticism of *The Philosophy of Right*. Nevertheless, he himself made similar use of the term, albeit for critical purposes. For Marx, like Hegel before him, the state constitutes a metaphysical concept whose empirical point of reference is the largely tautological reference just cited.[25]

One point on which there is a general misunderstanding of Marx's thinking on the state is of considerable significance for my alternative of political management. It concerns Marx's notion of the "withering away" of the state following on the contemplated revolution and subsequent dictatorship of the proletariat and transition into communism. Without addressing Marx's view of the possibility of substantial political and social change of the sort I have recommended in the absence of "objective conditions", it is important *not* to see Marx as an anti-political thinker, as Arendt in particular has argued. Marx's argument in support of the inevitability of the withering away of the state following the revolution is not anti-political, just anti-state. In point of fact, I have argued elsewhere that it is only in and through the elimination of the state, understood as the executive committee of the ruling class, that politics will be fully possible. By state Marx means *bourgeois capitalist* state, a distinctly modern and secular formation. It withers away after the revolution because the dominant (capitalist) class for which it functions as an executive committee no longer exists at all under the proletarian dictatorship.[26]

Without becoming embroiled in the always present disputations and controversies about what Marx meant and what the significance of his thought is for advanced industrial societies today, it must be clear that both Marx's critique of the state, and his optimism regarding the possibility of politics and the political in its absence, is important to my analysis. The major point of difference is the dependence of Marx's alternative society on a revolution which itself depends on "objective conditions" for its occurence. Even here, however, the contingent nature of such conditions, now or in the future, can readily be seen to defy rigid conceptions of determinism often (wrongly) ascribed to Marx. Still, I do not acknowledge that only some sense of urgency, socially perceived, will propel the sort of changes I recommend. On the contrary. It seems to me that it is precisely in the possibility of free choice, however circumscribed by the reality of economic downturn, that political management can become a preferred alternative in the public mind. When Society and its governmental/distributive mechanisms can no longer deliver the goods, there will doubtless be significant changes.

But to say this is not to argue that the right choices in the right direction will be made as a result. Indeed, some would say that such circumstances will increase the likelihood of a reversion to more traditional autocratic and dictatorial forms of domination. This may well be the case, but it is important to remember that the analysis offered here does not constitute a blueprint and is not intended to do so, for reasons that have already been discussed in an earlier chapter. Political management remains a possibility, but not necessarily a contingent one. At the same time, this is not put forward as a utopian theoretical treatise in impossibilities. It is an alternative which is very much needed and which is possible; it can and should happen. Arguments focussed on what will happen if the chance becomes a series of choices collectively undertaken over a substantial period of time often proceed from a fundamental lack of confidence in human possibility and a misunderstanding of human nature, such as it is. The real constraints on actualizing such possibilities are to be found within rather than outside us. The public all-too-often gets the social and political system that it deserves.

References

1 See Glendon Schubert, *The Public Interest* (Glencoe: Free Press, 1959). Schubert's scheme is based on Wayne A. R. Leys "Ethics and Administrative Discretion," *Public Administration Review,* Volume 3 (Winter, 1943), pp. 10–23. Also see Pendleton Herring, *Public Administration and the Public Interest* (NY: Russell and Russell, 1967, 1936).
2 See my "Rationality & Decision in Administrative Science," *Canadian Journal of Political Science,* Volume 6, No. 3 (June, 1973), pp. 271–294; "Science, Technology & Innovation: the Role of Commonsense Capacities," *Methodology and Science,* Volume 15, No. 3 (Fall, 1982), pp. 167–200; "Values: On the Possibility of a Convergence between Economic and Non-Economic Decision-Making," in *Management under Differing Value Systems,* edited by Gunther Dlugos and Klaus Weiermair (Berlin: Walter de Gruyter, 1981), pp. 37–71.
3 Max Weber, "Politics as a Vocation" in *From Max Weber,* edited by Hans Gerth and C. Wright Mills (NY: Oxford University Press, 1946), pp. 77–128.
4 See Joseph Tussman, *Obligation and the Body Politic* (NY: Oxford University Press, 1960). The incompleteness of Tussman's distinction between agents and members is a major theme of this study, and is developed here and in Chapters ten, eleven and twelve.
5 Wolin, *op cit* Nisbet, *op cit;* Salomon, *op cit;* Durkheim *op cit.*
6 Christopher Lasch, *Haven in a Heartless World* (NY: Basic Books, 1977).
7 Alan Thomas, "Audience, Market, Public: An Evaluation of Canadian Broadcasting," University of British Columbia, Dept. of University Extension, *Occasional Paper No. 7* (April, 1960). See Chapter 9, this study, for a discussion of this problem as it relates to higher education.
8 Lasch, *op cit;* and Sebastian De Grazia, *Of Work, Time and Leisure* (Garden City, NY: Doubleday Anchor, 1966).
9 Voegelin, *op cit,* p. 28. Also see generally, Michael Oakeshott, *Rationalism in Politics* (London: Methuen, 1967)
10 Voegelin, *op cit,* p. 29.
11 See my "Technocracy and Late Capitalist Society: Remarks on the Problem of Rationality and Social Organization," in *The State, Class and the Recession,* edited by Stewart Clegg, Geoff Dow and Paul Boreham (London: Croom Helm, 1983), pp. 152–238.
12 Note that this priority of member to agent not only serves to differentiate individuals from one another, but one over another of the same individual's functions. It is because every agent is first and foremost a member that *neither* can automatically be equated with citizenship. This is discussed further along in this chapter and in Chapters ten, eleven and twelve.

13 Notable exceptions to this rule in two party systems are labour and social-democratic parties, which are more likely to favour an instructed delegate model of representation in constituencies they carry.

14 Both the business management model and the levels conception of federalism are discussed in greater detail in Chapter ten.

15 See my "Elites, Meritocracy and Technocracy: Some Implications for Political Leadership," *op cit.*

16 Edelman, *op cit;* Schubert, *op cit;* Leys, *op cit.* Also see my "Discretion and Administrative Process," *Osgoode Hall Law Journal,* Volume 10, No. 3 (Autumn, 1972), pp. 117–139.

17 This is discussed at greater length in Chapter seven.

18 See *The American Ideology,* pp. 200–230; and David Lebedoff, *The New Elite: The Death of Democracy* (Chicago: Contemporary Books, 1983).

19 James Madison, "Federalist 10 & 51" in *Federalist Papers* (NY: New American Library, 1961). On the importance of political parties. E. E. Schattschneider, *The Semi-Sovereign People* (NY: Holt, Rinehart & Winston, 1960).

20 Thomas Hobbes, *Leviathan,* edited with an introduction by C. B. Macpherson (Harmondsworth: Penguin, 1968). Also see, John O'Neill, "The Hobbesian Problem in Parsons and Marx" in O'Neill, *Sociology as a Skin Trade* (London: Heinemann, 1972), pp. 177–208.

21 Agents often act like members, even when in agency roles and functions, in which case a *relationship* with members is sensible. Otherwise, even real communication with *constituents* is rare.

22 See my "Innovation: The Practical Uses of Theory" in *Social Change, Innovation and Politics in East Asia,* edited by Y. S. Yim, H. T. Wilson, and R. W. Wilson (Hong Kong: Asian Research Centre, 1980), pp. 9–29; and *Tradition & Innovation.*

23 Compare to the view of politics found in Bernard Crick, *In Defense of Politics* (Harmondsworth: Penguin, 1960), itself based on an interpretation of Aristotelian political science.

24 See my "Functional Rationality and 'Sense of Function': the Case of an Ideological Distortion," in *International Yearbook of Organization Studies 1980,* edited by Graeme Salaman and David Dunkerly (London: Routledge, 1981), pp. 37–61.

25 G. W. F. Hegel, *The Philosophy of Right,* translated with notes by T. M. Knox (London: Oxford University Press, 1967); Shlomo Avineri, *The Social and Political Thought of Karl Marx* (London: Cambridge University Press, 1968), pp. 21–22, 48–52.

26 This is discussed in *The American Ideology,* pp. 172–175.

Chapter 5
Problems of Institutional Polity

I

I have sought to locate a major source of our confusion about politics and the political in the collapse of the polis and its subsequent reconstitution as an urban *social* space. This loss of self-government is certainly a most important event in the history of human collective life. Aristotle catches the essence of this supreme problem when he attempts to recover an alternative to politics by favouring the production of good men rather than good citizens, inasmuch as this is possible. Later on, what remained of the Greek conception of the citizen as a man of wealth, thus a man of leisure, was supplanted by the Christian conception of wealth as property necessitating stewardship. The ironic upshot of this notion is that instead of leisure leading to politics as display, management of one's property in the Christian equation demands delegation to others who can "re-present" one's interests even though they are not directly (or necessarily) their own.

In the give and take between politics and polity, I noted the way that institutions often acquire the sort of permanence that speaks not only to habits of public obedience but to the vested interests of endless generations of incumbents. The key concept here, of course, is legitimacy, and it is the nature of legitimacy in general, and the unique properties of legitimation in advanced industrial societies in particular, that needs to be taken account of. The point here is one I shall raise in more detail further on, namely, that we need to provide for process and change not only within our political institutions but *through* them. This is a very tall order, particularly given the way institutions became a permanent part of a given cultural and social landscape, sedimented as they are into habits, attitudes and patterns of response to events in our collective life. All of this is to say that institutions must provide as an essential property of their own existence as activity and practice provision for their own peaceful and evolutionary supersession.

In the event, it is hardly comforting to realize that the percentage of governments of the world's nation- states based on representation and the rule of law has been declining steadily since 1960. The same can be said of the percentage of policy matters decided by representative bodies in advanced industrial societies. The steady decline in this latter instance, far from vio-

lating the rule of law, is increasingly seen to evidence its presence. This in
contrast to emergent nations in the so-called Third World, where concern
about the instability which representative democracy might cause frequently
marches hand in hand with the refusal to entertain all but the most authoritarian and oppressive notions of "legal" rule. There is a substantial difference, to say the least, between arguing that legality prevails in given political
systems, and claiming that therefore one can say of the society in question
that it is governed by the rule of law.[1]

A further point has also already been alluded to. It is the attitude, all too
readily encouraged by spokesmen for representative and constitutional government, that principles cannot always be translated into practice, therefore
always taken seriously, and the allied claim that our failure to realize a
higher level of adherence to either the representative or rule of law principles may justify scrapping attempts to insist so strongly on recognition of
their demands, requirements and ideals. Along with the tension already
noted between the rule of law and electoral representation in the advanced
societies, these constitute some of the most important matters which we
need to address when looking at political institutions as such.

It is essential that we *not* ignore the distinct possibility in all of this that
political forms and institutions may be *regressing* or *regressive* in the sort of
legitimacy they demand from publics. Infatuation with the doctrine of progress often leads us to assume a generally unilinear notion of improvement
which sees political "development" as the inevitable concomitant of technological advance. Yet it is difficult to escape the significance of contemporary
science fiction and futuristic entertainment in films and elsewhere, where
more technologically advanced powers *always* have variations on despotic
government, whether benevolent or otherwise. Whether this simply attests
to the failure of political imagination relative to the incessant technological
unfolding of possibilities and realities is beside the point. What is important
is the way it underscores the infatuation of consuming audiences with forms
of political and governmental rule which are totally at variance with what we
allegedly find extant in the advanced societies as operative institutions and
processes.

In this and the next chapter, I want to open out these and related points in
order to focus on some of the more salient matters affecting our politics and
government. While some of the problems which I isolate appear endemic to
any society based on one or another form of organized capitalist (or state
capitalist) industrialization, others seem less given in the system's root structure and more capable of alternation in line with concerns which are virtually beyond history, therefore *more* (rather than less) elemental from the
standpoint of a possible human nature. Perhaps the greatest paradox connected with provisionally resolving any of the problems I try to identify is

precisely the fact that such resolution cannot be carried out if the people themselves do not become more politically concerned and involved. The idea that anyone can do this *for* the people not only smacks of the worst sort of caretaking, but ignores the fact that agents are first and foremost members. Just because agents (and their henchmen in political and social science) refuse to acknowledge this point does not mean we must cease reminding them.[2]

II

An initial point only hinted at in the preceding relates to the requirements of stability and order needed to generate and sustain a modern industrial economy and society. Functional "system requirements" are clearly justified for many because they make it possible for us to isolate, so it is claimed, those requisites essential for development and civilized life. Freud has provided a tremendous amount of support for the idea that civilization (by which was meant European commercial and industrial society and culture in the nineteenth century) required a sublimation of sexual, aggressive and related instincts in order for stable collective life *in any form* to exist. Nowadays, it is more usual to hear this claim asserted in concert with a more culturally and historically specific one which argues that stability is necessary if we are to sustain the social and economic order on which present living standards and "life-styles" are based.

By this reckoning, political institutions have as their major purpose the constraining of the base appetites and instincts of men. Hobbes, Hume and Burke, each in his own way, favoured such a conception of proper collective life. It reflected in all these instances a rather hardheaded conception of human nature, since institutions had as their real object the pacification of the "animal" predilections in favour of reason and calculation or convention and tradition. The ease with which such a position could be reconciled with more "liberal" theories legitimizing the ascendancy of industrial capitalism has been pointed out forcefully by Wolin, among others. It meant that there was an immense ballast already available to those anxious to restrain the people in their name by the time that pressure from below forced steady extensions of the franchise after 1832.[3]

Today there exists a strong tradition in political science as a whole which prefers to see representation strictly harnessed to legality and convention. In a sense, such an interest is incontrovertible. The problem, however, arises when such a view is carried to the point of endorsing pacification and the priority of consumer or audience status over that of citizenship. This is

typically accomplished by pointing to the "dysfunctions" of political instability in and through the alleged *threat* posed by excessive involvement in
politics by the people. Such involvement is "destabilizing" because it agi-
tates and inflames, and also because it threatens to "politicize" other
spheres of collective life. Comparisons and contrasts are all too frequently
made to Third World countries in order to draw attention to what we are
getting ourselves in for by letting politics and the political off its short
leash.

The most recent version of this approach has benefitted from the post – 1973
economic downturn in most industrialized societies in the West. It stresses
the imperative need to avoid politicization in order to restabilize and get
back on track. It equates political activism, all too accurately it would seem,
with the presence of a social and economic surplus which makes such a
"luxury" possible in good times, but demands its suspension in bad ones. All
these views have in common a largely pessimistic view of human nature and
a fear of incipient disorder and collapse should "system limits" be too cava-
lierly tested. Again we must acknowledge Freud's central role, equating
civilized life with sublimation of the instincts, for the preference for settled
habituation and careful and limited rationalism often depends in key ways
on Freud for its ultimate support.

This is what made me stress the need to see Society as a culturally and
historically specific *form* of collective life rather than a synonym for it in
earlier chapters. Freud occasionally hypostasizes the particular properties
and requirements of his own form of collective life to the human condition
as a whole. While various individuals and groups have noted the way that
developments *within* society have altered or attenuated the relevance of
many of Freud's claims, they all too rarely realize that what they and he
have in common far outweighs the matters on which they differ. There is
something peculiarly social, or rather societal, about all such theories, and it
is in this sense that I would argue for making a careful distinction between
Society and the idea of collective life *per se*. In any case, it is in just such a
distinction that the sense of Aristotle's supreme problematic is to be discovered, for he realizes the essential difference between the good man and the
good citizen, and knows that the former is all too readily produceable at the
expense of the latter.

In effect, I would argue that Society is an extremely effective device for
producing good people but a disastrous one for producing good citizens. At
the same time that I make this claim, I want to emphasize that by good I
mean "ethical" only in the narrow societal sense presently operative. Durkheim stated that the social is moral and the moral is social, and by this he
meant not simply that morality or ethics has a collective source. He meant
that outside the confines of society terms like morality and ethics are mean-

ingless. What I would claim, however, relates to society in its more specific sense (Society).[4]

As a culturally and historically specific *form* of collective life rather than a synonym for it, Society tends to define the good person as someone who engages in occupational life, consumption and spectating, the last two unabashedly passive enterprises and the first increasingly so. In addition, it tends to equate politics with agency *rather than* citizenship, and views politics as at best a necessary evil required for steering the societal totality while distributing its material and psychic rewards and reinforcements. Politics as an affirmative display by individuals falls, largely as a consequence, under a number of possible headings, none of them complimentary. Apart from being destabilizing when engaged in by too many, it can variously be defined as frivolous, narcissistic, evidence of emotionalism or irrationality, or a sheer waste of time when carried out by individuals on, or virtually on, their own. Chapter seven explores these matters in more detail from the standpoint of political science as a discipline.

The idea and practice of the good citizen is effectively subsumed by that of the moral or ethical person, understood strictly by reference to Society. Idiosyncratic activity, however collectively supported it may come to be, is seen to threaten a societal agenda which views politics and active citizenship as a danger to economic, if not social, life. Underpinning all of this, as noted, is the idea that lying just beneath the surface in each individual is a cauldron of insatiable instincts which, if left uncontrolled, will blow the patina of civilization away without leaving a trace. In this belief, Freud stood shoulder to shoulder with Hobbes, Hume and Burke, to be sure. Passivity is as a consequence enshrined as the proper collective decorum in matters political, not so much because it best satisfies the requirements of convention and tradition, but because it is seen to constitute the only conceivable basis for effective rational calculation in the emerging form of collective life – Society.

III

This is hardly surprising. After all, Society's major institutions, virtually defining the contours of modernity itself, include the market, the firm, the courts, bureaucracy and meritocracy, experimental science and science-based technology, and the professions. All have in common a conception of reason as *rationality,* where the central property is a combination of ends-means instrumentalism and disciplined observation. The problem for anyone attempting to open out, or take advantage of, new spaces for the practice of politics is that this combination of properties consistently favours *organization* as the vehicle for resolving "political" issues. Wolin has drawn attention to the central elements running like a thread through the key institutions of modernity. His discussion of the parallels between method, formal organization, and constitutionalism and legalism shows forcefully that recourse to such vehicles or "means" was closely related to the determination to *reorganize* modern European societies following the French Revolution and Bonapartism.[5]

I would go a bit further, however, and argue that recourse to such means, far from generating a reified "technical phenomenon" of the sort suggested by Ellul, actually evidences the increasingly central role of disciplined observation, in combination with a manifestly *instrumental* conception of reason as rationality. On the first point, we are fortunate to have available to us the studies of Michel Foucault, in particular *Discipline & Punish*. It is the way that formal organization arose as a solution to both the threat and the reality of collective disorder that defines the contours and parameters of the then emergent form of collective life – Society. Capitalism, and later on capitalist industrialization, is only one among many important institutional realities that helped define these contours and parameters. What is important about capitalism in particular is the role it played first in dismantling feudal and mercantile institutions (with the notable assistance of science), then in building a culturally-specific form of collective life that was in many respects qualitatively new.[6]

Society as such has at its core the properties I have mentioned, and capitalism, particularly in its industrial variant, has been an essential vehicle supporting the growth of formal organziation as the pre-eminent technique for reinstituting order in and through this unique form of collective life. This is readily evident in the rise of the firm and the corporation as instruments for temporarily leaving the market in order to re-enter it on a stronger footing. Ordering the new societal space for purposes of maximization was seen to necessitate temporary exits for the purpose of creating work and labour relationships more in tune with traditional and conventional methods than the anarchy of the market could possibly guarantee. Wages and salaries as forms of remuneration provide a striking contrast to both market exchange on the one hand and fees on the other.

At the same time that I point to these developments emerging out of the new form of economic activity, it is essential that we not downplay the *continuity* that characterized the transition to modernity, particularly where the emergence of an "economy" is concerned. Not only was the firm, and later on the corporation, a movement in the direction of order and status, using the newly discovered vehicle of rational formal organization. There was, partly as a consequence of this economic growth and development, the need to extend the organizational principle to the activities of governments, as more and more functions were seen to be required to maintain social order. This contrasts strikingly with the less formally rational ways of organizing collective life, which capitalism in its early preindustrial phases stood squarely against. Indeed, it is mainly in this early phase that it makes sense to speak of the "liberating" role of capitalism.

Centuries later its industrial phase would depend heavily on the discovery of new methods and vehicles for ordering collective life along "rational" lines. In the event, it also came to depend on already existing institutions for its labour force. What gives the idea of "free labour" under capitalist industrialization such a hollow ring goes far beyond Marx's discussion of exploitation, degradation, and the extraction of surplus value. It is the dependence of industrial capitalism on organizational forms and practices designed to incarcerate the poor, the deviant, the criminal and the insane which gives the lie to much of Marx's discussion of "primitive accumulation." Not only did these institutions provide continuity by functioning as models for the organization of work and labour. Frequently, industrial production was *actually carried out* by individuals incarcerated in asylums, work houses. prisons and charnel houses. Continuity is underscored, then, because of this reliance during the transition to industrial capitalism on what were clearly *premodern* institutions and practices, ones which antedated the rise of capitalism itself in many cases.

What is important about this development, and those allied events which gave rise to the other institutions mentioned, is that the continuity it provided made it much easier to turn to the task of organizing once industrial capitalism had defeated its predecessor and established itself as a major basis for the emergence of the new form of collective life. Society at one and the same time functioned as the prototype ("Society") for the subsequent organization of work in firms, corporations and bureaucracies *given* the model of rational organization, while simultaneously completing itself in its mature phase precisely by reference to the bureaucratization of its work, labour, and civil sectors (Society). In the process, status supplanted contract while formal ("rational") organization redefined market relations. To be sure, here it is necessary not to fall into the trap of fetishizing the anarchic character of market relations, particularly given the reliance of such activity on disciplined observation, calculation, and a decidedly goal-oriented instrumentalism.

Nevertheless, there is a sense in which the changes that occurred constituted evidence of a clear discontinuity while yet relying on certain underlying institutional continuities of the sort mentioned. One of the more significant reasons why a formal organizational basis for the reinstitution of order on new "rational" foundations may have been virtually foreordained is implicit in industrialization as a phenomenon. It constituted, after all, an *extension* of capitalism backward, and thereafter outward, backward because it meant that now things (commodities) which formerly were produced in non-capitalist ways (guilds) would be produced capitalistically, outward because this extension backward inevitably carried with it the need to think in terms of organizing and searching out markets to make such production economically feasible. Such a development could not help but favour a heightened emphasis on the organizational principle as the major means for accomplishing a set of re-ordering priorities far beyond the confines of the market and simple exchange.[7]

Another property of this emphasis on organization as the ordering vehicle of European and North American industrialization underscored the dependence of industrialization under capitalist auspices on a movement *away from* the contractual nexus so central to the market and simple exchange toward status. Status constitutes the basis for power in any ordered system no matter whether its basis of legitimacy is alleged to be "traditional" or "legal-rational." Only meritocratic ideology in the present setting could lead us to believe that ours is an open society based on objective rationality, with merit the method of allocating functions in a societal division of labour that has overcome all forms of stratification based on ascription. One only needs to observe how the merit principle in practice so often finds common cause with tenure and job security, once an initial "probationary" period has elapsed, to make the point. The fact that the jobs, tasks or functions are often referred to as "statuses" lends further support to the idea that meritocracy in practice is synonymous with formal organization, structure and closure more than anything else.

What the prevailing ideology most needs to legitimize, as already noted, is the persistence and extension of hierarchy and authority to more and more spheres of life. The idea that any form of domination could be rational lies at the heart of Max Weber's ambivalence toward civil and industrial society in the West. Caught sufficiently inside the culture he sought to analyze so carefully, Weber found it impossible in the final analysis to deny the priority for his own thinking of either ends/means instrumentalism or disciplined observation. At the same time, it is highly likely that he understood that the consequences of incipient rationalization and de-magicalization must include the eventual "traditionalization" of ends/means rationality. The pace with which it was being embedded into organized structures meant that only the economic failure and ultimate collapse of capitalism could stop it from becoming *institutionalized* in the form of what Mannheim later called functional rationality. Since Weber believed capitalism to be virtually invincible, even in the face of the possibility of social revolution, it is highly likely that he expected that the legal-rational form of legitimacy, and the institutions that embody this form, would eventually become traditionalized as the central properties and artifacts of civilization as a *culture*.[8]

The normal tendency where any hierarchical structure is in place is to presume at least minimal competency on the part of incumbents. Social order is seen to require such a presumption, the moreso where it can be shown that incumbency is "rational" rather than arbitrary. In the case of politics and political institutions, the usual course is to either engage in such legitimizing activities, or treat this sphere as invariably corrupt, and exemplary of the worst aspects of human nature. Though this may sound as if it contradicts the prior presumption, it really constitutes its other side. It is the notion of "competence" which those with the latter attitude hold which is the point at issue here, because it relates very much to the way ability is increasingly seen to favour status, order and organization over contract, novelty and individuality. It would not be too much to argue that the public often seems to prefer managerial to entrepreneurial postures where democratic politics is concerned.

IV

It is when we turn to the matter of *political* rather than administrative and bureaucratic organization that we see the consequences of favouring the combination of ends-means instrumentalism and disciplined observation already alluded to. The institutionalization of political activities and processes only underscores Society's bias in favour of formal organization and functional rationalization as devices to manage the present form of collectivity. Weber plainly saw this in his discussion of politics as a vocation when he contrasted bureaucratic organization with the bourgeois politics of notables found in two party systems. This once again points to the tension and ambivalence already noted in his social and political thinking, particularly as this thinking reveals itself in his preference for a unilinear theory of progress. A politics of notables was, by this reckoning, simply obsolete when compared to the "progress" of functional rationalization.[9]

This bias in practice is a major reason why the ongoing process of "technocratization" of the political sphere often seems irreversible. Representation as a way in which members of legislatures put forward the needs and interests of their constituents has in the usual case been almost totally undermined in parliamentary systems by the requirement of party discipline in virtually all voting situations. Complementing this is the bias against deliberation and discussion, which it is argued, simply takes too much time, and in any case is *at best* a poor substitute for the expert knowledge that is really needed for political and governmental decision-making. The formal organ-izational principle in practice is too narrow a basis for ordering our political processes and practices, I believe. Indeed the terms "government" and "governmental" are increasingly understood to mean executive and admin-istrative rather than parliamentary and representative structures.

When it is remembered that the organizational principle in practice favours functional rather than substantial rationality in the way understood by Mannheim, we can perhaps better appreciate some of the more serious consequences of this unremitting effort to technocratize politics.

Increasing industrialization, to be sure, implies functional rationality, i.e. the organi-zation of the activity of the members of society with reference to objective ends. It does not to the same extent promote 'substantial rationality', i.e. the capacity to act intelligently in a given situation on the basis of one's own insight into the interrela-tions of events. Whoever predicted that the further industrialization of society would raise the average capacity for independent judgement must have learned his mistake from the events of the past few years. The violent shocks of crises and revolutions have uncovered a tendency which has hitherto been working under the surface, namely, the paralysing effect of functional rationalization on the capacity for rational judgement.[10]

What is important here is not only the claim that there are two types of rationality, but the assertion that there is all-too-often a zero-sum relation between the two where human judgement is involved. The price of overreli-ance on the organizational principle in practice – functional rationalization – is individual incumbents whose capabilities as individuals attenuate as a conse-quence of their dutiful participation in the organizational whole as "parts".

When one remembers that advanced industrial societies have made "suc-cess" more available to ever larger numbers of persons by dint of what Mannheim elsewhere called "success in a career" (and Durkheim positive individuation), the consequences of this zero-sum development, if true, are considerable. It means that the mode of rationality employed in one's oc-cupation is no longer peripheral or secondary relative to one's life, but is increasingly central to it. Occupational role and function serve to define, or at least substantially influence, the parameters of interest and the methods of thought and analysis applied to what is seen to be a problem. Common-sense capacities are redefined and reformulated in a way which, it is argued, does not normally conduce to reflection, deliberation and sensible judge-ment. It is the "other side" of this occupational function, relevant to discus-sions of "time off from work," which I focussed on earlier when I com-mented on the passivity of consumer and audience roles. From the stand-point of Aristotle's understanding of post-political urbanity as an urban *social* (or societal) space, it is easy to see how occupationalism, consumption and spectating belong together as essentially *prepolitical* activities.[11]

Let me develop this matter of the organizational principle in practice a bit further. Functional rationality would appear to be peculiarly organizational in the narrow sense, because it speaks to the combined impact of ends/ means instrumentalism and disciplined observation in producing what is nothing less than a cultural artifact of modern Western Civilization itself. While Weber treated bureaucracy as an organizational embodiment and prototype of the process of incipient rationalization, he did not formulate his concept of "formal" rationality in a way which lent itself to utilization in a direction similar to Mannheim's. Indeed formal rationality applies mainly to *capitalism* and *legalism,* and to an extent to the secularization of the world's religions, not to bureaucracy. To be sure, Weber's checklist of the ideal – typical properties of bureaucracy does include reference to formal and structural characteristics, but nowhere does Weber (or Mannheim) address the consequences for what he called "goal-rational" action of the fact that increasingly it was *the organization itself* which was fast becoming the relevant "actor" in the market, not the individual.

Revisions of established methods of thought as a result of this development begin, of course, in economics and political economy, and only later spread to other disciplines. The concept of simple exchange under market capitalism must be reformulated in order to take account of the existence and force of firms and corporations. Firms leave the market, organize labour, management, and functional expertise, in order to re-enter on a more secure footing. The individuals they organize and employ, for whatever purposes, are normally insulated from the market, a point not lost on Mannheim when he analysed types of success, as noted.[12] The question is less whether this happens than whether the result is beneficial and edifying to the individual concerned. If his interests are adequately protected and represented through established political and governmental institutions and processes, then such insulation may be deemed salutary. Where this is not the case, the problem of representation has consistently arisen. In both cases, however, the issue of political passivity is a real one, although only in the latter instance are the consequences of this sort of stultification directly harmful to one's individual and collective interests.

The fact that we inhabit an employee society where the major "rational" players are organizational units in public and private sectors, or somewhere in between, means that the individual may be required to reformulate, or even reproduce, himself should he move from individual to organizational employment. His individually-based goal-rationality, synonymous with what I earlier termed ends/means instrumentalism, may readily become instrumentally dysfunctional now that the relevant unit is collective in nature, and characterized by a complex and specialized division of functions. While such a contrast can easily be overdrawn, it does suggest that Durkheim's distinction between a normal and a pathological division of labour gives perhaps too much credence to professional vis a vis task specialization. One only needs to remember how anti-political Durkheim was, and how much he wanted a non-conflictual work place characterized by a pre-modern notion of "solidarity," to realize how he could see salvation in and through occupational rationality, combined with formal organization and the social sciences.

The idea that the meritocratic ideal in practice actually produces an objectively rational system of domination is itself perhaps its most blatantly "ideological" aspect. It is very much the ideology of no ideology for precisely this reason. The idea here is to stress the ideal, and downplay the sort of closed stratification order favouring status and long socialization which meritocracy in practice generates and sustains. The actually existing system inherits the mantle of legitimacy in ways Weber both anticipated and agonized over. It is at best apolitical, and often manifestly anti-political, in its attitude to politics, government and citizenship. Participation, even interest, in politics is seen to be actually or potentially dysfunctional because the people are ignorant, or confused, or irrational, or incapable of clear thought and judgement. Expertise and specialized capability is required because everything has become so "complex." Note the similarity between this line of argument and the contingency style of thinking so characteristic of the "political-culture" set.

One way of persuading the people that someone not accountable to them through governmental and political mechanisms ought to act in their name is to point to the need for objective expertise and the sort of planning rationality allegedly prevalent in firms and corporations not subject to democracy in any of its variants. Complexity fronts for vested interests whenever technocratic thinking endeavours to reduce political matters to administrative problems soluble by the right technique or method if we will only let the experts get on with it. Public enlightenment through formal schooling and constant attention to media is said to be helpful, but certainly not capable of even beginning to keep up with the exponential growth of knowledge that members of the public really *should* know if they are going to combine representative democracy with stability, improving living standards and low unemployment. Failing this, representative democracy in practice is alleged to function best when individuals confine their "political" activity to voting and being entertained as an audience, often by reference to the most superficial aspects of public life.[13]

V

The alliance of extended socialization processes for societal members with *both* meritocracy *and* role passivity is incontrovertible evidence of the political costs of such "objective" structural rationality in practice. It favours closure rather than openness, and status rather than real social mobility based on "merit," as noted. It supports the impression that rationality as such is an attribute of structures rather than of individuals. Indeed, one could argue that even its structural or organizational bias with regard to reason as rationality is excessively *formal,* to the point of constituting more a blueprint than any operative collective reality. Thus it is to role (or status) rather than to the individual *per se* that one looks for the disaggregated component parts of this formalized organizational rationality. Since the structure is thought to be the relevant acting unit for addressing (and comprehending) the issue of rationality, individuals figure in such a reckoning mainly as incumbents of a formally *pre-structured* whole, when not viewed as value-laden impediments to its goal-rational efforts.

Mannheim's conception of functional rationality is virtually synonymous with such an understanding, and is to be contrasted strikingly with what I have elsewhere termed "sense of function." Like reason itself, it is a mistake to allow central concepts like function to become the virtual property of those who equate it, for good or ill, with functional rationality. One of the most outstanding recent efforts to show the consequences of such an association for politics and citizenship in advanced industrial societies was Hannah Arendt's discussion of the contrast between division of labour and cooperation in *The Human Condition.* Formal bureaucratic organization is perhaps the best known example of functional rationality in advanced industrial societies, and both are to be understood in Durkheim's terms as manifestations of a modern, secular division of labour peculiar to Society as such. It is the difference between fitting into an *already* formed and structured whole, and building up some working whole out of the interaction and interest of individuals, that Arendt uses as the basis for distinguishing division of labour in the first instance from cooperation in the second.

Arendt's remarks underscore the problems inherent in allowing all collective activity to either become subject to, or be judged against, functional rationality and division of labour.

Division of labour is based on the fact that two men can put their labour power together and 'behave toward each other as though they were one.' This one-ness is the exact opposite of cooperation; it indicates the unity of the species with regard to which every single member is the same and exchangeable. Since none of the activities into which the process is divided has an end in itself, their 'natural' end is exactly the same as in the case of 'individual' labour: either the simple reproduction of the means of subsistence, that is, the capacity for consumption of the labourers, or the exhaustion of human labour power.[14]

Weber had addressed this dilemma, more from the standpoint of sociological method than anything else, when he contrasted bureaucracy as a structural ideal type with the "building up" of corporate groups and orders out of individual activity that must not be ignored, even given the prior existence of collective life. But Weber was too infatuated with bureaucracy as the organizational prototype for the rationalizing society, from which the only escape was reversion to pre-modern forms and to dilettantism – the intellectual antithesis of modern professional specialization for him.

Arendt's distinction recalls an earlier point I attempted to make when I contrasted bureaucratic with parliamentary and political party "organization" in an effort to protest the way that functional rationality has come to constitute the normative ideal, rather than simply an ideal type, for those desirous of organizing collective activity. The structure of bureaucratic organization can only be made subject to representative democracy if mechanisms are brought to bear on it from outside it. I shall argue further on that representation in any valid sense is not inherent in such structures in practice any more than it is in theory. Elected legislatures, and all the political and governmental institutions that go with them, are the crowning glory of modern Western societies as political systems. Even the rule of law must be kept in perspective relative to this immense and world-historical accomplishment lest it degenerate either into formal legalism or what Kirchheimer called "political justice." It is precisely in the tension between representation and the rule of law, as I suggested earlier, that Weber's ambivalent attitude toward legal-rational authority as peculiarly the product of modern Western Civilization presents its political face.[15]

The problem with division of labour in all its variations – including functional rationality – is that it is more the *product* of prior inventiveness and innovativeness, whether of a technical, social or political kind, than a spur to new ideas, processes and activities. As a model for political, and even governmental, organization, it is problematic because it favours a conception of rationality which sees it mainly as a property of formal structures rather than individuals. Instead of building up the interest and effort of active individuals into a collective for these purposes alone, bureaucratic administration understandably relies on functional rationality to formally predefine the whole into which incumbents must fit. While this doubtless makes sense where large-scale corporate and bureaucratic structures are employed for private and public sector activities respectively, this cannot justify importing it into the sphere of politics and citizenship as a normative ideal against which to contrast, measure and evaluate legislative, party and group organizations.

What makes this development in advanced industrial societies even more serious is the fact that it is occurring in tandem with the thoroughgoing subordination of cities to this same functionally rational model as *their* normative ideal. The rationalization of politics and government, whether for reasons of power, or because someone wants government to run in what is alleged to be a more "businesslike" manner, aggravates any effort to overcome the permanently bad estate that cities have fallen into since the dilemma that Aristotle first saw was further complicated by industrialization. Regressed to pre-political status with only intermittent exceptions since the rise of imperium in ancient times, the city finds itself even more obviously an urban *social* space as a consequence first of capitalism and the rise of the secular national-state, and thereafter of industrialization under capitalist (or state capitalist) auspices. Imperial and national state systems, as Weber pointed out in his analysis of pre-modern and modern bureaucracy, had little choice but to turn to clearly organizational approaches in order to achieve stable governance.

Seen in this light, Arendt's allegedly "idealistic" or "utopian" conception of politics as individual display may now be better appreciated. The idea that politics is evanescent, permanent only in its capacity to recreate itself anew whenever questions about public things and citizenship arise, only seems absurd when politics is equated with government, and government with institutionalized structures which essentially fix the parameters of political possibility in the name of stability and "rational" order. Organizational structures synonymous with functional rationality have thoroughly occupied the field in this regard. On the one side, representative institutions must ideally begin with, or at least aim at, functional rationality as the basic organizing principle in practice. On the other, residues in the political field which remain relatively unorganized are constantly held to account for any trouble which might conceivably arise from instability and disorder. Institutionalization itself is now almost totally subject to the model of functional rationality, just as Weber's analysis of conduct was required to favour a "rationalistic bias."[16]

Of considerable significance in all of this is Weber's equation of bureaucracy with legal-rational authority. Stability and order is to be realized in both instances by acquiescence in what can only be termed a new form of institutionalization, one more subject than ever before to conscious rational intent and design. Perhaps it is something other than the machinations of status and power groups which lies at the root of Weber's remark that politics in constitutional systems is, after all, "a slow boring of hard boards."[17] Given his equation of freedom with pluralism and an unending "antagonism of values," his view of alternatives to bureaucracy as dilettantism and a reversion to pre-modern forms can be seen in a somewhat different light. Without disputing conventional assessments, I would submit that Weber was far more aware of rationalization (and "legality") as a uniquely new process of institutionalization than most commentators acknowledge. That his treatment of politics in early twentieth century societies did no more than pose the problem in general terms can hardly be held against him.

A major institutional process whose effect is having grave consequences for the emergence of politics as citizenship and *active* representation in advanced industrial societies is public education. In effect, I argue that a central agenda of these societies operating through their schools is to simultaneously extend the period of what is called "secondary socialization" into the mid-twenties, while organizing the curriculum, as well as extra-curricular activities, with an eye to producing disembodied disciplined observers. Disembodiment occurs whenever the facts and techniques imparted can neither be back-referenced to reflection and contemplation nor forward-referenced to practice in the Aristotelian sense. It is this disembodiment which is central to the emergence of role (and status) passivity where the icons of successful *societal* interaction are based mainly on occupational function, consumption, and spectating. Such passivity is, of course, formed relatively early on in the experience of public education, where students are able to adopt the "audience-to-media" model from television watching to the classroom. This invariably downgrades the more active "member-of-the-literary-reading-public" model which prevailed earlier, and puts the two positions into what often approaches a zero sum game.

The idea that it should be interested in producing, as a central feature of its socializing agenda, disembodied disciplined observers only seems difficult to accept if we forget *the kind of* institutionalization processes that Society, as a culturally and historically specific form of collective life, favours. What all of the above role and status models have in common is *both* the demand for disembodied disciplined observation as a basis for "success" or effectiveness in societal life *and* an overriding a-or anti-political approach and preference. Even citizenship is fitted into the structure of rational institutions and the process of rational institutionalization in the emerging equation. It is in this socializing agenda that we see the increasing cooptation by legality and "rational domination" of the possibilites for citizenship. This constitutes nothing less than a modern day version of the tension Aristotle first addressed between the ethical requirements for the good man and the political requirements for the good citizen.

VI

An additional point about the consequences of Society's preference for passive a-or anti-political roles and statuses should be made before turning to the claim of many that a new form of representation compatible with this passivity has emerged in advanced industrial societies. It is the fact that with functional rationalization as the model of institutionalization, and extended secondary socialization of the sort noted, goes a tendency to particular types of speech intended to avoid politics and the political. Professional, managerial, and specialist forms of jargon are simply one side of the society-wide argot intended to blur, obscure, or define the world in non – or a – political terms. It is hardly surprising that political and social sciences, along with favouring social order over individual display, opt for the view that politics can now be found in virtually every instance of the use of language in a collective setting. Such a view obscures the boundaries between talk and speech and what has always constituted *political* discourse, and bears an all too obvious resemblance to Kant's equation of freedom with the decision to rise from a chair.

It is the way that all of these societally appropriate forms of talk come together in the context of modern, functionally rational, organizational and occupational life which requires us to ask how it is that such class and status fixed modes of communicative interaction manage to "succeed" to the extent that they do. The simple answer is that while we probably overestimate the amount of real communicative understanding that goes on between members, even what does occur is largely a function of "acceptance" based on a commonsense capacity to engage in interaction. Frequently what a person said can be accepted precisely because, in the context concerned, it does not have to be (or will not be) acted upon at all. Rules, records and other pre-existent bases of action, particularly under norms of functional rationality, exist which make it virtually unnecessary to have recourse in this and related contexts to what people actually say. To note that advanced industrial societies contain a massive amount of talk that *nobody* feels is necessary (or helpful) to act on is simply to point to the sort of excess that is bound to arise where "communication" may be valued but political talk held in contempt.

The contrast between the oral and the written traditions suggests itself at this point as a way of addressing the phenomenon of more talk and less saying. Speech as a deed suffers the same fate in a collective which sees it as an alternative to action that the individual experiences in any effort to generate political speech and community not subject to the model of functional rationality. Just as his parameters of possible activity are predefined by his organizational, occupational, and perhaps even his societal "membership," so also is he subject to derision for attempting to generate speech as a deed which is not subject to the written tradition. Bureaucratic rationalization and this latter tradition belong together, inasmuch as the key device for annihilating the possibility of politics has always been to persuade publics that it really is far more efficient to speak *in the written rather than in the oral* tradition, for reasons that Weber made clear when he implied that the oral tradition was synonymous with reversion to pre-modern forms.[18]

Yet it must be clear that the existence of representative institutions remains a necessary condition for the possibility of politics. Far from arguing that politics and representative institutions, or for that matter the rule of law, are in a zero-sum relation to one another, I would argue that the possibility of politics presupposes the existence of dynamic representative institutions. My complaint is not with institutionalization *per se,* which is in any case a normal, natural outcome of human collective existence and activities, but rather with the way that the organizational principle in the form of functional rationality has come forward as the only sanctionable model for such institutionalization. I believe that this particular organizational mode has had consequences in the political and governmental field which Max Weber probably anticipated in general outline but could not really know in any detail. In particular, it is the alliance between this pre-formed notion of action and the truncated conception of speech that tends to accompany such rationality which favours passivity in the occupational sphere as well as in consumption and spectating.

What I am saying is that a settled society is of value for the same reason that tradition is of value, but that this view of collective life on its own fails fundamentally to meet the criterion of excellence long ago formulated by Aristotle. Apart from the obvious fact that a great deal of this settled character is not the result of happiness, or even satisfaction with things as they are, is the way that emergent structures are effectively closing off real social mobility in favour of status. The assumption that publics have been led to accept is that this situation is the best we can hope for, given the overall complexity and unpredictibility of things. The problem here is that such an admission leads to an exaggerated deference to expertise, which has its inevitable counterpart in the desire to avoid the responsibilities of citizenship altogether. The idea here is that such activity, when not inconceivable because of the expertise allegedly required, is a form of work or labour, and therefore should be avoided by citizens in favour of consumption and spectating as an alternative to work, labour and occupational life.

In the event, the task as I see it is not to forward a utopian notion of politics which can only occur in the absence of representation and stable government. It is to realize something that will no doubt pass as heresy in the present context of public self-deprecation, namely, that it is just possible that the *quality* of public policies, even in areas adjudged to be complex and unpredictible, would be *improved* if public interest and consideration were encouraged and actually made possible by recourse to existing institutional mechanisms, the revival of established processes, and the discovery and utilization of the new public spaces that have recently emerged in advanced industrial societies. Clearly, this will require a serious re-evaluation of the iconic role played by functional rationality – the formal organizational principle in practice-in setting the parameters of what constitutes permissible methods and forms of collectively organizing political activities and functions. It is only in the presence of such re-evaluation that it will be at all possible to arrest the atrophy of political and governmental institutions and structures like legislatures and parties. It is this very atrophy which largely explains the increased recourse to legal and judicial remedies that has become the virtual hallmark of these societies.

One of the clearest consequences of these developments in political and social science, as I noted earlier, has been the fairly recent attempt to reinterpret political representation of individuals and interests so that it is no longer seen to be best served through formal elections to legislative bodies. This must be counted as serious a development as the already-noted equation of social stability and order with the decline of representative institutions and mechanisms and a consequent increase in recourse to legal and judicial approaches, and the rule of law generally. "Bureaucratic representation" is based on an argument that seems unassailable, *whether or not it is applicable to the particular country in question.* It asserts that the formal electoral mechanism produces elected representatives of the general populace who do not "reflect" that society's most salient *socio-cultural* characteristics. In many instances, it can be shown that the public servants who make up its permanent civil service better embody these characteristics than do the legislators to whom they are responsible under the doctrines of the rule of law and the supremacy of law. Even where the claim is not presently applicable, it is often argued that the society would be better served if it favoured such an outcome through the channels of public policy.[19]

The first thing to be said about such a notion is that it is a near-perfect embodiment of the very passivity that I have been bemoaning by reference to the role of the citizen vis a vis occupation, consumption, and spectating. To say that a people should be pleased by the fact that their most salient *ascribed* characteristics are better *reflected* in the civil service than in the elected legislature is to provide this passivity with theoretical and ideological legitimation. Instead of focussing on what candidates for election stand for and intend to support in the form of policies once in office, the emphasis here is on non-elected individuals who are either appointees or who fall under some civil service schedule of office in a standing bureaucracy. These individuals are looked at in terms of their origins and backgrounds, which is to say that they are viewed retrospectively rather than prospectively, thus with an eye to their past rather than to their present and future promises and possibilities. The fact that there is absolutely nothing even remotely political about either the theory or the practice of bureaucratic representation only underscores its real *societal* auspices, ones which cannot avoid favouring the passivity given in the roles and statuses discussed above.

A deeper problem is implicit in this blasé view of representation, sponsored as it is by political and social science. At a time when the role of representative mechanisms and functions is in manifest decline relative to the initiatives of bureaucrats, technocrats, regulators, judges and governments and oppositions demanding strict party discipline from elected members, such an endorsement of passivity is little less than a travesty. The fight for majority rule through formal elections resulting in representation of citizens and publics in legislative bodies was not easily won and is clearly not foreordained as the path which "political development" in the Third World will necessarily take. The idea that it might slip away from citizens in the advanced counties, whose preoccupation with personal and economic problems has led them to favour expertise, coupled with legal and judicial remedies, can no longer be discounted. It is difficult to deny the persuasiveness and power of those who seek to dissuade members of the public on grounds that the requirement of continued stability and order necessitates a wholesale delegation of their authority to non-elected officials, officials whose actions will be given at best periodic legitimation in and through occasional plebiscites.

To the claim that bureaucratic representation can function to the advantage of organized interest groups able not only to influence the course of legislation but provide information essential to its composition two things need to be said. First, no effective public management of and participation in government and politics is realistically possible where a virtual monopoly of initiatives, information and access resides with a group which, regardless of size, cannot help but operate as a relatively closed body of office holders honouring secrecy and discretion as it was understood at the time Weber wrote. After all, this is their proper obligation even in a democracy, and it is precisely this fact which *must* preclude their cooptation of the public sphere. Second, the purpose of representative democracy under the rule of law is only to support organized interests because they in turn reflect the needs and desires of individual citizens. Organized interests, regardless of their area of concern, have no right of access to government in the absence of this prior acknowledgement and recognition.

VII

A final point relates to suggestions that take their point of departure in the contemporary technological "revolutions" that have arisen as a consequence of automation, the micro chip, and biotechnology, among other developments. It is argued that finally technology has made it possible to put publics, and citizenship generally, back in the picture. Individuals, with a small investment, or supported by general tax revenues, can now effectively "vote" on a wide range of public issues without having to leave their homes or workplaces. Such a proposal is yet another endorsement of the sociologization of political activities and the public sphere generally, for it forwards the model of the consumer or member of a viewing audience as the ideal basis for generating the new pseudo-citizen. Passivity is once again ensconced in such a recommendation, in line with the nature of these essentially re-active a political behaviours. Politics and care for public things not necessarily beholden to Society and its socializing agenda are effectively dealt with by *being taken out of the public sphere altogether* in the new equation.

This becomes evident once the nature of "the vote" is seen to actually constitute a version of consumption and spectating in an even more blatant and sustained way than the mass media already requires of the people's representatives. After all, the vote is to occur mainly in homes, is to be on issues which are treated as if they stood alone relative to larger order problems and more sustained lines of policy, and would have the added effect of bypassing representative processes and mechanisms altogether. The government would allegedly "register" these "votes" and base public policies upon them. The problem here is that such an undertaking could not help but jeopardize policy development and continuity, while it polarized public opinion unnecessarily, often on matters where members of the public would need more information, more time, and more opportunity to reflect and deliberate. Note that this is not an argument against intense and sustained public participation in politics by citizens, only a claim that the public contribution to improved policies presupposes such pre-decisional concerns.

In addition to making what might be called initial decisions on public policy matters, there is the question of how policies, once formulated in legislation, would be executed, implemented, administered and enforced. I address several of these problems in the next chapter, where the concern is with the problem of discretion in politics, public administration and law. My point here is that the new type of direct democracy through on-line technology would make careful supervision of policy development difficult if not impossible. This is particularly true where new considerations arise that were absent when the legislation in question was first framed. Clearly, then, public participation and concern of the sort I have counselled cannot be expected to function as a substitute for representative mechanisms, processes, or institutions, but instead depends on the good health and functioning of legislative and party structures at every turn. This is not because members of the public are irrational, incompetent or congenitally apathetic and deferential. It rather underscores the extent to which the integrity of process, activity, interest, effort and display reflects the proper role of governmental and political systems in action.

Along with "outputs" their task is political education, and in this respect I would argue that the educative process is reciprocal and indicative of interdependence between agents and members. In the final analysis what such reciprocal action demonstrates is not only that agents are members but that members can be, and should be, agents. This interactive and interdependent process is ideally what *should* happen in the present circumstances of Society's dominion over individuals, citizens and publics in order to overcome this dominion. It points to what the surplus created by capitalist productivity should have led to but did not as a consequence of the system's capacity to forever extend the notion of perceived need far beyond the real necessities of life. Finally, it addresses the important difference between representation, and the emergence of new guardian classes in politics, administration, technocracy and the law determined to act on behalf of the public rather than in concert with it. These individuals and groups do not even view themselves as agents, but for the most part believe that representative democracy is fundamentally incompatible with the need for governments to make speedy decisions on complex matters of grave political, economic and strategic moment.

This argument, and present large-scale acceptance of it by citizens, is the most serious problem we face in attempting to generate a public sphere of political activity and possibility that takes account of the new public spaces that have emerged in the advanced societies, while at the same time reviving and resuscitating already existing representative mechanisms and processes.[20] The operative assumption in the latter case, which I believe is fully borne out by the present poverty of public policies, is that the mechanisms and processes were *never* intended to carry the load that is now pointed to in order to justify by-passing them with the help of the guardian groups cited. In contrast to those who fear the public will destabilize society and run amok if allowed to exercise its most basic mandate, I argue that this very undertaking has the best chance of improving the quality of public policies. Socialization for political sterility and incompetence cannot continue to be the major "latent function" of the schools and the media, whether by design or indirection. Its consequences, as noted, extend beyond initial self-deprecation to the sort of long term deference which presently characterizes Society's preference for passive non-political "social interaction" through occupational life, consumption, and spectating. This goes hand in hand with the emergence of the guardian groups cited, and it is to their power and influence in the public sphere that I now turn.

References

 1 See Otto Kirchheimer, *Political Justice* (Princeton: Princeton University Press, 1971) for the radical case. Weber never seems to have presumed any *necessary* relation between representative democracy and the rule of law, however close the correspondence. See Weber, *Theory of Social & Economic Organization,* pp. 124–132, 324–329 and *Law in Economy and Society.*
 2 An excellent critique of caretaking is Paolo Freire, *Pedagogy of the Oppressed* (NY: Herder and Herder, 1972); and *Education for Critical Consciousness* (NY: Seabury, 1973). I present an alternative to this all-too-characteristic feature of social science research practices in Chapter 8.
 3 Sigmund Freud, *Civilisation and its Discontents* (Garden City, NY: Doubleday Anchor, 1958); Wolin, *Politics and Vision,* Chapter 9.
 4 See Emile Durkheim, *Selections,* edited by George Simpson (NY: Thomas Crowell, 1963).
 5 Wolin, *op cit* Chapter 10.
 6 Michel Foucault, *Discipline and Punish,* (NY: Random House, 1978). Also see John O'Neill, "Defamilization and the Feminization of Law in Early and Late Capitalism," *International Journal of Law & Psychiatry,* Volume 5, Nos 3/4 (1983).
 7 See generally my *The American Ideology,* particularly Chapters 1, 2, 7–9.
 8 See my "Reading Max Weber: the Limits of Sociology," *Sociology,* Volume 10, No. 2 (May, 1976), pp. 297–315; and *Tradition and innovation: The Idea of Civilization as Culture and its Significance.*
 9 Compare Weber, "Politics as a Vocation," *op cit* to *Theory of Social and Economic Organization,* pp. 329–341 and *From Max Weber,* pp. 196–244, where Weber discusses *bureaucracy* as a vocation. I discuss this point and its significance in "Technocracy and Late Capitalist Society," *op cit.*
10 Karl Mannheim, *Man and Society in an Age of Reconstruction* (London: Routledge and Kegan Paul, 1940), p. 58.
11 Mannheim, *Essays in the Sociology of Knowledge* (London: Routledge and Kegan Paul, 1952), pp. 235–249; Durkheim, *The Division of Labour in Society,* pp. 401–409; DeGrazia, *op cit;* Thomas, *op cit;* Arendt, *The Human Coalition,* chapters on "the public and private realm" and "labour".
12 See R. H. Coase, "The Nature of the Firm," *Economica,* New Series, Volume 4 (1937), pp. 386–405.
13 Wilson, "Technocracy in Late Capitalist Society," *op cit.*
14 Arendt, *The Human Condition,* p. 123. Also see Wilson, "Functional Rationality and 'Sense of Function'", *op cit.*
15 Kirchheimer, *op cit;* C. B. Macpherson, *Democratic Theory* (London: Oxford

University Press, 1973); Macpherson, *The Life and Times of Liberal Democracy* (NY: Oxford University Press, 1977).

16 Arendt, *The Human Condition,* p. 200 on power. Weber's "rationalistic bias" is discussed in *Theory of Social & Economic Organization,* pp. 92–93. For commentary Wilson, "Reading Max Weber," *op cit.*

17 Weber, "Politics as a Vocation," *op cit* p. 128.

18 Harold Innis, *Empire and Communications* (Toronto: University of Toronto Press, 1950); Innis, *The Bias of Communication* (Toronto: University of Toronto Press, 1951). Compare to Arendt, *The Human Condition,* pp. 175–247.

19 In this regard see Norton Long, "Bureaucracy and Constitutionalism" in Long, *The Polity* (Chicago: Rand McNally, 1962), pp. 64–76 for one of the original statements of the position. Also V. A. Subramaniam, "Representative Bureaucracy: A Reassessement," *American Political Science Review,* Volume 61 (1962), pp. 1010–1019. For commentary, Wilson, "Elites, Meritocracy and Technocracy," *op cit.*

20 In this study I attempt to fuse some of the major concerns of political theory and comparative institutional analysis in the study of politics, on grounds that the present academic division of labour in the discipline seriously impedes the practical contribution (in the Aristotelian sense) that it might make. See Chapters 2 and 6 for a reference to Aristotle's understanding and its relation to present conceptions of practice and the practical.

Chapter 6
Discretion in Politics, Administration and Law

I

The fact that the discussion which follows constitutes a separate chapter should not be taken to mean that discretion does not count as a problem of institutional polity. Indeed, I shall argue in what follows that discretion as such needs to be understood in a very broad and wide-ranging sense if it is to function effectively as a device for studying the nature, possibilities and limits of political management. Only in this way will it be possible to address exercises of discretion as they occur in politics and law as well as in public administration. Focussing on discretion allows us to see the original understanding of the problem as it was formulated by courts, judges, and the legal profession. It also forces us to realize that its present redefinition clearly constitutes an attempt to rehabilitate discretion so that it no longer functions in a critical and negative way, but instead is seen to be necessary in many of its forms to dynamic administration in the public interest. A final upshot of this focus will require us to employ the operative notion of discretion in such a way that it reaches beyond bureaucratic administration to technocracy, political leadership, and even to courts and judges.

The basic assumption implicit in what follows is that careful drafting of legislation, and spirited supervision of those to whom its execution, implementation and enforcement is delegated ought not to be given up on just because the results of efforts in this direction so often fall short. Again, I would argue not only that this shortfall is part of politics and the political process, but that an adequate public response to it is absolutely essential to the good health and functioning of representative institutions. This means that I oppose present efforts, strongly supported by those in favour of technocratic management of government (and the economy), to play down the importance of the distinction between politics or policy and administration, not because I deny that the political element enters into administrative implementation, but because such a tack makes efforts to honour what is at base a sensible, and highly significant, distinction far less possible or acceptable. There is a difference between admitting that administration has unmistakeable political properties, and allowing this admission to justify giving up on efforts to enforce the distinction at all. This is especially true given the nature of the rule of law and the supremacy of law, for these doctrines constitute the cornerstone not only of legality but of representative institutions in advanced industrial societies.[1]

Apart from the reasons already advanced in past chapters for the public's tendency to support discretionary initiatives beyond what could reasonably be called the electoral mandate, there is a fairly recent development that has accelerated this tendency considerably. I have in mind the view, increasingly presented in public contexts, that today's political and military realities, as well as the emergence of an international economy characterized by countries behaving like firms in order to compete effectively, have contributed even further to "complexity" and the resultant need for speed which is already so central a factor in policy-making in advanced industrial societies. It is sometimes even argued that representative institutions, already difficult to defend in the present setting, have become thoroughly dysfunctional when measured against this requirement of effectiveness in the international economic arena. Japan is put forward as the example of a country which produces for an international market that it monitors carefully, and is therefore quite correctly evaluated as that nation-state which is the best at functioning *as a firm*. Representative institutions, and a whole host of political traditions associated with pluralism, voluntarism and minimum state interference in matters economic, are viewed as liabilities precisely because of their preference for openness, deliberation, and representation.

The idea that there is a problematic tension approaching a zero sum game between representative democracy and competitiveness in newly emergent international markets has been able to trade on the on-again-off-again injunction to governments to behave in a more "businesslike" fashion. In most cases what is being offered as a basis for good government functioning resembles in its major outlines nothing so much as the necessarily restricted options that have arisen for democracy in responding to economic crises, environmental disasters, and global war. This is a telling indictment of many of the corporatist schemes and models now being offered as ways of dealing with the problem of maintaining comparative advantage in the new economic circumstances. Representative democracy, already on the run in the ways indicated, is now assumed to be almost totally dispensable. The fact that Western societies have traditionally viewed economic activity as a *means* to the attainment of non-economic values of a political, social and cultural kind is all too readily forgotten in the haste to be *au courant* with the latest in corporatist thinking.[2]

Another issue to be contended with arises as a corollary to the developments outlined above. It is the serious damage being done to the possibility of responsible political management by citizens and publics as a result of efforts to actually operate governments as if they were businesses. As already noted, very few businesses operate, or ever operated, in the way that those encouraging this move on government's part allege. One wonders how successful they would have been had they followed the excessively formalistic and highly structured blueprints that have been forwarded to governments as the best way of functioning efficiently and effectively. Corporatist and technocratic approaches cannot be fully appreciated in terms of their present appeal if this past history of infatuation with business models is not known and its consequences understood. For it is here that we can see clearly just where the notion that efficiency and effectiveness preclude, or at least require the substantial alteration of, representative institutions and government access to organized and unorganized publics originated.

The initial form that recognition of the need for speed and expertise in the face of this emergent complexity took was executive centralization and central government concentration. This accords closely with the view of efficient and effective government as government formally structured along functionally rationalistic and bureaucratically hierarchical lines. After all, the idea that governments ought to be run like businesses strongly implies that they should be structured and organized in the ways that large corporate, oligopolistic and managerial undertakings are organized. The added observation that business organizations are not typically subject to the responsibilities that accrue to governments in representative democracies only underscores the fact that the real planning horizon for such governments is all too often the next election. This is a real problem which citizens and publics must seriously consider, and it is one which becomes less and less likely to be so considered the more representative institutions, and the political element generally, are allowed to atrophy in favour of the more passive types of roles and statuses already discussed.

Another reason behind the movement toward order, status and closure in advanced industrial societies is probably more germane to European countries. While North America shook off or refused to acknowledge the influence of many feudal and mercantile economic institutions and practices, these institutions have continued to exist and be factors in European development, even into the present. Without becoming too carried away by the claim to uniqueness on the part of settlers in the "new world", it must be clear that pre-modern institutional forms were closely associated by these settlers with the very countries and cultures which had proscribed, and ultimately transported them, to North America and Australia. The point here is that bureaucratic rationalization is much better able to blend into pre-modern institutional forms of organizing where these forms still possess residual legitimacy. In the case of North America and Australia, bureaucratic development was less able to trade on these pre-modern forms and practices, which meant that a new basis for legitimizing organization separate from that of tradition, convention or the routinization of charisma was needed.[3]

Only in the case of the United States, however, was this requirement for a new basis of legitimation met by a revolutionary break and a fresh start. To be sure, this has probably served to make legitimation on meritocratically rational grounds *easier* there than in countries like Canada and Australia, where residues have remained important as both a reminder and a part of their respective evolutions as members of the British Commonwealth. The blending of mercantile and early corporatist forms with modern, secular and *formally* meritocratic administration in Canada has made it virtually impossible to understand Canadian society by reference to right-left and capitalist-socialist labels and epithets. Weber's distinction between pre-modern and modern bureaucratic organization is very useful in providing a frame of reference which addresses the contrast between traditional and legal-rational grounds as bases for legitimizing bureaucracy and functional rationality in the public sectors of all the advanced countries. Since legitimation is a matter which is very closely tied to discretion, it is important to relate it to discretionary exercises in all spheres of institutional polity, including the legal and judicial system.

II

Discretion can only formally take place where some person or group is acting on the basis of pre-existent legislation.[4] This legislation, usually in the form of statutes, but often in the form of rules, regulations, orders, and instructions to administrative bodies, is the basis for the claim to legitimacy that those exercising the discretion offer. In particular, it is to specific sections, phrases, and clauses that administrators, as well as politicians, political appointees, and judges and magistrates point when they are asked to justify a particular line of decision, whether of a political, administrative, regulatory or judicial nature. In the case of judges and magistrates in common law countries, the injunction to function independently of politics and public administration has led to a parallel system of case law based on *stare decisis*. Again, however, only in the United States, and to a certain extent in Canada and West Germany, have high courts been permitted to go beyond the interpretation of statutes to challenge their legitimacy through the aegis of judicial review.

The idea that courts and judges, of whatever standing, ought to have the power to nullify acts of the peoples' representatives presupposes the existence and force of some written document which has the status of a constitution. This constitution, in turn, is treated not as if it were a statute, but rather as if it were a "higher law" against which the statutory exercises of legislatures are to be measured and evaluated. West Germany is the sole example among countries whose legal system is a product of the Code Napoleon rather than the common law of a system which allows for considerable judicial review of legislation. This provision for review was put in place after World War II, and has functioned in the main as a defender of civil rights and liberties and an arbiter of the division of powers between federal and state *(Land)* governments. Canada, firmly within the parliamentary tradition, as well as the common law, has for some time treated the British North America Act as a constitution for purposes of arbiting its federal system as well. More recent extensions of judicial initiative are responses to the patriation of this document and its formal declaration as a constitution with an entrenched charter of rights.

My reasons for discussing courts and judges at the outset relates to the fundamental incompatibility between parliamentary supremacy and the presence of a constitution which is considered to be a higher law. The paragon case, cited time and again, of what is likely to happen whenever some document is given this sort of status relative to legislation is the United States, for in this extremely important instance the idea of the supremacy of their constitution over acts of Congress led to a dispute as to which of the three "branches" was to be the *final* arbiter and interpreter of its meaning. Though the possibility of review and nullification resided in a statute providing for its appelate jurisdiction rather than in the constitution itself, the United States Supreme Court was able to legitimize its claim over that of the Congress, in no small part because it was, after all, *statutes* that were being scrutinized. For different reasons it was also able to make its claim stick against the president and the executive branch, probably because at a critical juncture in the court's development after the Civil War there was a series of relatively weak, and in some cases ineffectual presidents.[5]

Code law systems on the continent of Europe and in Japan for the most part continue to honour the historical reflex associated with the French Revolution, and Bonaparte's consolidation of it. Here courts and judges are not in fact independent, are seen to embody the interests of Society as such, and are for the most part strictly enjoined from anything but the most rigid interpretation of statutory enactments. The reflex to which I referred was the fact that courts and judges had been strong supporters and defenders of the *ancien regime* prior to the French Revolution. The Code Napoleon harbors a suspicion of courts and judges, and grants to the legislature a near-total monopoly of the power to make law. There is to be no parallel system of judge (or bench) made law, since judicial decisions can only be legitimated by careful reference to an operative statute of the legislature, not by pointing to an earlier judicial decision as is the case under *stare decisis.*[6]

Parliamentary systems in Great Britain and the Commonwealth, with the slight exception of Canada in the ways indicated, lie somewhere in the middle between the United States at the one extreme, and countries which honour the Code Napoleon at the other. There are two component parts of the rule of law running parallel to one another, but judges and magistrates are not permitted to review and nullify acts of the legislatures in question. The presence of parliamentary supremacy limits the courts to interpretation, admittedly of a broader type than in Code law countries, but nonetheless far short of the powers potentially available to the federal judiciary in the United States. While parliamentary systems claim to possess constitutions, and to operate under constitutionalism and the rule of law, these are not predominantly written documents and are not viewed as a "higher law" above legislative enactments. Indeed, the British "Constitution," and by attribution those of other commonwealth countries, is comprised of statutes, rules, regulations, orders, and judicial decisions, along side unwritten conventions and traditions, and historic documents. Lacking the status of a higher law, these countries (with the exception of Canada) exhibit a parallel system of judge made law and the power of interpretation, but not the power of review and nullification.

The status of legislation *vis-a-vis* the rule of law is an important consideration when studying both legitimation and representation. Where courts and judges are permitted to review and nullify, this activity amounts to the performance of a guardian function by non-elected individuals whose positions are secure given the committment to the political independence of the judiciary. Where judges are seen to depart from precedent, their good reasons cannot abjure the fact that some form of discretion has been exercised, even if it is called equity and alleged to be essential to the rule of law. Judicial independence amounts to a grant of tenure not totally unlike that which follows the period of probation prior to a permanent appointment in the scheduled civil service. In this respect judges do not differ that significantly from their counterparts in the Code Law countries, who are in fact scheduled civil servants in no way "independent."[7]

The way in which discretion has acquired its new respectability relative to the way it was traditionally understood is of the greatest importance. It is, I submit, directly linked to the emergence of a contemporary "rational" notion of deference tied to claims of complexity and the need for expertness and speed. Discretion is a key concept because the way it is worked out in political, administrative and legal practice serves to effectively define the parameters that seek to supplant representation, or make sure these mechanisms and processes do not function in practice the way they are supposed to in theory. A central fulcrum in this regard is the interface between law, legislation and the judiciary. I have tried to show how different systems have dealt with this interface because I believe it is an indispensable starting point for examining discretion in politics and public administration as well as in judge-made law. While the remarks that follow certainly do not presume that *any* representative system, or any legislation, automatically constitutes and epitome, I would claim that representation and the central role of legislatures is the most important single element in our modern political heritage, and is almost *always* to be preferred to other modes of policy-making.

The reason that I feel so strongly about legislatures, and the political parties and organized interest groups that go along with them, is that these institutions are the cornerstone of any hope for political management as their necessary complement. Greater public participation has been frustrated at every turn first by the modern Judaeo-Christian conception of wealth as property necessitating stewardship, and thereafter by the rise of commercial, but particularly industrial, capitalism with its demand for hard work and long hours under difficult conditions. Once this system had "succeeded", in the sense of producing a surplus sufficiently continuous to be above subsistence for most, the foundation was laid for the development of the sort of passivity, apathy and deference given in the priority of consumer and audience roles, and further heightened by the need for speedy decision-making under conditions of complexity and unpredictibility. Austerity and economic downtown provide yet another excuse for deference, in this case through a plebiscitary system that confines citizenship to choosing the alternative to the present party in power. That this choice is often a negative one is evident from the fact that many or most are actually voting *against* the party in power rather than for the opposition.

While one might argue that two party systems provide for a higher level of long term stability in government acitivities than multi-party systems, this is usually the sort of statement made by partisans of the former speculating about what effect the latter would have on the country they come from. Multiparty systems not only generate more formally organized party structures, particularly of the centre and left, than do two party systems. They normally "represent" particular interests or factions in a direct way unlike the indirect representation interest groups secure as a consequence of their status and influence over political and administrative activities in two party systems. Indeed, it has been suggested that most parties in multi-party systems more closely resemble well-organized interest groups in two party systems than they do political parties in these systems. While one might argue that this view is a bit extreme, it does draw attention to the two major methods of representation in advanced industrial societies. It seems to me that in *both* instances a political situation exists within which discretionary activity by non-elected officials and judges can be maximized. In what follows, I want first to compare in more detail the old and the new view of discretion, then focus on the three key areas of politics, public administration and law in order to show the form it takes, and some of the political consequences for representative institutions.

III

The effective power which the capacity to exercise discretion confers is in direct proportion to the felt need for government and law in given areas of collective life. The greater the share of activities in the total society carried out by or on behalf of government, the greater the opportunity for discretion by politicians and public administrators. If a society is particularly litigious, or committed to the notion that their constitution is, after all, a "higher law", then this will increase the likelihood of judicial discretion. A difficulty with the stupendous rate of growth of government in the advanced societies is implicit in the idea of a democratic mandate. Because we live under representative institutions and the rule of law, every extension of government activity is automatically presumed to accord with the interests of the people. It is their representatives, it is pointed out, who are responsible for this growth of government and public administration, and, in the recent Canadian case, even for the increased volume of activity which the judiciary must carry out. The public is thereafter assumed to consent to these developments.[8]

Whereas businesses and industries are increasingly required to honour an extended conception of "social" responsibility beyond (and occasionally opposed to) that which is normally owed to shareholders, governments are presumed for the most part to be socially responsible because they reflect the policies of the formally elected representatives of the people, either directly or through the actions of those appointed and scheduled officials who are in theory "accountable" to these representatives. It is this issue of responsibility and its relation to accountability which is at the heart of discretion in politics and administration in the advanced societies. I have already pointed out how consequential has been the new revised attitude toward discretion where public and civil servants are concerned. The fact that instead of speaking of responsibility and accountability we so often speak of "responsiveness" suggests that aspects of the rule of law connected with public control of politicians and, indirectly, of administrators is in a serious state of atrophy, if not eclipse. Bureaucratic "representation" of the sort already discussed is alleged to guarantee such responsiveness, at the same time that it justifies diminishing concern about the collapse of the rule of law as it relates to discretion.

An indirect beneficiary of these developments, ironically, has been the courts and judiciary, and the legal profession as a whole. Whenever the legislature finds that it has been bypassed, for whatever reason, by executive, administrative, or judicial bodies, the result will be an atrophying of those properties of the rule of law that relate to popular sovereignty. Since this latter doctrine finds its most basic and proximate meaning in the doctrine of legislative supremacy in all representative democratic systems, the possibilities of meaningful public understanding and control diminish accordingly. It is at this point that legislatures find themselves in a situation which, though largely initiated by their respective executive and governing groups, carries through to other aspects of public life. Rendered impotent as such by the demands of party discipline, the initiative soon enough passes from the executive or governing groups internal to the legislature to administrative, regulatory and civil service bodies outside it which are theoretically "accountable" to it. The decreasing ability of the legislature to remedy a situation in which the lion's share of legislative drafting is already occuring in ministerial bureaucracies leads to the increased likelihood of unwarranted discretion.

For the crisis of modern Western representative democracies we need therefore look no further than the legislature, and the way the people have allowed it to progressively lose more and more of the power that goes with its major function.[9] Legislative drafting, wherever it occurs, is all too often careless and occasionally thoroughly incompetent. This provides the basis for an immense amount of potential discretion beyond the amount which anyone expects as a result of unanticipated and changing conditions. After all, if the legislation could specify precisely and anticipate fully, there would be no need for administrative implementation at all. But admitting this must not lead to the sort of cynicism which all too frequently seeks to justify *less* concern about these matters because, after all, some discretion is necessary and inevitable. Another consequence of poor legislative drafting is that it goes hand in hand with a lack of concern on the part of the legislature and its leadership groups with the supervision of public administration in all its guises. Lack of resolve on the matter of legislative drafting breeds a similar lack of resolve where the supervision of public administrators implementing this (and other) legislation is concerned.

It is at this point that the public will frequently seek a judicial, legal or litigious remedy for this difficulty, in many instances actively supported by leadership groups in the legislature. Individually, it will be argued that this is the only way to secure rights of a *political* character no longer defended by legislative bodies. There may even be pressure to give the judiciary a broader mandate to interpret legislation, one which approaches judicial review. To be sure, nothing better indicates the relative position of the two bodies of law than the presence or absence of effective judicial review. At the same time, judicial review has proven to be relatively ineffective in protecting the public against administrative discretion in the United States. The proposal for an *ombudsman* in common law countries reflects the inability of these countries to really control such discretion in the absence of legislative (or executive) will, while it underscores the lack of applicability of devices within Code Law systems like the French *Conseil d' Etat,* which accomplishes this objective with a relatively high level of reliability. The idea that the courts should be constantly scrutinizing legislatures with a critical eye is itself a notion that goes far beyond their responsibility to protect the civil rights and liberties of individuals and minorities.[10]

All of this is made the more interesting by the fact that the assault on discretion was originally a *joint* effort of legislatures and members of the judiciary in common law countries. This is not intended to downplay their very different reasons for concern, even though *both* institutions were heavily dominated by members of the legal profession, who took a dim view of the effects that complexity, rapid change, and the tremendous growth of public administration were having on the role and status of both legislation and bench made law. The result, quite in contrast to Code Law countries, was an excessive reaction to discretion *per se* which became known as the "extravagant" version of the rule of law because of its committment, at least in theory, to the so-called "non-delegation" doctrine. This doctrine was clearly impractical inasmuch as it began with the assumption that the exponential growth of public administration could be contained within the bounds of doctrines which had been formulated far in advance of the conditions that had made such growth inevitable. As a result of this impossible mandate, it became quite common to accept the practice of clearly unwarranted and excessive discretion alongside a theory which was opposed to *all* discretions as inherently a violation of the rule of law.[11]

K. C. Davis captured the essence of this problem when he argued that the very failure to distinguish necessary from unnecessary discretion could not help but lead to this great gap between theory and practice. The result might well be described as one in which both theoretical and practical developments are vastly wide of the mark, one on the side of excessive zeal, and the other on the side of the realization that very little of what is supposed to be problematic can be held to account. So long as discretion *per se* was thought to be the issue, no real effort to deal with the problem could be hoped for. It was simply too all-encompassing. Yet recognition of the importance of the distinction between necessary and unnecessary discretion raised serious difficulties for the legal profession, and for its members in the legislature and the judiciary in common law countries. Any argument in support of discretion on grounds that some was needed in the public interest for whatever reason was tantamount to acknowledging the inability of both legislatures and courts to keep pace with contemporary developments. It also underscored the challenge to traditional conceptions of both the rule of law and "justice."[12]

It is from this perspective that we need to examine carefully efforts to mediate between the extreme view which argues that no delegation by the legislature to administrative bodies should occur, and the equally extreme notion that there really is little use in trying to enforce any control whatsoever over this process given the impossibility of effective control of even a small portion of the discretion exercised. In addition to the theory of bureaucratic representation, the other major basis for retrenchment, mainly in support of this latter notion, has been the view that effective control of discretion depends on prior processes of "secondary socialization." Their job is to produce or generate competent administrators who understand, or will at least make an effort to understand, the difference between necessary and unnecessary, thus legal and effectively illegal, exercises of discretion. Again the problem is back-referenced to education and training, simultaneously expected to do the least and the most to make the system a going concern. In neither case, let it be noted, are we dealing with what could even remotely be called a "political" solution, for it would appear that the legislature, that agency most capable of such a solution in theory, lies near death in a comatose state.[13]

The sensible approach to the problem of discretion must be on the order of the one proposed by Davis, albeit with substantial amendments and caveats. Davis acknowledges that discretion is inevitable for reasons virtually given in the very existence of public administration as an implementer, executer and enforcer of legislation. But having said this, he does not as a consequence give up the ghost, even to the extent of seeing the job of producing "socially responsible" administrators to lie in prior processes of secondary socialization. Instead, he distinguishes necessary from unnecessary, warranted from unwarranted, discretion in a way guaranteed to frustrate anyone looking for a cut and dried approach to a most complicated problem, one which is endemic to representative democracies today. Having made this distinction, he then suggests ways of enforcing it which are both internal and external to public administration. The crux of his argument is that good, warrented or necessary discretion can only be realized where the relevant bureau, board, agency, commission or tribunal is required to police itself. It is futile, Davis argues, to rely on the legislature to do this, since the very complexity and resulting requirement of speed, expertise and consequent centralization puts an added burden on it when it cannot even realize effective supervision under existing conditions.[14]

While I would be the first to applaud Davis for his committment to such an approach, there is a sense in which it is little different from the emphasis on prior secondary socialization already discussed. Though there is an extended discussion of external (as well as internal) checks in his book *Discretionary Justice,* it is clearly the processes of *self* confinement and structuring which are supposed to be central to distinguishing the wheat from the chaff of discretion. To the extent that his argument makes practical sense as a realistic suggestion, particularly in the *absence* of effective external controls, it presupposes precisely the sort of prior socialization in the right values, attitudes, and behaviours that is endemic to the sociological approach to politics and government. It effectively rationalizes or legitimizes what actually occurs, much like what takes place with the alleged social responsibility of business. It does this by arguing, in effect, that because such prior socialization has occurred, the administrative outcomes which take place in real life situations must be *appropriate almost by definition.* This line of thinking is all too reminiscent of the focus on ascribed characteristics and preference for passivity and lack of external controls implicit in the idea and practice of bureaucratic "representation."

I am not arguing the Davis' recommendations reduce entirely, or even mainly, to this. What I am suggesting is that any meaningful effort to distinguish between warranted and unwarranted discretion in ways that promise to achieve the split *in practice* must begin with legislatures rather than letting them off the hook like Davis (and everybody else) does. To be sure, twentieth century developments may have rendered legislative bodies, as such, puerile in the absence of parties, executives and public administrators, for reasons that will be discussed in the next section. But all this means is that the revival of representative institutions, complemented by public interest and concern and the emergence of new public spaces in advanced industrial societies, depends on the people themselves as much as on their representatives. Persuading party leaders and their well "disciplined" members (save for the odd "free vote") to undertake a revival of legislative authority seriously threatens their control of the legislature as a forum for rubber-stamping policies jointly generated by the leadership of the governing party, political appointees, and top technocrats and bureaucrats. This, we are told, is what is required, organizationally speaking, if we want efficient and effective government in a complex, unpredictible, and highly interdependent world.

IV

It may seem odd to extend to the activities of political leaders and their parties the name of discretion. What makes this extension absolutely necessary, however, is the way efficient and effective government under party discipline has fundamentally compromised the original notion of representation that is implicit in Western political institutions. The mechanism of formal election continues unabated, but does so in the context of a system of parliamentary organization based on party discipline which appears in many significant respects to have violated the constituency based system of representation found in most two party systems. The point here is that the discretionary mandate permitted to elected representatives in two party systems presupposed that the individual would represent his constituents to the best of his ability *and judgement*. In effect, what has happened is that control of the individual representative's political (and politically relevant) behaviour has passed from his constituents to the party leadership in the lower house of parliament. The system of discretionary representation succumbed very quickly, it will be noted, to the requirement of organization and leadership as prerequisites for efficient and effective government in most two party systems.[15]

This description does not, of course, apply to the American political systems, where institutional competition based on a Tudor and Stuart model effectively cross-cuts and fragments the organizing power of federal and state political parties. But this is no endorsement whatsoever of the deadlock that often arises when the separately elected legislatures and their respective executives engage in a standoff. The original notion that the best government was the least government motivated this institutional competition, one that originated prior to the real development of political parties, even in England. Nowadays such a view hardly can be said to serve the interests of citizens and publics, and is in many respects no less regressive than the idea of turning social services over to private enterprise and vacating the regulatory arena altogether. Indeed, the problem with any system which is premised on deadlock is that its leading or governing elites are often better able to guarantee a monopoly over citizens and publics than would be possible under parliamentary two party government. The significant exception to this generalization is the fate of organized interest groups, who often benefit from the fragmentation of the power to govern and make laws found in the American systems.

While federalism might be argued to provide a constructive kind of jurisdictional fragmentation conducive to better government, it simply proliferates the number of governments under conditions in which such an option cannot generally be avoided. There are usually very sound territorial and

cultural reasons for federal governments, but this on its own does not necessarily guarantee an open political system in which it is possible for representation to survive against the rhetoric of efficiency and effectiveness. In
fact, it may well provide yet another basis for institutional competition,
particularly where each jurisdiction is the monopoly of one of the two political parties in a two party system. In the American Case, the sheer number
of states, coupled with the post-World War II demands of Western leadership, have led to the collapse of federalism as a competition between jurisdictions in favour of centralized government and extensive federal initiatives. In Canada, by contrast, the presence of a ten-to-one province to
federal government ratio has resulted in a more consistently balanced competition than in the United States, with its fifty-to-one ratio.[16]

Where it is multi-party systems like those found in Western continental
Europe that are in question, the presence of well organized parties, particularly of the centre and left, allow for a far greater differentiation in types
and styles of citizen and public participation than one generally finds in two
party systems. This is reflected in party structures, which are more permanent in multi-party systems than is the case in two party systems. In the
latter case, party organization is lamentably almost non-existent save for the
brief periods prior to and during formal elections. In contrast, multi-party
systems exist as *bona fide* structures reflecting the various types of participation (and employment) available there. This situation is, however,
blunted in its impact to some degree by the party list system that operates in
place of the constituency based method of representation found in two party
systems. While one could argue that the effective eclipse of this method of
representation as a consequence of party discipline has served to diminish
the difference between the two systems in practice, it would be better to
focus on the sense such an electoral system is likely to make in those small,
homogeneous nation-states with long established political conventions that
make up a significant portion of those countries with this form of party and
electoral system.

What is central to the arguments offered in support of the superiority of
each system over the other bears importantly on representation. It is frequently argued that whereas multi-party systems achieve superior representation of citizen and group interests because of the sheer number of parties,
two party systems sacrifice such representation in favour of the stability
which is argued to arise out of minimizing differences in the search for a
majority of constituencies, if not votes. Spokesmen for two party systems
note the tendency to unstable coalitions which is always a possibility in
multi-party systems, in contrast to the occasional minority governments that
take place in two party parliamentary systems. The American equivalent to
this would be institutional competition, jealousy and deadlock between le-

gislative and executive "branches", whether or not it reflects political party differences between them. Supporters of multi-party systems focus instead on the way that their parties reflect real differences in the society better than the major contenders in a two party system forced to seek after a majority of constituencies as a basis for governing. Recourse to coalition governments is seen to be a lesser evil when compared to the failure of the dominant parties to meaningfully represent societal interests.

The fact that spokesmen for two party systems *criticize* the main contenders in multi-party systems on grounds they resemble interest groups in two party systems is seen as evidence of the failure of parties in the latter systems to properly represent. Supporters of multi-party systems see this as a strength rather than a weakness, but it is quite clear that such systems are best able to combine relative stability with this more direct form of representation where established conventions and traditions serve to mellow the always-present temptation to conflict and non-cooperation. In both cases at issue here, one cannot avoid dealing with the comparative success of organized interests in achieving their goals, either directly as in the first instance or indirectly as in the second. Multi-party systems, after all, are mainly comprised of parties which reflect the *dominant occupational interests* in society to the extent that each can speak with one voice (business, labour, agriculture, civil service and government). The question is really whether these interests are any less successful when they operate indirectly on major political parties (particularly in the United States) than when they are directly represented as a party in a coalition government where they must often compromise, or at least trade-off preferences, in and through the law-making and governmental process.

Another issue relates to the opportunities for small, medium, or up and coming interests to get the ear of government. In this case it could probably be argued that two party systems provide for greater scope for such groups, if only because the governing coalition in multi-party systems, and the legislature as a whole, is likely to reflect the monopoly position held by those occupational interests on which parties are so often based in such systems. Parties seeking a majority of constituencies in two party systems, on the other hand, may find it problematic to become too closely tied to one or a few interests prior to contesting an election. This is more likely to happen *after* a given government has been established and finds itself in power, if only because organized interests are often indispensable sources of expertise for governments, ministries or caucuses attempting to formulate statutory legislation. The American situation also lends itself to such arrangements, subject of course to the institutional split between legislative and executive branches that is always at least as important as partisanship in these matters. Here it could readily be argued that the sheer competitiveness and existence of plural centres of power allows better access to a wide range of groups than is the case where parliamentary systems operate under conditions of tight party discipline. Parliament becomes little more than what one commentator has called a "policy refinery" efficiently processing policies and decisions of the governing party, in contrast to the United States, where branches as well as parties regularly compete and challenge one another.[17]

As noted, a serious obstacle to any attempt to realize dynamic representative processes in the midst of demands for efficient operation and effective attainment of goals is the combination of political tensions, military threats and skirmishes, the emergence of an international market system where nation-states must behave like firms, and massive taxation, equalization, and transfer functions on the domestic scene. Both deliberative legislative bodies and the division of functions found in federal government, not to speak of heightened political involvement by citizens and publics, appear little less than an archaic residue of times past, a hangover of how things were done before we learned how to mange consensus and generate a social economy based on occupationalism, consumption and spectating. Politics and citizenship is seen as an ever-present threat to good decision-making in government for this among many other reasons, rather than a central vehicle for improving processes of policy-making in line with the way representative institutions were supposed to function. This assessment, I readily admit, flies in the face of the conventional wisdom on these matters, and requires extended comment for this reason.

The standard argument begins with the assumption that representative institutions are inherently time-bound to a period prior to the onset of full-fledged industrialization, urbanization and the emergence of mature industrial societies. As such they are in a fundamental sense obsolete, and can only be kept relevant to contemporary realities by constant adjustment and a substantial act of will. Here it is necessary to recall the alliance between the social-scientific preference for a focus on prior socialization as a sufficient condition for adequate "representation," and the present emphasis on passive and non-political activities like consumption, spectating and most of occupational life *rather than* citizenship. To be sure, this is closely related to the increasingly closed and status-based phenomenon of formal meritocracy discussed in earlier chapters. What it all amounts to is an endorsement of the idea that political and governmental institutions and activities at best exhibit a "lag" relative to societal developments, and at worst are little more than an anachronism. Let it be noted that this line of thinking is promoted both by those who oppose significant change and by those who favour it. In all cases it is the view that such institutions are obsolete which leads to calls either for their streamlining in the ways mentioned or for their wholesale abolishment.

I believe that such claims are historically challengeable and in any case fail to make analytical sense. While being the first to support the idea that citizens and publics must seek to overcome the failure of advanced industrial societies to become more constructively political by taking advantage of new public spaces which are opening up, I do not see this activity as one which occurs as an option to working through normal representative channels using the instruments of parties, organized interest groups, and the mass media. This is because representation is not for me a matter of whether it is possible to secure direct, as opposed to indirect, impact. Indeed, one of the problems of the direct approach which I alluded to when I discussed computer voting at the end of the last chapter is the fact that this approach undermines *process* at the same time that it favours a variation on direct democratic techniques which, given the technology involved, further exaggerates the non-deliberative "vote" as the essence, *rather than a last step,* in the exercise of the *activity* of citizenship. Note once more how such an approach leads to a situation in which citizenship, so defined, looks less and less different from the other manifestly non (or anti) political activities cited above. It is the mere *registry* of a vote and nothing more.

It is essential to revive the constituency basis of representation on which two party systems originally depended, even if it occurs at the cost of the efficiency and effectiveness normally associated with well-disciplined parties in parliament. The American example, because it fails to achieve such efficiency in the normal course of domestic, and occasionally foreign and military, policy considerations, ought not to be counted better as a consequence from the standpoint of public and citizen inputs. While one might argue that this arrangement redounds to the distinct advantage of certain organized interests, this should not lead to excessive infatuation with the idea and practice of deadlock where lesser agencies should function to *delay* passage of legislation, Multi-party systems may achieve better representation of *dominant* occupational interests in society, but this does not address the chances of other interests. Similarly, the availability of several forms of citizen and public participation given the nature of party structures in such systems should not lead us to ignore the effects on policy-making of near-compulsory membership in coalition governments where representation may be purchased at the price of needed stability.

Politicians in leadership positions under the regimen of strict party discipline simply possess too much of what I have called discretion. This was originally justified in the Burkeian formulation on grounds that constituents were not, after all, voting for someone like themselves whom they could instruct at every turn, but rather for someone who warranted this discretion because he was electorally responsible in a broader sense. The resulting party discipline is not only a central characteristic of two-party parliamentary systems, but of multi-party systems based on government by dominant coalitions as well. Only in the American case do we see an example of the failure of this discipline to achieve the efficiency and effectiveness coincident in the narrow sense with parliamentary government. In this latter case, it matters little whether the system is two or multi-party in nature, for in both instances the executive, or government, is formed out of the leadership of the majority party, or dominant coalition, in the lower house of the legislature, rather than as a result of a separate election like that which takes place in the United States. The presence of this discretion is real and consequential, and might be said to have expanded in the absence of citizen and public interest and participation. Delegation to non-elected officials is the major upshot of this vast discretion to organize, decide and implement free of all but the most occasional constraints in the form of elections.

V

In turning to legislative and governmental delegation to non-elected appointees and scheduled officials, I concentrate on a development which seems no less inevitable for us than it was for Max Weber. Weber saw bureaucratization as the leading edge, organizationally speaking, of what he believed was an inexorable process of rationalization and consequent de-enchantment. On the other hand however, Weber, speaking within the auspices of sociology rather than against them, could simultaneously view bureaucracy as the only alternative to dilettantism in the field of administration. In his list of the (presumably) affirmative characteristics of bureaucracy, Weber cites "precision, speed, unambiguity, knowledge of the files, continuity, discretion, unity, strict subordination, reduction of friction and of material and personal costs." By discretion Weber means the capacity, good sense and willingness to be discrete in the utilization of the knowledge bureaucrats have, not a power of initiative or room for manoeuvre under delegated legislation. The meaning, both in past times and today, that jurists, legal scholars and legislators have given to discretion is not, however, unrelated to the original notion assumed by Weber. For it is in their monopoly of actually or potentially relevant knowledge in the policy and implementational field that the claim of indispensability of these salaried non-elected career officials finds its justification.[18]

The point about seeing discretion *both* ways where the activities of bureaucrats and technocrats are concerned is that it allows us to fix on the extent to which the allegedly objective claim of expert knowledge requires a power of discretion for its active utilization and deployment. The conventional legal and juristic view of discretion in the common law presupposed that the presence of discretion could be corrected by the development of stricter standards and more precise criteria, combined with better supervision of process and behaviour. Legislatures and courts stood together in this evaluation, the first trying to achieve greater definiteness in its statutes and allied instruments, the second concerned to improve the procedures used to carry out obligations under this delegated legislation.[19] This latter function was a more pronounced activity of American courts than it was in other common law countries, where a stronger role was often played by the government as parliamentary executive. It is the idea that discretion is a form of *power* complementing, buttressing, and occasionally substituting for the formal authority conferred by the people on their elected representatives, whether in the presence or absence of a claim to objective expertise, that requires attention.

Specialized expertise and a monopoly position regarding knowledge relevant to policy and implementation is therefore of little significance where it is not accompanied by *the power, opportunity, or tendency* to act independently and in the absence of either prior instruction or subsequent accountability. To be sure, the problem of unwarranted discretion by non-elected officials may well be aggravated considerably by the fact that the elected representatives of the people are themselves engaged in forms of what I have termed discretionary behaviour. It is in this sense that one might characterize the problems arising out of administrative discretion as partially the result of a "double delegation" from the people. An attitude of laxity or contempt toward their responsibilities to the people can become a fixed attribute of a country's political elite. It would be most surprising, in the event, if this attitude did not either carry over into public administration, or constitute a *cause celebre* for administrators secure in their power and anxious to play the role of public guardian. In either instance, it is not the notion of objective knowledge *per se* that is being challenged here but rather the essential incompleteness of a doctrine which assumes that its possession carries with it an automatic basis for a justification of action.

Today the point of view toward administrative discretion is in a state of flux in many of the advanced societies regardless of their legal and juridical heritage. I noted already the tendency to evaluate the exercise of discretion by administrators less as an irresponsible escape from the provisions of legislation that could perhaps have been more precisely drawn, and more as a necessary activity reflecting the lack of expertise among legislators and politicians, combined with the complexity and unpredictability of events. Without in any way attacking the view that the present situation often necessitates such exercises of discretion, we can nevertheless refuse to accept either the theory of bureaucratic representation on its own or the view that discretion can be overcome by prior (and ongoing) secondary socialization in the right values, norms, and attitudes. While Davis accepts the need for an expanded conception of discretion based on the view that *some* discretion is frequently warranted and necessary, and therefore should be "legal," he leaves too much to the internal and self-policing functions of confinement and structuring for my taste. After all, one might argue, if legislatures were incapable of framing more precise legislation, for whatever reason, or of supervising delegations to administrative bodies in an earlier period, how can we expect them to improve their efforts now that these bodies are engaged in ongoing attempts at self-confinement and structuring in addition to their normal acitivites?[20]

There is no alternative in the present circumstances in which we find representative institutions in the advanced countries to insisting on self-confinement and structuring of the sort Davis recommends. This needs to take place, however, alongside public efforts, through the electoral mechanism and in other ways, to improve the drafting of legislation and the supervision of administrators acting under delegated legislation. To treat self-confinement and structuring as sufficient would be akin to settling for an *internal* audit of a public agency. My point here is not that the public, or given majorities, can constitute a check in the sense of being "correct" simply because they are the public, or a majority, in given circumstances. It is instead addressed to the futilitarian notion that such efforts are hopeless because, it is argued, there will always be exercises of discretion (or "bad" discretion), and therefore why try to control a relatively small percentage of it? This attitude is of the utmost significance to understanding the reasons for apathy and indifference on the part of individuals whom one could have expected to be politically active, or at least consistently concerned, about public matters.

It is the view of political economy and psychoanalysis together that political interests and concerns not directly related to one's own life situation provide evidence of "neurosis" which is the greatest barrier to public participation in matters where the public is absolutely necessary to the healthy functioning of representative institutions. This only seems peculiar so long as one fails to acknowledge the extent to which Freud's ideas and concepts, often interpreted by others, have been sedimented in every day conceptions of mental and emotional health. Along with this goes the view of political economy, adopted by Marx, that politics and government are mere "superstructures" relative to the mode of production in given societies. The two notions together now effectively undergird the contemporary understanding of political interest and participation in politics. When combined with what can only be termed the fetishization of objectivity, particularly as it relates to expertise of a technical and scientific kind, the result has been to effectively legitimize and rationalize public and citizen apathy and indifference.[21]

Though we may be willing to acknowledge the possibility than non-electoral forms of representation are regressive, and as a result insufficient *at best*, it is far more difficult to acknowledge the fetishistic character of the claim to objectivity based on the monopoly of a particular form of knowledge. If intellectuals can dismiss such an observation on the grounds that these are, after all, nothing more than *knowledge-claims,* the general public is usually not in a position to produce such a formulation. This is not a consequence of their "intelligence," but rather a function of the degree to which their "secondary socialization" has been successful rather than unsuccessful. The preference for roles that are passive rather than active, massifying rather than individuating, focussed on consumption and spectating as the supplement (or complement) to occupational life rather than on citizenship, are the hallmark of the advanced societies. One is compelled to wonder how long this political *regression* can continue before it has permanent consequences *even in the economic and cultural spheres of collective life!* The place to begin the movement toward public activism, and the insistence that representatives fulfill their mandate and honour reciprocity and real interdependence, is with the discretion exercised by non-elected officials. It is likely to be more effective to work backward from this double delegation, if only because insistence on better standards and supervision of delegated legislation is more likely to lead to changes in the way we pick legislators then electoral changes are to the appointment and scheduling of non-elected officials.

While I certainly would not want to say that precisely formulated statutes will eliminate the need for legislative and governmental oversight of administrative action, it will probably make the job considerably easier in the normal case. But it is the all-too-numerous instances where statutes are framed imprecisely, whether because of lack of time or expertise or because of inability to secure a majority or gain cabinet (or caucus) agreement, that the need for careful and consistent oversight arises. Thus there is something akin to a sliding scale in the relation between the drafting of legislation and its effective oversight. Failure to be precise, often accompanied by *explicit* provisions delegating a power of discretion to administrative bodies, argues for a *greater* oversight. Though Davis seems to presume that such oversight will follow from the self-confinement and structuring efforts of administrative bodies themselves, this claim can easily be challenged by his view of what often necessitates these latter efforts – the legislature's inability, rather than simply its failure, to be more definite.[22]

Though numerous commentators have noted that "political" reasons of the sort mentioned, rather than just considerations of time and expertise, help explain the vagueness and ambiguity of much legislation, this claim can be carried too far, particularly in parliamentary systems, but even in the American case. The underlying problem remains the determination to be efficient and effective, whatever the cost to democratic and representative institutions and processes. This is probably the ultimate sanction for the double delegation, and is dangerous to liberty inasmuch as it not only leads to public self-deprecation in matters political, but fails to meet the most important function which only representative democracy can really perform in large national-state systems.[23] I have in mind the view of political processes as a vehicle for political education. By education I do not simply mean education in the process, although knowledge of and respect for these processes is of the utmost importance. Political education for me is a reciprocal process between members and agents, agents and members, members and members. It is because agents are first and foremost members that the failure of political education in and through process may well be generating politically regressive behaviours, reflected in passivity, apathy, indifference and excessive deference to administrative and allied forms of expertise *on the part of politicians as well as the electorate.*

Again, however, it is the public impression that government must function in what is alleged to be a businesslike manner that reinforces the view that efficiency and effectiveness are values at last equal to those sponsored by representation. The fact that the two are seen to be in a zero sum relation to one another guarantees that democracy and representative institutions will come out the loser. I would argue that here one must carefully distinguish efficiency from effectiveness so that the real significance of the latter term can be seen to *require* process and political education, rather than speedy decision-making. The paramount importance of such process and education is to be contrasted to the sort of direct democratic devices like referenda, initiatives and recalls that it is argued can be brought into being much easier given the advent of automated electronic technologies for "voting." Not only are such devices manifestly non, or even anti-political, as noted. Their ultimate rationale for encouraging the sort of isolation and passivity that goes with such exercises of "citizenship" is precisely that they provide for a speedy *registry of opinion.* Anyone who could seriously offer such devices as ways to improve the process of politics and government is already so totally socialized in non or anti-political roles as to be virtually useless (if not dangerous) to the concerns of this study.[24]

VI

A final point of concern will require me to extend this discussion of admini-strative discretion so that it comprehends a phenomenon which is in one sense a part of this problem in the contemporary setting, but also constitutes a dangerous new departure in its own right – technocracy. Technocracy is to be distinguished from bureaucratic administration in a number of respects. First, it indicates that the public sector-private sector distinction so central to political economy and public administration has collapsed as a conse-quence of the increasing role of the state in the domestic and international economy. Second, it points to the heightened importance of science and science – based technology in production, research and development, and even administration and service activities in many spheres of collective life. A third factor is the emergence of giant, often multi-national, economic aggregations whose power is matched only by their interdependence with one another. Fourth is the emergence of operations research, systems theo-ry, and game-theoretical modelling techniques complementing increased reliance on automated-electronic and robot technologies. Finally, there is the fact that a central aspect of the experience of secondary socialization in the advanced societies is the tendency to confer rationality on structures rather than on individuals. I have already argued that this sedimentation of rationality into structures carries with it a preference for less active, or thoroughly passive, roles like consumption, spectating and often occupa-tional life itself.[25]

Technocracy is an approach to governing premised on the view that societies can be seen as systems in need of professional management. It emerges as a direct consequence of executive centralization in government, as Meynaud pointed out a generation ago.[26] Like bureaucracy in the Weberian formula-tion, it is equally at home in the public or private sector, even if it feels it can make its strongest contribution where these functions are blurred, or col-lapsed together, thereby providing for *state,* rather than merely governmen-tal, direction. It is equally adaptable to all legal and judicial systems, and can even be found, albeit in truncated form, in non-democratic and non-representative systems as well. In two-party systems governed by parlia-ments under the requirement of party discipline, it benefits from the control the governing party has over the legislature, and the political process as a whole, while in multi-party systems characterized by coalition governments, or in the American system during periods of presidential-congressional deadlock, it often benefits from the confusion and the inability to act. It also benefits from dissociating itself from public administration, on grounds of its more elite guardian status and its capacity to combine functionally expert knowledge with the knowledge of systematic management. It hastens to add that it is strictly subordinate to politically elected leaders, and has as its only concern the staff function of running the organization of government and administration.

Technocratic knowledge claims therefore do provide legitimation for both advisory and managerial roles. Though technocrats often employ the politics-administration dichotomy in an effort to justify their real influence by purposely diminishing its importance, they no longer honour the distinction even in the breach. Indeed, technocrats have gone beyond the distinction between input and output functions on which the concept of modern bureaucratic administration is based. Theirs is a manifestly *political* administration, not in the sense of encouraging public concern, interest and participation, but rather in the form of a thoroughgoing cooptation of public power as it is formally expressed through the representative mechanism. Politicians may rely on the skills, capacities and expertise of bureaucrats and other public administrators, but this power remains theoretically as well as practically incomplete in the absence of the politician. Technocrats have no such problem, for they believe that the society is a *system* to be managed and operated by governments. Since their theoretical understanding of the society is alleged to be complete, it is only a "convention" that really requires them to act through politically elected leaders.

It is hoped that the messy business of parties, interest group conflict, and formal elections can be contained, kept to a minimum and ideally made into a routine affair. While it really matters little which party or individual governs, it is better for their notion of efficiency and effectiveness if there is as much stability and continuity as possible. Only in this way will it be possible for them to maximize the application of the systems concept to society in the form of professional management. Technocratic management, it must be clear, is the absolute antithesis of political management as I have defined and discussed it. It treats all roles and statuses related to Society and the social as inherently preferable to those which even hint of politics as something involving the people in processes that serve to educate and enlighten both them and their agents. The best arrangement is plebiscitary democracy, if we must have the formal trappings of democracy. Where political parties insist on challenging the prevailing notion of functional rationality as an attribute of structures, it is best to try to substitute primaries for nominating conventions.[27]

A final concern on the part of technocrats is to place representation as a value and an objective at loggerheads with the rule of law. This is a prospect which is most attractive to politicians as well as bureaucrats, because it provides an unchallengeable basis of legitimacy for activities which may violate the spirit not only of legislation which is presently in force but of electoral promises. Even where no explicit or latent appeal is made to legality and the rule of law, it frequently functions as a justification for short-circuiting or ignoring altogether aspects of politics and government as process which are absolutely essential to representative democracy. One of the most serious problems that the advanced societies have is precisely the presence of a power of discretion that allows politicians, and the bureaucrats and technocrats who benefit from a double delegation of public power, to downplay or ignore altogether these processes. Even when written into statutory and organic law as a requirement of governmental activity, they are frequently interpreted in ways intended to reconcile their formal observance with the requirements of efficiency and effectiveness in pursuit of speedy decision-making under complex and unpredictible conditions.

On the other hand, nothing that has been said thus far about the relationship between representation and the rule of law is intended to challenge their mutual indispensability and essential complementarity in all the advanced societies. My major concern in drawing attention to instances in which the rule of law, in the truncated form of "legality," stands in irretrievable opposition to representation has been to show how significant is the dependence of representative institutions and processes on specific conventions and legal provisions defending their indispensable role in democratic societies. Here I have in mind statutes and allied legislative and administrative instruments, supplemented by judicial decisions. The issue is therefore not of a simple either-or nature, but rather relates to whether the rule of law shall have as one of its basic attributes the defence of representative institutions, or whether, on the other hand, it will favour a different set of values whose actualization effectively bypasses these institutions, for whatever reason (e.g. complexity, need for speed, expertise, stability, judicial supremacy, national security etc.). Institutions of polity require legal, as well as traditional and conventional, supports, and this should be forthcoming not only from legislatures, but from courts and judges in common law countries as well. This latter need is particularly acute in countries where the idea of a written constitution as a "higher law" is wholly or partially operative.

Representative institutions clearly possess a double aspect when considered in this light. They are (and should be) undergirded by the rule of law in several of their most central aspects, while at the same time setting unchallengeable limits to the degree to which any agent may convoke "legality" as a device for short-circuiting representative processes or ignoring them altogether. It is imperative in this regard that the distinction between crisis and non-crisis government be maintained.[28] This is just as important a matter where elected representatives are concerned as it is when considering the problem of discretion as it relates to administrators, bureaucrats, technocrats, and justices, judges and magistrates. To some extent this problem with agents arises out of the way that institutionalization *per se* all-too-often engenders passivity, apathy and deference to agents on the part of citizens and publics. This is complemented, to be sure, by the very nature of institutionalization throughout our formally meritocratic societies, where "rationality" is being sedimented and institutionalized, mainly under norms of functional rationality. Such traditionalization is difficult to reconcile with public interest and concern, particularly in circumstances where agents, regardless of political party or preferences, know that form is being purchased at the expense of substance. Representative institutions cannot for long perform their real public and citizen functions where such developments lead to the emergence of the political, administrative, and judicial guardians mentioned above.

Much of the justification for the claim that we live in times more complex and unpredictible than anyone has ever experienced is to be discovered in the phenomenon of "information". This is at the very least paradoxical if only because information overload logically justifies *more* participation, deliberation and process, *not less.* "Information", however, acquiesces in a system notion of organized efficiency and effectiveness where the society is treated as if it were one giant organization requiring professional management. Because there is alleged to be more information than ever before, it is argued that only those expert in separating the wheat from the chaff can be permitted access to it. The idea that any sort of collective sense of order demands application of the model of the formal organization writ large points to the overpowering influence of functional norms of rationality in our thinking. It also serves to emphasize how alien to politics and the political such an understanding and such priorities really are. What is required in the present circumstances is for politicians to stop turning to the experts rather than to the people when issues of a political nature arise. This only exacerbates the difference between agents and members, while it furthers the impression among non-elected agents that politics is a nuisance barely to be tolerated *by politicians* when it interferes with system planning.

One is compelled to raise once more a question which is absolutely central to this discussion, namely, what representation is supposed to mean. Is it a device, once institutionalized, for making participation difficult or impossible, or is it an instrument for giving the widest possible scope to participation in recognition not only of the limits of public delegation but of the need for process as political education? To the extent that representative institutions are viewed as *substitutes* for public interest and participation in politics and government, they will be formalized in ways which may damage them irretrievably even though they do not violate legality and the rule of law. The fact that citizens and publics may readily agree with politicians, bureaucrats and technocrats that efficiency and effectiveness are the real goals, and that this requires stability rather than effective representation, makes it extremely difficult to persuade them that their continued input is absolutely essential to sensible, politically rational policies. True, this will take more time in countries where time is money, but this is the *raison d'etre* of process as a device for political education.

There is no substitute for such process and education, whether by direct techniques of registration or by administrative discretion and technocratic initiatives. It is hard to know where to begin in all this, but the answer is clearly not to allow the rule of law an unfettered sway over the need for the heightened operation of these processes. The effective ambit of the representative function is in a period of serious shrinkage in the advanced societies for a number of reasons, some sensible, most unacceptable. Politically elected representatives of the people have got to open up public and representative processes, if only to see what they have been missing all these years. They too are members, and as such reflect the society's infatuation with specialized knowledge and expertise, particularly as it bears on scientific, technological, professional and managerial matters. They also embody, almost without regard to ideology or political party, the view that collective life is best ordered by reference to norms of functional rationality, and that these norms can be found either in the proper operation of businesses and industries, or in the systematic functioning of the state as a formal organization writ large. There are no easy mangerial techniques available to us to resolve the problems of discretion raised in this chapter, but a start must be made somewhere, and soon.

References

1 A. V. Dicey, *The Law of the Constitution* 10th edition (London: Macmillan, 1959, 1965); John Dickinson, *Administrative Justice and the Supremacy of Law* (NY: Russell and Russell, 1959).

2 Macpherson, *Democratic Theory;* Macpherson, *The Life and Times of Liberal Democracy.*

3 I discuss Weber's two forms of, two routes to, and two types of bureaucracy, found in *Theory of Social & Economic Organization* pp. 329–341, *From Max Weber,* pp. 196–244 and *Law in Economy & Society,* pp. 322–348, in *Tradition and Innovation,* chapter 5. Also see Helen Constas, "Max Weber's Two Concepts of Bureaucracy," *American Journal of Sociology* Volume 52 (1958), pp. 400–409.

4 Kenneth Culp Davis, *Discretionary Justice* (Baton Rouge, Louisiana: Louisiana State University Press, 1969) V, pp. 4–5, 21, 25–26; and H. T. Wilson, "Discretion and Administrative Process," *Osgoode Hall Law Journal,* Volume 10 No. 3 (Autumn, 1972), pp. 117–139.

5 Chief Justice Marshall, of the United States Supreme Court, made the strongest case for the necessary tie between the idea of a written Constitution as a "higher

law" above acts of the legislature, and the need for judicial review in *Marbury v. Madison* 1 Cranch 137 2L. Ed 60 (1803).

6 Henry Abraham, *The Judicial Process* (NY: Oxford University Press, 1962); Bernard Schwartz, *The Code Napoleon and the Common Law World* (NY: New York University Presse, 1956); Richard Wasserstrom, *The Judicial Decision* (Stanford- Stanford University Press, 1961).

7 Henry Friendly, "Judicial Control of Discretionary Administrative Action," *Journal of Legal Education,* Volume 23 (1971) pp. 63–69; Albert J. Reiss, "Research on Administrative Discretion and Justice," *Journal of Legal Education,* Volume 23 (1971), pp, 69–76; Joseph Steiner, "Judicial Discretion," *Cambridge Law Journal,* Volume 35 No. 1 (April 1976), pp. 135–157.

8 The difference between consent and consensus is all too easy to underestimate or ignore altogether. Even consent theorists all too readily focus only on the obligations of *agents*. That this is the source of one of our most serious misunderstandings in representative democracies must be clear from my effort to address the obligations of *the public* for the vitality of the political system. This is implicit in the distinction between citizenship and membership, and my corollary refusal to allow the assumption to stand that agents are automatically or necessarily better citizens than *other* members. See Pitkin, "Obligation and Consent," *op. cit;* Tussman, *Obligation & the Body Politic;* Alexander Bickel, *The Morality of Consent* (New Haven: Yale University Press, 1975), Chapter 10.

9 Aristotle, *Politics,* at 1179 b 20–1181 b 12–15 and 1252 a 1297 a 7 sees legislation as a device by which to *complete* our human nature in and through citizenship in the state as a body politic or constitution.

10 W. W. Crosskey, *Politics and the Constitution in the History of the United States* (Chicago: University of Chicago Press, 1953, 1980).

11 Dickinson, *op. cit.* But see Theodore Lowi, *The End of Liberalism* (NY: W. W. Norton, 1969), pp. 298–299, where he suggests an imperative need to return to the rule of non-delegation scrapped by the American Supreme Court after 1937.

12 Davis, *op. cit.* pp. 27–51.

13 Daniel Gifford, "Decisions, Decisional Referents & Administrative Justice," *Law and Contemporary Problems,* Volume 37, No. 1 (Winter, 1972), pp. 3–48; H. T. Wilson, "The Problem of Discretion in Three Languages," research document, Judiciary Study, University of Paris, March 1980.

14 Davis, *op. cit.,* pp. 52–96 at pp. 56–61.

15 The logic of the discretionary model rested on the existence of a constituency system which was *thereafter* aggregated in a legislative body. Party discipline undermines the intention of this system severely, and as a consequence suggests that a turn toward instruction is no less sensible and necessary than a paramount concern for the drafting of legislation and the supervision of all those exercising delegated authority under it.

16 Note that most of the growth areas for government action in Canada under the *British North America Act* have been in the provincial rather than the federal jurisdiction – health, welfare, local services, education, and the administration of justice.

17 Richard Van Loon and Michael S. Whittington, *The Canadian Political System,*

3rd edition (Toronto: McGraw Hill/Ryerson, 1981), pp. 616–665. Note that the chapter on parliament as a "policy refinery" is the *final* one of the book (19 of 19).

18 Weber, *Theory of Social & Economic Organization,* p. 337 on dilettantism as the alternative to bueraucracy; and Weber, *From Max Weber,* p. 214 on the affirmative characteristics of bureaucracy.

19 Ernst Freund, "The Use of Indefinite Terms in Statutes," *Yale Law Journal,* Volume 30 No. 5 (March, 1921), pp. 437–455; Davis, *op. cit.,* pp. 97–141.

20 Wilson, "Discretion in the Administrative Process," *op. cit.,* and "The Problem of Discretion in Three Languages," *op. cit.,* responding to the implications of Davis' proposal at *op. cit.,* pp. 58–59. Self-confinement and structuring in response to legislative vagueness, for whatever reason, cannot overcome the obligation of the legislature to supervise these activities by reference to all its normal powers (appropriations, legislative modification and amendment, appointment (or approval) of key personnel, and investigation). This is *the* central feature of the doctrine of the supremacy of law – that authority may be delegated (under controlled conditions) but *not* the responsibility for its exercise. Self confinement and structuring can be understood as a *method* of interpreting a statute which is *necessarily* subject to regularized periodic scrutiny by the legislature.

21 Robert Lane, "The Decline of Politics and Ideology in a Knowledgeable Society," *American Sociological Review,* Volume 31 No. 5 (October, 1966), pp. 647–662; and my critique in *The American Ideology,* chapter 2, "Knowledge & the Problem of Rationality."

22 This suggests that *the legislature* ought to be compelled to confine and structure itself in the way Davis has suggested for public administration, regulation, administrative law and process, and public enterprise. Only the general public, through its participation in and along side process, can make this happen, for special and vested interest publics have no incentive to do so. The only way the general public can do this is to realize and appreciate the difference between membership and citizenship, and the allied fact that agents are not necessarily better citizens than *other* members. This is discussed in more detail in Chapter 10.

23 Wayne A. R. Leys, "Ethics and Administrative Discretion," *op. cit.,* is a case in point. This study is an attempt to respond to the so-called "political" element in a way which does not use this observation as a device for *avoiding* the need to offer analysis and alternatives. Also see Wilson, "Discretion in Administrative Process," *op. cit.,* section on politics. Grant McConnell isolates two basic approaches to political factors in American governmental history – the organizational and the legal – in *Private Power and American Democracy* (NY: Alfred Knopf, 1965), pp. 280–292.

24 The idea of running government like a business is undeniably American in spirit and animus, as is evident from the *Hoover Commission Reports* in the 1940's and their not-inconsiderable fallout in the United States and Canada in particular.

25 Wilson, "Technocracy and Late Capitalist Society," *op. cit.* Also see Jean Meynaud, *Technocracy* (London: Faber & Faber, 1965).

26 Jean Meynaud, "The Executive in the Modern State," *International Social Science Bulletin,* Volume 10 No. 2 (1958).

27 David Lebedoff, *The New Elite: the Death of Democracy* (Chicago: Contemporary Books, 1983).

28 This distinction becomes more and more difficult to defend in practice for reasons already cited. Once the idea of crisis was extended from war to environmental disasters, and thereafter to economic depression, pre and post war, as well as wartime, responses to war, and continuous fiscal participation in mature capitalist economies not excluding wage and price controls, the stage was set for an alliance between the permanent expansion of government and the organizational principle of functional rationality. The latest phase of this alliance is now to be discovered in the idea of the business model, but adapted to the need for nation-states to function totally or sectorally as firms for purposes of competition in the international market. For a critical assessment of the concept of crisis, see my *Tradition and Innovation,* Chapter 1, section 2.

Chapter 7
Is a "Practical" Science of Politics Possible?

I

Few would object to the idea of a practical curriculum in the study of politics. Most would probably applaud just such a bias in the discipline known as "political science." To be sure, it can be argued that some areas of the discipline are *already* more relevant (thus presumably more practical) than others to an understanding of ongoing public affairs. Two examples that come immediately to mind are public administration and local and municipal politics. Here it would seem to be the diminished role of thought or theory in these areas which helps account for such an assessment. In the first case, it is assumed that administrators simply "carry out" or "execute" policies made by elected officials, thereby avoiding the complexities and intrigues of politics in favour of the simplicity and straightforwardness of "administration." While the dichotomy between politics and administration may be less acceptable in academic circles today than it was in the past, this assumption continues to fuel popular (and occasionally even official) thinking on the matter.[1]

In the case of local and municipal politics, it is precisely the baseline conception of politics as corrupt and venal which is often employed in order to discredit academic and scholarly efforts at understanding. The argument is that knowledge of a practical kind is available *only* to practitioners, or sound investigative reporters with good connections. While such a claim can be made for attempts to study all forms of government and politics, it rarely achieves the same effect that obtains when assessing how one gains a practical understanding of politics in local and municipal jurisdictions. This fact has an important bearing not only on public conceptions of how our political and governmental system works, but on the way political scientists view research and scholarship in their own discipline. It would not be too much to argue that a veritable "status order" has emerged in both public perceptions and in the discipline of political science. In the latter case a clear majority of those in the discipline have quite definite, if unstated, ideas about what fields are more and less prestigious, and where research in given areas fits into the hierarchical scheme of things.

All of this generates a strange result in the public (as well as the academic) mind, one which I shall call the "inversion effect" for want of a better term. The more distant the jurisdiction, the more important its endeavours, activities and peccadillos, the more immediate the less important – except when one must become "personally" involved because a local or municipal decision or policy is seen to affect one's self, family, property or neighborhood. Even in this latter instance, however, the bias about the practical already cited holds sway. "Getting involved" means becoming a participant or practitioner of one kind or another rather than seeking an academic understanding of the relevant issues. One may run for public office, join a citizen's pressure group, or engage in a variety of less continuous efforts to secure a desirable outcome or avoid an undesirable one. The fact that elected officials in municipal jurisdictions can so readily aspire (often successfully) to federal or provincial office only underscores the high percentage of the citizenry often found in metro-urban areas.

While local and municipal politics may offer a more immediate route of *potential* access to the individual in search of political understanding, it shares another limiting characteristic with more remote jurisdictions – particularly in Canada. I have in mind the sort of secrecy about the way decisions are made and implemented which has nothing whatsoever to do with matters touching on national security, such as they are. In effect, it is precisely the way that democratic politics "works" which constitutes a *barrier* to its understanding apart from the knowledge of practitioners and good investigative reporters. This only reinforces the feeling that academic concerns are irrelevant while it underscores the essential amorality of politics and the political in general. This attitude toward academic understanding has been aided and abetted by political scientists and political sociologists whose effect, if not their intent, has been to convince many that our choices are limited to either dicatatorship and totalitarianism or "politics" (and business) as usual.[2]

The way the inversion effect operates in political science is worthy of careful attention for reasons that have already been suggested. What is important here is to appreciate just how interdependent and mutually-reinforcing public and academic versions of this phenomenon have become in recent years. Academic political scientists all-too-often assume the viability of a status order which places research into remote and distant jurisdictions on a higher plane of prestige than the study of more immediate – and accessible – ones. Possible or actual familiarity breeds contempt! Thus as a rule those who study either federal politics or federalism *per se* stand above those studying provincial affairs, while the latter have a status superior to students of local and municipal politics. The tendency for those who study local and municipal affairs to end up at the low end of the totem pole is further reinforced by the correct, but often misleading, legal status of these jurisdictions as "creatures of the province" (or state). That this status holds can gainsay neither the central importance of the *functions* performed nor their range, occasion and sheer number in the contemporary setting.

Both public and academic assumptions on these matters have received consistent and continuing support from the recent prime minister of Canada, those in his government and in Parliament, as well as appointees, superbureaucrats and civil servants in Ottawa. Few ideas could lend more ready support to a politician or bureaucrat with centralization on his mind than the currently popular notion already cited that the federal bargain is best understood as a relation between *levels* of government rather than coordinate jurisdictions. The fact that the provinces allow the federal government to collect taxes for *both* jurisdictions under a convention ensconced in legislation serves to reinforce this idea. While no one would argue with the claim that the functions of government have grown exponentially in *all* jurisdictions over the past forty years, it is important to point out where most of this growth has been and what jurisdiction is constitutionally "responsible" for it.

It is the fact of vastly heightened *provincial* responsibilities in the areas of health, education, social services and law enforcement that necessitates a substantial revision of the existing accommodation on the matter of tax collection, for reasons which have been clearly and forcefully presented in two recent reports. What makes this observation all the more germane to our concerns here is the answer to the question which jurisdiction has the lion's share of responsibility for implementing and carrying out these programmes and functions: localities and municipalities. When this added factor is considered, the full consequences of the view of the federal bargain as a relation of levels is brought home. With the important assistance of the policy-administration dichotomy – the other major fiction encouraged by contemporary governments in order to obscure the reality of technocratic political administration – this view places those jurisdictions at the "administration" end of the hierarchy in the lowest status, and those at the "policy" end in the highest. The fact that a levels approach to federalism phantasizes the provinces themselves as appliers and executors of federally-framed programmes only underscores the above points about the consequences of such thinking and the impact on Canadian attitudes of *American* developments. It also indicates the extent of our acquiescence in the organizational principle of functional rationality, the central ordering principle of our civilization as a culture.[3]

One might go further and even hypothesize that the very growth of federal government, while to some extent unavoidable, has been aided and abetted by such public and academic understandings of political process and relations between jurisdictions. A "levels" concept supports the association of remoteness with importance already alluded to, while it provides a more ready avenue for models and frameworks *precisely because* the distance and lack of access is seen to be so considerable. This, in turn, promotes a lower estimate of those very areas, programmes, functions and jurisdictions which are close by and about which we might readily find out more, albeit as participants or practitioners rather than observers and academics. In one sense, the result to date looks more and more like the proverbial self-fullfilling prophecy. What is to some extent now true becomes the more true as a result of public and scholarly acceptance of the levels notion, while what is hardly true or not yet true at all can be counted on to become true with the passage of time.

If this argument gives a new slant to the idea of what it really means for local and municipal jurisdictions to be "creatures of the province," then such a bias may constitute a necessary corrective to prevailing assumptions. While an argument can be made, as noted, in support of the *limits* to understanding available to the non-participant to and/or non-practitioner of local and municipal affairs, a similar claim is just as valid for the effort to understand federal or provincial politics. The question we have to ask at this point is why the mass media focus so heavily on the federal, and thereafter on provincial, jurisdictions and activities. Perhaps they too honour a status order of sorts, such that better or longer-serving reporters, analysts, interviewers and commentators are promoted first to provincial then finally to federal affairs. This would give them a central role in the self-fulfilling prophecy, and tempt anyone unaware of public apathy and academic hyper-specialization to go overboard to the point of seeing the inversion phenomenon and the assumption of levels as part of a grand conspiracy perpetrated on the people by its various "elites."

II

One way of looking at the issues already touched upon would require us to determine whether politics is rational or irrational. Here politics and its study would part company if only because this assessment would require us to give *good reasons* for our answer, even if we argued that politics was irrational. The two best known proponents of this latter position in the twentieth century are Max Weber and Harold Lasswell. Weber defined politics both "as a strong and slow boring of hard boards" and as a major basis for the exercise of charisma, thereby making a distinction between an ethic of responsibility and one of ultimate ends. More important was his defense of the well-known distinction between facts and values. Facts, while perhaps necessary to good decision-making, are clearly insufficient, particularly in the ethical and political sphere. Weber has been criticized, justly I think, for mystifying politics and the political. It was his view of the "free" society as one characterized by the antagonistic clash of competing values which seemed to leave leaders with such a wide ambit of discretion in all but the most stringent legal and/or traditional settings.

Harold Lasswell provides a parallel, but somewhat different, characterization of politics and the political in his *Politics: Who Gets What, When, How*. I would argue that it is precisely his narrow concept of reason and the rational which led him (with Weber) to equate politics with the irrational *because* of its concern with goals, objectives, needs and maximizing criteria generally. Clearly, any adequate comprehension of politics must see the rational element in the *interrelation* of personal and societal values, means and ends, facts and values, the administrative and the political, preparatory to and following upon choice and decision. Instead writers like Weber and Lasswell have tended to start from a highly formal model which: (1) *presupposes* the above dichotomies; (2) *invents* a notion of technical, instrumental and calculating behaviour which is unrealistic because isolated from self-interest, ends, values and the political. Admittedly, it is the very imposition of such formal models on politics *by academics* which is the hallmark of the disciplined observer, the person who studies politics rather than becoming involved as a participant or practitioner.[5]

Weber and Lasswell provide erstwhile support for a view already alluded to which is a corollary of the inversion effect. As a result of seeing distant events as more important *because* they are less (or non) accessible, the role of *both* mystification and the rational disciplined observer, with his frameworks, models and concepts, is heightened in both the public and the academic mind. This is the ultimate conundrum for the study of politics: the gap between what politics "is" and how we can learn about or study it. Thus, a feeling that remote jurisdictions are and must be more important is nicely complemented by the impact of study and understanding, relative certainly to its role in making sense of local and municipal politics. To be sure, the importance of study in the understanding of political activity in faraway (thus presumably superordinate) jurisdictions serves to underscore the perceived *absence* of possibilities for potential participation and practice by publics while it points to the way officials in these jurisdictions often promote such an image of any central political system. In the latter case, the levels approach to the federal arrangement aids and abets a view of federal politics as *both* institutionally organized (therefore amenable to analysis by "models") *and* irrational. The alleged reality of irrationality in the federal political sphere is, however, more likely to be the subject of academic and scholarly interest than any other jurisdiction, with the result that such be-

haviour acquires a legitimacy of sorts far less available to local and municipal jurisdictions. Just as imperium supplanted the city-state, so also does the
inclusiveness of central authority underwrite its present legitimacy for citizen and scholar alike.

Is this gap between theory and practice unbridgeable? If so then the question of the role of reason and the rational as orienting concepts for the study
of politics arises. If the study of politics is *inversely* related to participation
and practice such that the role of frameworks, models and concepts is the
greater the more remote the jurisdiction, then the practical value of political
science by almost any canon of relevance comes into question. This means
that political knowledge and political experience are in what amounts to a
"zero-sum" relationship to one another. In effect, we are compelled not
only to acknowledge the existence of two discrete phenomena here – knowledge and experience – but also to see them as distinct, and often mutually
opposed, kinds of endeavour. That this admission can be seen to hold for all
fields of social inquiry, given their dependence on formal intellectual con-
structions, is scant consolation when the difficulty of even *describing* extant
political institutions and governmental practices is taken into account. It was
precisely these sorts of concerns which appeared to motivate those political
scientists, particularly in the United States but elsewhere as well, who initiated and/or helped carry out the so-called "behavioural revolution" in the
study of politics.[6]

At the outset I suggested that public conceptions of relevance are *directly*
related to academic interests in the study of politics, then went on to argue
that the relative absence of such interest in local and municipal affairs reinforced a public perception of politics there as venal, corrupt and essentially
amoral. Thus politics in *all* jurisdictions is viewed by publics as something
effectively beyond their control, albeit for very different reasons depending
on the jurisdiction in question and the issue at hand. No matter how important (remote) or unimportant (near and immediate) publics and academics
might score various jurisdictions given their acceptance of the federal bargain as a relation between *levels* of government, the result is invariably a
public sense of impotence and contempt and an academic committment to
specialization, professionalism *and the promise of practical relevance*. I am
going to argue in what follows, certainly not for the first time, that this latter
development on the part of academic political scientists – the behavioural
movement – reflected the *triumph* of public apathy and indifference about
politics and the political more than any effort to resist this development.
Behaviouralism recast this apathy in the form of a "science," or rather an
ideology of scientism, whose unstated committment was nothing less than
the technocratic concern to convert political issues into administrative problems soluble by elites and cadres of experts.[7]

Most non-academic attitudes toward political theory would probably be skeptical of its relevance to practical politics. Only under certain conditions, they would argue, could theory be justified on practical grounds. The distinction between normative and empirical theory was to be of central importance to behaviouralism, because it became the basis for contrasting the bad theory (normative) of "traditional" or "classical" political theorists with the good theory (empirical) of the behavioural movement. Normative theory was either too prescriptive, too historical, or too institutional, while empirical theory, as it came to be known, promised a scientific approach in which frameworks, models, methods, hypotheses and their testing, and generalization would result in explanatory and predictive knowledge. The basic assumption was that these concerns constituted an attempt to make theory relevant to practice and to practical improvements, thus that behaviouralism was superior to traditional approaches on practical, as well as academic, grounds.

If such a promise also served to underwrite the emergence of a new professionalism based on technique, specialization, scientism, and publicly and privately funded "research," then so much the better. It is important, at this juncture, to realize just how dependent behaviouralism was on both the fact/value and ends/means distinctions in Weber and on his view of politics and the political as essentially irrational, albeit comprehensible by means of "rational" theories, models, frameworks and concepts. A corollary characteristic of the behavioural "mood" equated professionalism with science and *both* with the practical and relevant. This signified a redefinition of practice and the practical away from an Aristotelian emphasis on ethical concerns toward an *instrumentalist* conception whose technical and strategic possibilities were available to those who made political decisions. Implicit in such professionalism and scientism was a committment to the value of value-neutral *intervention* on behalf of power-holders as a clear alternative to the forlorn hope of politicizing apathetic publics. This also reflected behaviouralism's preference for a scientistic (Plato) rather than a truly scientific (Aristotle) approach to politics as discussed in Chapter two.[8]

All one has to do to appreciate the consequences of such a direction on the part of political science is to consider the public and institutional costs of this research as the material expression of social scientific professionalism and scientism in Society as a whole. Behaviouralism's embrace of the above-noted redefinition of practice and the practical can only really be understood as a development emerging out of the tension between professionalism and political and social reform in the United States which reached its zenith during the progressive era from 1900 to 1914. By 1920 a conservative temper had taken hold, and the reformist zeal which seemed so "natural" a bias of up-and-coming professionalism on the part of political scientists and sociologists rapidly became suspect. Professionalism opted for research over reform, the university over local government and the settlement house, thereby engendering a split which became unequivocally hierarchical in nature, particularly following its limited, but nonetheless real, successes during the depression and World War II.[9]

C. Wright Mills has referred to *both* phases of political science and sociology under this professionalizing imperative as a manifestation of "liberal practicality." It was the later institutionalization of these disciplines in governments and corporations, as well as in universities, which led to their shift away from reform and change toward administrative manipulation and control. The result not only served to keep pace with changes in liberal ideology which were themselves responses to changed conditions between 1900 and 1960, but led to a wholly different approach to "social problems" like poverty, crime, race, ethnicity, marginality, deviance etc. One way of making sense of the collapse of laissez-faire and the rise of unions, the welfare or service state and the social sciences themselves would require us to see such developments as a *response* to these very difficulties. Such a response would be "successful" precisely to the extent that it contained the conflict and disorganization by maintaining the basic societal, economic, and governmental framework intact in the fact of unanticipated problems. In these changed circumstances, liberal practicality increasingly came to demand that academic researchers take their cue from large organizations both public and private when formulating "social problems" worthy of study. This served to reflect the new dependencies of behavioural research in particular as it was taking shape in political science, sociology and the behavioural and administrative sciences during the 1950's and early 1960's, while it indicated the real bias of any profession once it has achieved minimal recognition.[10]

III

Any assessment of behaviouralism's practical relevance must recognize just how significantly Society and its institutions have redefined practice and practicality, and how this change has been reflected in behaviouralism. I already contrasted Aristotle's conception of practice and prudence with modern and contemporary understandings, drawing attention to the absence of an ethical or moral component in the latter. Behaviouralist thinking reflects the influence of a conception of the practical and prudent absent not only of an ethical dimension, however, but of an intellectual and theoretical one as well. Thus what is termed "practical" more closely comports with what Aristotle called "productive" knowledge than anything else. The technical bias and instrumental orientation of productive knowledge is therefore to be distinguished from practical and theoretical knowledge by the absence of *both* ethical and contemplative concerns. Redefinition of the practical along the lines of the technical, instrumental, strategic and productive was thus achieved by first dismembering it from ethical concerns, and thereafter from thought and theory.[11]

The attempt to recast what thought and theory should contribute to the study of politics, as noted, saw its role strictly in terms of a scientistic bias favouring productivity and output. "Theories" must be structurally decomposed into testable, falsifiable hypotheses if they are to *fuel* the research efforts and desired outcomes of professional political (and social) science. The result was termed "empirical theory," in clear contrast to the normative theory so central to the behaviouralist critique of theory in traditional political science. Indeed, behaviouralists claimed that careful analysis of pre-behavioural political studies demonstrated a near-total absence of a scientific (read scientistic) committment to empirical methods, findings, and generalizations in favour of historical and institutional descriptions either of political and governmental activities and events or the thinking of "great" political theorists. It was therefore the alleged lack of "practical" relevance which served as a support for the behavioural redefinition of theory, now seen as a central element in the methodical production of "empirical" knowledge.[12]

Although theory was clearly redefined in the ways suggested, the matter of the ethical component in practice was confronted and dealt with in a different way by behavioural political scientists. Here it was the ideal of value-neutrality so central to professional objectivity and detachment which served to justify both a *scientistic* and a *productive* and *interventionist* approach to knowledge and knowing. While the role of thought and theory was redefined, ethical concerns were effectively sidestepped by a discipline determined to tacitly legitimize the claim that such matters were, after all, the province of political, bureaucratic and corporate decision makers. An additional point of some importance was the observation that utilization of the "public" knowledge produced by the discipline could be of no concern to the professional, for the very complexity and interdependence of the social division of labour makes controls here impossible even where they might be desirable. This had the not-wholly unintended effect of legitimizing the political scientist's perception of himself as a possible or actual *means* to externally defined ends, the classic definition of the technical expert as eunuch. This combination of the professional detachment of the scholar as "scientist", and the promise of relevance through the redefinition of both practice and theory, was thought more than sufficient to realizing Mannheim's (if not Aristotle's) objective of a scientific politics. In what sense could one argue that this objective has been realized?[13]

No doubt it was the naïve conception of "science" as a pursuit which was presumed to guarantee practical outcomes favouring human betterment which not only provided support for behavioural research, but helped legitimate many of its actual social effects. Scientism is notorious for its failure to distinguish the scientific from the technical, with the result that the nature and function of theory in science has been consistently misunderstood. One is tempted to argue that it is mainly on the matter of professional detachment as an idealized research protocol, and the resulting distinction between men of knowledge (staff, advisors *etc*) and men of power that science and behaviouralism concur. Professional recognition by those at or near the top of key institutions in North America and Western European societies led to and reinforced academic and intellectual *integration* into a social division of labour whose stratification order was legitimated mainly or exclusively on meritocratic grounds. It is more than a coincidence that such legitimation was now being provided with increasing frequency by those very disciplines which mistakenly viewed this integration solely as societal and governmental recognition of their efforts as professional, scientific, and ultimately (if not immediately) practical and relevant.[14]

In a sense this was the real purpose of behavioural political science in the eyes of those who defined the practical and prudent in technical and strategic terms. It was therefore less the actual effectiveness of the sorts of interventions encouraged or carried out by behaviouralists than their committment to invoking such a model of the relation between knowledge and power which would prove most helpful to decision makers anxious to have citizens, clients and employees "internalize" such conceptions. A careful look at most interventions by social scientists will show that much of the success claimed, even on the basis of the most superficial notions of practice and the practical promoted by those at or near the top of institutional hierarchies, cannot be taken at face value. It is thus not only a question of the redefinition of the practical and its consequences for ethical and intellectual concerns, but also the problem of analyzing and judging the significance of the results achieved *given* the objectives of those who paid for and made use of the research in question which is at issue.

The only significant exception to this argument can be discovered in the effects of organizational interventions, particularly in business, but occasionally in the public sector as well. Even here, however, it is necessary to keep in mind the more explicit committment by managements, bureaucracies, and politicians to making sporadic or consistent use of such research and consulting in order to legitimize changes they did not feel free to carry out in the absence of recommendations from inside or outside experts. It is clearly the integration of such research, with its professional and scientific claims, into the mainstream of organized institutional decision-making which underlines the real meaning of the ideal of professional detachment and objectivity, while it underscores the way the division of labour protects the disciplined observer from having to confront either his stake in the social structure or the way his knowledge may be interpreted or utilized.

It is hardly inconsistent to argue that behavioural political science's intervention effects were at one and the same time controversial and usually out of the control of those who actually produced the research on which intervention was justified. Yet this is clearly central to understanding the paradoxical character of the legitimating function for disciplines all-too-often deluded by their own rhetoric. Their models of social and political change have proven "relevant" only in a very narrow sense because of the notion of practicality they honoured. This led not just to cynicism in the guise of objectivity by some academics, but to sincere disillusionment on the part of numberless others. Any analysis of the effects of interventions allegedly based on behavioural research cannot ignore this disillusionment when assessing what was actually accomplished and how it was or was not related to the values, intentions and objectives of many academics totally committed to the goals of the behavioural movement. A great deal of the present disenchantment by academics formerly supportive of behaviouralism in political and social science (and their students) can be traced to what this committment to a science of politics and society was perceived to have actually produced.[15]

Where the objective was alleged to be a practical outcome favouring democratic and representative values in the political sphere, the legitimizing function was more complicated, particularly where national security and/or other cultures were concerned. Only by institutionalizing the research function itself could the illusion of progressive improvements in the realization of such values be maintained in the face of the redefinition of practice already discussed. As an element of the institutional structure in many advanced industrial systems, academic research and scholarship had now become "normal practice" in all sectors of civil society, not just universities and research bureaux. Indeed, I have argued elsewhere that there is a definite point beyond which one can no longer refer to the preferences and protocols resulting from the operation of the social and behavioural sciences without acknowledging their deep sedimentation in normal organizational and societal practices. While they reflect the model of success through disciplined observation first made operational by laboratory science and market capitalism, it is their role in bringing about the totalization of civil society and the triumph of secondary group values which underscores their real function, and the ideological nature of objectivity and value neutrality along with it.[16]

All of this has a great deal to do with the mutual *interdependence* (rather than exclusivity) between professionalism and social and political reform. Earlier I mentioned the post World War I schism between these two phases of the progressive movement, and went on to contrast two successive kinds of "liberal practicality" that had issued from professionalism in political and social science between 1900 and 1960. This must not, however, be allowed to obscure the point that behavioural and allied forms of research and political and social reform constitute two sides of the same coin. Interdependence means mutual need based on the essential incompleteness of either enterprise without the other. Both research and reform presuppose the desirability of *completing* Society understood as a culturally and historically specific *form* of collective life rather than a synonym for it. Both are as a consequence unabashedly interventionist, where by intervention is presupposed both a truncated norm of rationality based on ends – means (instrumental) thinking and an incremental model of social change premised on what Popper has called "piecemeal tinkering."[17]

There is not necessarily anything peculiar in the dependence of social structures on systems of knowledge for their legitimation. Even the sedimentation of these systems and their reflection in ongoing organizational and social activities only constitutes a present day version of the development of culture as a system of shared values. It is rather the specific character this process has taken in industrial societies which is worthy of note. Meritocracy appears more as an organizational and status-based version of the productivity ideal originally touted as the substructural basis for legitimizing Western capitalism. Habermas has noted the unique nature of capitalism as the first system of collective life able to legitimize and rationalize itself *from below* as well as from above.[18] In its later, more developed, phase this very society would achieve the ultimate in legitimation by inverting the ideological role of "nature" relative to reason and the rational. In the event, what is natural increasingly came to be defined by reference to what is rational rather than the reverse. This inversion constitutes a final phase in the emergence of civil society as an artificial totality. However suspect the modern concept of nature may be, its residual loyalty to a standard of reality at variance with the homocentric values of modern Western civilization pointed to possibilities nowadays less and less available as a result of the very "success" of Society's normative agenda, an agenda which increasingly depends upon the political, social, behavioural and administrative sciences.

IV

Supporters and critics alike have noticed the fact that problem formulation is all-too-often subordinated to method in behavioural political and social-scientific research. This tendency for the tail to wag the dog is highly significant for appreciating the social and political consequences of the new practicality and its relation to "research."[19] The behavioural movement in political science constitutes an important case study of a sustained effort to comprehend politics and the political from the perspective of the disciplined observer. Scientism and professionalism provided the ideological ballast underwriting the redefinition of practice, then theory, while method and technique became a crucial vehicle which formalized, standardized and thereafter legitimized behavioural research in the eyes of publics, universities, corporations, governments and funding agencies. Given in such an active approach, as noted, was a thoroughgoing attack on pre-behavioural (or non-behavioural) political science for ignoring its proper tasks or performing them badly.

The view that "traditional" political science was not only intellectually sterile but practically irrelevant provides us with some useful insights into the consequences of the new liberal practicality in operation. The fact that behaviouralism often opted for advising and assisting power holders in one or another sector of the organizational society meant that in these instances it had opted for system rationality, an incremental and piecemeal approach, and a professional and scientistic preference for detachment, albeit in the service of intervention rather than for its own sake. Behaviouralism's wholesale acceptance of Society's reformulation of practice and the practical is what made it possible for it to argue that non-behavioural political science was both practically irrelevant *and intellectually sterile* as a consequence. Its successful merger of detachment with an active committment to intervention, however piecemeal, often had the not-wholly-unintended effect of legitimizing its own approach at the expense not only of traditional political science but of political experience as well.

Nevertheless, behaviouralism did give consistent aid and comfort to all variations on the inversion effect already cited. This endorsement of a particular status order favouring the study of more remote jurisdictions to ones nearer at hand further underscored the difference between its view of practicality as detachment and intervention and the experience and "practical" knowledge of the politician. At the same time behaviouralism had no way of supervising or controlling the information it produced, even if individual researchers wished to do so. In some instances, as noted, researchers simply opted for a staff function advising organized power holders in administrative, bureaucratic and managerial positions. This constituted a substantial retreat from politics and the political into organization and bureaucracy, with the result that *both* voting publics and their elected representatives were often alienated from behavioural political science research.

What made such a response sensible was the clear technocratic bias such a committment entailed. Earlier I made reference to this bias' core concern – that political issues as much as possible be converted into administrative problems soluble by expert professional staff and bureaucrats in the upper reaches of public (and in some cases private) organizations. Depoliticization was an unavoidable by-product of the success of the behavioural movement in operation. This was evidenced no less by its technocratic preferences than by its disdain for publics (unless powerful and highly organized) and politicians (unless supporters of behavioural research, which many were not). Where depoliticization was not thought feasible or desirable, the effect was to overemphasize the distinction between facts and values, with the result that the relevant public issues were mystified and the "irrational" nature of politics and the political exaggerated.[20]

This general comment is not intended to ignore or downplay behavioural political science's participation in the inversion effect, and its manifestation in a status order which puts federal topics above provincial topics and provincial topics above the study of local and municipal affairs. Here I noted the way that public and academic support for a "levels" conception of jurisdictions and relations between governments tended to coalesce with the policy-administration dichotomy. Thus behavioural political scientists can be expected to be progressively less interested in a given jurisdiction the closer it comes to their immediate circumstances because: (1) these jurisdictions should ideally be "carrying out" federal, and thereafter provincial, policies (e.g. administration); (2) but often do so in a way which underscores venality and corruption *precisely because* such "political" behaviour is thought to be the preserve of "higher level" jurisdictions, particularly central governments.

This perception, apparently justified by public attitudes and understandings as well as the practices of present-day governments, combines with the inversion effect in political science to play down higher – level venality and corruption in favour of theories, models, frameworks, concepts and research into politics at this "level" and the next one down. Local and municipal jurisdictions receive little or no legitimation for their alleged "irrationality" because the levels concept places them at the bottom of the status order (e.g. administration) from the standpoint of *both* politics and its study. Regardless of the gap between politics and political science in *all* jurisdictions, the status order functions as a *differential legitimation order* which is strongest at the "top" and weakest at the bottom. The more remote and detached, the more amenable to legitimation through detached, and presumably disciplined, observation. What is legitimated at the top, and to a lesser extent in the middle – the "irrationality" of politics – is left high and dry at the bottom by a levels/status order concept that equates politics with activity at the top end and administration with activity at the bottom.

The inversion effect guarantees that both public and academic *interest* will be directed away from local and municipal affairs in the absence of an immediate problem calling for participation and direct action, while it simultaneously mystifies and legitimizes federal, and to a lesser extent provincial, politics. To the extent that knowledge and improved performance depend upon or are related to interest, public apathy and indifference will be a key factor in assessing policies in all jurisdictions. However, it must be clear that even consistent legitimation for federal policies functions as a support for this apathy and indifference rather than constituting evidence of public participation. Media representations of the issues, however accurate and insightful, can have only a limited impact on individuals who all-too-often associate the evening news with everything but citizenship. This is why interest in public affairs is rarely a sufficient condition for active public participation. Citizens often become interested in media reports, discussions and analyses of public issues because they confirm a sterotype and/or provide legitimation. Otherwise, the news on its own functions as entertainment, down-time, or constitutes one of many daily habits carried out in a less than fully conscious state.[21]

The question posed in the title of this essay has still not received a direct answer, perhaps because too much is at stake in the meanings we give to terms like "practical" and "science" for a direct answer to be very helpful. Behaviouralism claimed that it could offer a practical science of politics allegedly based on the model of activity in science and the professions. In a sense it did succeed in doing this, but only by acquiescing in a formulation of practice and the practical which denuded it of both its ethical and its contemplative dimensions. The price of this acquiescence is certainly not something apparent to the naked eye. In a sense, one might argue that no price was paid at all, if only because behaviouralism reflected the emerging social and political reality in quite specific ways. Thus it was by and large a product of the very developments it sought to render transparent through dispassionate analysis. This would help explain why it simultaneously attacked what it called traditional political science, while offering little in the way of anything more than mild methical palliatives to established or emerging liberal practicality.

Too much a creature of the values of society as it had taken shape by 1950, the behavioural "revolution" rarely if ever even achieved the sorts of reforms which late liberal practicality still honoured, however often in the breach. The price of acquiescence seemed no price at all, and perhaps there was no price for the heady professionals and careerists who eagerly sought status, prestige and recognition. That this recognition carried with it thoroughgoing integration into the cultural and occupational mainstream of Society as the emergent *form* of collective life was nicely papered over by behaviouralism's allegiance to the meritocratic ethos which is the indispensable basis for merging value – neutrality as a research protocol with intervention as a "practical" strategy. There is very little beyond this to be said against behaviouralism in political science, if only because: (1) the difficulties addressed are a property of all social, behavioural, and administrative sciences; (2) even traditional political science was not immune to the criticisms arrayed against behaviouralism, particularly given the history of the American committment to a "science" of politics.[22]

This raises the issue of what possible suggestions one might put forward in the effort to mobilize efforts at social and political change which are neither too "revolutionary nor too piecemeal and incremental. In what follows I try to show how making *Society itself* transparent can constitute a basis for social and political changes which combine the virtues of the piecemeal method with potentially system-wide consequences. A first step is to realize that Society, as noted, is a *form* of collective life rather than a synonym for it. A second step is to acknowledge the fact that there is a *dialectical* relationship between Society and knowledge about it. A third step is to see how and why ideologies and systems of knowledge might be "correct" renditions of social and political reality, if only because even the most mundane description of human acts and events participates in implicit theoretical understandings which presuppose criteria for delineating correct and incorrect versions of this reality.

In the final analysis, the desire to realize a *science* of politics which is simultaneously practical is probably unrealistic. Not only do social scientists exhibit a persistent failure to distinguish science from technology when discussing this idea. There is also their fundamental misunderstanding of the role of contemplation and speculative thought in the *success* of the scientific enterprise. The only conceivable way that science in its generic sense could be construed as directly and concertedly "practical" would require nothing less than this very confusion between science and technology, coupled with a misreading of the role of thought in science. Science on its own is rarely "practical", even in the most narrow and instrumental sense given the term today. It is certainly not in a position to challenge effectively the uses to which pure and applied scientific work is put, even if individual scientists wished to do so. Thus the Aristotelian conception of practice and the practical which presumes an ethical as well as a contemplative dimension is lost to both scientific and social scientific work.[23]

This being the case, the question of ethics and its relation to politics and the public sphere must become a function of political management. Academic political science, even were it not so enamoured of remoteness in its effort to generate and sustain differential status and legitimation orders, could never hope to substitute for the sense of citizens and publics, in concert with their elected representatives and other public officials and employees. Indeed, I have argued that political science has played a central role in supporting the inversion effect amongst publics and citizens, and that such support has given aid and comfort to the "stability" theorists who all-too-often see mass apathy as a *sine qua non* for the successful operation of democratic political systems committed to the rule of law.[24] Political management begins with the assumption that management and managing is an appropriate metaphor for a system of governance. In the event, the rule of law and representation mediate between leaders and practitioners on the one hand and citizens and publics as participants on the other.

Yet this assumption only makes sense if it is understood to presuppose another. Management for me is not a top-down affair premised on a model of society as a *rational social organization*. It is a dialectical interplay of persons whose roles change from one part of the system to another, and who remain open to dialogue and discussion in their continuing concern for the care of public things. Expertise remains important from the standpoint of information prior to *and following upon* decisions, but such a realization cannot be allowed to obscure the need for an open circulation between citizen and representative functions and roles. Thus it is not simply the need for communication between "levels" occupied by permanent incumbents of "citizen" roles at the bottom, and officials as "agents" who are the product of a narrow circulation of elites at the top. It is the idea of collective life itself as *an experiment* which fuels the idea of political management.[25] Care for public things becomes synonymous with the self-maintenance of an organism by the reciprocal interaction of its parts, but with a very important proviso. Those parts need not, and cannot, be frozen into fixed roles which ascribe political leadership to a few and consign the large mass of citizens to apathy and a sense of futility, coupled with *reactive behaviour* in and through occasional elections which are all too often little more than plebiscites.

References

1 See Herbert Simon, *Administrative Behaviour,* 2nd edition (Glencoe: Free Press, 1957) where the distinction between facts and values, means and ends, is made the conceptual basis for the dichotomy between administration and policy. Also V. A. Subramaniam, "Fact and Value in Decision-Making," *Public Administration Review* Volume 23 (December 1963), pp. 232–237, an important attempt to

operationalize Simon's model. For a critique of this model in *both* its phases and a not-inconsiderable bibliography of materials by Simon, his supporters, and his critics, see my "Rationality & Decision in Administrative Science," *Canadian Journal of Political Science* Volume 6 No. 3 (June, 1973), pp. 271–294.

2 This attitude to the way politics "works" offends the new elite. See Lebedoff *op. cit.*, and note how much it resembles the progressivist revulsion with and retreat from politics at the turn of the century in the United States. See Eric Goldman, *Rendez-Vous with Destiny* (NY: Knopf, 1952).

3 Wilson, *Tradition & Innovation,* particularly chapter four.

4 I take issue with any attempt to associate the presence of elites and elite acco-modation with a conspiracy in "Elites, Meritocracy and Technocracy: Some Im-plications for Political Leadership," in *Political Leadership in Canada,* edited by Hector Massey (forthcoming).

5 Weber, "Politics as a Vocation," *op. cit.;* Harold Lasswell, *Politics: Who Gets What, When, How* (NY: Meridian, 1958).

6 Robert Dahl, "The Behavioural Approach in Political Science: Epitaph for a Monument to a Successful Protest", *American Political Science Review,* Volume 55 (December, 1961), pp. 763–772; Heinz Eulau, *The Behavioural Persuasion in Politics* (NY: Random House, 1963); Robert Presthus, *Behavioural Approaches to Public Administration* (University, Alabama: University of Alabama Press, 1968). For a critique in the Straussian tradition on something of a case by case basis, Herbert Storing (editor), *Essays on the Scientific Study of Politics* (NY: Holt, Rinehart and Winston, 1962).

7 My argument against Voeglin in chapter two would suggest that his exclusivist position regarding the interaction between the symbols of everyday life and those of political science actually *encourages* the sort of false concreteness, truncated rationality, and hypertrophied relevance which professionalism and scientism impart to this sort of political science. Voegelin would likely categorize this movement, beginning with Max Weber, as gnosticism. See Eric Voegelin, *Science, Politics and Gnosticism: Two Essays* (Chicago: Henry Regnery Co., 1968); and *The New Science of Politics,* chapters 4–6.

8 See chapter two, where I contrast being scientific (Aristotle) from being scien-tistic (Plato) on the basis of whether the animus is scholarly rigour appropriate to *its* subject matter (Aristotle), or slavish emulation of the methods and techniques of *other* sciences and practical arts (Plato).

9 Bernard Crick, *The American Science of Politics* (Berkeley: University of Cali-fornia Press, 1959).

10 C. Wright Mills, *The Sociological Imagination* (NY: Grove Press, 1959); Robert Lynd, *Knowledge for What?* (Princeton: Princeton University Press, 1939); and Lynd's attack on the methods employed by Samuel Stauffer in *The American Soldier,* in "The Science of Inhuman Relations," *The New Republic* (August 27, 1949).

11 W. D. Ross, *Aristotle* (NY: Meridian, 1959), pp. 183–184.

12 Dahl, *op. cit;* Robert Dahl, preface to *Modern Political Analysis* (Englewood Cliffs, N. J.: Prentice Hall, 1963). David Easton, *The Political System* (NY: Alfred Knopf, 1953) is an extraordinarily prescient work by almost any standard of comparison in the area of philosophy of method and approach in political

science, and should certainly be read carefully by anyone interested in these matters.

13 Karl Mannheim, *Ideology & Utopia,* translated and edited by Lewis Wirth (London: Routledge, 1954) chapter titled "Prospects for the Scientific Study of Politics." Also see my "The Meaning and Significance of 'Empirical Method' for the Critical Theory of Society," *Canadian Journal of Political and Social Theory,* Volume 3 No. 3 (Fall, 1979), pp. 57–68; and "Critical Theory's Critique of Social Science: Episodes in a Changing Problematic from Adorno to Habermas," *History of European Ideas* (forthcoming).

14 Weber clearly sensed the tie between legal-rational authority as a legitimate basis of domination and sociology's rationalistic bias. See Weber, *Theory of Social & Economic Organization,* pp. 126–132, 324–341.

15 I discuss the technocratic character of social science as a research, methodical/technical, and theoretical enterprise in "Technocracy and Late Capitalist Society," *op cit.* But see especially H. P. Dreitzel, "Social Science and the Problem of Rationality: Notes on the Sociology of Technocrats," *Politics and Society,* Volume 2 No. 2 (Winter 1971–72), pp. 165–182.

16 *The American Ideology,* chapters 2, 5, 8–10; *Tradition & Innovation,* chapters 2–4.

17 Mills, *op. cit.* This equation of research with reform was initially put forward by Emile Durkheim in *The Division of Labour in Society,* prefaces to the first and second edition and conclusion, and has realized its strongest recent statement in Karl Popper, *The Poverty of Historicism* (London: Routledge & Kegan Paul, 1957). For critical commentary, see my *The American Ideology,* chapters 5 and 8; and "The Meaning and Significance of 'Empirical Method' for the Critical Theory of Society," *op. cit.*

18 Jürgen Habermas, "Technology & Science as Ideology," in Habermas, *Toward a Rational Society* (Boston: Beacon, 1968), pp. 81–122; and my response to *both* Habermas & Popper in "Science, Critique & Criticism: the 'Open Society' Revisited," in *On Critical Theory,* edited by John O'Neill (NY: Seabury Press, 1976) pp. 205–230.

19 Mills, *op. cit;* Howard Becker, "On Methodology," in *Sociological Work* (Chicago: Aldine Press, 1975).

20 Dreitzel, *op. cit;* Wilson, "Technocracy & Late Capitalist Society," *op. cit.*

21 Alan Thomas, "Audience, Market, Public," *op. cit.* On the notion that citizenship is simply one among several passively ascribed role options available for affirming membership, see chapter 10.

22 Crick, *The American Science of Politics.* I would submit that the social-scientific framework which most fully expresses, and thereby legitimizes, the conceptions of concreteness, rationality and relevance found in the interventionist mix of research and reform in these disciplines is to be found in Talcott Parsons, *The Social System* (NY: Macmillan, 1951).

23 Popper, *op. cit;* Wilson, *The American Ideology,* chapter 5; Wilson, "The Meaning & Significance of 'Empirical Method' for the Critical Theory of Society," *op. cit.*

24 Bernard Crick, *In Defense of Politics* (Harmondsworth: Penguin, 1960); Gabriel Almond and Sidney Verba, *The Civic Culture* (Boston: Little Brown, 1965).

25 This project is very different from Popper's idea of social technology in *The Poverty of Historicism,* as I make apparent in *The American Ideology,* chapter 5

Chapter 8
How to Make Social Science Responsibly Political

I

In this chapter I argue that a most important basis for a possible politics in advanced industrial societies can be found in the pervasive and influential role of social-scientific research operations in these societies.[1] If political science as an academic discipline participates in the problem of inversion, and conceptualizes political structures, processes and mechanisms in terms of levels in the ways indicated, this need not imply that the social sciences as a whole are inapplicable to the effort to bring political management into being as a possible political practice. As a matter of fact, I want to suggest in what follows that the social sciences are at present essentially incomplete empirical and observational disciplines excessively biased toward polity and against politics, but that there is a sensible and useful way to remedy this which cannot help but serve the interests and objectives of political management.

As an introductory point, consider the protocols that allegedly guide the actual production and generation of social-science research. Value neutrality and objectivity, the essence of the detached observer as impartial spectator, are central artifacts in this enterprise, and are assumed to manifest themselves in certain behavioural and formal ways. Whether the choreography and staging constitute anything more than window dressing intended to legitimize an attack upon, or defence of, a position about which one has definite ideas is almost irrelevant to my point. What is important is to see the social, behavioural and administrative/managerial sciences as *activities* carried out by academically trained persons, whether for strictly scholarly or for policy purposes, rather than simply as *knowledge* comprised of concepts, frameworks, models, theories, generalizations and "research". This is not intended to downgrade the knowledge content or component in these disciplines, but instead addresses a very important, though for the most part ignored, institutional property of Society as a culturally and historically specific *form* of collective life rather than a synonym for it.[2]

What I have in mind here is the fact that the social, behavioural, and administrative/managerial sciences are not, after all, mere observers of a societal reality that they do not themselves participate in. On the contrary, these disciplines constitute central vehicles for rationalizing and legitimizing Society's ascendancy over more and more aspects of collective life in advanced industrial societies. By focussing on these disciplines as *activities* carried out at least in part in tacit or explicit defense of Society as a culturally and historically specific form of collective life, one is compelled to see them not simply as a neutral and objective means for observing social interaction but as a *form* of social interaction in their own right. Were these disciplines in their active and policy aspects restricted to the practices of academics working in, or from, a university setting, it would be easier to take issue with my argument regarding their central role as a legitimizing agent. The point here is that Society is a *sociological* (or social *etc.* scientific) collective in large part because its civil practices are premised upon and legitimated by the protocols and choreography of these very disciplines.[3]

One does not, in other words, need to be formally trained as a social scientist to exhibit this form of life. Indeed it is central to successful civil behaviour, understood as a set of formalized rituals between strangers occupying recognized occupational and organizational positions in a *formally* meritocratic work system. That this work system and its values and protocols are becoming more and more influential as forces in non-work settings cannot be denied. The social sciences and related disciplines are thus a central model for social interaction when not a mode of social interaction in their own right. Their reciprocal interdependence with Society is revealed by the role of self and other observation in managerial, executive, and bureaucratic work, no less than by the realization that these disciplines in practice are a form of social interaction in their own right rather than simply a neutral and passive means for accumulating objective knowledge about social interaction. To defend a broader-based definition of these disciplines based on reciprocity and interdependence is to underscore the legitimizing functions of disciplined observation and allied protocols as simultaneously the means of acquiring societal knowledge and the mode, prototype or model for civil behaviour in this very society.[4]

II

Even assuming that the preceding argument makes a good case for revising our one-sided view of the social sciences in their relation to Society, what follows from it that is relevant to political management as a possible political practice? The first thing is to recall the discussion of social science as a defender and legitimator of *meritocracy* in earlier chapters. Here it was argued that it is precisely the way these disciplines "fit into" the very social structure whose values and protocols they seek to justify and rationalize that helps explain their central role. In this sense, they may appear to possess a duplex character, but this is readily dispelled once one realizes that disciplined observation is a *cultural artifact* premised on the commitment to *active intervention* in and through knowledge. It is through this central protocol that the social sciences seek to acquire objective knowledge following what they perceive to be the lead of the natural sciences. And it is in this very commitment that the social sciences mistake themselves, for they are not duplex at all. They are the ideological light infantry of a culture whose form of life includes commitment to the belief in objective "facts of life".[5]

My inspiration for this view of the social sciences can be discovered in the work of the phenomenological sociologist Alfred Schutz. Schutz was concerned about social-scientific knowledge as an expression of a scholarly, *rather than a commonsensical,* mode of rationality. He believed that the contribution of such disciplines, while significant, was not without cost. Writing in the 1930s and 1940s, Schutz believed that the price of becoming knowledgeable in a social-scientific way was that one sacrificed the less formal, more substantive knowledge acquired through participation in and experience of a culture or subgroup therein. To a considerable extent the two forms of knowledge and knowing were thus seen to be in a relation of mutual exclusivity by Schutz. While today one could make a strong case for my claim that the social sciences as formally practiced by academics are merely the tip of the iceberg in what is unabashedly a *sociological* society, it must be clear that to date it is almost solely in the work, market and civil sectors of this society that sociological models of knowledge and behaviour have displaced commonsense modes.

Schutz' advice may seem absurd to us precisely because of the nature and extent of our indebtedness to social-scientific approaches to life and the world, but it is compelling and overpowering in its simplicity and good sense. He called it his "postulate of adequacy" and described it in the following way:

Each term used in a scientific system referring to human action must be so constructed that a human act performed in the life-world by an individual actor in the way indicated by the typical construction would be reasonable and understandable for the actor himself, as well as for his fellow man.[6]

The implications of the postulate are admittedly radical, if only because were it seriously honoured in the actual research practices of social, behavioural and administrative/managerial scientists, it would polarize and render dialectical what is now a one way, formal and highly structured (and stratified) activity. Such a proposal could only be dismissed on its face, however, by someone commited to the view of subjects as passive objects whose job is to confirm or disconfirm social-scientific hypotheses about them.

It is precisely my commitment to radicalizing and politicizing Schutz' postulate of adequacy which has required me to go substantially beyond simply recognizing it as a formal, epistemological complaint. My purpose has been to treat this postulate as the basis for an alternative *mode of action* in advanced industrial socieites. What makes the act of radicalization unmistakably political is the way it *mobilizes* the observed person or respondent as an *active* participant in dialogue with those who are observing, surveying, interviewing *etc.* him, rather than simply a passive "subject-as-object" responding to the choreography and formal and behavioural cues brought to bear on him. The way in which this act of mobilization is made the basis of a possible politics is simple. Participants to social research activities must not only find social-scientific renditions of their behaviour, attitudes and responses "reasonable and understandable" in a logical or epistemological sense, but must also *agree* that such constructs actually capture the meaning and sense of what they did, believed *etc.*

This difference between seeing a description or explanation as accurate, correct and sensible with regard to *actual* behaviour, feelings, attitudes, etc., and viewing such constructs as logically and epistemologically meaningful as *formally possible* lines of action, thought and belief is absolutely fundamental to the notion of "responsible" politicization in the title of this chapter. It is as a consequence of this that the requirement of agreement carries with it a promise of dialogue, however truncated. Respondents cannot, in other words, even know whether they agree or disagree with social-scientific constructs of their responses until the researchers in question address the individuals or groups with their findings. Thus, social scientists cannot confine themselves merely to instructions to potential and actual respondents regarding how best to carry out their tasks in their role as research subjects. This is (or should be) standard social-scientific practice, and is not what I have in mind when I speak of radicalizing and politicizing the postulate of adequacy.

The proposal rather addresses the obligations of social science researchers once the research activities have taken place or (in the case of longitudinal and panel studies) are already underway. As a form of social interaction rather than solely a means for studying social interaction at an alleged distance from it, social science research thus comprehends a latent function that is at least as important as the manifest function of accumulating and applying knowledge construed as a commodity. This latent function is premised on the requirement of communication and dialogue, and presupposes the primacy of equality at the level of commonsense capacities and knowledge. However much its manifest function presupposes, and takes its point of departure in, the hierarchial structures of a formally meritocratic societal status order, the latent function is potentially *destructuring* in its effects on this very order. It allows the research act to function as an *opportunity* to cut through the power, status and deference orders that are virtually built into the society that sponsors, supports and sustains social research.[7]

If we begin by assuming that the model of social-scientific interaction with research subjects *should* seek to maximize communicative equality and *mutual* understanding, then the question of why this rarely happens takes on a new significance. Paolo Freire encountered this question as a practical problem (in the Aristotelian sense of the term) several years ago in his efforts to provide a basis for educating Brazilian peasants who were "illiterate". In the event, he realized how fundamentally hostaged to formal literacy requirements the idea of commonsense intelligence was. Freire was determined to distend the communicative capabilities of his subjects from the assumption that such capabilities were worthless in the absence of the ability to read and write. Far from seeing formal education as a force for liberation, Freire realized that in the hands of educational authorities committed to the existing power and status order such "enlightenment" made communicative equality and mutual understanding virtually impossible. Indeed, the picture of the educative act which these authorities supported was anything but liberating, either in effect or intent.[8]

If this discussion seems irrelevant to the issues I have been concerned with in this chapter, this probably indicates not only how distant we feel other cultures to be from our own experience, but how superior we believe ourselves to be. Having thoroughly internalized the ideology of progress as a linear process of development attested to by our technological and scientific prowess, we construe Latin American experience as irrelevant because it is, after all, the product of a culture which is conspiciously "behind" our own. The result of such thinking is the same kind of one way, top-down asymmetrical approach that is embodied in present social-scientific research operations *within* advanced industrial societies. Thus they can benefit from what we can "teach" them, but not the reverse. What we know is *ipso facto* valuable to them because we define what is valuable by reference to what we do best. What they know is irrelevant to us, both because it is "behind" our own development, understood and defined in the narrow way indicated, and "culture-bound" largely as a consequence. What we know, as Weber pointed out, is presumed to have universal value, while what they know (if anything) is likely to be of value to them, if it is of value to anyone.

Freire's "pedagogy *for* the oppressed" attacks the same sort of "banking" concept of knowledge as a commodity to be accumulated and distributed by educational "authorities" which is embedded in the asymmetry of the professional-lay distinction as it works itself out in "normal" social science research. When he says that people cannot learn exclusively or in the main from being *taught* as passive objects, he simultaneously addresses the issue of the essential passivity of respondents behaving correctly under the standard social-scientific research regimen. It is the fact that communicative equality *disrupts* the normal proceedings of both social science and formal education which underscores the bias of professionalism as it works itself out in the assumption that knowledgeable experts act and take initiatives while research subjects or students "take in", accept or respond passively. It is the built-in guarantee of hierarchical communication which indicates *how* these functions are embedded in a formally meritocratic status order.

I say *formally* meritocratic because the order or structure in question is not the result of an objectively rational allocation of responsibilities, tasks, powers and rewards as meritocratic theory might have us believe. Indeed, few properties of our civilization as a culture or form of life in its own right are more controversial than the idea of "rational domination" so central to meritocracy, bureaucracy, sociology and education. In an earlier chapter I stated that our culture has effectively inverted the relationship between reason and nature. For the first time reason is a standard for judging what is "natural" rather than the reverse. It is quite clear to me that the central role of the disciplined observer as an impartial spectator accumulating objective knowledge at a distance is the key to understanding the meaning of this inversion. To the extent that reason is equated with objectivity realized in and through formally rational choreographies like professionalism, research and public education, nature is viewed as the property of the subject driven by irrational values, biases, feelings, desires *etc*.

What makes the idea of rational domination at one and the same time compelling and paradoxical is given in the question that it inspires us to ask: How can *any* form of domination possibly be rational, and what would such a system look like if it were even conceivable? The idea of rational domination is central to the claims found in meritocratic ideology, claims that are essential in any effort to legitimize the kinds of professional-lay relationships already alluded to above. Social science research, functioning both as objective accumulator of knowledge about its culture and central legitimator of this very culture, expresses and embodies in its normal practices the essence of rational domination. This concept is the lynchpin of meritocratic ideology and as such constitutes an overpoweringly successful basis for legitimating power and status hierarchies in advanced industrial societies today.

Society thus has a vested interest in sustaining and protecting the social sciences and related disciplines, albeit only if they disavow an Aristotelian conception of practice and prudence in favour of disciplined observation preparatory to (someone else's) active intervention. It is as a result of this

conditional interest that social scientists will invariably find themselves occupying positions in one or another formally meritocratic structure. This
occupancy will be publicly legitimated not only by social-scientific identification with the professions, but by identification with science as well. Professionalism and scientism together constitute the central ideological ce-
ment underwriting the public (and often the governmental and managerial)
view of these disciplines as responsible producers and guardians of expert
knowledge. The public defers to the èsoteric nature of these pursuits because it identifies them with their confidence in the traditional professions
and their respect for the perceived accomplishments of the natural
sciences.

Again, I am not taking issue with the fact of social-scientific research, either
in its active dimension or in terms of its knowledge claims. What I am
suggesting is that the one-sidedness of these disciplines is not necessarily
serving the interests of citizens and publics when it cloaks itself in the mantle
of professionalism and scientism. The problem really lies in the social scientist's steadfast refusal to view critically the processes, practices and protocols which make it possible for him to acquire "knowledge" of social behaviour and social interaction. In effect, the ways in which *his knowledge is
acquired* is central rather than peripheral to the social, economic and political reality in which he finds himself while in the act of studying some small
part of it.[9] While the social sciences are not themselves dialectical, it is
important that the social-scientific researcher realize the unique nature of
his dialectical relation to Society. As a citizen and member of the public no
less than anyone else, he must not allow his support for the one-sided norms
of professionalism and scientism to lead him to underestimate the constructive possibilities of responsible politicization lying latent in the present manifest practices of normal social science.

Professionalism and scientism thus constitute the key vehicles of legitimation allowing social scientists to operationalize the concept of rational domination in and through the normal practices of their respective disciplines.
Reason and nature are typified as the observer and "subject-as-object" respectively. The social scientist, with his "banked" professional and scientific
capabilities, constitutes an authority who dictates the pace and direction of
the research proceedings, while subjects as objects are understood to be
(and view themselves as) passive potentiality, mere raw material presently
available to confirm or disconfirm social-scientific hypotheses about them.
The social scientist, taking his cue from both professional and scientific
canons of conduct, finds it difficult not to adopt either an exploitative or a
caretaking approach to his subjects-as-objects, and frequently adopts *both*
in his effort to generate objective knowledge about forms of social interaction which rarely if ever include *the research act itself.*

If the exploitative approach mirrors natural science's commitment to a
"domination of nature," where nature is construed as passive potentiality
awaiting human definition and consequent transformation, the caretaking
approach is more subtle. Here the problem I am addressing is not dependence on what may in fact constitute the superior knowledge of the professional practitioner in his area of expertise. It is rather the tendency for this
legitimate dependence of clients, patients, students *etc.* to be *generalized* in
a society whose governing ideologies include professionalism which is problematic. Thus the professional relationship, which is almost always a *hierarchical* relationship of a formally meritocratic kind in advanced industrial
societies, becomes a basis for unconditional deference to professional opinion across a wide range of issues, problems, and assumptions to which the
professional's capabilities have little if any relevance.[10] His citizen and public roles, on the other hand, are vastly more important. While his contribution admittedly may benefit in the contemporary setting from his professional, scholarly and scientific knowledge and capabilities, it is the clear
priority of *commonsense* capabilities more evenly distributed across the general population which cannot be dismissed, allowed to atrophy, or subjected
to manipulation if the possibility of political management is to be actualized.
It is in this sense that radicalization of Schutz' postulate of adequacy presents itself as the basis for a responsibly political social science.

III

Let me develop my emphasis on the need for dialogue and reciprocity in the
research act a bit further. Clearly the idea that reason is a property of *being
human* rather than coming from a particular culture or occupation is central
to its sense. Commonsense capacities become fundamental rather that peripheral in the new equation, while professional, scientific and scholarly capabilities are now understood to be *superstructural* because dependent in all
cases on commonsense understandings for their ultimate sense, meaning
and significance. This means that everyone inhabiting a professional, scientific or scholarly role not only possesses commonsense capabilities, but depends on these capacities in every day life like anyone else. To the extent
that political management depends on these abilities, interests and experiences, individuals who happen to have occupational qualifications will be
better able to participate and contribute if they acknowledge their existence
and central importance in their own lives. Far from constituting a zero sum
game, I am arguing that superstructural and substantial modes of knowledge
and knowing are functionally interdependent in fundamental ways, and that
this fact has been almost totally ignored by a formally meritocratic (or mer-

itocratizing) society too enamoured of and deferential towards professional and scientistic approaches to knowledge and action.

The proximate ways in which the professional-lay distinction might be constructively addressed in the normal practice of social science research depend fundamentally on the latent function of dialogue and reciprocity mentioned earlier. The advantage of the "anti-method" I am proposing is that radicalization of Schutz' postulate of adequacy will allow us to combine the possibility of Society-wide changes in thoughts, attitudes and actions with what is undeniably a piecemeal and incremental method operating at the microcosmic rather than the macrocosmic level. Instead of having to settle for either a total systems approach or one premised on "muddling through", reforming social science research practices in the ways suggested promises to realize the advantages of both approaches while avoiding some of their inherent disadvantages.[11] One of the most important things coming out of all this is the realization that *both* of the above alternatives constitute opposite extreme instances *on the same continuum*. Both are archetypal instances, related to real-life situations and events only in the most formal way. Far from being "unrealistic", my proposal is eminently realistic because realizable in ways which make significant political gains for all concerned without necessarily sacrificing the legitimate objectives of professional and academic social science.

Once social researchers have met the initial requirement of communicating their findings to respondents, I stated that respondents must not only *understand* what was being produced in the form of explanations about their thoughts, beliefs, attitudes, actions *etc.* but must fundamentally *agree* with these findings. The issue of majority vote or consensus regarding both understanding and agreement would need to be ironed out, preferably on a case by case basis, but this itself would constitute a constructive episode in the process of responsible politicization. The difference between understanding and agreement is crucial. A person can (and often does) understand such renditions in terms of what is *formally possible* as a line of action, conduct or belief, but this need not imply agreement that what is formally possible is the way he actually thought or acted. Normally, to be sure, the two aspects are collapsed into one experience for an individual. Nevertheless, it is possible for understanding and agreement to be separated where a person is more reflexive and self-analytical, not only in the initial stages of recognition but later on as well.

What if it turns out that any given finding is unacceptable? Clearly agreement must be reached as a precondition for publication of the research, and this agreement must be sought in an individual by individual manner. Only if individual respondents agree in advance to bind themselves to a majority rule or consensus decision regarding the accuracy and sense of any given

findings can their individual preferences be absorbed into a collective decision. If they do not agree with any particular rendition, their responses must
be deleted from the sample as a precondition for publication. Even here,
however, their counter-statements would have to be published alongside the
research itself, and generally accorded the same status in every other way.
Thus it is conceivable that if social scientists do not themselves modify their
findings, or admit to the possibility of interpretations like dissenting respondents *in the actual text of their study,* their sample could fail to meet requirements of significance and be less (or in) valid in other ways. This would
certainly condition the research effort and radically alter the nature of the
researcher-respondent relationship.

What therefore appears to be a mere precondition *could* function as a basis
for restructuring social interaction in advanced industrial societies. No longer just a "means" for accumulating knowledge about social interaction
where the behavioural, interactional and political aspects of the research act
itself is ignored, this "latent" function could make social research a prototype for dialogue, reciprocity and communicative equality in its own right.
Even when subjects "agree", some dialogue has occurred under these "new
rules" of sociological method.[12] In all cases the phenomenon of research as a
form of social interaction has been taken account of and preserved in its
experiental aspects. And this, in the final analysis, is precisely the moment
of the act of disciplined observation that needs to be preserved, if only to
counteract the tendency to treat such activity solely or mainly as a method of
studying, observing and recording that which is occuring external to it.
Whatever its claims are, disciplined observation is an activity in the world,
one which has become a central rather than a peripheral *function* of social
life within and around the expanding ambit of civil society itself.

The possibility of an emancipating social science thus carries with it much
more than a reform of social research practices in the relevant academic and
professional disciplines. It could come in time to function as a prototype not
only for responsible societal analysis and critique, but for politically responsible change as well. This is why I have called it an anti-method. Its effects
can in general be comprehended as potentially and actually counterstructu-
ral in their impact, rather than simply destructuring. Not only will radicalizing the postulate of adequacy in the ways suggested act to undercut the
false distinction between the research act and the "knowledge" generated
out of it. It will also meet Arendt's very sensible criterion for the political as
that which is permanent only in its impossibility as anything other than a
recurrent but evanescent phenomenon. What Arendt means by politics
must be counterposed against polity, not because one can (or should) displace the other but because both are necessary and are mutually interdependent with (rather than mutually exclusive of) one another.[13]

From the standpoint of the relation between Society and the social sciences, the importance of this proposal can be surmised from the way in which it seeks to update Durkheim's demand for a professional moral code among sociologists. The demand was first articulated in his doctoral dissertation in 1893, but constitutes a concern which preoccupied Durkheim during the rest of his life. Durkheim's overzealous attack on "dilettantism" is best understood as a response to his times, but his demand for a moral code appears tame in light of the events of the past 90 years. In effect, Durkheim felt that the very presence of sociologists committed to normalizing the abnormal division of labour in concert with occupational groups was sufficient to the industrial problem as it existed at the turn of the century. He may have been right, judged from within the confines of his own commitments and general line of thought. It is certainly true that his demand that sociology work actively in behalf of trends favouring normalization and against trends standing in its way has had a far stronger impact on the development of the social sciences (and Society) than the idea of value neutrality has as anything more than a research protocol honoured as much in the breach as in the observance.[14]

Today Durkheim's demand needs to be updated in line with the actual centre effects of the social sciences throughout the work, market and civil sectors of Society, and elsewhere as well. To be sure, this impact is itself reciprocal, if only because there is a sense in which Society as a culturally and historically specific form of collective life rather than a synonym for it *needs* the social, behavioural and administrative/managerial sciences. Also, developments in the above-noted sectors of Society have until recently been instrumental in generating those academic and professional disciplines whose job it has been, following Durkheim, to protect the emergent form of collective life against either the persistence of archaic and traditional remnants or the threat of incipient collapse and even revolution. Only in the past few years has it made sense to speak of the social sciences and related disciplines as centre effects because of the way their theories, concepts, frameworks, models and research *mirror,* rather than only describe externally, the social, economic and political reality that initially produced them and made them possible. In effect, this form of knowledge no longer seems in the least bit strange to anyone acquainted with or part of what could be termed the middle class experience in the urban areas of North America.[15]

To update Durkheim's original moral code is to recognize this interdependence, bordering on a dialectical relationship, between the social sciences and Society. In order to meet the needs of the present situation, however, something fundamentally more critical is required. My proposal not only carries with it the distinct possibility of a substantial and ongoing, *but es-*

sentially constructive, critique of the social sciences. It also seeks to redress
the bias of Durkheim's demand away from polity toward politics. Durkheim's confidence in the social sciences need not be fundamentally challenged, so long as the issue of dynamizing citizens and publics is not ignored
in favour of the now-conventional professionalism and scientism that Durkheim understandably honoured and believed in at the turn of the century.
Reformism on its own is the inverted mirror-image of professionalism and
scientism in sociology and political science, and its major function has consistently been to favour established structures, whether in the public or
private sector, over citizens and publics. Indeed the social sciences are re-
markable for precisely the manner in which they have isolated, and thereafter aggregated, the responses of citizens treated as passive respondents –
the veritable raw material for confirming or disconfirming hypotheses,
whether of an explanatory or an interventionist nature, about them.

No matter how committed social researchers are to resisting top-down intervention in the name of citizens and publics, their normal practices, combined with the reality of a highly fragmented societal division of labour,
make the realization of this goal almost impossible so long as they adhere to
conventional ideas about the relation between knowledge and policy. Built
into the scheme as it presently stands is a set of funding and related dependencies that invariably biases social science in the direction of the kinds of
piecemeal and incremental reforms that are desired by those in control of
given organizational and occupational hierarchies. What results from the
working out of this dependence syndrome is that social scientists usually
have little or no effective control over the way their research is "used". In
effect it is the *instrumental* nature of the social sciences in their relation to
societal structures that replicates the unfortunate instrumentalism these disciplines adopt toward thought and theorizing in their own professional practices. This latter commitment helps explain the ascendancy of the social
sciences, while it indicates the price paid for this recognition.[16]

Overcoming the means/end split as it has been institutionalized both within
social science and in its relation to the society in which it finds itself means
addressing the reflexive and political moment in Society which is covered
over by professionalism, scientism and meritocracy. Ironically, it is only by
destructuring in the ways suggested that the above splits can be overcome.
Overcoming one split means overcoming the other; they interact recipro-
cally with one another in this regard. The idea is to make social science
research a central manifestation of an in-process critique whose effect will
be to sunder the spatio-temporal distinction between thought, communication and change presupposed by reliance on causal reasoning and causal
explanation. But this is not to argue that encouraging the political moment
will have the effect of undercutting polity and structure, for the two mom-

ents are in a dialectical relationship, not one of mutual exclusivity. What I do claim is that it is only by radicalization of the postulate of adequacy that the political moment can become a real possibility interacting with polity and structure. And this will not take place until and unless both means-end splits are challenged by an approach like mine which *merges* the piecemeal and incremental with the potentially revolutionary in and through the research act itself.[17]

It is because social scientists have developed too much of a vested interest in the non or a political character of polity as structure that politics as individual citizenly display and collective process must emerge and take shape in the advanced societies. This will constitute a fundamental challenge to the wanton hypocrisy of the present formal meritocratic model in operation. This model all-too-often endorses intervention and reform as a professional, scientistic and bureaucratic *control* on change. Such control is deemed necessary in large part because of the threat commonsense capacities operative in the public sphere pose to meritocracy in practice. It is because meritocracy in practice more and more resembles the fossilized and petrified system of formal rationality so clearly prefigured in Max Weber's attack on rationalization and de-enchantment in the West that the political moment is essential if polity itself is to be preserved from a similar fate.[18]

The point here is that destructuration, and the consequent overcoming of the twin splits which make thought a means in the social sciences *because* the social sciences themselves are viewed as instruments by those in positions of power and authority, cannot help but bring a number of key assumptions about superiority and subordination into serious question. Perhaps most important in this respect will be the probable consequences for the concept of "rational domination" in practice, as well as the disembodied notions of objectivity and neutrality so central to its legitimation. To bring the conept of rational domination into question as an objective possibility in social life is to underscore the truncated character of norms of rationality that claim objective status as a neutral and indisputable basis for the present meritocratic stratification order. It is the central role of the social sciences and related disciplines in legitimating meritocracy given their vested interest in professionalism and scientism which makes advanced industrial societies so non or a political in character. This in the face of an almost exponential growth in government and public sector activity.

Polity cannot do the job alone, nor was it ever intended to do so. This is another way of saying that the representative function so central to the operation of politics in the advanced societies cannot be expected to carry the load on its own. Unless the political leadership the system produces is balanced by public participation, the representative function will be totally pre-empted by the rule of law and constitutionalism – a necessary but clearly not a sufficient condition for the health of collective life. Fixed conceptions of government equate its health with criteria of efficiency in operation all-too-rarely honoured in the observance even by large-scale manufacturing, commercial and financial organizations in what is euphemistically called the "private" sector. Such criteria are legitimated by polity's vested interest in structure, stability and predictibility and order, in line with Crick's interpretation of Aristotle and Almond and Verba's conception of "civic culture".[19] The reality, however, is as different from its ideal as meritocracy in practice is from the meritocratic ideal. This is no accident, a point not lost on political management. I have argued that the social sciences can contribute to the development of a responsible politics through radicalization of Schutz' postulate of adequacy. It remains to encounter possible objections to this proposal.

IV

Taken as it stands, adherence to the postulate of adequacy in the ways suggested would put the brakes on much of what passes for research in the social, behavioural and administrative/managerial sciences today. Yet the question of how social researchers can continue to stand in support of un-distorted (or less distorted) communication while relying on public deference to professional and scientific choreography and protocols must be asked. If these trappings indeed constitute the preconditions, along with objectivity, neutrality and authority based on "rational domination", for accomplishing their "normal" work, then might not awareness of some of their less sanguine consequences lead to a revision of present practices along the lines suggested? This is not a question that can be answered in the abstract, but only practically on the basis of the actual conduct of social scientists should such radicalization become acceptable as a legitimate option *within* "normal" sociology and political science.[20]

Earlier I argued that it was necessary to see all forms of superstructural knowledge and activity (professions, sciences, scholarship *etc.*) as interdependent with commonsense capacities in quite specific and continuing ways. In pursuit of this point, I referred to the fact that individual occupants of such roles are also citizens and members of publics, and that this realization cannot help but underscore the importance of the commonsense and the *sub*structural. In effect, social scientists as citizens might readily resist social scientific understandings of *their own* thoughts, beliefs, attitudes, feelings values and actions, taking umbrage at the way subjects-as-objects are pre-defined as passive respondents whose isolated, and thereafter aggregated, responses become the raw material for confirming or disconfirming hypotheses about them. This ability to take the role of the other is of course a central feature of proper market, work and civil behaviour in advanced industrial societies, yet it is one that is constantly being undermined by the presence of public and private status order hierarchies premised on formal meritocracy, with their claim to legitimacy based on rational domination.

In a corollary to his postulate of adequacy, Schutz carried this observation further, drawing attention in the process to the fact that the actor's knowledge of the world is no less a datum for the social scientist than his actions. Referring pre-eminently to the *possibility* of agreement between social scientists and their subjects, he *presumes* that similar world views and interpretations are not only possible but "likely". "What makes it possible for social science to refer at all to events in the life-world is the fact that the interpretation of any human act by the social scientist *might* be the same as that by the actor or by his partner."[21] It is this fundamental underlying "kinship" which cuts across the role structure, however hierarchical and however legitimated, to bring individuals in possession of both substructural and superstructural capacities together. The social research situation is one of the most important places where this enterprise of collective self-examination of the two capacities, their presuppositions and interrelations, can take place.

Looking at specific problems of implementation *without* necessarily presuming the sort of mutuality and identification which would likely take place once the proposal had been fully accepted, we can cite the following problems. Though the list cannot claim to be exhaustive, it does try to address what I believe to be some of the most important difficulties which would occur in both the initial and the continuing phases of the attempt at implementation.

(1) Researched subjects are so *illiterate, ignorant or stupid* about the nature of social science research, if not in more general ways, that it is unlikely that they can function as equal members of the proposed interaction situation.

(2) Researched subjects might be *hostile* to the social research enterprise and give their consent only to sabotage, or attempt to sabotage, the situation. They might in effect be put in too powerful a position to influence the outcomes of social research or to stop it from taking place altogether.

(3) Researched subjects might be *indifferent* to what was said about them, in particular the generalizations reached on the basis of isolating, then aggregating, their responses. This might lead them either to give their consent *pro forma* or waive the opportunity to participate in the ways the proposal recommends and would make possible.

(4) Social scientists might fail (or refuse) to inform subjects of their rights, or might take advantage of the impact on subjects of professional and scientistic protocols

and choreography. This might influence individuals to participate even if it were
contrary to their perceived interests.

(5) Social science is so heavily dependent on established, formally meritocratic,
institutions for its recognition, access, funding *etc.* that the possibility of radicalization in the ways suggested must be considered minimal, even where a
substantial number of social scientists engaged in research support it.

A thoughtful look at the first alleged difficulty should dispel it unequivocally. It is precisely the sort of claim that can only be taken seriously so long
as researchers refuse to radicalize the postulate of adequacy in favour of
normal social science. It begins by assuming precisely what I have taken
issue with by reference to commonsense capacities themselves, namely, that
intelligence and ability is exclusively or mainly a function of professional,
scientific or academic training and certification. The fact that this is absurd
must occur to the healthy common sense of even the most professional and
scientistic social researcher, yet it is the sort of realization which is resisted
precisely because of its potential consequences for the vested interest in
hierarchical and asymmetrical ways of doing social science research so important to the vast majority of social scientists.

The issue of hostility, and consequent infiltration and sabotage, by individuals "masquerading" as respondents cannot be ignored. At the same time,
their influence would not likely be consequential in groups of any size. Also,
respondents themselves would be to a large extent self-selected, particularly
if the suggested "moral code" had become a matter of public knowledge
through the mass media. These individuals would likely view such subver-
sion critically, unless it made sense to them. In this latter case, social science
researchers themselves would need to consider what was going on, and it
would become a legitimate and necessary part of the social research setting,
not something extraneous to it. Where social scientists had not made such an
option available to their research subjects, the purpose of such infiltration
might well force everyone to consider it, *regardless of what was ultimately
decided.* Where the researchers had already shown their willingness to consider it as an option, sabotage of the proceedings would likely be cut short
by the vast majority of respondents.

Indifference is another consideration, yet is no less valid as a response to the
possibility of the radicalizing option than concern and interest. Indeed, indifference in the research setting provides an all-too-relevant parallel to
apathy toward public issues in Society at large. Here it is the "right" to be
apathetic which is central, even if it means waiving the opportunity to participate actively in favour of the normal role of the subject-as-object. The
reason for underscoring this particular "right" must be clear. We must never
attempt to overcome the structures of rational domination by making use of
any of these structures, or the values that guide them and make them pos-

sible. To take advantage of existing inequities, asymmetries or protocols in pursuit of their overcoming is to make a mockery of the exercise and all it stands for. In the event, it becomes just another, newer, form of caretaking, and bears an all-too-poignant resemblance to Lenin's "post-revolutionary" organization of Russian society.

The possibility that social science researchers might fail to inform subjects of the radicalizing option is a real one, but one whose likelihood would be minimal where this option had become public knowledge. As for the impact of professional and scientific protocols and choreography, the result could well be deference, but it might not. Remember that individuals are gathered together in the research setting, and it is highly unlikely that *someone* would not be aware of the possibility of the radicalizing option. In the event no one was aware, the social scientist's failure to inform them of it could be counted a violation of trust and confidence on his part toward his research subjects. If anything like a code of ethics existed for social scientists, even an informal one, his failure to notify subjects of this option could redound to his disadvantage. He may not be allowed to publish results unless he returns to the group, gives them the option, then follows the "new rules" should they choose to adopt them.

The dependence of social science research on established institutions for recognition, access, funding *etc.* is a serious stumbling block, one which could only be overcome if a substantial body of social scientists were willing to honour the proposal as a possible option on which given subjects would have to reach a decision in the research situation. Even here, however, too much depends on authorities in the universities, in government buraux, in firms and in funding organizations. That these authorities might be as fearful of the possibilities of radicalization as many political scientists are of politics and the political, as opposed to polity, must be clear. The only thing that might be argued in such a circumstance is that social science is too valuable and necessary for any authority to turn its back on its practitioners where they support the proposal. On the other hand, it is precisely the disorganizing effects which might make them wish to turn their back on the social sciences, convinced as they were for the past century that such a challenge was unthinkable and determined not to tolerate it now. Where social scientists themselves gave little support to the radicalizing option as a basis for a possible politics, the problem of research proposals being denied recognition, access or funding would arise far less frequently.

One practice which would be intolerable from the standpoint of the proposal is virtually endemic to many forms of participant observation. It is the practice of studying, observing and recording individuals who are not aware that this is happening. Needless to say, in many (but not all) cases *someone* knows this is happening, but again this sort of enterprise is an example of hierarchical thinking based on rational domination as a privilege beyond criticism. Such practices are at best one step removed from conventional survey and formal research, and therefore are impermissible because they preclude the possibility of even conventional subject-as-object status. This would be my reason for condemning the "obedience to authority" studies carried out, albeit with the best probable motives, by Stanley Milgram. The problem in this case is that he had to engage in duplicity and legerdemain in order to point up what are admittedly findings of the first order. Milgram discovered that many individuals will administer shocks to others, even when the latter screamed or cried out in pain, when told to do so by those perceived to be in professional or scientific authority. The point here is that the screams and cries were faked, like the entire "experiment", in order to see how far individuals would go even if it violated their sense of rectitude and compassion.[22]

The argument I would favour in all instances where such techniques were being called for in order to acquire knowledge not apparently available by other means is that any practice that violates openness, reciprocity and mutuality is suspect no matter which side of the research situation it emanates from or what the justification for it might be. All I am saying is that the categorical imperative (like charity) begins at home. No one should become a means to the production of findings that will allegedly "help" them, and others like them, at some future date. This is the legacy of the disciplined observer making himself believe that he is "outside" that which he investigates. Whatever the source of such an assumption, it clearly favours a caretaking approach to individuals which really denies them their status as subjects and deprives them of the opportunity to take an active role in their lives as rational beings with commonsense capabilities. Furthermore, it can lead to exploitation where such research is implemented by some "user" operating independently of the researcher. It is all-too-reminiscent of the view of man as a non-rational and sentimental being found in Durkheim, and later so central to the work of Elton Mayo and the Human Relations movement in industry.[23]

Any conclusion to such a proposal must again favour radicalization because it dynamizes a key situation by reviving the commitment to the capacities of individuals as citizens, regardless of their location in the social (and occupational) division of labour. In this effort it points to the need to rethink our reliance on the written tradition, not only where the mode of exposition is written, but where it takes the form of speech. The problem today is that too much of what could constitute a basis for constructive dialogue is buried beneath megatons of institutional and organizational structure dedicated to cutting real speech down where it is not cut out altogether. The only place it seems to me that speech and the oral tradition is allowed to survive is in circumstances where it is virtually petrified into formal one way decrees and "statements of fact" from authorities.[24] This is even becoming a problem in areas of collective life outside the widening ambit of the market, work and civil sectors. Our great problem in advanced industrial societies is that we accept the idea that we must *speak* in the written tradition because time is money and it is wasted on any form of communication which questions criteria of efficiency and productivity.

Political management is committed to discovering situations where there is a possibility, however slim, of excavating politics and the political from the dead weight of formal meritocracy. The idea of reason as a humanly distributed possession of individuals in collective life, rather than the property of those trained in superstructural modes of knowledge and knowing, is central to this effort. So is the idea of merging piecemeal and revolutionary objectives, beginning "locally" and taking the existing structure of society as a working given. A final reference to the proposal's commitment to openness, honesty, dialogue and reciprocity should underscore the fact that we now have a real opportunity to overcome archaic assumptions, values and patterns of action which have for too long allowed us to ignore politics in favour of polity. It is precisely social-scientific recognition of the central role of their disciplines which should lead them to take more serious account of the citizenship of their practitioners, as well as their probable resistance to being treated as passive respondents in the ways indicated.[25]

Once the possibility of an option of the radicalizing sort is accepted, it becomes easier to question the value of professional and scientistic protocols and choreography in the absence of the political moment. After all, what is the point in accumulating knowledge behind the backs of those who will allegedly be its beneficiaries, using techniques that we could not tolerate as citizens if we were required to submit to them. It is the fundamental disjunction between the alleged ends or goals of social science research and the means used to acquire such knowledge which necessitates radicalization of the postulate of adequacy. Such radicalization constitutes one situationally appropriate form that political management might take in the social research situation in advanced industrial societies.

References

1 This is a very much modified and amended version of an essay titled "Anti-Method as a Counterstructure in Social Research Practice," which appeared in *Beyond Method: Strategies for Social Research* edited by Gareth Morgan (Los Angeles: Russell Sage, 1983), pp. 247–259. Note that I address the need to make the social sciences *responsibly political* rather than politically responsible, the

latter objective being too clearly tied to traditional concerns and even "symbolic reassurance."

2 Marx made this point most persuasively when he insisted that natural science be understood as a form of human *industry* in *Early Texts,* edited by David McClellan (Oxford: Basil Blackwell, 1962), section on "private property and communism."

3 Thus social science as a *form* of social interaction rather than solely a neutral means for dispassionately observing social interaction at a distance from it is paralleled by the idea of Society as a culturally and historically specific *form* of collective life rather than a synonym for it. See my "Functional Rationality and 'Sense of Function': the Case of an Ideological Distortion," *op. cit.,* and *Tradition & Innovation* for development of these parallel, and dialectically interrelated, notions.

4 Wilson, *Tradition & Innovation,* chapter 3.

5 *Ibid.,* chapters 4 and 5.

6 Alfred Schutz, "The Problem of Rationality in the Social World," in *Collected Papers, Volume Two,* edited and introduced by Arvid Brodersen (The Hague: Martinus Nijhoff, 1964), pp. 64–88 at p. 85.

7 Robert Merton, "Manifest & Latent Functions," in Merton, *Social Theory & Social Structure,* 2nd edition (NY: Macmillan, 1957), pp. 19–84.

8 Paolo Freire, *Pedagogy of the Oppressed* (NY: Herder & Herder, 1972); Freire, *Education for Critical Consciousness* (NY: Seabury Press, 1973).

9 Harold Garfinkel, "The Rational Properties of Scientific and Commonsense Activities," in Garfinkel, *Studies in Ethnomethodology* (Englewood Clifts, N. J.: Prentice Hall, 1967), pp. 262–283 at p. 262. Also see Wilson, "Rationality & Decision in Administrative Science," *op. cit.,* for application of Schutz' and Garfinkel's critique of behavioural and positivist approaches to the administrative sciences and organizational analysis.

10 Stanley Milgram, "Some Conditions of Obedience and Disobedience to Authority," *Human Relations,* Volume 18 (1965), pp. 57–76; Milgram, *Obedience to Authority: An Experimental View* (NY: Harper & Row, 1974); Randall Collins, *The Credential Society* (NY: Academic Press, 1979); and Wilson, *The American Ideology,* chapter 9.

11 See Charles Lindblom, "The Science of Muddling Through," *Public Administration Review,* Volume 19 (Spring, 1959), pp. 79–88; Popper, *The Poverty of Historicism;* Wilson, *The American Ideology,* chapter 5; and Wilson, "Rationality & Decision in Administrative Science," *op. cit.*

12 My proposal is thus *not* a counter concept of interpretation for sampling the latest trends in social theory, like Anthony Giddens in *New Rules of Sociological Method* (NY: Basic Books, 1976). Far from simply *using* a modified form of Durkheim's famous *Rules of Sociological Method* (NY: Macmillan, 1964), I honour the original intention of the author to pursue a mode of active and industrious inquiry by attempting to update the original demand so that it now possesses a reflexive, as well as a disciplined observational, component. See my "The Meaning and Significance of 'Empirical Method' for the Critical Theory of Society," *op. cit.,* and "Critical Theory's Critique of Social Science", *op. cit.* for elaboration.

13 Arendt, *The Human Condition,* p. 200.

14 Durkheim, *The Division of Labour in Society,* preface to the first edition, chapter one and conclusion; Wilson, *The American Ideology,* chapter 8, and 4 on Durkheim's sociology of knowledge and its relevance to the now well-known "Popper-Kuhn" controversy.

15 Burton Bledstein, *The Culture of Professionalism* (NY: W. W. Norton, 1976); Collins, *op. cit.*

16 Wilson, "The Meaning and Significance of 'Empirical Method' for the Critical Theory of Society," *op. cit.*

17 This is directly related to the need to merge thought, analysis, concern, evaluation and action discussed in chapters 10–12.

18 Wilson, "Elites, Meritocracy & Technocracy," *op. cit.;* Weber, *The Protestant Ethic and the Spirit of Capitalism* (NY: Scribners, 1958), concluding paragraphs.

19 Crick, *In Defense of Politics;* Almond & Verba, *The Civic Culture.*

20 See Claus Muller, "Notes on the Repression of Communicative Behaviour," and Jürgen Habermas, "Toward a Theory of Communicative Competence," both in *Recent Sociology, No. 2* edited by H. P. Dreitzel (NY: Macmillan, 1970), pp. 101–114 and pp. 115–148; and my response in "Notes on the Achievement of Communicative Behaviour and Related Difficulties," *Dialectical Anthropology* (forthcoming).

21 Schutz, *op. cit.,* pp. 85–86.

22 Milgram, *op. cit.,* but see Martin Wenglinsky, "Review of Milgram's *Obedience to Authority,*" *Contemporary Sociology: A Review of Reviews* (1975), pp. 613–617.

23 Durkheim, *The Division of Labour in Society;* Elton Mayo, *The Human Problems of an Industrial Civilization* (Cambridge, Mass: Harvard Business School, 1933).

24 Felix Kaufmann, *Methodology of the Social Sciences* (New Haven: Yale University Press, 1944), on knowledge protocols and "statements of fact." Kaufmann figures prominently in much of Garfinkel's work.

25 Note the difference, once again, between my active political concern and that of both Habermas, in *op. cit.,* and *Communication and the Evolution of Society* (Boston: Beacon Press, 1979); and Karl Otto Apel in *Transformations of Philosophy* (London: Routledge, 1980). There is a considerable difference between the employment of theoretical analysis as a *substitute* for political practice at the one extreme, and the idea of a responsibly political (as opposed to a politically responsible) social science at the other.

Chapter 9
The University as a Training Ground for Citizenship

I

The need to carefully consider the contribution that universities in the advanced societies can make to political management and its allied concerns has only been heightened by the post World War II emergence of relatively open access to higher education facilities. From a situation in which the university's political role was mainly defended on the grounds of its status as an elite institution with a leading societal responsibility because of its privileged position, it now finds itself functioning more and more as a vehicle for social mobility and integration. Instead of being viewed strictly in terms of leadership based on privilege, the university can now be better comprehended as a social institution whose function appertains as much to participation in societal concerns and objectives as it does to leadership in these endeavours. In many countries, universities are increasingly treated, for better or worse, as extensions of the public school system of the country, state, or province. This is made all the easier when increased access and enrollments are undergirded by the public nature of higher education in almost all of the advanced societies save for the United States.

The effect of open higher education is to encourage students who might otherwise not go to university to stay in school. This is not to argue that there was not an initial pressure to open out these facilities. I am, however, concerned with the impact that this new informal requirement or expectation is having on young people whose process of secondary socialization is effectively extended into their early, and in some cases, their mid, twenties. In some countries an undergraduate degree is no longer considered sufficient, and students are encouraged to continue on for a further degree or certificate in business or professional studies. While there may be clear instances in which one can demonstrate the specific function and value of studies beyond secondary public education, much of it seems tied to the notion that higher education will have a maturing, as well as an edifying, impact on the young. Without challenging the need for such an option in these societies, one is nevertheless entitled to wonder about the consequences for innovation and novelty of arrangements which encourage some of our brightest young people to remain in what is increasingly an extended version of secondary public education well into their twenties. It is the perpetuation of dependence and tutelage, even in the face of the most readily defensible cases for extended tuition, that constitutes the "other side" of Society's socializing agenda in these matters.

The recent austerity throughout Western Europe and North America provides ample evidence that the desire and demand for higher education is not simply a function of affluence. When the economy is bad, higher education, instead of being desired for the access to better paying, higher status jobs that it brings, is seen as the best guarantee of eventual employment while yet providing an alternative to job-hunting under austerity conditions. However poor the forecast for the employment of university graduates, it rarely has the effect of encouraging young people to forego the experience if it is available to them, particularly when the alternative is to hit the job market with only a secondary school degree. University managers and executives who seriously expected that economic downturn would lead to a *decline* in undergraduate enrollments can scarcely be forgiven for their naïveté and lack of empathy and commonsense understanding. This is as much the result of being safe and snug in tenured or otherwise secure jobs as it is a function of the so-called "generation gap." One of the major properties of the norm of functional rationality in practice is precisely this formalization of meritocracy as a substantive ideal in and through provisions for job security throughout large organizations in the advanced societies.

The point about all forms of education available to the young, including higher education, is therefore what its latent, and often its manifest, purpose is and what it means. To say of the primary and secondary grades that students are being "socialized" for adulthood as much as they are being trained in specific subject matter areas simply begs the question. Once we discover that aspects of this logic have become the basis for defending more higher education, or at least more open access to these facilities, it becomes all the more necessary to find out exactly what students are being socialized in and for, and why. If it is argued for one reason or another that longer periods of secondary socialization are needed, then we need to consider these claims carefully in the light of the nature of Society as a culturally and historically specific form of collective life. Why should such an extension be necessary, and what precisely are both its benefits and its costs? The idea that people are living longer than was the case in the past, and are as a consequence putting off (or avoiding altogether) the sorts of decisions that go with adult status is unpersuasive. This strikes me more as a rationalization for an already accomplished state of affairs than anything else.

One point of considerable significance bears on the "cooling-out" function of extended secondary socialization just mentioned. Employers have traditionally believed, not without reason, that young people are best kept in some form of schooling at least into their twenties. The effect of this tuition is supposed to improve the likelihood that they will pass into young adulthood *before* undertaking full-time career employment, to the benefit of all concerned, particularly the employer. The difficulty here is that adulthood is in most instances simply postponed as a result of such a strategem. It is, after all, as much a social and cultural process as it is a physiological one, so simply encouraging young people to undertake more schooling only serves to put off the problem, not to resolve it. That the problem is dealt with in a formalized context characterized by dependence and tutelage, rather than in a broader societal setting, probably aggravates it more than anything else. Universities in particular perform a function of incontestable significance to employers, and to Society as a whole, when they provide the organizational basis for extending secondary socialization well beyond the age of first majority. Its significance is to be discovered in its preference, implied or stated, for passive non or a political roles, whether in occupational life, consumption or spectating.[1]

In order to fully comprehend this important development, it needs to be correlated with the decline of confidence in apprenticeship methods of training on the part of a vast number of business, commercial and industrial endeavours throughout the advanced societies. While Western Europe certainly retains a greater role for practical on-the-job-training than is true in North America, the drive to meritocratic formalization, with its preference for closure and status, has become much stronger there since 1960. If it seems somewhat ironic that the openness and availability of institutions of higher education should be so consistently correlated with functional rationalization, formal meritocratization and closure, this is readily explained by the animus of extended secondary socialization itself. Like Durkheim's reference to free occupational choice in a situation of essential "normlessness" or anomie, the option is conditional, and has as its purpose the subordination of the individual to new controls expressive of the emergent form of (organic) solidarity. In this context, specificity of training still relates in large measure to the acquisition of experience in a given line of work (now much disparaged), rather than to the possession of formal cerfiticates, diplomas and degrees. In the absence of such experience, Weber's bureaucrat could hardly avoid being as pathological as he is regularly conceived.[2]

The decision to forego apprenticeship and allied methods of on-the-job training may have been inspired by changes in the nature of organized work which began to take shape in the 1920's and 1930's. This process was delayed, to be sure, in certain industries and certain countries, and in many instances never took place at all. Nowadays the performance of Japan and many EEC countries, particularly in medium to high-technology industries,

frequently confounds this earlier decision. Having reached its highest level
of development in the United States and Canada, this preference for extended formal education probably is as much for financial reasons as for
anything else. Young people were now to be kept in school at least until they
had achieved an undergraduate degree, in all cases at their own expense or
that of their parents or the general taxpayer. Employees did not, as a consequence of this, provide a delayed version of apprenticeship, but expected
that greater maturity, coupled in some instances with business and professional training, would more than make up for its absence. This line of thinking would appear to have fundamentally misfired, even from the standpoint
of their own objectives, particularly once it became clear that European
recovery would mean that North American employers could no longer take
the in-migration of vast numbers of practically trained engineers and tech-
nicians for granted.

It is in the context of these developments, coupled with Society's socializing
agenda, that the present and future political role of the university needs to
be considered. As a vehicle for mobility and integration, its main thrust
seems increasingly to favour a merger of the strictly scholarly and the immediately practical. Indeed, it may be more accurate to say that it is in the
process of generating a third alternative separate from either one. This
alternative is no longer even remotely a side effect relative to the role of
scholarly and scientific studies on the one hand and vocational and technical
studies on the other. It is a centre effect from which it is more and more
difficult to escape, regardless of economic conditions, practical interests of
an entrepreneurial and technical kind, or what should be the vigour and
excitement of youth. As for those who do opt for vocational and technical
training, or for no further training at all, they often acquire the income
necessary for a satisfactory middle class living standard, even if this income
is more the result of institutional und public sector contracts in periods of
economic downturn. But it is the universities that supply the vast majority of
individuals who will inhabit the formally meritocratic positions characterized by salaried full time career status, tenure, and a vast range of perquisites and benefits not available to all those who are officially "outside" the
system.[3]

None of this is intended to disparage the university for doing what Society,
and its employers and general taxpayers, expect it to do for them, usually
with public monies (save for the United States). The point is rather to be
clear on the conditions within the university, as well as between it and
relevant elements in its environment, that bear on how well it will be able to
perform these functions. And it is precisely because of its role in providing
opportunities and avenues for both mobility and integration that it already
constitutes one of the most important of the new public spaces which have

opened out in recent times for the activity of citizenship. Students in process, regardless of how temporary their stay in university, constitute a leading force of central significance not only to the care and concern for public matters, but for innovation in ways of addressing and dealing with issues through politics and the political. An elitist approach based on controlled access to higher education in earlier times may have allowed the university to function as both a vehicle for and an embodiment of power in Society at an earlier stage in its development. Today, however, we can only salvage, and seek to revive, established representative institutions by encouraging the politicization of new public spaces where the issues are either to be discovered, or where they are most likely to gain clear discussion and understanding.

II

Let me turn now to those aspects of higher education and the university that help explain the reasons for its structural, organizational, and relational properties. The objective here is to underscore the relationship between structure and function, but at the same time to suggest that all-too-often the structure is inappropriate, if not counterproductive, to the function. It is not always the case, for example, that the function can be designated as mistaken once the societal agenda and goals have been articulated. It makes little sense to rail at systems of higher eduction simply because they express in microcosm the goals of a society which is considered to have severe problems virtually insoluble by reference to available mechanisms or techniques. I am concerned here to offer an analysis of the university setting which will allow us to begin immediately, as I did in the case of the social sciences in an earlier chapter. If universities are to become new public spaces, along with others, complementing established institutions, then analysis must try to discover in present relations and ways of doing things an opportunity to fix on those areas where change should be encouraged to this end. I want to delineate some structural properties and historical facts about the university that bear on its mission in advanced industrial societies.

Perhaps the most visible characteristic of the university considered as a structure is its bureaucratic organization. Apart from the extent to which such organization has become coincident with the norm of order in Society is the way that bureaucracy has been associated with fiscal responsibility where the spending of public monies is concerned. This may seem strange, since bureaucracy, and public administration generally, is forever being critized for the costs of governments. But closer inspection reveals that this is frequently an attack on the *objects* of such expenditure rather than on the effectiveness of the methods employed to secure fiscal responsibility. The historical case on this matter was made with great force by Max Weber, when he observed in a different cultural and temporal context that bureaucracies are without peer when it comes to financial responsibility, *regardless of the cost of maintaining them!* As a matter of fact, Weber cited this as one of the many advantages of bureaucratic organization and management, even though modern bureaucracy would itself have been inconceivable in the absence of a money economy. Thus, when people attack bureaucracy for its power, its distance, and particularly its costs, they are really attacking the form of collective life that requires its extensive utilization, and so must pay for it.[4]

One of the most interesting, if least understood, peculiarities of bureaucratic organization in the university bears on the fact that in several important respects it does not constitute simply an imposition of the bureaucratic form on activities related to higher education, but provides us with a rather unique variation on this structural form. Universities are *professional* bureaucratic organizations rather than conventional ones because they evidence a reversal of the usual relationship that can be seen to obtain between line and staff roles. Indeed, I have suggested elsewhere that it is the influence and impact of precisely this organizational experience, particularly when coupled with the ideology of professionalism, that helps explain why technocrats as a group favour the modification of governmental administrative structures in the direction of professional organizations like the university. For the most important upshot of this reversal of line and staff functions in the area of higher education is revealed in the fact that generalists or managers typically occupy *staff,* rather than line, functions, while specialists trained in academic disciplines are usually found in line positions. This reversal of roles is the key to understanding the difference between a standard bureaucratic structure in either the public or private sector, and a professional organization.[5]

In the case of the university, this reversal is important because it attests to an uncompleted state of affairs, at least in North America. What I have in mind is the fact that historically the university was under the careful scrutiny not only of governing boards comprised of leading figures in the society, but was often managed internally by figures who were only marginally related at best to academic and professional pursuits. One of the most important and persistent features of the university from its origins in the middle ages has been its consistent and continuing professional and practical bias. It was only in the period following the onset of industrial capitalism that a sufficient surplus was generated to make it possible for defenders of the university like Cardinal Newman to speak on behalf of the esoteric pursuits of the higher learning. Few realize how intensely practical the university was in the period from the higher middle ages to the mid-Nineteenth Century. They only see the studies engaged in at an earlier time (theology, law) as impractical from the standpoint of the *present day,* and fail to relate such studies to the needs of the times in which they were justifiably prominent for their practicality.[6]

Faculty control of the university is at the best of times a conditional matter, but it ceased to be of central significance in North America with the growth of the surplus and a view of practicality which excluded academics in favour of individuals with business experience or loyalties. It was the effective *recapture* of the American and Canadian university by the faculty in the period from 1890 to 1930 or 1940, best evidenced in the heightened policy role of university senates relative to governing boards, which set the stage for the contemporary university in these countries.[7] In Britain and Western Europe the tradition has been somewhat different, combining various forms of state or public control with a highly elitist tradition of scholarship, almost always based on the class system. Integration of the middle and upper middle classes into academic life occurred faster on the Continent than it did in Britain, where this development is largely a post- World-War II phenomenon. This is probably because capitalism, and capitalist industrialization, had a greater impact on landed aristocracies and other pre-industrial remnants there than it did in Britain until recently. In all instances however (including Canada), the pattern into the 1960's was to follow the lead of the United States on the matter of its commitment to more open access to higher education.

The present problem, well reflected in the student uprisings in North America and Western Europe in the mid and late 1960's, is that faculty were able to recapture a modicum of control of academic, and occasionally even administrative, policy from boards and Society as a whole, but did not extend and complete this "revolution" to the benefit of students. I would argue that this failure or refusal in several national-state settings after World War II was instrumental in maintaining the loyalty of former undergraduates to the ethos of consumption, and the passive conception of leisure as "time off from work" that flows from it. Students failed fundamentally to benefit from an earlier recapture whose effect was to vastly increase the size and scale of higher education undertakings in the United States, while maintaining students in a position of dependence and tutelage. Students became little more than a clientele, or a poor and/or dependent clientele, at a time when the prestige of academic status in universities was increasing due both to wartime accomplishments and the post-war desire to significantly expand higher educational facilities. The basis for associating such an expanded constituency with an extension of the secondary public education system was firmly in place.[8]

In post-war Europe, old traditions were to some extent revived, but were increasingly subject to the new definition of the situation which had been imposed on Europe by the United States and the Soviet Union. European post-war reconstruction was, after all, overseen by the four powers. In Western Europe, the pre-eminence of the United States was impossible to deny, the more because of the continent-wide impact of the Marshall Plan. No matter what the blandishments of a private enterprise approach to the higher learning amongst Americans were, they were unsuccesful in imposing such a notion on countries with a long tradition of public, and in some cases state, control. To be sure, there was insistence in the West German case that this state or public control be exercised by the states rather than by any central authority. But the basic motif was left in place, in no small part because the association of state or public control with academic compromise was overdrawn. Too many of the allied countries, and those under occupation until 1944 or 1945, had similar traditions, albeit with differing institutional arrangements (like Britain, France, the Netherlands, Denmark, and Norway for example).

When I say the *"recapture"* of the university by faculty, I mean to allude to the fact that faculty control had been a regular characteristic of the university from its origins to the mid-nineteenth century, regardless of the formal or real role of the state in the early modern period of European development. At about the same time that the "higher learning" was emerging as an esoteric activity to be supported as much for its results as for its prestige, American universities were established in the states on the basis of land-grants, and a distinct emphasis on agricultural, technical and practical arts were favoured from the outset. This coincided everywhere with the sudden rise in status and prestige of the natural sciences, which quickly became the model for disciplines with lesser claims to public attention and support. Scientists began to challenge established scholars in classical, historical, theological and philological studies for the title of leading discipline, and a clear distinction was drawn between the arts and sciences, probably in order to protect scholarship in the above cited areas from serious institutional challenge. This challenge, and the split that issued largely from it, was probably the basis for the development of "faculties", as well as the idea of specific curricula leading to degrees, certificates *etc.*

One of the major characteristics of faculty in the natural sciences is typically their preoccupation with the kind of research which links them with other scientists in other universities and other areas of Society. The system of scientific *communication* is infinitely more sophisticated than anything found in other disciplines, and its basis is not necessarily the universities where given researchers find themselves. Identification with scientists elsewhere indicates the far greater role of professional cross-university linkages than intra-university ties to other faculties. Partly this is a function of the nature of scientific research, its need for extensive funding, and its system of communication, identification, and prestige and reputation. It is in this research/service distinction that one discovers the prototype for most of the problems that *other* disciplines have in reconciling research, teaching and service as the three major functions of university faculty. It is clearly the basis for the "cosmopolitan-local" dichotomy that one commentator found so problematic some years ago. At the same time that I note these developments, however, I must stress that this impact on other disciplines has not caused scientists in universities anywhere near the same trouble that it has those disciplines which often consider science a model of intellectual and professional endeavour.[9]

One of the most impressive characteristics of science as a research and scholarly enterprise is the way that it manages to *combine* research and instruction through the aegis of laboratory, mathematical or theoretical apprenticeship. It is the only university-based discipline which does this so extensively, and it is absolutely central to science's intergenerational continuity, "success" and standing in the country. It is a central element undergirding the system of communication, identification and prestige and reputation in science. Lacking this model of apprenticeship, which is the single most important function carried out by scientists *within* discrete university communities, other disciplines can at best offer the highly motivated student reading courses and small seminars. To be sure, a parallel cosmopolitanism is also absent, which is to say that other disciplines are *more* dependent on the decisions of those who direct universities than are scientists. When this fact is added to the failure of these disciplines to deal effectively with the three university requirements of research, instruction, and service, the dilemma for students is only underscored. Unlike students in science, those in other disciplines are largely left to the vagaries of chance and inclination in the absence of tried and tested techniques and methods which effectively combine research with instruction while providing the basis for what *Society* has come to expect will be service.

It is the fundamental difference between being taught and having the opportunity to learn that I have in mind by this distinction.[10] To the extent that the university experience for undergraduate students favours tutelage and dependence, both in the instructional and in the residential situation, it will unavoidably lend aid and comfort to that panoply of passive roles which I have already associated with non (or a) political and non-innovative behaviours. It is not, then, simply the length of the secondary socialization experience so much as its fundamental nature that is important in assessing its consequences for our societies. In scientific subjects, particularly where laboratory experimentation is a central aspect, students not only are able to merge research and scholarship with instruction, but as a consequence of doing this come to view the learning environment as one in which they participate actively.[11] It is one of the dilemmas of our time that students most actively involved with such research are frequently those least interested in matters political and governmental. While many of the remarks which follow are no less applicable to scientific students than to non-scientific ones, they probably are more directly relevant in most instances to the latter than to the former.

III

The result of the unfinished "revolution" in higher education is only underscored by the fate of students in a system where legislators, governing boards, university managers *and faculty* generally see eye to eye. In effect, the main consequence of the recapture of the university by academic faculty has been the full integration of academics into the societal structure as occupational members. Even (or rather especially) where faculty unions have come into being, their objective is to protect the faculty share within the universities against the demands of any and all competitors. Collective bargaining is a successful device for rationalizing the heretofore pluralistic and diverse reality of the university power structure, by superimposing on established institutional practices a labour-management grid. Neither students nor hard-working faculty benefit very much, if at all, from this development, and it must therefore be considered a device for shoring up faculty privilege against the demands of students. At the same time it accomplishes societal integration of a kind, by adopting a variation on the model of negotiation already in place for primary and secondary school teachers in the public educational system.

What is problematic in all of this is the way it serves to freeze the student's status rather than to allow students to benefit in fundamental ways from the recapture of higher education by faculty. If the university and higher education are integrated into the larger society in direct ways by the greater availability of these facilities for the general population, the appropriate method of internal management and accountability requires recourse, as noted, to the organizational principle of functional rationality in practice. The most damaging upshot of continuous recourse to this principle or norm can nowadays be seen in what I shall call the *organizational* conception of university membership. The essence of this conception is that the only people who are members are those who are *organizational members,* in the sense of receiving either a salary or wage on a regular basis *as employees.* In this equation students cannot help but be clients, or rather the dependents of clients, rather than members. The vagaries of their tutelary and dependent status, coupled with generational differences and the fact of their temporary stay in the university, all conspire to favour a view of them as an *external* clientele, or the dependents of one, rather than members of a community of scholars.[12]

To be sure, this notion of "community of scholars" can be argued to be unrealistic because it appertains to only a small percentage of students in an age of mass, or at least more open, higher education. My point is not to attack this function, but rather to suggest that it does favour an organizational conception of membership and a view of all students as external clients rather than internal members. In addition to this there is the relationship between tutelage and dependence, extended secondary socialization processes into the mid-twenties, and the disciplinary and control functions performed in the university setting by bureaucratic structure to be considered. Up to now I have emphasized the role of bureaucracy and functional rationality as an instrument for guaranteeing more responsible utilization of public monies from general tax revenues and allied sources. But it is important not to underplay the significance of bureaucracy as a form of rational domination. While we can acknowledge some of the claims that Weber made regarding the *organizational* rationality of bureaucracy, we must not ignore the consequences for those dependent upon it of its claim to the mantle of objective rational domination. Power, control and dysfunctional disciplinary properties clearly emerge from its failure to maintain the substantive ideals of meritocracy when these ideals are converted into practice.

The idea that a member is one who contributes services for which a wage or salary is received certainly makes sense from the standpoint of bureaucratic functional rationality. After all, universities are seen as secondary structures in civil society rather than primary groups, so the imposition upon them of the model of a society in microcosm rather than a community can be readily understood. Without overstressing the established distinction between community and Society as anything more than the range of possible orientations available in *any* collective setting[13], one can say that strict adherence to power, discipline and control as vehicles of the instructional situation may not be the best approach to higher education. On the other hand, the large majority of undergraduate students would not be in university at all if access to higher education had not been improved, and many may not now wish to be there at all, even if it is seen as a minimum condition for future salaried employment "outside". Perhaps it is true that only the small minority can learn in an atmosphere more akin to community than to Society, and its microcosm bureaucracy. The fact that extended secondary socialization must mean an extension of the idea of publicly supported schooling into the university years would appear to make an even stronger case for continuation of established structures and relationships.

What I would like to stress, however, is the effect the organizational conception is having on the student/faculty relationship, and how this relationship plays an important role in the young adult's approach to his life afterwards. The first thing to be said is not that huge enrollments preclude a primary group relation between students and faculty, but rather that a certain notion of the proper function of the university and higher education already needed to be operative in order to justify such vastly expanded enrollments. Students are looked after in large universities more and more in terms of their needs (and powers) as consumers and audiences, which is to say that extended secondary socialization provides the possibility that they may be able to avoid or escape their own *political* development as human beings altogether. In its place we get a massive catering operation providing entertainment, shopping, fast food and counselling that more resembles a social service station and a glorified secondary school than anything else. This is only complemented by the role of the university as *in loco parentis* for resident students. The bond between students and faculty is sundered *initially and continually* by the organizational conception that treats one as a member and the other as a client. Since this, along with scholarly and scientific research, is supposed to be the university's *raison d'etre,* it constitutes a fact of major significance.

This is probably aggravated by the employee status of the faculty, even in situations in which it is possible for faculty to gather in the lion's share of public or private monies that fund a particular institution. Once faculty come to view themselves mainly as salaried employees, *either* a labour-management *or* a professional model has the effect of underwriting an organizational (and societal) conception of work and non-work activities. At the same time, however, it is necessary to be aware of what the consequences of faculty professional or union organization are for those other functions taking place on university campuses, whether directly related to the research and instructional situation or not. What typically emerges, particularly in an austerity setting, is not a number of unions bound together by promises (and practices) of mutual solidarity. Instead, higher education's integration into Society is characterized by the appearance of *a hierarchy* of unions and/or associations, with the faculty getting the lion's share as noted. When this is coupled with the effect secure status through tenure, complemented by union or professional provisions, has on incentive and quality output, particularly in research, the price of making the university part of an extended secondary socialization experience available to everyone becomes apparent.

The situation in which a hierarchy of unions and/or associations becomes an established part of higher education serves to suggest in no uncertain terms how unavoidable *student* organization might be in the circumstances. Faculty, already in possession of a tenure-for-initial merit arrangement, find this convention insufficient in the light of a combination of mass access to higher education, with its demand for faculty, and hard economic times. So they move from an already existent position of strength to an even stronger position by supporting professional or union organizations, and the imposition on the university of a labour-management model of collective bargaining whose effect (if not its intent) is to assist in its thorough-going *rationalization* into a *system* of higher education. This scheme violates the principle of no overlap between labour and mangement in every instance in which it is superimposed on a university whose charter grants its academic senate supreme authority in all matters of an academic nature. What is worse, faculty *use* their existing position of strength to solidify it by another, rather different, strategem, one which has the effect of guaranteeing their pre-eminent power, status, and remuneration at the top of the hierarchy of unions and/or associations.[14]

In a technical sense, it would probably be more accurate to refer to a plural hierarchy of unions or associations, if it is kept in mind that they do not reach the same heightes or (by implication) depths on the matter of their respective power, status or remuneration. Integration into Society is manifested by the existence of many unions or associations, and even more by the fact that some are either branches of, or affiliated with, unions outside the university. The public will find it difficult to follow many events and developments in higher education short of official policy pronouncements so long as it has a simplified view of the contemporary university in advanced industrial societies. This is especially evident in the *competition* between unions, usually within the same hierarchy, for relative positioning. Faculty sit atop what is clearly a teaching and instructional hierarchy, using part-time teachers and graduate students as virtual slave-labour by paying them on a course by course, rather than on a "package", basis. Since this practice goes hand in hand with the devaluation of the faculty member as anything more than a public educational employee whose sole job is to teach, staff the odd committee, or run a department, it indicates a situation which should be of the gravest importance to the taxpayer.

The second hierarchy is actually headed by the one group whose overall role in Society has *not* led to its professionalization or unionization – university managers. This group is to be distinguished from university executives, who may or may not have advanced degrees and once have been academic faculty, but who are on their own atop all hierarchies, and as often as not view themselves as links between a given university, its board of governors, and the central, state or provincial legislatures. University managers are frequently casualties of the line-staff reversal I already cited as elemental to the difference between universities (and hospitals) and standard bureaucratic organizations. In almost any other public or private sector organization, these people would have many of the same responsibilities and function in a *line* capacity on all matters relating to decision-making and formal authority. But in universities they are *staff* rather than line personnel, regardless of how senior, how secure, and how well paid. Staff and line, as noted, often can be seen to come together at the very top of the university in its executive group, where certain vice-presidential tasks will frequently be carried out by individuals without the Ph.D. degree and with no prior experience as academic teaching faculty.

University managers are responsible for actually running the university as an administrative organization, and frequently find it impossible not to be involved in academic policy matters, either because of unavoidable overlap or because of lack of initiative from faculty. They have in common with management virtually everywhere in advanced industrial societies an absence of formal union or professional organization as an occupational group. Perhaps this speaks more to the importance of management in general, and to its ubiquitiousness wherever an organizational society of employees is found, than anything else. It certainly is not reflected in the line-staff inversion, for university managers are generally (and understandably) rewarded by remuneration, often in consequence of their lower status and their lack of ultimate (line) formal authority on all university matters, whether academic or administrative in nature. Like their brethren outside the university, managerial personnel are rarely organized, and indicate the indispensability to *any* complex organized process, like higher education has become, of a permanent, stable and secure internal management group. Not surprisingly, their lack of *de jure* tenure or security is generally more than made up for by their actual permanence and continuity.[15]

Below university managers are the administrative and clerical staff. If the first group is mainly men, the second is invariably made up of women. This group clearly needs some sort of job security where competence is not in question, since they, in common with all groups in a weaker position in their respective hierarchies, generally get the leavings of the top groups. This has fundamentally to do with the ambivalent status of administrative and clerical personnel. Though they are technically below university managers in power, status and remuneration, their position is as much a product of their subordinate status *vis a vis* faculty as it is to top internal management. This is because university managers are not organized, and frequently only exist as a "P & M Group" in a sense which is wholly unrelated to collective efforts. Their salaries are usually not rationalized like one would find amongst most

scheduled public and civil servant groups, and they do not bargain collectively. It is therefore to academic faculty, with its *twin bases* of established
pre-eminence, that we must turn if we are to really understand the reasons
why a union may be fully justified for administrative and clerical staff, even
(or especially) given its general inability to improve its position significantly
in common with dominant groups and functions.

A final hierarchy is tied to the outside, generally in more direct ways than
either faculty, part-time instructors, or graduate students. I have in mind the
maintenance, caretaking and cafeteria and food service groups. To be sure,
here one frequently discovers differences in status, power and remuneration
as severe as those which characterize faculty, part-time instructors and graduate students. In some cases cafeteria and food service groups will not be
permitted to organize at all by the caterer, in clear (and consequential)
contrast to maintenance and caretaking personnel, who are frequently in
unions with ties to extremely powerful external labour organizations. This
situation is roughly equivalent in the extreme case to that of non-unionized
workers in occupations in the catering and food service areas outside the
university. These functions and occupations are also made up of a majority
of women. This is complemented by the frequent inability of the individuals
to speak the official language effectively as a consequence of being recent
immigrants to the country in question. Such groups also need unions, but
university budgeting tends to be organizationally based, so they frequently
end up with the leavings no less than do secretarial and clerical staff, along
with part-time instructors and graduate students. This discrepancy is only
accentuated in difficult economic times.

This extended discussion of the university as a formal bureaucratic organization with hierarchies of competing occupational groups is highly germane
to any adequate understanding of its practices by students and by taxpayers.
The sheer complexity and range of functions and occupations brought together in the contemporary activity of higher education may speak to societal integration and the reality of a significantly extended secondary socialization experience for an increasing number of people. But it only underscores the confusion over the relationship all this activity bears to the original primary functions of the university – scholarly research, undergraduate
instruction and graduate training. In the case of undergraduates in particular, the problem with an organizational conception of membership is that
one side of the central relationship justifying the vast amount of monies
allocated to higher education is virtually excluded from membership and
assigned the status of clients, or dependents of clients, while the other side
increasingly views itself as employees whose main task, particularly in hard
economic times, is to realize job security and monopolize the lion's share of
operating revenues.

The way the organization-based conception of membership excludes students certainly gives the appearance of a greater kinship between the different employee groups than any, taken singly or collectively, would have with students. This is no doubt compounded by the age, and in most instances generational, differences between students and almost everyone else, as well as by the fact that students are temporary inhabitants, both in terms of the length of the academic year and the number of years it takes them to complete their studies. What is important to notice, however, is the way that these facts have been mobilized, along side the reality of an extended period of secondary socialization, in order to justify treating students *at best* as clients and at worst as immature and apolitical consumers in urgent need of more schooling before being released on Society and the economy. Anyone who argued that the organization of Society should properly lead to longer and longer periods of tutelage and dependence for more and more young people must now begin to see the severe costs of such an undertaking, however inevitable it is believed to be.

A point I wish to make about the consequences of this emphasis on employment and the primacy of employee status bears directly on the relationship between the organizational principle of functional rationality and formal meritocracy and the organization-based conception of membership. It is the fact that these two notions are not necessarily compatible with one another, and have certainly proved to be at loggerheads on a fairly regular basis in the university. What I mean here is that functional rationality and formal meritocracy, whatever we may think about them as functional realities, are not necessarily benefitted, and are often even hindered, by the organization-based conception of membership in operation. This is because of the absence of the now traditional discipline and control devices characteristic of most bureaucratic systems, at least to some extent. The organization-based conception of membership, as a consequence of this absence, leads to fragmentation rather than integration. Only when the matter is brought to a head through the negotiations and decisions of faculty unions or associations and university executive management is it really possible to speak of rationalization and integration, but this itself serves only as a framework for the continued existence of the fragmented occupational system.

This might be judged a very good thing relative to the alternative of a highly structured system of functional rationality until the relation between means and outputs is considered. One of the pervasive problems of loosely coupled and decentralized organizations relates to the possible dysfunctions of this structure for their major output responsibilities.[16] This becomes all-too-clear in the case of the universities, where the student's present clientele status as "loss leader", as well as the fragmented status of the university as a series of hierarchical unions in competition with one another, can only be justified by arguing that this is, after all, what is meant by societal integration. The problem with this notion as it affects undergraduate students is that these people receive only extended dependence and tutelage rather than even legitimate clientele status, forget employee status as an organization member. Thus it could be argued that the avowed purpose of even extended secondary socialization is not served well by this practice, since the individuals so catered to acquire at best a tangential acquaintance with what it means to be an employee and none whatever with what it means to be a powerful external client, like, for example, governments, business associations, professional groups *etc.*

Indeed, one could argue that as a consequence of not being a member in any meaningful sense (or rather not being perceived to be a member by those who call the tune), students are fundamentally excluded from a development which confirms all the worst hopes and dreams of Durkheim's occupational and functionally specialized society.[17] However problematic this development may be, it is becoming ever clearer that the way "rationality" is being institutionally embedded as a traditional and conventional method of acting and behaving is generating a significant change in the relation of employees to customers and clients throughout advanced industrial societies. I would argue, in effect, that the output functions (products, services *etc*) of a vast number and range of large organizations are being challenged frontally by the rights of employees as consumers and members of Society *without regard to outputs!* This development, as I have argued elsewhere, is directly germane to invention, innovation and new ideas in Society, and goes hand in hand with the idea that extended dependence and tutelage is necessary and can be justified.[18] Unfortunately for undergraduate students, the security that university members have achieved now seems less and less available to them both "inside" and "outside", even though they have been socialized in dependence rather than in initiative.

Perhaps it is precisely the fact of the increasing organization of Society outside the university which accounts for the fragmenting effect of unions and associations of various kinds on the university itself. It is now quite standard for people to speak of the university as an organization of employees with students outside it as dependent clients. Thus it happens regularly that university bulletins will state that on a given informally observed holiday classes will not be held but that the university will nevertheless be open!. What often tends to be forgotten where the university, or rather the multiversity, is willing to do anything the Society wants done for it and can pay for is that higher education is more than simply an organized activity or pursuit. It is an *institution* with a long and distinguished history of service to humanity, but service most often based (like science) on its freedom and autonomy from immediate social and economic pressures and demands rather than its subordination to them. Undergraduate students, and Society as a whole, are effectively robbed when the institutional function is subordinated to every conceivable societal and economic demand and pressure, whether in the name of expediency, efficiency, effectiveness, costs, or "social conscience".

Integration of the university into the present reality of advanced industrial societies must not, in other words, occur at the cost of the university's persistence as an institution. Emptied of its practical role in the Aristotelian sense, the university becomes progressively more and more *de-institutionalized* as it becomes more and more organized, whether this organization is a product of internal systematization (organizational principle), or the result of the university becoming a meeting point of various occupational and functional groups (organization-based conception of membership). To be sure, this is not to argue that the two organizational imperatives are totally irreconcilable. I am rather concerned with the effect on what is supposed to be the university's output functions of the societal demand or pressure for integration into the public educational system through an extension of the formally organized process of secondary socialization. An interesting feature of this development in all cases is the essential contradiction between being in a protracted period of tutelage and dependence while being regarded as neither a member nor an employee nor part of a powerful external clientele. While I would certainly prefer more viable alternatives to such extended schooling, the point is that the present system is not even managing to accomplish *its* objectives, regardless of what we might think of them.

Thus secondary socialization as the successful production of passive apolitical individuals is not occurring at anywhere near the rate that is desired. At the same time, this allegedly negative development is probably a good thing for advanced industrial societies. A point that needs to be emphasized, however, relates to what these individuals are left with when such socialization through the medium of higher education fails. In a sense, as Habermas has pointed out more than once, the system as a whole is so dependent upon its ability to "deliver the goods", on "performance", that its failure to do this at various times may itself constitute the reason behind the corresponding failure of secondary socialization. Mannheim argued that the orientation to "success in a career", as opposed to political or economic success, depended not only on an economy capable of sustaining a good standard of living for a large number of people, but also its ability to do this over a long period of time. A career orientation, in short, presupposes precisely the ability to plan for the future by taking the economy and its delivery systems pretty much for granted. Lack of confidence in the systems's ability to deliver the goods, in this latter event, is obviously going to redound to the disadvantage of secondary socialization.[19]

In the case of undergraduate education and training in particular, the result of such negative perceptions only leads to mass defection from the university and higher education where it is thought that this additional period of socialization is optional rather than necessary. Once a proportionately large number of students come to believe that it is in reality part of the experience of public education and schooling, rather than something that is discretionary, the same patterns of action are far less likely to repeat themselves with regularity. Students in a very specific sense no longer feel themselves to be independent young adults, and understandably come to see higher education as a natural continuation of schooling. When the system fails to deliver the goods, or rather the careers and jobs, the result is no longer defection *en masse* because advanced industrial societies are simply too organized and structured at the total systems level to permit the luxury of believing in a real alternative almost anywhere to the closed society of functional rationality and formal meritocracy. The contest between the market and the firm is ultimately no contest at all for the large majority of students, who often see failure to complete university as permanent consignment to the economic scrap-heap.

Problems inside the university thus provide a blurred and somewhat distorted, but nonetheless generally accurate, microcosm of problems outside the university. Important in this regard for undergraduate students is the fact that the university is no longer a discretionary option to be used to distinguish oneself through the aegis of extended tuition and certification. Thus conditions inside the university are directly affected by, and may even constitute a fairly direct reflection of, external realities. Where the economy is significantly affected this does not, however, generate the sort of response which would have been appropriate in an earlier day. Students often seem to understand the situation better than those who govern and manage the university, if the current heavy enrollments, and requests for admission all out of proportion to available facilities, is any indication. It is precisely because of the way young adults are viewed and treated in advanced industrial societies that I tend to emphasize *using* the university rather than repudiating it. While I take back nothing I said earlier about the terrible dilemma we have gotten ourselves in to by over-valuing higher education, while allowing the trades and vocations, and the apprenticeship method, to atrophy in favour of the development of a credentialist society, we must nevertheless begin incrementally with the institution as it stands.

If the university for students (and the public) constitutes an increasingly compulsory aspect of extended public schooling beyond the secondary grades, and therefore has the appearance from this perspective of a formal bureaucratic organization, it is seen as a set of competing occupational groups by many or most members of these groups. It may not even simply be a place of work, except to the extent that it provides the institutional setting within which both integrating and disintegrating activities take place. Not being members, undergraduate students in particular can only experience frustration, especially if they realize that they are the raw materials that are to be transformed in and through this process of socialization.[20] It might well be argued that the sort of politicization that occurs in universities whenever occupational groups come together and compete for limited resources is a good experience for students, even apart from what they learn or do not learn during their temporary stay. I would second this point of view only so long as students, particularly undergraduate students, are included into the reckoning as members rather than treated like clients. The pale substitute that is available for students under the name of "university politics" must be expanded into the opportunity not only to learn rather than simply be taught, but to participate rather than watch.

In an employee society where the most available and tempting form of success is success in a career, extended secondary socialization, and with it protracted dependence and tutelage, is the order of the day. What gives the biggest lie to Durkheimian positive individualism is precisely the regularity with which it can be successfully produced through long-term secondary socialization processes which have the sanction, if not the active support, of key elements of the society in question. I have already argued that this development at best truncates the emergence of political interests and consciousness if it does not annihilate them altogether, in favour of more passive roles appropriate to "passage" from higher education into careers and occupational life. Yet it is in the institutional reality of the university that one phase of the drive to heightened interest and participation must begin. It is, in other words, the very fact that students correctly view university as part of their formal schooling rather than a discretionary option which requires us to *utilize* this situation as an opportunity to generate citizen interest and concern, as well as reflection on the responsibilities of membership in a form of collective life worthy of careful scrutiny. So long as students are denied membership in the university, this will not happen.

This is clearly the best way to reconcile the organizational principle in practice with the organization-based conception of university membership which presently excludes students. It will also achieve a reconciliation between the university as a human system concerned about the status and well-being of its respective occupational groups, and the university as an instrument of societal and governmental expectations, requirements and demands. Thirdly, it will provide a basis for carrying through the "revolution" which allowed faculty to gain control of much of what passes for academic policy in higher education today, without, however, carrying their new status, power and remuneration through to students. Finally, it will allow us to begin to actually take advantage of the fact of extended secondary socialization to turn around the present preference for consumer, audience and passive occupational and career roles in support of the responsible politicization of some of the most potentially inventive and innovative people we have in Society. If the space outside looks problematic for all because of problems with the performance of the economy, then higher education must be viewed as even more than the "holding pattern" that students presently assume when they decide to go to university.

IV

When I argue that we must proceed incrementally, I mean not only that the present structure, but also the commitment to more open access to higher education, must be taken at least initially as a given. Undergraduate education and training is perceived by students, as well as an increasing percentage of the public, as part of required public schooling for individuals desirous of careers in many occupational areas. But incrementalism in the foregoing also appertains to process and procedure as well as to values and goals. Indeed, I would be false to my overriding belief, expressed throughout this study, that process and procedure is a central value of the system not only in theory but in operation if I did not acknowledge this. Thus the objective in what follows is upon maximizing the possibilities of undergraduate students becoming *de facto*, if not *de jure*, members of the university. In aid of this, I focus almost exclusively on undergraduate students in the same way I have done throughout this chapter. In doing so, it must be emphasized that I do not thereby argue that undergraduates are more deserving of attention than either their compeers who go directly to work from secondary school or those in graduate or professional studies within the university. I am rather concerned about the combination of their large numbers, their extended tutelage and dependence, and the serious consequences that result from their particular clientele status.

The first reaction one might justifiably have to the organization-based conception of university membership, and the consequent consignment of undergraduate students to the status of clients, would be to recommend that students imitate the prevailing practice of occupational and functional organization by themselves unionizing. As the university's "loss leaders", it might be argued that such a strategem can only aid their objectives of membership. The difficulty with such a suggestion, however, lies in the very status of students as one side of the relationship that constitutes one of the *raison d'etres* for the existence of the university and higher education. What

I want to argue is that students, though certainly not members of the university as it is presently comprehended in its organizational conception, are unavoidably members of the university as an *institution* with a long history and a highly significant contribution to collective life in Western societies. While this may serve to constitute litte more than hair-splitting, it is a distinction worth noting, particularly in light of what it leads us to conclude about the attempt to achieve inclusion as members through the aegis of collective bargaining organizations.

In almost every instance where the benefits of student organization can be demonstrated, these benefits can be seen to be as well or better served by *not unionizing* and instead choosing some other more local method of organization more appropriate to the conditions of the university in question. Since students constitute one side of an established *institutional* relation at the centre of higher education, the arguments I have made against unionization of faculty, while no basis for critizing student unionization, suggest that another mode of organizing be employed. Undergraduate students could derive just as much benefit from alternative methods not tied to central structures or based on the legal status of the union as a collective bargaining agent. The best way to reconcile the institutional, research and participatory functions of higher education to the advantage of undergraduate students would be to proceed incrementally and locally so that the benefits of smaller size and immediate contact with conditions would be maximized whenever this was felt to be necessary. The truth is that unionization may secure the occupational and economic needs and interests of faculty, but it probably compromises the educational function irretrievably, particularly in circumstances where the economy is not operating at its best.

A basic problem with achieving organization of students relates not only to large numbers and the undesirable option of student unionization, but also to the temporary status of undergraduate students. The answer to this problem would require us to try to maximize the local character and attributes of the particular university in question by stressing the need for greater continuity between various class years than presently exists. Alongside this might be a greater overall amount of time spent in university studies in any given academic year. The academic year should probably be at least ten months long if the period of study is to remain four years in length. Arguments regarding the need for students to contribute to the financing of their studies by working during the summer (as opposed to part time during the academic year) are nowadays *less* persuasive than they used to be. Costs are so high and good jobs often so scarce that a great deal of this argument loses its steam in the present context. Continuity from class to class could be improved significantly by a longer and more intense year, one which would combine educational, training, cultural and citizenship functions, activities and obligations.[21]

Another important point in favour of a local emphasis in the effort to achieve more continuity and a more intense experience relates to contacts with the "outside". To date, students either make these contacts on an individual basis, or allow university members, whether faculty or managerial staff, to do it for them. Students need to initiate a great deal more contacts and communications with significant communities of opinion that are important to the functions, activities and requirements of the university experience than they presently do. Part of the problem is the fault of students themselves, but part of it is linked to tutelage, dependence, and the perpetuation of the *in loco parentis* function already noted. Students all-too-often concentrate strictly on entertainment when they take the initiative. In some systems students are given a basic allotment on a yearly basis which their councils may spend for virtually any purpose. Students simply perpetuate the public stereotype of them as immature adults-in-waiting who need constant management and are incapable of allocating funds for which they are responsible to any meaningful use when they fail to take advantage of this opportunity to exercise their rightful role as central institutional members and actors.

The emphasis on concentrating and lengthening the university experience is therefore not directly associated with the claim that students simply need more instruction. It relates to other functions of responsible adult life which students are all-too-often denied *in spite of* their efforts rather than as a consequence of them. The present system of extended tutelage cannot be justified on any grounds, certainly not on the grounds that students required to spend four or five *more* years in public schooling should have their adult-in-waiting period extended accordingly. I want to argue that *no* body of evidence can justify withholding adult status from university students for this added period of time. The result has become all-too-predictible in the contemporary setting, where extended lifespans are seen to justify longer periods of dependence relative to the rest of animate nature than human beings already exhibit. Responsibilities are often matters which no group of young people are eager to take on, especially given the mess which they perceive their parents to have created. Whether such an assessment is true or false is not the issue. It is rather whether we can any longer afford to not take advantage of this crucial period of development amongst the young people in advanced industrial societies.[22]

It is for this particular reason that I feel it necessary to simultaneously argue for student organization, continuity and responsibility while opposing recourse to collective bargaining and a unionizing imperative. Apart from the problems which will invariably arise as a result of union disenchantment with adults-in-waiting who are not employees and do not have steady work, the model basically violates many of the things that I believe could be rendered functional in the university setting for political management by undergraduate students. Neither is the emphasis on the particularistic and local properties of specific universities a mere sop to the "small is beautiful" crowd. One of the most important aspects of any participatory effort must begin by recognizing that membership, to be meaningful, must be referenced to local institutional properties. An appeal to membership which focusses on large aggregate systems not only fails as persuasive rhetoric, but ignores the really important factors that account for and make sense of attachment to and identification with a given university as an institution. The same is true of the abstract notions of membership which are found throughout Society today.

One of the most useful things that might be undertaken in an effort to maximize the possibility of meaningful institutional identification and membership relates very much to the university curriculum, in particular to pedagogy. I have in mind the need for universities to organize themselves on a pedagogical and "mode of learning" basis as well as along disciplinary and faculty lines. Undergraduate students need to be able to opt for *different ways of learning* particular subjects that interest them, whether this takes place on a course-by-course basis or relates to a full fledged programme of study. Many students want to learn certain subjects by instructional methods of a conventional sort, either because they are required subjects in a given curriculum of study or because they are introductory courses which have a heavy component of rote memorization. Other courses and subjects lend themselves more readily to forms of learning which are less conventional in an instructional sense. The permutations and combinations are immense, but the point in all this is that the course or subject matter should dictate the method or pedagogy which faculty employ. This in contrast to the present situation, where all-too-often standard pedagogy effectively determines how courses and subjects will be taught.[23]

I am tempted to argue for reviving or bringing into being the college system within universities as a basis not simply of residential and administrative organization, but of both substantive and pedagogical differentiation. While the latter two concerns may not be easy to reconcile, it is imperative that faculty and university managers, in concert with students, begin to seriously consider the continued viability of the university as a mere bureaucratic organization where line and staff functions have been inverted to the advantage of faculty alone. There is very reason to believe that variation in pedagogy and ways of learning can constitute at least as relevant a method of internal organization as organization on the basis of disciplines and/or faculties. Indeed, I would argue that overemphasis on the latter approach actually shores up the existing structure of privilege while it underwrites rather than challenges the notion of membership presently operative. This undertaking is well worth doing, and I do not propose it as an "experiment" or believe it to be in the least bit utopian. In fact, I believe that our failure to restructure the university along pedagogical lines will lead to an even greater amount of de-institutionalization than we already experience.[24]

I said earlier that students are not members of the university in the way it is presently conceived and understood by practically everyone both inside and outside it. I then contrasted to this the fact that as an institution of long standing and great pre-eminence, students are clearly members because they constitute one side of the relationship that is the real *raison d'etre* of higher education, today no less than in the past. It is with precisely this distinction in mind that I propose to revive the university *as an institution* in the ways indicated. While many would argue that a proposal of this sort cannot help but be more costly than the present system, I would respond by contrasting short and long term costs, both economic and social. Undergraduate students must have an opportunity to combine education, learning and research and scholarship with practical concerns and knowledge, and this cannot be accomplished to long as they are viewed and treated as dependent external clients rather than members. Every argument about the inevitability and/or desirability of mass higher education supports my claim that young adult status and responsibilities must not be deferred just because the experience of public education has been extended to require one or more university degrees.

Membership in an institution as one side of a relationship which is central to any justification for its continued existence and growth requires that this institution provide students with an intensive experience of the sort suggested. The best basis for improving the likelihood that citizenship will be actively practiced in the university setting, and later on in life, is to provide students with the kind of opportunities to be responsible members not only from the standpoint of the learning situation, but as participants in university management and in the effort to keep the university in tune with practical realities in the Society as a whole. Socialization for adulthood today too much resembles a catering or baby-sitting operation characterized by one way authority and discipline, and by a preference for passive roles in occupational life no less than through consumption and spectating. There can be little doubt that such socialization fails to answer pressing needs in advanced industrial society in favour of supporting what are often thoroughly wasteful and dysfunctional values, habits and modes of behaviour. The situation is more serious by far than most people would like to believe, but I am convinced that the way to improvement lies in political management, and that the university, like social scientific research practices, is an extremely important vehicle for confronting the problems I have raised here.

Failing these proposals, or others also concerned with reviving the institutional character of universities and higher education, we can expect the continued production of apolitical individuals decreasingly capable of sound judgment in circumstances in which this skill may be more and more necessary.[25] In its place we shall have functional rationality and formal meritocracy coopting our present form of collective life even more than it already has. The investment in undergraduate students that I am supporting here is nothing less than an effort to resuscitate substantive rationality as the grounding of all other forms. It is a well distributed *human* property which is absolutely essential to innovation of a social and cultural, as well as a technical, kind, but which has been ignored or downgraded, largely as a result of our increasingly obvious societal commitment to viewing rationality as a property of structures rather than of individuals. Just as I have argued that pedagogy must serve substantive problems and needs of disciplines in universities, and that this therefore requires us to acknowledge the central role of pedagogy in organizing the university as an institution, so also would I suggest that structures must serve individual needs if the society is to be viable. Political management is indispensable for system viability now and in the future, and institutions which support it must be revived and initiated.

References

1 The term "cooling out" is taken from Erving Goffman's, "Cooling the Mark Out" in *Psychiatry,* Volume 15 (November, 1952), pp. 451–463.
2 Durkheim, *The Division of Labour in Society,* pp. 229, 403, 407; Weber, *Theory of Social & Economic Organization,* pp. 329–341; *From Max Weber,* pp. 196–244.
3 Burton Bledstein, *The Culture of Professionalism: The Middle Class and the Development of Higher Education in America* (NY: W. W. Norton, 1976); Randall Collins, *The Credential Society* (NY: Academic Press, 1979); Wilson, The American Ideology, chapter 9.
4 Weber, *Theory of Social & Economic Organization,* pp. 338–339; *From Max Weber,* pp. 204–209, 214–216.
5 Amitai Etzioni, *Modern Organization* (Englewood Cliffs, N. J.: Prentice Hall, 1964), pp. 74–93 on the difference between standard and professional bureaucratic organizations; Wilson, "Technocracy and Late Capitalist Society," *op cit; The Academy and its Clients: Conflicting Perspectives on the Contemporary University,* report to the Commission on Relations between Universities and Governments (Ottoawa, 1970); Wilson, "Academic Bureaucracy," *Queens Quarterly* Volume 78 No. 3 (Atumn 1971), pp. 343–352.
6 Jacques Barzun, "Tomorrow's University: Back to the Middle Ages?", *Saturday Review,* Volume 52 (November 15, 1969), pp. 23–25.
7 Thorstein Veblen, *The Higher Learning in America* (Boston: Huebsch, 1918).

8 See Stuart Ewen, *Captains of Consciousness* (NY: McGraw Hill, 1976); and David Noble, *America by Design* (NY: Oxford University Press, 1977) for analyses of the environing reality which was developing in the United States at the time. Note that the post War II return of veterans, while closing the generation gap, actually served to underscore the distinction between faculty and students, while it accelerated the turn toward the truncated notions of relevance which had to some extent been established during wartime.

9 See particularly John Ziman, *Public Knowledge: An Essay Concerning the Social Dimension of Science* (London: Cambridge University Press, 1968); Diana Crane, *Invisible Colleges* (Chicago: University of Chicago Press, 1972); Michel Polanyi, "The Republic of Science," *Minerva,* Volume 1 (1962), pp. 54–73. Compare to Thomas Kuhn, *The Structure of Scientific Revolutions,* 2nd edition (Chicago: University of Chicago Press, 1970). Also see my critique in *The American Ideology,* Chapter 4; and Alvin Gouldner "Cosmopolitans and Locals", *Administrative Science Quarterly,* Volume 2 (1957–58), pp. 281–306, 444–480.

10 Harold Taylor, *Students without Teachers* (NY: McGraw Hill, 1969) remains one of the most articulate statements on this subject.

11 Note again Marx's point in the *Early Texts* about natural science as a form of human industry rather than solely a mode of knowledge and knowing.

12 Wilson, *The Academy and its Clients;* "Academic Bureaucracy," *op. cit;* "The University and Society: Issues for the 1980's" (unpublished paper, 1980).

13 John O'Neill, "Scientism, Historicism and the Problem of Rationality," introduction to *Modes of Individualism and Collectivism,* edited by John O'Neill (London: Heinemann, 1973).

14 The point here is that the similarity between secure positions in universities and in the civil service has blurred considerably in those countries where higher education is part of the public or state sector. After a brief "probationary" period, admission to candidacy, or some variation on it, virtually guarantees that tenure will in due course be granted. Everyone in the same rank marches forward on the backs of a small minority of university faculty, whose rewards are consequently lessened by the requirement that they be spread throughout a rank in equal amounts *regardless of merit!* This is the essence of what I have in mind elsewhere is this chapter when I address the fact that organizations in general, and universities in particular, are viewed as places of employment where *employees* are the first, if not the only, consideration. This also underscores my earlier point about the negative consequences of the organization-based conception of membership for the university's *output* functions. Also see generally Richard Mandell, *The Professor Game* (Garden City, NY: Doubleday, 1977).

15 Francis Rourke and Glenn Brooks, *The Managerial Revolution in Higher Education* (Baltimore: Johns Hopkins, 1966); Van C. Morris, *Deaning: Middle Management in Academe* (Urbana: University of Illinois Press, 1981).

16 Karl Weick, "Educational Organizations as Loosely Coupled Systems", *Administrative Science Quarterly,* Volume 21 (1976), pp. 1–19.

17 Durkheim, *The Division of Labour in Society;* Durkheim, *Professional Ethics and Civic Morals* (London: Routledge and Kegan paul, 1957). Robert Presthus, in "The Political Role of Interest Groups," in *Elite Accomodation in Canadian Politics* (Toronto: Macmillan, 1973), pp. 140–170 at pp. 140–143 notes that struc-

ture follows function. One might readily reformulate the hierarchy of competing unions and associations as a competition between variously organized *interest groups*. I would argue that the consequences for the university are not-dissimilar to what interest group proponents *would like to do* to parliamentary systems under party discipline. These therefore constitute parallel concerns for political management, and relate in different ways to the issue of openness, access, and institutional functioning.

18 See my "Innovation: the Practical Uses of Theory," in *Social Change, Innovation and Politics in East Asia,* edited by Y. S. Yim, H. T. Wilson, and R. W. Wilson (Hong Kong: Asian Research Service, 1980), pp. 9–29; "Science, Technology & Innovation: The Role of Commonsense Capacities," *Methodology & Science,* Volume 15, No. 3 (1982), pp. 167–200; *Tradition & Innovation,* Chapters 2 & 4.

19 Jürgen Habermas, "Technology and Science as Ideology," *op. cit.,* pp. 95–105; Karl Mannheim, *Essays in the Sociology of Knowledge,* pp. 247–249.

20 A focus on students as "raw material" is all-too-appropriate a metaphor given its origin in organization theory and analysis. See for example, Charles Perrow, "A Framework for the Comparative Analysis of Organizations," *American Sociological Review,* Volume 32 (1967), pp. 194–208; James Thompson, *Organizations in Action* (NY: McGraw Hill, 1968). This is related in the Canadian case to the all-pervasive nature of American influence in higher education, as discussed in my "Continentalism and Canadian Higher Education," *Canadian Review of American Studies.* Volume 1, No. 2 (Fall, 1970), pp. 89–99.

21 The summer job routine has the effect of perpetuating tutelage and dependence, and perhaps even the intent. It extends dependence over a longer period at a critical juncture in the development of young adults, and guarantees terrible confusion to no constructive purpose whatsoever. It creates a "back and forth" situation, where dependency alternates between home, school and employer, thereby sustaining a collective self-image as poor clients, or rather their dependents. This likely induces an overly conservative attitude to job security, and misplaced or inappropriate motives in the pursuit of degrees and certificates. This probably redounds to Society's distinct disadvantage, but is readily understandable, not only because of the above factors, but because of what students observe of the behaviour and priorities of all "organization members" in the university, particularly faculty.

22 One is tempted to term the present situation one in which aspects of neoteny are revived, and thereafter transferred to Society. The exercise is a failure, and a danger we can no longer view with equanimity.

23 Howard Becker, "On Methodology," *op. cit;* C. Wright Mills, *op. cit.*

24 This idea of organizing a university's college system on the basis of a *pedagogical,* as opposed to an administrative/residential or subject matter basis, was first suggested to me by Professor James Gillies of York University, Toronto. For an excellent proposal to revive the apprenticeship approach to undergraduate education, see David Bakan, "A Plan for a College, with Commentary," *Canadian University and College* (June, 1969), pp. 30–34, 42–43.

25 See Karl Mannheim's justly famous contrast between functional and substantial rationality, one which emphasizes their zero-sum relation in industrial society, in *Man and Society in an Age of Reconstruction,* p. 58.

Chapter 10
Citizens, Agents and Members in the Modern Territorial State

I

While it might have made just as much sense to title this chapter "Is Man a Political Animal?," I would prefer to begin with the presumption that this is in fact the case and go on to give my reasons. My agreement with Aristotle in particular on this score will be evident, I hope, from the way I approach some of the major issues and concerns of political theory like human nature, sociability and gregariousness, animality and rationality.[1] It is important to be clear on what politics and citizenship mean, and how these activities are to be distinguished from other forms of activity and behaviour in a collective setting. It is also necessary to stress the difference between politics and theorizing or thought, in much the same way I did in chapters two and seven. In the event, it should be possible to address the question around several intersecting themes, for example, the difference between the collective (social) and the political, the idea of incentives and their practical sense, the concept of constituency as it relates to *both* representation and participation, and the notions of citizenship, membership and agency.

I argued in chapter two that it was largely as a result of the collapse of the city as a city-state, and its transmogrification into an *urban social place* with the transfer of governance to the imperial centre, that it became possible to separate the good man from the good citizen preparatory to absorbing the latter into the former. It would now be possible to consider the actual *production* of good men as a way of *avoiding* the issue of politics and citizenship in favour of governance and law. I would argue that it is in this confluence of the ethical, the legal, and the governmental that we see the beginnings of the idea of the territorial state in the West as an option to politics and citizenship. This process of change is repeated again and again, not just once, even though the Hellenic and Hellenistic experience is in a certain sense archetypal. Rome provides the best example of this shift, one which had occurred long before the Republic was formally transformed into an Empire following on the assasination of Julius Caesar. Territoriality and physical, geographical space time and time again cause cities, city-states, and countries to expand, whether for offensive or defensive reasons. With this the idea of the space of language, talk and lively silence is challenged by a fundamental revision in operative notions of citizenship, membership, and constituency.

The idea that the state and government ought to be supreme over and against any exercise of politics and citizenship that would attempt to stand against its notion of proper collective order has generally been justified in the name of public safety. Its effects on citizenship are not difficult to isolate, at least in general terms. Citizenship is no longer an act by an individual whose conception of the good man and the good citizen are one and the same. Nor do those around him any longer challenge this separation, for it seems to go hand in hand with the production of collective order from the centre outwards. Citizenship is now the result of proper socialization and becomes virtually synonymous with aspects of culture rather than constituting a constructive challenge to their hegemonic claims. An emphasis is now to be placed on coverage of the "general population," or at least some significant part of it. It is not the numbers *per se* which are important in the reckoning here, but rather the idea that the state and its governing groups look first at the general population before segmenting some section(s) of it away from the whole, whether for reasons of privilege or deprivation.

What goes hand in hand with the idea that the franchise becomes less and less meaningful the more it is extended is the separation of agents and members ensconced in law and assumed in ethics. *Raison'd etat* and *realpolitik* are only some more recent ways of conceptualizing, and presumably justifying, agency as delegated authority. This follows unavoidably, so it would appear, from the essentially passive reformulation of citizenship as the result of socialization and training rather than a challenge to established ways of thought and accepted values. Wolin's discussion of the changed view of space in the shift from city-state to imperium needs to be correlated with the separation of the good man from the good citizen, for it is as a result of this separation that it becomes possible to redefine citizenship in ways compatible with ethics and legality, while transferring the activity itself to agents who are now seen to constitute a group distinct from members.[2] Alongside this goes not only a revision of what it means to be a member, but a change in the notion of constituency away from speech and language toward territory. Instead of citizenship pertaining to political space and membership to other aspects of collective life, citizenship now becomes a form of membership, while political space is annihilated in favour of territorial governance under ethical and legal norms.

The space of language is a space where thought and action are seen to be fused, at least to the extent that speech is understood to constitute *a deed* rather than an alternative to doing. The dichotomy between thought and action, particularly in the form of the distinction between theory and practice³, is seen to justify not only a separation between agents and members, but one between theorists and practitioners as well. Indeed, no attempt to explain the shifts and changes already cited would be complete without an appreciation of the central role of thought, theory and advice in buttressing the preoccupations of agents over and against members. Initiatives undertaken need only be referenced to the mass of individuals occasionally, whether by vote or through other mechanisms of consensus formation. Legitimacy is provided not only by the delegated responsibility of agents to lead, but by the expert knowledge and understanding which thinkers and theorists may now put at their disposal to utilize as they wish. Socialization in citizenship becomes synonymous with learning to be a member, where by membership is meant a grasp of the correct ethical values and respect for legal norms, in contradistinction to citizenship in the city-state.

Innis, among others, has drawn attention to how this transmogrification of the notion of space away from language toward territory created the "dead" space of imperium, and with it the emergence of the written tradition as a vehicle of rule. The oral tradition is preserved in the main as the basis for the language of conversation, gregariousness, sociability, and "public opinion." Laws, rules, government as rule by agents (or perhaps, by those that do not even consider themselves as agents) supplants the idea of politics as citizenly display characterized by real individuation through speech as a deed. Imperium, with its unavoidable reformulation of space as territory requiring governance as *coverage,* cannot help but prefer the written tradition over speech, which above all, must not be considered a deed. Speech can only be granted the status of a deed when it *violates* the requirements of orderly "civic" (read civil) behaviour by transgressing written rules and orders carefully circumscribing what is permissible in speech. Long before propaganda was viewed as part of the written tradition operating through established or underground media, it was speech as a deed which violated the requirements of proper speech as formulated in written codes, rules, and orders.⁴

Modern representation might therefore best be understood as a device initially intended to *overcome* developments toward governance in the written tradition based on legal rules and ethical norms. It is an attempt, as I argued earlier, to achieve a delicate equipoise between the need for stability and order in collective life, and the idea that some form of speech as action should underpin and dynamize processes of institutionalization as they relate to membership, citizenship and constituency. Legality and the production of citizens as ethical persons properly socialized in the cultural requirements of the particular collective in question was not challenged in any fundamental way by representation, nor was the idea of the separation of and distinction between agents and members. Neither was the redefinition of citizenship as a passively ascribed form of membership in a particular collective viewed critically. In effect, representation was an effort to dynamize the existing pattern of order by giving significance to the possibilities for change through process rather than in place of it. Institutions and institutionalization were good and necessary, but not at the cost of a totally passive conception of politics as polity.

The idea of citizenship as something which is ascribed to a given category of person, rather than something which needs constantly to be achieved, must be discussed at greater length. This is what Arendt has in mind in her understanding of politics as display, what she calls *power,* and it explains why it cannot and should not demand permanence like the instruments of violence. When it does agents forget they are members, treat citizenship as a form of membership, and insist that their agency be seen to constitute proof of their good citizenship when precisely the opposite may be the case. Dead territorial space, and passive citizenship as membership under the dominance of socialization, ethics and law, preempt the space of power as the language of possibility, and citizenship as an active display addressed to the hegemony of the state and governance. This eventually comes to accord nicely with the illusory notion of achievement manifested in formal meritocracy, since in this case socialization produces a person who effectively appropriates a right to occupy organizational positions. The dead side of institutionalization carries the day under the banner of achievement and merit no less than does the politician who is able to successfully equate his formal agency with good citizenship.[5]

This means that it is not enough, as suggested earlier, simply to insist that agents see themselves first and foremost as members. Agents must also honour a notion of citizenship which is equated with display rather than solely with membership, even if this requires them to challenge the preference of the state and its governors for passivity, however much this passivity occurs through the operation of representative processes and practices. This is no easy matter, to be sure, for there are always ways of justifying keeping politics and citizenship on a short leash, though usually these justifications seek to inspire a fear of instability and disorder, and support legality, behaviour, and conformity to correct models of proper socialization. Agents are most truly members when they show their commitment to life in this way, by resuscitating in their own minds what it could be like to be a citizen as distinct from (or in addition to) being a member. The idea of citizenship as an ascribed and passively acquired form of membership is what allows both the people and their governors, even in representative democracies, to rigidly distinguish agency from membership by adopting an hierarchial and *organizational* conception of order which allegedly necessitates this very division of functions.

II

To acknowledge the need for cooperation, and to accept the difference between agent and member functions, fails to reach a matter that I consider to be of the utmost significance in what has been said thus far. As I argued in chapter five, sense of function is radically different from division of function or division of labour. Politics requires organization, and stability and order are in fact desired by a people in far greater proportion than many want to acknowledge. But this does not mean that organization, stability and order ought to be treated as self-justifying ends of human activity. Clearly these objectives are justifiable because they make other activities not only possible but, in the ideal case, more likely to happen. Division of labour, as opposed to cooperation, favours role fixity and rigid structural differentiation. This in contrast to "sense of function," where structure follows from and realizes its sole justification in and through function. Sense of function is cooperative because it does *not* require us to constantly *presume* the competence of those in leadership and other superordinate positions in Society, as is the case with (formal) meritocracy in practice under norms of "functional" rationality.

Division of function is therefore synonymous with functional rationality no less than cooperation is with sense of function. Indeed, Mannheim's notion of functional rationality is better understood as *structural* rationality, because it fundamentally fails to honour the priority of function in practice. There is nothing necessarily wrong with either the concept of function or the concept of role that nowadays is so often used interchangeably with it. It is role fixity, functional rationality and formal meritocracy that threaten the dynamism of representative systems where the only alternative to them is non-democratic modes of governance, however legalistic they are alleged to be.[6] In effect the problem with division of labour is that fixity and permanence are equated with proper functioning, when it must be clear to all that this is yet another instance where functional (read structural) rationality has successfully coopted the notion of institution and institutionalization. These notions no longer appertain to adaptation and to the emergence of values, customs and conventions, but instead are alleged to be synonymous with an organizational conception of order. This concept is no less stratified and hierarchical than its predecessors, but is legitimized by reference to the idea and practice of rational (meritocratic) domination.

This means that *form* pre-empts function in the person of structure and division of labour. Functional rationality is structural and formal because it is based on a manifestly organizational conception of role and function. To be sure, this is reinforced by the tendency to treat citizenship as a form of membership, where such membership is ascribed and granted once and for all either at birth, majority or as a result of "naturalization." All of this dovetails nicely with the concept of the modern state, with its operative notion of space as territory to be covered by codes, rules, laws and proper socialization. People are subjected to an ordering principle which in recent times has become the sign of a culturally and historically specific *form* of collective life as noted. Society in this reckoning needs to be seen as formed and structured because its purpose is the maintenance of a notion of order which equates silence with consensus. The oral tradition, once primary, is now seen to be derived from the written tradition no less than the primary group is a surrogate for the secondary group because it is seen to be produced by it. The citizen as member is in no real position to challenge this set of fixed assumptions, save for specific protests on "issues," or by himself becoming an agent.[7]

The view of agency and membership as a fixed, organized, and structured relationship of a formal kind may be necessary to the perpetuation of the good aspects of the modern territorial state, but it certainly is not sufficient. Indeed, one has to accept the *structures* themselves as indispensable to good government in order to make an argument in support of the claim that certain functions are themselves indispensable. Even if we accept such an assertion, it has been pointed out that this says nothing at all about the structures presently performing the functions. But I want to challenge the idea of functional prerequisites and functional indispensability precisely because this sort of claim has almost always been used to justify existing structures and ways of doing things rather than challenging them. It is but one more argument in support of passivity, premised as it is on the idea that the structure itself can only permit a certain amount of fluidity and process before citizenship as political display gets out of hand relative to "law, order and good government."

The tendency to equate citizenship with membership as a passively acquired and ascribed property of individuals inhabiting a state's territorial space is central to any understanding of the relationship between state and Society. In effect it is precisely this passivity as a recipient of various roles in the social structure which gives the lie to the claim that citizenship as it is presently understood is political at all. It becomes only one of many *societal* roles to choose from, along with occupational life, consumption and spectating, and "leisure," or rather time off from work. This is why Arendt was correct to equate its practice in the context of advanced industrial societies with behaviour rather than action, in a passage which must stand as definitive on the matter.

The unfortunate truth about behaviourism and the validity of its "laws" is that the more people there are, the more likely they are to behave and the less likely to tolerate non-behaviour. Statistically, this will be shown in the levelling out of fluctuation. In reality, deeds will have less and less chance to stem the tide of behaviour, and events will more and more lose their significance, that is, their capacity to illuminate historical time. Statistical uniformity is by no means a harmless scientific ideal; it is the no longer secret political ideal of a society which, entirely submerged in the routine of everyday living, is at peace with the scientific outlook inherent in its very existence.[8]

Society as a culturally and historically specific form of collective life, rather than a synonym for it, relies on an organizational conception of collective order to make it possible for citizenship to be reformulated as a form of membership. Passivity underwrites and makes possible the perception of citizenship as one among a number of societal roles to be carried out selectively and from time to time as an expression and an embodiment of proper socialization in the correct ethical, legal and conventional norms. Role structure and fixity coopt processes of representation on the one hand and institutionalization on the other, since passivity and choice of this sort is only available *within* a structure which is presumed not only to be fixed but objectively rational in the way it allocates its functions and the rewards that go with incumbency and performance. Agents take advantage of this bias toward passivity and ascription, with citizenship one of many role "options," not only to associate themselves with objective rationality, but to justify their claim to the status of superior citizens by comparison with the mere member who votes under the same everyday understandings that he uses when he works, consumes and spectates.

Agents buttress their claim to both "rationality" and "success" by appealing to the idea that expert advice can reconcile the need for representation and process with the need for efficiency and effectiveness in the generation and implementation of policy "outputs." In this endeavour, they are given massive aid and comfort from the social, behavioural and managerial "sciences" in ways that Arendt has alluded to in the excerpt cited, and elsewhere in *The Human Condition*. Even political science, in its contemporary rather than in its Aristotelian (and Voegelian) rendering, generates an icon of false practicality in order to ingratiate itself with the powers that be. The discussion in chapters seven and eight was intended to shed light on how the realities of the present advisory and consultative role of these academic and professional disciplines might be dynamized in support of representative processes *and* citizenly display. As a *form* of social interaction central rather than tangential to the advanced industrial societies they claim to be studying objectively and dispassionately, these disciplines and fields of research and study increasingly undergird the apolitical character of collective life under the sway of *structural* rationality and formal meritocracy.

The model of coverage and location given in the notion of government as the peopling of dead territorial space is paralleled almost perfectly by the "laws" of behaviouralism to which Arendt alludes.[9] Just as passivity is underwritten by the formulation and classification of ethical, legal and even conventional rules of action in advance of action and in anticipation of its challenge to order, so also with the aid and comfort *implicit* in the social, political, behavioural and managerial "sciences" when not explicitly directed to advice and expertise. Both aim at coverage, with the status of the citizen as member faithfully replicated in the role of "subject as object" of (and to) academic and professional research and knowledge. It is the absence of the interactive and participatory in these asymmetrical practices which make them indispensable to any effort which encourages the view of citizenship as a societal role within a fixed order governed by the canons of structural rationality and formal meritocracy. The citizen as member is permitted to choose which "role" he will play, so long as he exhibits proper socialization as it is discovered in ethical norms, legal codes, and accepted conventional practices.

As I suggested before, this cannot help but lead to (and enforce) a situation where the territorial state, with its dead space and its preference for the written over the oral tradition, and Society become one and the same. Coverage of those who people the territory necessitates that the oral tradition-language and speech as a deed – be reformulated as a derivitive and a surrogate of the written tradition on which "rational domination" clearly depends in its preference for role passivity, socialization and choice. Behaviour becomes all the more desirable when it can be shown that it conforms to the expectations and requirements of the citizen as member making role choices within the confines of space as place, space as territory to be covered. I have in mind here the space of structural rationality and formal meritocracy, with their claim to rational domination based on an organizational conception of collective order. It is this conception of space as place on the part of the citizen as member that makes it possible for the territorial system of government as coverage to work. It supports the supremacy of the written tradition over and against speech as a deed, and encourages talk that observes itself as an accompaniment of behaviour where each reflects and embodies the idea of objectivity and rationality found in rules, laws, records and files.[10]

The tentative answer to the question posed rhetorically at the beginning of this section must therefore be that of course man is a political animal. This is not to say that human beings are not collective and cultural animals as well. What is at stake is the distinction between these aspects of human nature, coupled with the need to appreciate the nature of citizenship, with its requirement of lively political space. Ethics, law and convention are important properties of human being in the world, but are different because they reflect and embody mainly (if not exclusively) membership rather than citizenship. The power of political space resides not in the permanence that its transmutation into territory and structure confer on it, but rather in its capacity to be recreated anew by dint of its very evanescence. This calls for a revival of discourse which in turn requires that speech and language be viewed as a deed rather than an alternative to it. Man's capacity for and interest in collective life in most of its manifestations must not be allowed to co-opt the field of our understanding regarding the needs of politics and the political, for these cannot be met in and through government alone, and may even be hindered by its view of agency and its treatment of citizenship as a form of membership.

III

The fact that I have shown citizenship, with its notion of space and language, to be in a most difficult situation relative to state, Society and government does not contradict my claim that man is a political, as opposed to simply a collective, gregarious, cultural animal. Because this possibility is covered over or lies dormant does not in any way negate my point about politics as citizenly display being "natural" to human beings in the same way that other qualities expressive of membership are seen to be. It is precisely because sociability and citizenship as display need *not* be in a zero-sum relationship that I oppose the way the question regarding man's nature is usually framed. It is not a question of being *either* a social *or* a political animal which is at stake here, for man is clearly and convincingly both. Because present conditions have suppressed man's political dimension does not make it any less natural than sociability. What it indicates is the presence of a hierarchy of activities in the human scheme of things, with politics and citizenship, along with contemplation and reflection, at or near the apex and other collective activities arranged along a vertical continuum on the basis of the extent to which they do or do not distinguish us from other forms of animate life.[11]

The hierarchical conception, unfortunately, has been retained in modern territorial states in the form of rigid formal structures expressing and embodying, political, administrative and legal authority. Rather than constituting a relatively fluid arrangement of possibilities for and instances of cooperation, the emphasis has been for the most part on the equation of citizenship with a form of membership, and the corollary division of functions between agents and citizens as members. Only agents get an opportunity to exhibit what is alleged to constitute good citizenly display in these circumstances, while the original hierarchical conception based on an evaluation of what activities are more or less uniquely human is suppressed in favour of role choices and options *where all roles are equal.* It must, however, be clear that all roles and functions are not equal. Yet the representative system can only be dynamized from within and without if we are willing to accept the fact that it cannot bear the load that our guiding assumptions and practices have put upon it. Citizenship is not a passively ascribed form of membership in Society, and agents must not be the only persons in a position to display themselves as political animals.

I would go even further than most, and argue that in the case of the modern parliamentary system of the United Kingdom, and the Tudor System of separated institutions of representation and power in the United States, these structures were *never* intended to carry the load presently assigned them. It is not simply the increase in the quantity and nature of functions performed by governments, but the interaction between this event and the rise in the complexity and status of occupational life which has been absolutely indispensable to generating feelings of incompetence, powerlessness, alienation and apathy found throughout the general publics of advanced industrial societies. When I say general publics I mean to take issue with the view, all too readily accepted, which asserts that there is no general public but only special interests and organized publics. Notions like this reveal the true loyalties of political science and the social sciences, for they take advantage of the present state of public stupefaction with the role of politics and government in collective life as a whole. It is this set of conditions that largely accounts for the unwillingness of citizens to view the political as a most human expression of humanness, and it is the "sociologization" of politics which has largely justified and defended incipient and continuous depoliticization.

I shall look at the issue of constituency and constituents in more detail in the next section, but suffice it to say here that the parallel between the idea of space as territory to be covered, and the reliance of social-scientific "laws" on the existence of large behaving populations, is what underlies our present inability to take the problem of incentives seriously. We need to reflect on the relationship between size, population and conformity to behavioural norms of socialization to a far greater extent than we have to date.[12] In the field of politics and in the exercise of citizenly display there is nothing better suited to good practice than careful thought and reflection. By this I do *not* mean expertise and functional rationality but rather commonsense rationality, which I understand to be a well-distributed set of capacities and possibilities which we possess by virtue of being human. This does not mean that we can equate their possession with citizenly expression but rather that there is a possibility for such expression because man *is* a political animal *regardless* of present conditions. It is to citizenship as mere membership that we must turn in order to understand how passive consent under these conditions has been equated with the will of the people.

I have argued elsewhere that a most important property of advanced industrial societies is the way they are able to avoid confronting the demands of the hierarchy of activities, properly understood, by an appeal to an expansive conception of need coincident with infinite desire. Arendt noticed this when she addressed Society as an "artificial realm" which deifies collective behaviours of a labouring and consuming kind. Macpherson argued that it constituted the essence of capitalism's core assumption and values because it "capitalizes" on man's capacity to persuade himself that need and desire really are one and the same. The original observation on this matter belongs, however, to Hegel, who pointed out the contrast between human beings and other forms of animate life on this matter of need in 1821.

An animal's needs and its ways and means of satisfying them are both alike restricted in scope. Though man is subject to this restriction too, yet at the same time he evinces his transcendence of it and his universality, first by the multiplication of needs and means of satisfying them, and secondly by the differentiation and division of concrete need into single parts and aspects which in turn become different needs, particularized and so more abstract. . . . This multiplication goes on *ad infinitum;* taken as a whole, it is refinement, i.e. a discrimination between these multiplied needs, and judgment on the suitability of means to their ends.[13]

Hegel goes on to discuss the sense of abstract liberation present in such an expansion and multiplication without however addressing himself to the issue of citizenship as display. Indeed, Hegel finds a likelihood of reconciliation between this tendency and institutional limits in his theory of the state as the highest form of "ethical life." Marx would later point out how empty an abstraction Hegel's state in fact is relative to the reality of civil society. The very process by which industrial capitalism institutionalizes the expansion and multiplication of needs is coincident with civil society rather than the state in Hegel. This is evident from Hegel's correct equation of this process with the rise of ends-means or instrumental rationality, first by individuals in the market, thereafter by firms as "collective persons." In civil society so understood, the only kind of individuation compatible with the interests of those who govern and direct these forces is the personhood of occupational life and its reverse side – consumption and spectating. Durkheim more than anyone else knew how important it was to reconcile individuation with values and behaviours which would support the emergence of Society as a culturally and historically specific form of collective life.

This equation of personhood and individuation with occupational life takes shape in civil society as a panoply of fixed and structured roles. In what Arendt calls the labouring society, citizenship as membership is equated mainly with the superstructure that the capitalist surplus allegedly makes possible, therefore with consuming, spectating, or "down time". Only in the case of agents do we equate politics with work or labour, and here what I have in mind is the Christian notion of stewardship noted earlier. Instead of viewing wealth as an opportunity for citizenly display, it is construed as property requiring careful management. Instead of entering into political space, individuals in such circumstances delegate the political, now understood as an occupational function or role, to elected representatives who are seen as *their* agents. They perform the function, do the work, and are permitted a position in the hierarchical structure of formal meritocracy which accords nicely with the false function of functional rationality. At best, this particular exercise of citizenship by agents focuses on the combined activities of insuring technical progress and distributing and managing the social welfare apparatus of late capitalism. At worst, it constitutes nothing less than a zero-sum game between agents and citizens as member.

Persuading individual citizens that political concern is not farce or entertainment in the absence of some specific interest, economic or otherwise, is no easy task. Particularly in periods of austerity or economic downturn, but at other times as well, the feeling that one should enforce a strict division between occupational and private life is itself in serious danger of collapse, however much it may be desired. This is undergirded, to be sure, by the demands and requirements of conformity, which stipulate that individuation occur through behaviour rather than action. By making individuation more "available," since it was now equated with occupational performance and success in jobs and careers, Durkheim clearly meant to resuscitate the solidarity of fixed and hierarchical structures, with the proviso that they be adopted to the needs of modern industrial organization and technology. Only the initial choice of the workman is to be voluntary, because the sole purpose of freeing the individual from old values and traditions that are obsolete is to subordinate him to new socialization and controls. Civil society constitutes the dead life space of the territorial state under norms of formal meritocracy and functional rationality, where citizenship must be a form of membership if agents are to function as stewards.[14]

It is in the final analysis the lack of confidence in human possibilities, premised on a pessimistic conception of human nature, that underpins the continuing emphasis on fixed and structured roles which are seen to be equivalent save for the distinction between agents and citizens as members. Members have a wide range "options" which are seen to be virtually interchangeable, but it is the distinction between agents and members which underwrites such a passive conception of function compatible with formal meritocracy and functional rationality. The significance of the hierarchical notion applied to human being and activity in the world is lost to structures whose real justification is the imperative need for stability and order. Passivity and sociability are seen to go together inasmuch as the citizen as member is understood to have his role options and possibilities *ascribed* to him rather than achieved and displayed by him. Such an idea of citizenship is the bureaucratic *open sesame* in any territorial state for the opportunity to behave and conform, to consume and spectate, and even to participate in occupational life to the extent that this is possible. Thus the notion that citizens are either natural born or naturalized so pre-eminent in the common law, and the somewhat different sanguinary basis found in code law systems and variations upon it.

What I am saying here does not contradict my earlier point about man being "naturally" a political animal. To address the present ascribed nature of citizenship, when it means nothing more than membership, is to focus on the range of activities that *both* agents and members view as valid activities for members when stability and order based on a pessimistic view of human nature is operative. This is different from arguing in favour of something which is *also* "natural," but is presently suppressed because its exercise constitutes an *alternative* to passive role ascription which is seen to threaten stability and order. What is most dispiriting about this situation is that citizens, well socialized in the equation of citizenship with membership and the fixed hierarchical separation of agents and citizens as members, themselves accept and enforce it. So long as the system can deliver the economic goods, any attempt to resist the demands of behaviour and conformity is met with scorn and derision. Only when the system begins to fail in this its almost only basis of legitimation do alternatives suggest themselves, but even here the association of real individuation with instability and disorder figures prominently in the negative assessment of such activity by members.

One of the most important conceptions buttressing the view of citizenship as an ascribed status, ironically enough, is to be discovered in that tradition of political theory concerned with natural rights, natural law, and the social and political contract. I consider these notions to be indispensable doctrinal bases justifying and legitimizing passivity over display, behaviour over action, conformity through occupational life, consumption and spectating over real individuation. To say that human beings are "naturally" one thing or another can be defended and rendered sensible if and only if such "nature" is not necessarily always to be discovered in present structures and practices.[15] This is a somewhat different point of emphasis, to be sure, from the earlier pessimistic view of human nature. What they have in common all too often is their *results,* namely, that the present state of stability and order under law and convention depends on man being conceived either as too evil to be trusted with an active notion of citizenship or too naïve and innocent. It is this latter view which has often been a guiding assumption for natural rights and natural law theorists. Just showing that such rights exist in the background, even to the point of adopting a metaphoric and analogical conception of law in support of such a view, is often considered sufficient.

While it would no doubt be possible to address the lack of fit between such notions and present institutions, operative social-scientific norms of research frown on any such attempt to displace rather than defend present structures by refusing to focus on "functional requisites." These disciplines, not excluding political science, are committed to an organizational conception of collective order and stability, and this conception has no place in it whatsoever for "horse and buggy" notions from antiquity or the early modern period like natural rights, natural law or social and political contract. This in spite of the fact that such notions more often than not can be blended with pessimism and cynicism of the sort already cited to counsel against the exercise of real citizenship. Display in the present collective order is variously assessed as narcissistic, silly, pretentious, frivolous, or just plain mistaken. Besides, what is the point of criticizing a system which is, after all, seen to be delivering the goods to most of its members, particularly when such an alternative is viewed mainly as a device whose effect, if not its intent, is to *hinder* the territorial state's superintendence of technical progress and social welfare, alongside the "delegated" superintendence of the economy by dominant firms and corporations.[16]

Few things better illustrate the deadness of territorial space relative to the idea of possibility in the space of language than the view that man's sociability is in a zero sum relation to his capacity for citizenly display. Thus the fact that man is naturally a sociable and gregarious animal is seen to preempt and effectively dictate what the nature of citizenship *must be* under these circumstances. Citizenship becomes membership because this is seen to be the only way man's political naturalness can be allowed to express itself that is compatible with the stability and order that sociability and gregariousness allegedly demand. Here we see clearly the indispensability of the fixed and hierarchical notion of structure first articulated in the modern context by Maistre, Bonald and later by St. Simon and Comte. We also understand the treat to hierarchy that an emphasis on the range of human activities and possibilities poses for the modern conception of stability and order, a conception so essential for the emergence and development of industrial capitalism in the West. The effect of all of these theories, whether intended or not, has been to elevate and permanently to franchise the territorial state that is nowadays virtually coterminous with Society itself. Small wonder that Marx in particular took such issue with any claims of naturalness which saw present institutional developments, in particular the state and civil society, as evidence for such a claim.[17]

IV

The truth about nature and naturalism whenever it is applied to the claim that man is "by nature" a political animal is that real human development requires us to *go beyond* present notions of gregariousness and sociability in order to demonstrate that this is the case. The present either-or zero-sum conception keeps us in effective tutelage to our worst fears and greatest apprehensions about ourselves, while it denies the real hierarchy of activities and the need to integrate and develop them all together. We are so fearful and apprehensive about the threat this will invariably pose to collective order that we elect, and increasingly appoint or just hire, agents, not only to perform such activities under the guise of work, labour and occupation, but to further persuade us that we cannot be trusted with such "responsibility," whether because of our capacity for evil or our naïvete and innocence. It is to the notion of collective order discovered in Society's organizational imperative, and to the needs of industrial capitalism for such order and discipline, that we must turn if we are to fully comprehend the rise of the modern territorial state, with its preference for law and convention, its suppression of the space of language in favour of citizenship as membership, and the rigid distinction between members and agents.

It is not only possible but necessary in the light of the foregoing to limit the otherwise legitimate charge of fetishism to claims which equate what is alleged to be natural with either what presently is, institutionally speaking, or with what can never be. If the idea of incentives seems misplaced with regard to the discussion thus far, it is only because we equate incentives with money or some other form of value appropriate to the social and economic system that we live under. The purpose of any incentive relevant to politics and the political must be to encourage individuals to take political as well as economic risks. This probably implies status and prestige risks as well, for in the culturally and historically specific form of collective life in which we find ourselves, citizenship as achievement and display is viewed in the various ways that I have mentioned. Public confidence does not need to be heightened simply because one or a few of its "members" has something important so say. Such improvement requires a collective self-assessment which goes beyond Holmes' famous "can't help" dictum – his belief in *both* popular sovereignty in principle and democratic elitism in practice.[18] Present institutional arrangements in the political and governmental field simply can no longer carry the load *we* have put upon them.

This is not simply an assessment of the institutions, for I have argued off and on throughout this book that they are sufficient to the practical task under two conditions. The first is that we *use* them to create the citizen anew as someone not subordinate to either the role choices of members or the rigid distinction between agents and members. The second is that in pursuit of this goal we be mindful of the new public spaces which are becoming more and more available for the exercise of politics and for citizenly display. It must be clear by now that by spaces here I mean the space of language and action, of speech as a deed, rather than *territorial* space (place). That this is not a moot point is best evidenced by the way we have allowed the idea of space as territory to inhibit our own political development. Once formulated as a problem of coverage, the only way to make politics coincide with the interests of late capitalism is to "democratize" all action into behaviour, all "sense of function" into fixed role structures of functional rationality and formal meritocracy, and to make of citizenship one amongst many available versions of membership in the form of role options or choices.

That the new spaces I have discussed thus far – media protest and single issue politics, local and municipal or "grass roots" public affairs, the opportunity for reform of political science and of the social, behavioural and managerial disciplines, and the contemporary university and higher education – are intended to function in the main as a *supplement* to established mechanisms rather than a substitute for them needs to be given extended attention for a number of reasons. Many have argued that such a position acts to defend obsolete and outmoded institutional arrangements that are at least two centuries old, when what is needed is new institutions appropriate to Society's need for functional expertise and meritocracy in the interests of both speedy and sound decision-making. I want once again to state what many will consider a heresy – that the reason we need dynamic representative systems and lively political parties is not so much to mollify the people, but because popular decisions expressed through the political process are generally *better* decisions and make more sensible policies. To argue that citizenly display is compatible with full utilization of present institutional arrangements, however, is not to argue against the need for change.

There is a point beyond which, given the present socio-economic order, political and governmental change simply cannot go, for reasons that both political economy since Harrington and Locke, and Marx, made apparent.[19] My concern for fully utilizing present institutional arrangements is not simply to arrest their atrophy and incipient formalization for its own sake, but because it is only through functional utilization that we can mold them to our purposes and prepare the ground for larger order changes as conditions warrant. "Progress," if it makes any sense at all to use it in the sphere of politics and government, must mean adaptation to available conditions and possibilities *as they emerge*. For me, the problem of allowing the newly emergent public spaces to coopt partisan politics and representative mechanisms and processes is not the fear of instability and disorder, as I hope I have made clear. It is rather that they are not a substitute as they stand and will only be formalized and absorbed into the already formalized system in due course, with no clear advantage to *human* political development. Indeed one of the greatest problems of these alleged alternatives is precisely the fact that they serve the interests of emergent elites whose concerns are clearly a or anti-political, as Lebedoff has recently pointed out.[20]

With the exception of participation in local and municipal affairs, they are nothing less *on their own* than a device to *bypass* existing arrangements, thereby not only leaving these arrangements intact, but reaffirming the equation of the citizen as member and the distinction between agents and members. A derived point in criticism of these new spaces as alternatives is the way they effectively underwrite the view that citizenship as membership is only one among many roles available to the societal member. Politics becomes theatre, entertainment, a media smash, but only so long as the audience as well as the participants is interested. On their own media protest and single issue politics in particular reaffirm the view that our present political and governmental institutions have little or nothing to offer the citizen in terms of his time, energy, interests, and values and principles. At the same time that they do this, they favour passivity and a "quick fix" approach to politics when everyone knows that there are no final solutions in collective life, nor should we want there to be. Representative institutions must be dynamized, both from within and without, by citizenly speech, action and display, and this means that the new spaces that are opening up for the possibility of politics must not be seen as an alternative to the existing system if we are really interested in change.

One of the problems with mass media already alluded to resides in its capacity to turn politics into a spectator sport or a consumable commodity in the absence of dynamic representation. The passivity endemic to such "participation" by the public not only fits the role structure and the idea of options, including citizenship. Mass media politics is perfectly compatible with the concept of space appropriate to the territorial state, as well as its preference for the asymmetry of the written over the oral tradition as a vehicle of communication. Direct democratic "votes" of the sort I discussed in chapter five are an excellent example, for here those who push such an idea, whether as a substitute for or a complement to existing institutions, either consciously or unconsciously have a consumerist and/or an audience model of the public in mind. Process is slower because it needs to take account of the fact that opinions and sentiments change with the passage of time and as a result of reflection and deliberation. Direct devices like referenda, initiatives and recalls are immediate, and, as a result, often the result of knee-jerk reflexes more than anything else. This will be even more the case once the public is able to register their "vote" from home and the office with the indispensable assistance of video data terminals and allied auto-electronic equipment.

To some extent, it is possible to see in the extensive use of polls and polling by government not simply the attempt to discover and anticipate public opinions and sentiments on "issues" of the day, but mainly an effort to *further* short-circuit utilization of existing processes under the guise of delegated authority from the people, combined with extensive and far-reaching exercises of discretion by politicians and judges and magistrates, as well as by civil servants, technocrats, political appointees, and regulators. Polls require a reflex reaction, and in any case are carried out on what may or may not constitute a very accurate "population universe sample." This is less problematic for me than the way such an approach shows how much in common this short-circuiting of representative and partisan processes has with the interests of the territorial state in dead political space, the written tradition as an asymmetrical model of speech, and the view of space as territory to be covered, whether in reality or in principle, by direct media and related techniques and devices of this sort. Because the people have been socialized to see themselves as the passive recipients of the combined efforts of the territorial state and the large corporation, such devices are accepted with gratitude as evidence of popular sovereignty and the reality of democracy when they constitute nothing less than the suppression of the political dimension in collective life.

Another surrogate for the dynamization of representative and partisan institutions has existed alongside these institutions for a considerable period of time in many democracies, and is often considered as legitimate a way of engaging in politics as parties, legislatures and elected executive bodies. I have in mind interest groups, pressure groups, trade associations and lobbyists, and it is precisely the recent interest in such groups as possible *substitutes* for electoral politics, but particularly political parties, that demands discussion. The emphasis in such organized groups on function and occupation may appear to contravene the established focus on territorial representation of which I have been critical, but it is important to realize just how dependent on this latter system of representation these groups are. They work within the established structures of government and seek to influence the law making and implementation processes, either by lobbying and influencing key figures or by dint of the monopoly of functional and technical expertise they claim to possess. They are a complement to the ongoing delegation of power over the economy that is an unavoidable upshot of the development of a mature capitalist system. At the same time, they speak to what many now believe to constitute at least a complementary basis for representing the public.

The difficulty here is that such a conception begins by acknowledging that there really is no public but only specialized publics. Since this is argued to be the case, what is the point of trying to improve existing representative and party structures, or even to support the further development of the newly emergent public spaces already cited? Such groups offer no alternative to the present system, and in fact will only accelerate the processes of depoliticization given in the equation of citizenship with membership and the fixed distinction between agents and members. They focus on the notion of concrete, usually economic, interest, and argue not only that representative democracies guarantee their right to organize and petition the government, but that theirs are the only real interests to be represented. They contrast themselves to unorganized, inchoate, and irrational "public opinion," and often go so far as to argue for their right to have a constant and privileged access to government. Much of this derives from the unavoidable delegation of responsibility for running the economy that takes place in all advanced capitalist systems. But they also claim to possess monopolies of knowledge, skills and techniques, and experience appropriate to their functional and occupational basis of organization.

This is not to deny that a great deal of their "success" must be ascribed to the size, prestige or importance of their membership. I am more concerned, however, with the way that they use the existing territorial system of representation, with all the properties I have mentioned, in order to achieve their own objectives and interests. In fact, it would not be too strong to argue that these groups actually encourage the developments that I have argued will lead to the breakdown of the representative and partisan nature of democratic political systems if present trends continue. Their major objective, when it comes to suggesting alternatives to existing representative democracies that do not allow them sufficient points of access, is frequently to encourage the fragmentation of the policy making function, particularly in parliamentary systems of cabinet government. They resent the power of initiative which elected, appointed and scheduled officials have in these systems, and encourage fragmentation where the existing system is not sufficiently malleable. No less significant is the way they downgrade parties and legislatures for failing to engage in effective policy making while often benefitting from this very failing and only wishing for more.

From the standpoint of my dual concern for making the maximum functional use of existing institutions, while acknowledging the present *supplementary* role of the new public spaces that are emerging relative to these institutions, theirs is a decidedly a or anti-political bias. They are at least as committed to the citizen as member as most agents and members are, and are no less concerned about the destabilizing effects of politics and real citizenship than was Durkheim when he advocated a functional and occupational basis for governments in industrial societies. Regardless of the amount of competition between them for status, power, recognition and ideally interdependence with government, their basic mode of organizing and their goals and objectives are sufficiently congruent to tempt them to come forward as an *alternative* to the present system. It is their correct assessment of the consequences for representation and partisanship of the present executive, administrative and even judicial discretion and power of initiative found in parliamentary systems in particular which leads them to put themselves forward when in fact they often depend on the present confusion and are no more capable of governing than were Durkheim's functional and occupational associations.[21]

Theirs is no less the space of territory than the parties and legislatures they simultaneously revile and depend upon. The concrete interest allegedly present in specific groups is offered not simply as a distinguishing property of one particular group over the inchoate and unorganized public, such as it is, but of the aggregate of interest groups who together will guarantee a merger of private and public interest as well as of expertise and representation. In the final analysis it is their claim to more sensibly and meaningfully represent the public, now reformulated as separate and distinct publics, than parties and legislatures, and even executives, which requires serious reflection. Why doesn't everyone get organized along the lines of the special interests that are most important to them, and petition the government like we do? Of course the question answers itself. The argument for the superior representative power of all groups taken together is only rhetoric, and in any case is unrealizable because of the very things that are needed in order to successfully organize and gain access. Taken individually and in terms of the shifting coalitions outside their special areas of legislative interest, their purpose is to achieve a balance of interest forces in any particular situation while avoiding the responsibility for governing that is necessary in all representative democracies.

Political parties, it would seem, no longer aggregate interest groups in ways that they find acceptable. This has led to attempts to secure access to centralized executives, technocrats and civil servants while at the same time arguing that the impotence of parties and legislatures shows the hopelessness of any view which does not equate the public with the politics of concrete interest groups. Not surprisingly, their emphasis on function and occupation, and their acceptance of the idea that citizens are really only members who have chosen a particular role option, reveals itself in the way that their alleged alternative presumes the priority of occupational life and consumption in terms of the groups that are at the centre of the representation which is offered. Interest groups and allied organized entities rely on the very problems the territorial state is having in order to justify their alternative, but no more want the responsibility for public policy decisions than business does when it accepts its privileged position in all capitalist societies, while allowing governments to take the blame for policies that may readily have resulted from their advice and intervention. Theirs is no real alternative, but if it were it would be a retrograde step in any effort to provide a new basis for political development in advanced industrial societies.[22]

V

In this final section I want to focus on the idea of constituency, because it is absolutely indispensable for an adequate understanding of the problems and possibilities to be discovered in present-day representative systems. It is, after all, nothing less than the key organizing concept of the modern territorial state, with its emphasis on representation as areal coverage of populations and interests. More precisely, it is the operative notion employed to *reconcile* area on the one hand with populations and interests on the other, on the assumption that coverage is the key prerequisite to representation. I have mentioned interests alongside population in order to underscore the difference between groups with a national as well as a sectional interest and those whose concerns are exclusively or mainly within one or a few constituencies. In a certain sense, it is the way that organized interests have taken on a national significance which has served to *further* erode constituency representation in modern states. It is the dominant role of party discipline in two party systems, whether federal or unitary, which has effectively undercut the vaunted promise of constituency-based representation by which large territorial states justified their support for a discretionary rather than an "instructed-delegate" model of representation.

In multi-party systems, as noted, party structures, at least of the middle and left, tend to be more permanent than parties in two party systems, which only have a fixed structure directly before, during and after an election or during conventions. Parties in multi party systems often more closely resemble interest groups, and even civil service structures, than those in two party systems. In place of the latter's obligation to seek to garner majorities in over half the constituencies reporting, the former are normally reconciled to coalition governments. Electoral systems tend more often than not to parallel a country's political party system, with the constituency basis, as a rule, national in multi party systems, and local and regional in two party systems. These differences generally go hand in hand with the fact that two party systems normally characterize large territorial states, while multiparty systems are usually discovered in small, relatively homogeneous countries. West Germany, to be sure, constitutes the major exception to practically everything I have said in this paragraph, a fact readily explainable by the way in which it was created, following the end of occupation in 1949, as an amalgam of American, British and French governmental and political institutions.

The first premise of the idea of constituency, wherever we find it, is that the people as a whole cannot govern themselves but must be represented by their agents. I have argued that agency is only problematic where it is seen to constitute an alternative to membership. The result of such an equation is that citizenship is understood to mean a passive role option available to members, who elect, appoint or employ agents to perform the functions that pass for citizenly display. Agency in such circumstances comes to be understood in its legal variant as a discretionary grant of authority and power rather than a trust, the moreso where party discipline in two party parliamentary systems renders the operative norm of constituency-based representation at best of secondary importance. Only under direct democratic techniques available in small countries at the so-called "grass roots" level is it really possible to control grants of agency and delegations of power. The instructed delegate model employed by parties of the left in diverse systems is an attempt to reproduce, under conditions of constituency representation, a replication of this control over agency found in non-representative direct democratic techniques and practices.[23]

The point is that democratic national states, of whatever legislative, partisan and electoral stripe, cannot escape the problems that arise out of efforts to represent the people's will and the public interest. A realistic understanding of the importance of constituency is absolutely essential to an appreciation of what these problems are and how best to deal with them. If we therefore *begin* by recognizing the indispensability of constituency to effective and meaningful representation, it will allow us to focus our attention on the varous ideas and methods presently in use to represent the people where they are alleged to be incapable of (re)presenting themselves. It is really a question of whether existing systems of representation, based on various notions of constituency, function to inspire public interest and participation, or seek to retard and frustrate it by underwriting the idea of a fixed one way delegation of authority to agents, who in turn are responsible only relatively rarely through the mechanism of formal election and in other ways. On the whole, it would seem inescapable that present systems have as their major effect, if not their intended outcome, to retard and frustrate the representational possibilities of both established institutions and the new public spaces that I have argued are essential if these institutions are to be at all viable.

In effect, existing mechanisms shore up the already dominant tendency to equate citizenship with membership, where by membership is meant a range of permissible role options that one exercises alongside the performance of an occupational function. It is the idea of citizenship as *ascribed* which makes its equation with membership so "natural", just as it is the view of politics and the political as one form that man's natural sociability and gregariousness can take that makes it possible to view it as one amongst many societally sanctioned behaviours. Constituency, in the event, can be seen as a device for facilitating the effective management and control of the people of large, concentrated, or variously diverse territories at least as much as it is a method which permits them to be effectively represented under present notions of agency and delegation. It is in *both* senses, then, that I believe we need to reflect on operative methods of representation through the aegis of constituency in all advanced industrial societies characterized by democratic government. There is a great deal of value in seeing in the idea and practice of constituency a thoroughgoing embodiment of the organizational principle in general applied to the management of territorial states, particularly when popular understandings of what constitutes the proper functioning of the representative system are taken into account.

Having been continuously socialized in the belief that they are an inchoate, amorphous mass to be "covered" through various forms of constituency representation, it is hardly surprising that the people are aware only of the "opinions" they, or a sample of them, are alleged to hold on issues of the day. Their passivity as respondents only confirms the consequences of a view of citizenship as membership already cited. Nowadays individuation is seen to inhere in occupational performance and success, this being the form most "available" in advanced industrial societies. That this is no less true for women than for men raises serious questions which it is beyond the scope of this study to examine. Alongside this non or anti-political conception of individuation is the view that only organized interests, particularly of the economic kind, constitute concrete "actors" in the political field. The public interest, and the idea of a general public, remains acknowledged almost solely as a "normative" construct by citizens no less than by agents. Even agency loses its status as a mode of individuation to the extent that these individuals must subordinate themselves to parties, groups, the media and countless advisors. The remaining scope for individuation in advanced industrial societies, once occupational life has been taken account of, reduces itself to "off-work" activities focussed on consumption, spectating and leisure.

The only alternative which increasingly appears on the horizon is one that is on the whole available to only a restricted few, although the numbers are clearly growing. I have in mind individual recourse to judicial bodies and to legal process generally. Here what is sought is a range of legal rights and liberties which it is the job of the law to protect and serve. This includes economic rights of a proprietary and contractual kind as well as torts, and is to be contrasted to civil rights and liberties which are also the responsibility

of courts and judges under the rule of law. My assessment of this development sees it as problematic only to the extent that such avenues are thought
to function as a *substitute* for political rights and the responsibilities of the
elected representatives of the people and their delegates and agents. It is
problematic as a substitute because such rights and liberties can only establish the individual's status as a societal member, never as a citizen. This
is no criticism of such approaches to individuation. On the contrary, this is
precisely what the courts and legal process are supposed to do in a representative democracy. My complaint is with those who expect too much from
this approach, particularly now when courts and judges are so often encouraged from all sides to go beyond interpreting legislation to reviewing and
nullifying it, even in countries where the latter is an established practice, like
the United States and the Federal Republic of Germany.[24]

A major device for dealing with the problem of representation as it arises in
large, or culturally diverse, territories is, of course, federalism. Here it is the
idea of two coordinate jurisdictions, each with some sphere of exclusivity,
which is supposed to guide the political and legal organization of a given
state. The citizen may be a member of one state, where membership is
ascribed in the manner already discussed, but he votes in two legal jurisdictions, as well as in local, municipal or metropolitan elections where such
entities are "creatures" of the state or province. Federalism can arise for a
number of reasons, but the major ones are sheer size of territorial expanse,
internal regional characteristics of a distinct kind, or the prior existence of
separate cultural, ethnic, linguistic or tribal peoples that wish to federate for
one reason or another. Since the division of power is so important to the
success of federal states, there is a tendency for such states to favour written
constitutions, or organic laws of some superordinate legislative body to the
same effect. In the event, a more active role for higher judicial bodies is
often called for, the objective being to arbitrate this division of political
functions under conditions of competition and change. This need not always
be the case, as is attested to by the case of Switzerland in particular, but here
most of the responsibilities mentioned are carried out by the Federal executive.

Federalism thus recognizes the need to counteract the tendency to make
relevant electoral constituencies coincident with the borders of the state
itself. Federal states which have arisen mainly as a response to size and
regionalism are normally characterized by two party systems and a local
constituency basis of representation. This in contrast to unitary states lacking a clear internal division based on cultural differences, where multi-party
systems and proportional representation are normally the rule.[25] Proportional representation, in effect, treats the state as the relevant constituency,
and is more viable as a consequence in small states and/or ones with rela-

tively homogeneous populations and settled traditions. In both federal and unitary states there will be provision for *residential* voting and representation, and it is here as things presently stand that the notion of citizenship as membership seems most viable. I tried to argue against such a conception of local and municipal politics in chapter seven, on grounds that the urban city may be a key factor in *restoring* the political space of language in the face of national-state and international territoriality. Suffice it to say here that, to date, the combined effect of one residential and one or more legal constituencies for representation has been to function more as a tool for coverage and a device for management than anything else.

Though all three conceptions of constituency mentioned thus far constitute modes of representation in democratic societies, they differ substantially from the "grass roots" approach as a basic value, however unrealized in practice it may. Here the view, which to some small extent inspires territorially and regionally based forms of federalism, is that the government which can best be trusted is the one closest to the people. Such a view is nostalgic to the extent that its conditional validity rested on the assumption that societies needed little or no government activity in the state or provincial, but particularly in the federal, or central, government jurisdictions. Nowadays the scope of government welfare, fiscal, monetary, and contracting and subcontracting activity alongside foreign affairs makes such a view almost anachronistic. This is why I have argued that it is mainly in the urban city that it will be necessary to begin the process by which citizenship can come to constitute a viable form of individuation, one of inestimable assistance to representative institutions and processes as well. At the present time, one could make a strong case for the claim that local, municipal and metropolitan government and politics is both the least understood and the most potentially significant for the general populace.[26]

A popular misunderstanding, already noted, which is all too readily encouraged by those who govern from the centre in federal systems, is that federalism is an hierachical arrangement of *levels* of government rather than one characterized by two coordinate jurisdictions. It is so easy to slip into such a way of conceptualizing federal systems that one tends to forget how fundamental the retention of some sphere of mutual exclusivity in each jurisdiction is to the viability of the division of functions. A conception of federalism based on levels tends to work against the view that each jurisdiction has its sphere of exclusive political responsibilities, and therefore an exclusive responsibility to represent the relevant constituents on matters within their respective spheres of authority. The tendency from the centre is often to see the "lower level" jurisdictions as vehicles for carrying out public policies framed at the centre. Thus the desire to increase the number of shared as against exclusive jurisdictions in order to break down or com-

promise the *political* viability of states or provinces. In some cases this has
gone so far as to undermine the substance of state or provincial functioning,
even in areas where this jurisdiction is supposed to have exclusive authority.
When one remembers that, with the exception of foreign affairs and military
defense, the main areas of growth in demands on government have been in
the state or provincial jurisdictions (law enforcement, health, education,
welfare), this situation becomes all the more disquieting.[27]

It is not only doubtful whether we shall ever be able to reconcile a mass
franchise with direct rule, but doubtful whether we should desire such an
outcome even if we could secure it. I have already mentioned several examples of direct democracy in order to suggest that it is precisely this emphasis on *passive registration* rather than either display or process which
provides the strongest case against them. Direct democracy makes sense
only when the range of issues and the number of citizens involved permits
deliberation and process to occur. Attempts to use contemporary "post-
industrial" technologies to try to turn the tasks of governing into a version of
the town-meeting writ large simply underscores the gap between technology
and representation while it reaffirms a passive conception of citizenship as
membership based on consumer and audience models of societally sanctioned behaviour. In our effort to look realistically at possibilities for citizenly display both within and alongside established representative mechanisms, we must be very careful not to forget that the ultimate defence of
representative democracy is not only the superiority of its decisions but the
superiority of its processes as well. Neither grass roots representative democracy nor direct democratic techniques are realistic options in the present
situation, and cannot be counted upon to halt the further atrophy of existing
representative and party systems.

A final point concerns one issue which cross-cuts the question of constituency and the constituent. It is the nature of majorities and the relationship
between citizenship, membership and majority rule. Dahl has provided us
with a useful classification system by distinguishing Madisonian, populist
and polyarchal democracy in his *Preface to Democratic Theory* and elsewhere.[28] The importance of his analysis for me lies in the dilemma of how
one reconciles constituency representation as an individual voter with majority rule in practice. For example, riding organizations in two party systems where more than two parties are running may be faced with a situation
in which the winner fails to secure anywhere near a majority. Those who
voted for other candidates, therefore against the winner, find their vote
lopped off and not reaggregated later. Only in multi party systems under
proportional representation does the problem not arise in anywhere near as
serious a form, because here the constituency is the nation-state itself. Riding organization in federal systems, as noted, clearly sacrifices important

aspects of representation to stability and order. The alleged advantage of the riding basis of constituency is that it permits a higher likelihood of stable government than is the case in multi-party systems, where coalition formations and frequent instability is often the order of the day.

To lop off even a *minority* at the riding level, no matter which jurisdiction is involved, raises serious problems of representation, particularly in light of the overwhelming impact of party discipline on the ability of elected members to represent the interests of their constituents. When one considers instances in which majorities may suffer the same fate, the absence of some sort of back-up system of proportional representation seems particularly harmful. On the other hand, if the purpose of the constituency system is really stability and order rather than forms of representation not compatible with these priorities, then the Madisonian recommendation that any democracy spread across a great expanse be broken down into a sufficient number of constituencies to minimize the influence of any particular faction or group of factions makes sense. Seen in this light, the Madisonian equation is more readily compatible with polyarchal than with populist democracy, for the objective is no longer to maximize a single notion of majority rule and popular sovereignty, but to *divide* in the interests not only of stability and order but of good management as well. The result is a view of representative democracy committed to *using* the existing bases of constituency in order to increase the likelihood that as many individuals and groups as possible will be in the winning coalition, at least some of the time.[29]

The gravity of a situation in which majorities are frozen along ideological, ethnic, religious, cultural and linguistic or regional lines is self-evident. Legitimacy must not be based on a concept of majority rule which is not sufficiently fluid to have room in it for a vast number of persons, particularly those with intense views, but others as well. Legitimacy must therefore give first priority to process, and must seek to reconcile representative institutions with the need for inclusion in the winning coalition, particularly where views are held strongly by groups in a segmental relationship to the rest of the polity. When the nation-state itself is the constituency, it makes sense to value proportional representation, especially in situations in which there is a tradition of coalition government. Constituency as an internal mechanism makes stability and order more likely because it cross-cuts blocs and groups which always are like-minded on given issues, and promises something other than confrontational majorities and minorities. But is stability and order so much to be preferred that systems without these electoral divisions should be thought the less of for it? Possibilities for citizenship as I have defined it exist in all representative democracies, but this is no reason to ignore the need to dynamize relations between politics and polity, whether in and through established institutional processes and mechanisms, or alongside them in the new public spaces that are beginning to emerge.

References

1 Aristotle, *Politics* 1252 a 1–1253 a 38; W. D. Ross, *Aristotle* (NY: Meridan Books, 1959), pp. 231–233.

2 Sheldon Wolin, *Politics & Vision* (Boston: Little Brown, 1960), Chapters 1 & 2.

3 Wilson, *Tradition & Innovation* (London: Routledge, 1984), Chapter 3.

4 Harold Innis, *Empire and Communications* (Toronto: University of Toronto Press, 1950); Innis, *The Bias of Communication* (Toronto: University of Toronto Press, 1951).

5 Arendt, *The Human Condition* (Chicago: University of Chicago Press, 1958), pp. 175–247. So much for Weber's notion that *ideally* bureaucratic office-holding would be based on free contract, *without a right of appropriation!* See Weber, *Theory of Social & Economic Organization,* pp. 333–334, nos. 4, 6 and 9; *From Max Weber,* pp. 202–204, nos. 3–5.

6 Otto Kirchheimer, *Political Justice* (Princeton: Princeton University Press, 1971); Bernard Schwartz and H. W. R. Wade, *The Legal Control of Governments* (Oxford: Clarendon Press, 1972).

7 Wilson, "Functional Rationality and 'Sense of Function': the Case of an Ideological Distortion", *International Yearbook of Organization Studies 1980* (edited by Graeme Salaman and David Dunkerly (London: Routledge, 1981), pp. 37–61; and Innis, *op. cit.*

8 Arendt, *The Human Condition,* p. 43; Sebastian DeGrazia, *Of Work, Time and Leisure* (Garden City, NY: Doubleday Anchor, 1966).

9 This is not to say that "laws" cannot have a sense amongst peoples who refuse to be tied to one place. Note in particular George Sabine, *History of Political Theory* (NY: Henry Holt, 1937) where he discusses (chapter 11) the "law" of the folkish people (Teutons) of Germany, and carefully distinguishes it from both convention, and the law of territorial states.

10 See Stanley Raffel, *Matters of Fact* (London: Routledge, 1979). This distinction on the matter of speech as a deed *versus* the written tradition all too readily captures Weber's ambivalence about the bureaucratic "vocation" in its relation to the *dys*functionally rational principled (value rational) actor. See Weber, *Theory of Social & Economic Organization,* pp. 115–132 at pp. 115–118.

11 Arendt, *The Human Condition,* pp. 116–117, 123, 126–127, 131.

12 James Madison, *Federalist Papers* (NY: New American Library, 1961), nos. 10 and 51; Alexis De Tocqueville, *Democracy in America,* 2 Volumes (NY: Alfred Knopf, 1945). See my *The American Ideology,* Chapters 7–9, reference to levelling of status groups, Society as a whole, and bureaucracy and meritocracy; and "Technocracy in Late Capitalist Society," *op. cit.*

13 G. W. F. Hegel, *The Philosophy of Right,* translated with notes by T. M. Knox (London: Oxford University Press, 1967), no. 190; Arendt, *The Human Condi-*

tion, pp. 27–28, 38–50; C. B. Macpherson, *Democratic Theory* (London: Oxford University Press, 1973).

14 Emile Durkheim, *The Division of Labour in Society* (NY: Macmillan, 1952), pp. 228–229.

15 See Quentin Gibson, *The Logic of Social Enquiry* (London: Routledge & Kegan Paul, 1960), Chapters 1 & 2.

16 See Charles Lindblom, *Politics & Markets* (NY: Basic Books, 1977) chapter titled "The Privileged Position of Business."

17 See Shlomo Avineri, *The Social and Political Thought of Karl Marx* (London: Cambridge University Press, 1968), pp. 43–52.

18 Samuel Bachrach, *Democratic Elitism* (Boston: Little Brown, 1965), foreward and introductory remarks.

19 See James Harrington, *The Commonwealth of Oceana;* and John Locke, *Second Treatise of Government.*

20 David Lebedoff, *The New Elite: The Death of Democracy* (Chicago: Contemporary Book, 1983).

21 The exception of global war needs to be mentioned here, in light of Avery Leiserson's, *Administrative Regulation* (Westport, Conn: Greenwood Press 1975, 1942), a case study of reciprocal *self*-regulation between American interests with strong stakes in wartime contracting and subcontracting.

22 Compare Arthur Bentley, *The Process of Government* (Chicago: University of Chicago Press, 1908) and David Truman, *The Governmental Process* (NY: Alfred Knopf, 1951) to E. E. Schattschneider, *The Semi-Sovereign People* (NY: Holt, Rinehart & Winston, 1960).

23 See Joseph Frascona, *Agency* (Englewood Cliffs, NJ: Prentice Hall, 1964); Roscoe Martin, *Grass Roots: Rural Democracy in America* (NY: Harper & Row, 1965); Grant McConnell, *Private Power and American Democracy* (NY: Alfred Knopf, 1965), especially pp. 91–118.

24 Henry Abraham, *The Judicial Process* (NY: Oxford University Press, 1963); Bernard Schwartz, *The Code Napoleon and the Common Law World* (NY: NYU Press, 1956); Bernard Schwartz and H. W. R. Wade, *The Legal Control of Governments* (Oxford: Clarendon Press, 1972).

25 K. C. Wheare, *Federal Government* (London: Oxford University Press, 1946, 1958). The most prominent exception to this latter rule is, of course, the United Kingdom.

26 See Jane Jacobs, *The Economy of Cities* (NY: Random House, 1969).

27 Functional Rationality expresses and embodies an organizational approach to the problem of order, and is best captured in the view that Society should ideally endeavour to approximate a bureaucracy writ large as much as possible. Concern about the fate of the nation-state as a potential or actual *firm* in the anarchy of the emerging international market has served to further underwrite this concern.

28 Robert Dahl, *Preface to Democratic Theory* (Chicago: University of Chicago Press, 1956); Dahl, *Polyarchy: Participation and Opposition* (New Haven: Yale University Press, 1971).

29 Dahl, *Preface to Democratic Theory,* pp. 63–84, Appendix pp. 84–89, and pp. 124–151.

Chapter 11
Some Arguments Against Political Management

I

The idea of a public capture of its own institutions and processes of representation only seems absurd if we ignore the fact that these institutions are not only geared for such redefinition and reformulation, but urgently need it. I have tried to show how this necessary development needs to be complemented by recognition of new public spaces for the display and activity of politics heretofore not thought to be particularly "political." The examples cited suggest that the main thrust, when all is said and done, will need to be focussed on traditional governmental and political institutions however, not so much because this provides for more continuity and is therefore "safer," but rather because these institutions must first be fully utilized before it is possible to even conceive of realistic alternatives where lines of societal and economic development are deemed to demand it. I cannot overemphasize the importance of not short-circuiting these institutions of representation given the clear tendency to political *regression* in both the advanced societies and in the world as a whole. It is perhaps this tendency which requires us to acknowledge the all-too-unfortunate correctness of recent science fiction, where technically and economically advanced societies are always characterized by either benevolent despotism or tyranny.

While those with a technocratic, managerial or elitist frame of mind, as well as others, might object to my use of the word regression to explain such contemplated, it not anticipated, developments, my reasons are quite straightforward and, I think, readily comprehensible. My conception of "progress" or "development," to the extent that I have one, is based on the evolution of *political and governmental* institutions rather than economic and technical ones. Thus *any* form of government which substitutes the discretionary rule of one or a cadres of non-elected officials or judges for that of elected officials is to be considered regressive. To be sure, I have argued that representative institutions, still formally if no longer substantively viable, are in urgent need of public assistance and concern. Some of this assistance can occur through their maximal utilization to secure debate and deliberation rather than sheer "output" for its own sake, as in parliamentary systems, or institutional deadlock, as one often finds in presidential systems. In all cases the objective is the process as well as the outcome. While I would agree that it is conceivable that good process could yield bad outcomes, I think it is far clearer that efficiently (or inefficiently) produced outcomes in the absence of good process are self-feating in all representative democratic systems in the long run.

Representation is a complicated way of securing the public will and interest on issues of moment, but I would argue that it is not only unavoidable if there is to be democracy in large systems but necessary if the best outcomes are to occur. It may once again seem strange for me to argue that the public's decisions are often better *in an objective sense,* and not just because it "ought" to be represented. I would go even further and argue that it is madness to waste this incomparable resource in favour of occupational or material life in whatever its manifestations.[1] I do not rest content with the idea that it is morally right that the public should be self-governing through its representatives. I claim that this is an objective property of human development so central that its absence or loss consigns the relevant society to outcomes in the policy field which are not only morally bad and socially pernicious but objectively inferior. Meantime, the atrophy of process which such incessant short-circuiting and manipulation has brought about underscores the increasing difficulty of realizing this "new instauration" with every passing year.

The key factor underlining the situation we face is of course the equation of citizenship with the passive acquisition and manifestation of membership in its many forms, and the relation this bears to Society's view of property and capital as a resource requiring stewardship rather than providing the basis for politics. Coupled with this, to be sure, is the failure of the capitalist surplus to generate such possibilities, even if they seemed to some to be the self-evident best outcome of all this enterprise, accumulation, investment, production, innovation and growth. The answer lies in what is required of societal members in order to keep the system in constructive equilibrium and provide the basis for growth.[2] Few things have been more central to industrial capitalism in its mature phase than the necessity of subjecting mass populations to overlapping roles and functions concerned with perpetuating the system's economic and technological output, whether in the sphere of occupations and careers or in the areas of consumption and leisure. System stability and rationality presuppose a continuing fit between these variegated roles and functions if the performance claims touted by the system of secondary socialization are to have any meaning and effect.

None of this is to argue for a zero-sum view of the relation between political development and economic and/or technological advance. Such a suggestion is thoroughly incompatible with my view of relations between the political and governmental and the societal and economic. Also, there is the question of economic and technological progress themselves, for it is not self-evident, or even demonstrable, that these alleged processes can be said to possess objective content and validity, even within given historical periods and epochs. While an institutional infrastructure for advanced industrial society is emerging as a basis for the sedimentation of "rationality" in structures, this infrastructure permits us no assurance that the economic and technological outcomes being generated are guided by factors any the less arbitrary than could be discovered of parallel outcomes in so-called "primitive" cultures. It is important when analyzing these developments not to be so caught up in the rhetoric that produces us as well-socialized societal members that we ignore the contingent nature of technological progress in particular. Here what turns out to be important is the role of capital allocation decisions in all industrial systems, whether based on corporate or state capital, or a mixture of the two.[3]

Thus my objective throughout has been to argue that it is possible to secure a higher level of political development without sacrificing any necessary material comforts. Indeed, I would argue that a more rational organization of collective life so that it no longer resembles what we today call Society is unlikely in the absence of political management, or some variation on it. The present suppression of politics, the political and the public as citizens, apart from their status as members, means that we are not only less developed than we could be but less developed than we need to be. As a matter of fact, I would argue that in light of the problems already cited and discussed we are becoming progressively less developed every day. Our difficulty in accepting the strong likelihood that we could have a materially abundant society which shares its surplus with those less fortunate and at the same time is characterized by some form of what I have called political management arises out of our tendency to equate Society with collective life itself rather than seeing it as a culturally and historically specific *form* of collective life. We assume that the present mix of "role sets," where citizenship is equated with membership, is absolutely essential to our present form of material life when this is true only in the most limited and superficial sense.

What I have in mind by the distinction between what is materially necessary and what is presently available to consumers, audiences and occupationals in advanced industrial societies is evident from an earlier discussion. Here I noted industrial capitalism's reliance on the individual's willingness to permit an infinite expansion of the category of need by those who direct the processes of need satisfaction. Much of what is said to be needed is clearly not necessary, yet it is the opposite assumption that has, until recently, made the fortune of late capitalism. While one might argue that public "interference" in the mechanisms of institutional delivery systems can only lead to instability and disorder in the ways so often pointed to to dissuade the public from its "irrational" views and criticisms, my argument is that only public controls and effective supervision of representatives, complemented by direct action where this is appropriate and comports with the rule of law, can actually succeed in realizing a much needed equilibrium between political development on the one hand and economic and technological development on the other. The present disequilibrium becomes all the more problematic when it is realized how dependent an allegedly "objective" thrust in technological innovation is on the accelerated production of experts and specialists, complemented by technocratic co-optation of processes of representation and policy making in governments.

There is a sense in which one could argue that economics, and economic development as a priority, has for far too long had a monopoly of the process of technological innovation in Western societies. By this I mean to point to institutionalization in general, and non-economic institutions of a political and cultural kind in particular, as prerequisites for the sorts of social or collective innovations so necessary to achieving the equilibrium we need. The idea of a gap between the economy's present monopoly of technique and technology, and the needed assertion and affirmation of politics and the political as both process and display is not new. What has not really been addressed is the fact that this equilibrium is absolutely necessary if we are ever to bring economic development and representative democracy into line with one another. The necessity of doing this is based on the objective superiority of the public rather than any set of moral imperatives, as noted. We have only a short time to rectify this situation in order to offer a timely constructive example to Third World countries, as well as a beacon to peoples presently living under totalitarian and despotic governments. Our superiority from the standpoint of production, consumption and leisure, however clear, is no substitute for political management and the needed equilibrium, nor can we expect it to be in the future.

II

In what follows, I want to look at a series of arguments that have been produced and promoted, as often by the people as by their agents, experts and by thinkers and scholars, regarding the alleged hopelessness, meaninglessness or danger of political management and the needed equilibrium. Here we shall discover that a good deal of the argument against political management is premised on a conception of rationality which *begins* by assuming that reason is *not* a well distributed capacity which people ordinarily can be presumed to possess simply by dint of being human. The point about any redefinition of reason as rationality that fails to organize itself around this presumption is that it ignores precisely what it needs in order to make *its* claims intelligible. Thus, the equation of rational capacity with institutional training and certification, found in professional and technocratic views, with a power position in some organizational hierarchy, as in managerial and bureaucratic views, or with scholarly and scientific background and performance, as in the intellectual view, only makes sense because there is a foundational capacity lying beneath such superstructural "effects" to which their producers, along with everyone else, must continually return.

The problem becomes both more significant and more urgent when it is remembered that the public in all the advanced societies ordinarily defers to such individuals and groups, and that this normally makes good sense where those in question are speaking as experts of one kind or another on some matter where expertise on its own is highly relevant. The problem arises from the fact that individuals frequently permit a legitimate claim to special knowledge to shade over into areas where such considerations should not have any such claim to deference. This is all too evident in the myriad of issues that governments are required to encounter and deal with in and through political process. Turning to one or another of the groups cited to legitimize public policies is at best self-serving where the purpose is to short-circuit debate and deliberation in the name of output and efficiency. At worst, it contributes further to the atrophy of representative institutions and mechanisms while it conditions members of the public to view citizenship as a role option to be rarely if ever exercised. Instead, the bundle of functions that might be needed and required are turned over to representatives, bureaucrats, technocrats, regulators and judges and magistrates on grounds that they are the relevant "occupationals" to perform this work in advanced industrial societies.

This view of government and law as simply another part of Society's complex division of labour is what underwrites this de facto *permanent* delegation while effectively justifying public passivity. Such a perspective on politics and governance makes it all the more likely that significant numbers of the public can be kept in a state of suspended animation about such matters, while at the same time supporting the position that a hierarchical or scientific version of rationality is superior in an objective, rather than simply a functional, sense to "public opinion." Note that it is only as a consequence of a situation in which the field of reasonableness is coopted by the special and superstructural rationalities that it is even conceivable that the public could accept its views as mere "opinion." There is an all-too-familiar reminder of Plato's contrast between knowledge and opinion in *The Republic* evident in this distinction, and it is problematic precisely to the extent that Society's division of labour is itself seen to possess objective validity, and therefore to apply to governmental and political structure and processes as well as to other areas of collective life.[4] Every point of emphasis in the development of human personality cited by the social and behavioural sciences only underwrites and extends these developments, hardly a surprise given the clear *societal* bias of these disciplines.

I would put the issue in the following way to highlight its gravity while suggesting an approach to its resolution. How is it even possible for the public to understand and appreciate arguments produced by those in the superstructure in the absence of reason as a well-distributed *human* resource? This question, and the discussion leading up to it, may seem unsatisfactory to those anxious for a methodical or strategic problem-solution fix based on causilinear and serial-sequential approaches and assumptions. I have purposely addressed the problem as I see it without recourse to such approaches and assumptions for the same reason that I take issue with any notion or norm of progress based mainly or exclusively on economy and technology. Paolo Freire put the matter most convincingly when he noted that no attempt to lead or direct the public can be expected to do anything more than perpetuate the present tutelage. The essence of the problem is the requirement that any proposed solution in the existing modes begin by assuming that such passivity is going to continue. This definition of the problem in a certain sense predefines its own range of possible "solutions", and is unsatisfactory for this very reason. "Objective conditions" may be appealed to, but certainly not Marx's (or Lukács') proletariat.[5]

To the argument that the mass media and the onset of video data terminals and personal home computers are likely to reverse present trends, my answer is the same as it was earlier when I drew attention to the limits of direct democratic techniques *whenever* they cease to be occasional supplements and come to function as substitutes for representative democratic processes. A major difficulty with the mixed presidential and cabinet system brought into being after the French Constitutional Convention of 1958 was precisely the way that President de Gaulle employed direct techniques as a way of circumventing the assembly and the legal government of France. This example is only the tip of the iceberg, as it were, when compared to the ongoing redefinition of politics and public issues as part of entertainment and leisure in a collective that rigidly bifurcates work and non-work activities on the basis of roles and role sets in the ways noted. Passivity is enshrined, while privatization and the absence of discussion and deliberation combine with it to make the very idea of public matters meaningless where it cannot be fitted into the societally biased requirements of order and function. The fact that these matters are being dealt with superstructually on the basis of functional rationality only underscores the political poverty of such an understanding of reason and the reasonable.

If no set of suggestions which simply perpetuate the sort of passivity and tutelage on which the equation of citizenship and membership is based will "work," and if all efforts to design and implement conscious strategies and techniques based on the presumed superiority of superstructural modes of rationality cannot hope to succeed, then what does this tell us about the way we have conceptualized the problem? Beyond what I have already suggested, it tells us that Society is not only a culturally and historically specific form (or mode) of collective life rather than a synonym for it, but that forms or modes of collective life always *include* all the ways that have been produced or generated within them in order to comprehend them, whether through theory, experience or disciplined observation. If this is so, then one can expect only a limited amount of assistance from intellectual and professional disciplines *independent* of prevailing forms, biases and assumptions. It is therefore hardly surprising to have to acknowledge the very conditional validity and ability of such activities and endeavours from a practical perspective. Practicality in the Aristotelian sense is so different from our present equation of the practical with the technical, the methodical and the strategic and tactical that it is often difficult for us to see how these differing conceptions of reason and rationality can ever be reconciled.

The answer might be said to lie in "objective conditions" only in the most superficial sense, because here we are essentially invoking Hegel's equation of the rational and the real, albeit in a different guise. While this clearly gets around some of the not-so-obvious problems raised by strategic or methodical approaches that presuppose only a very limited conception of the problem-solution fix, its invocation suggests that there really is no solution at all, if only because there can in the strict sense be no possibility of getting outside these conditions in order to affect them in ways that do not comprehend the inclusion of those doing the manipulating as well. Perhaps this is the best thing that can be said of such an approach, namely, the way it turns us away from major reliance on causilinear and serial-sequential notions of problem and solution which presume both the possibility and the desirability of *final solutions*. The fact that there are no final solutions in collective life and living underscores the importance of politics and the political, understood as both process and display, while it points to the unsatisfactory nature of proposals which begin in the assumption, often found in mathematics and technology, that final solutions are not only possible but desirable.[6]

Appeal to objective conditions comes at too high a price, however, if this is all that reliance upon it can offer anyone seriously interested in reviving representative institutions and processes while providing for the emergence of the new public spaces indicated. It is a counsel to leave things as they are, or perhaps a reference to the *possibility* that some proposed intervention or suggestion might work after all because the time is "right" for it. But since there is no way of knowing this in advance, or acting as if one were outside the system when he clearly is not, it still does not allow for advance planning, particularly given unanticipated and unintended conditions. In the present circumstances of international and national-state developments in advanced industrial societies, such reliance is all the more problematic because of the very pace of change and development, and our inability to generate contemplated cause and effect scenarios with confidence due to institutional, technical and related forms of complexity. Thus the issue is less whether foreknowledge of objective conditions provides for advance planning and successful intervention, and more whether once they are known there will be sufficient time to take action to modify or change them in line with desired collective political and social options.

Schelling addressed this dilemma as a unique property of advanced industrial societies over ten years ago in an effort to show that neither claims to foreknowledge of future conditions nor "beneficent" motives and intentions suffice to make sense of such efforts any longer. The point was to show that planning presupposes either that the system in question remains pretty much as it is, or alters only in response to a finite and limited number of factors allegedly known in advance. In addition to this sort of limitation, which simply affirms the inclusion of economics as well as the social and behavioural sciences within Society, there is a rather different issue related to time and temporality. The very appearance of a likelihood of an undesired development in Society may *ipso facto* indicate that things have gone too far and that it is *already* too late to intervene in an attempt to change or modify incipient developments. The implication of Schelling's remark is that now more than ever before Hegel's observation that the owl of Minerva rises only at dusk is intended not as a counsel of futility, but rather as a goad to the development of new steering techniques and strategies which do *not* presuppose exclusion, but require us to acknowledge the limits of functional rationality and the urgent need for citizenship and participation apart from the ascription of membership.[7]

What is at stake is the need to realize that objectivity and the objective as both means and end is only wrong or misplaced where it fails to take account of the real object – the whole. There is also the very cogent criticism of contemporary expertise in all its manifestations because it encourages the public to take a dim view of itself and to exaggerate the *objective* contribution that expertise and knowledge can really make to policy issues and questions. Politics combines the comprehension of questions regarding how life is to be lived with more immediate problems concerned with appropriate institutions of government and governing in its understanding of practice and the practical, and it is most unfortunate that this Aristotelian insight has been lost in the modern territorial state. There are *two* Aristotles on this score, and they are certainly complementary, however incompatible they may be in the ways already noted. This is evident from a careful reading not only of the *Ethics* and *Politics,* but of *The Constitution of Athens* as well. And it is Aristotle's original attempt to reconcile the good man and the good citizen which I have found most helpful in addressing the present situation, where citizenship is equated with, rather than distinguished from, societal membership.

Our problem is different from Aristotle's, not so much because of the growth of economy, industry, commerce and technology, but rather because of the effects these developments, along with many, many others, have had on efforts to improve the possibility of democracy in large systems jointly dependent on representation and the rule of law. Formulating the problem this way, just like redefining what constitutes my basis for progress in collective life, allows us to see yet again why present problem-solution notions are unsatisfactory. One is forced to wonder whether in the prevailing situation we ought not to count ourselves fortunate *precisely because* economics and the social, behavioural and managerial disciplines are so incapable of realizing their announced goals and objectives. I say this not in any spiteful sense, but in order to reaffirm the substantive basis of reason as a human property, well distributed, which we can no longer afford to employ solely for occupational and material purposes on the argument that the public is inept, and must look to elites in the superstructure – in almost every case non-elected – in order to have these roles and functions carried out under norms of efficiency and related notions of effectiveness.

III

In this section, I want to focus on egoism and the claim of self-interest in order to address what has been alleged to constitute another major property of the human condition standing in the way of political management. This issue is quite different from those criticisms which arise out of superstructural claims to special status undergirded by public acceptance. For in this latter case we are dealing with what is alleged to constitute the most easily identifiable property of "human nature" – egoism or self-interestedness. It is said to constitute an immovable obstacle to political management precisely because of its "naturalness." Here a number of interrelated themes and concerns which have been a staple of ancient, medieval and modern political theory in the West come together. These themes and concerns require careful analysis in the light of contemporary conditions and possibilities, not because they are either true or untrue, but because their very voicing points to the power of ideas and concepts, particularly when they simultaneously come from the superstructure and are on the whole fully endorsed by the general public in the societal substructure. The reciprocal character of this exercise in collective self-legitimation has only been made more problematic with the emergence of the claim to "rational domination" already cited.

A major argument against the possibility of political management is the claim that egoism and self-interestedness are incompatible with the alternative proposed because no such collective order could possibly survive the demands of selfishness. This argument ignores the fact that a similar claim was made earlier in modern Western development regarding the alleged incompatibility between individual-centred interests in accumulation and comparative advantage and the development of Society as a new and desirable form of collective life. Both arguments failed to take account of the extent to which individuation, in whatever form, is a collectively produced and sanctioned phenomenon almost by definition. This being the case, it becomes apparent that the real issue is not the disintegration of collective life from within as a consequence of self-interestedness, but rather whether there are forms of collective life that are more desirable than others given the preference for one over other modes of individuation. In this understanding, individuation can take on many forms of what might be termed self-interest, and self-interest in turn is seen to be no less collectively produced and sustained than individuation. The power of ideology is seen to argue for possibilities in the future that the very development of past and present collective forms fundamentally disputes.[8]

Much of what I am addressing here has its origins in the natural rights and natural law tradition of political and social thought. Thus the apparent tie to "nature," where nature is seen to be diametrically opposed to human institutions, which are understood to be "unnatural" *because they are human.* The paradox is that human beings are alleged to possess rights by nature which *their own* institutions have effectively sabotaged. Men are considered to be naturally entitled to rights which are backed up by laws of nature, but the idea of a natural entitlement has somehow been lost with the growth and reciprocal dynamism of human institutions, particularly modern institutions which make claims to legitimacy premised on their alleged superiority from a rational standpoint. The idea, more and more accepted in advanced industrial societies, that rationality inheres in structures rather than in individuals further exacerbates an already problematic development arising out of the way that institutions "cover over" man's essential nature. For here the claim is made that institutions no longer point to their durability and continuity as grounds for legitimacy, but to their aggregate and structural reasonableness *as well*.

The difficulty with arguments like these is that they no longer serve the cause of investing formally and functionally rational political and governmental institutions with renewed vitality in the ways I have addressed and recommended. When I argued earlier that man's nature as a political animal was effectively covered over by the success of legitimacy claims from institutions of modernity like science, science based technology, capitalism, industrialization, and the rule of law and bureaucracy, I meant to argue *against* the historical reference of natural rights and natural law because such doctrines have served as ballast for the growth of *Society* as a peculiarly apolitical organism more than anything else. Thus the reference for their utilization in virtually very case is prebourgeois and precapitalist structures based on prebendal and patrimonial administration. The growth of specifically *societal* institutions was probably given more aid and comfort by the work of Locke and Rousseau, however different their arguments are, than by any other modern political theorists, because of the emphasis placed in each case on the priority of the new collective form over any other way of ordering.[9]

One way of taking account of this influence would require us to look carefully at the concept of contract or compact that figures so prominently in natural rights and natural law thinking. Creation of such an "historical fiction" perhaps served the purpose, in Locke's case, of underlining the trusteeship function of governments *vis a vis* the *prior* compact that had *already* brought individuals together in a collective setting. But it did so at a very high price, as Wolin has pointed out in his analysis of the conformist properties of Lockeian and post-Lockeian liberal thinking. Endorsement of this relationship between the collectively societal and the political created the basic argument that would legitimize the subsequent atrophy of politics and the political in the face of the gigantic unfolding of Society and economy. Once again, the success of this latter project and its desirability and necessity in no wise required such atrophy, particularly after it became apparent that the further growth of the institutions cited above could no longer occur in the absence of a strong and continuous government presence. It was at this point that the concern for stability and order, now correlated with Hume's habits of obedience, should have given way to a far greater concern for *political* development.

In the case of Rousseau, the matter is, if anything, even clearer, for here we see a complementary endorsement by the very absence of an alternative to the legislator as Society itself. Even though Rousseau begins with a radical attack on institutionalization as an artificial encumbrance whose effect is to distort what human beings are by nature, he ends by underscoring a serious gap between his ideal of citizenship in the *polis,* and the far from simple life that was even then beginning to emerge in Western Europe. A parallel development in Rousseau's thinking which underscored this gap between his idealization of the city-state, and emerging realities and possibilities against which the ideal was at best nostalgic, was his reaction at an early date against the institutional cooptation of rationality and reasonableness. It was his equation of reason with the self-interest and negative individualism of Locke which led to a fullscale reaction against the idea of reason as a basis for collective life. Rousseau's problem lay in the fact that the then-prevalent view of reason as an individual property coincident with utility and best advantage was itself an institution central to the emergence and develop-ment of modernity for which he had no alternative.[10]

It was to some extent the confused status of nature and the allegedly natural relative to human beings and their institutions which has left us uncertain of the role these various theories played in actively legitimizing the emergence of "rational" institutions. One thing that is clear is the way that reason, understood as calculation aimed at maximizing one's utilities, itself comes to be institutionalized following Western industrialization. Thus it was not simply that a new view of self-interest which equated it with rational calcu-lations and individuation had come forward to challenge more "traditional" institutions, or even that this new view had itself in due course been insti-tutionalized. It was rather the way that reason and rationality were dis-tended from man's nature and treated as some perverse or artificial attri-bute, while at the same time being understood solely as a property of indiv-iduals rather than institutions, which served to sanction subsequent structu-ral developments only later acknowledged as instances of "rational domina-tion." Reason and nature only much later make an accord with one another, but by then superstructural auspices and modes of training had thoroughly coopted the very base that made sense of the claim and its subsequent acknowledgement.

Nature thus stands unreflexively for what Hegel called the concept in its nonconceptuality, while at the same time being viewed as a central deter-minant of human nature, albeit not the only one.[11] We are tied to nature because we are a part of "everything else" while yet being able to know this, and it is this latter aspect which points to that part of us which is distinct from nature, in the metaphysical if not the Biblical sense. Natural rights and natural law thinkers saw nature as the basis for asserting the individual's rights in the context of his apparent suppression by institutions, and tended to back this up by pointing to prior contracts or compacts which his fore-bears had allegedly entered into as rational individuals determined to esta-blish the basis of collective life and government once and for all. Political economy saw things in a way far closer to the utilitarians, since for them nature and our membership in it ultimately constrained our development rather than legitimizing and facilitating it. They felt it necessary to follow the lead of Hume, who once referred to natural rights, natural law and contractarian thinking as "nonsense on stilts." In a sense, the entire reference to nature ceased to be a very useful basis for thought and argument once industrialization and the subsequent growth of Society began to make its claims in support of the individual as the bearer of a rationality seen to be coincident with self-interest and egoism.

My emphasis on nature in the earlier discussion about now man can simultaneously be viewed as distinct from nature and yet be frustrated by his institutions from expressing his nature as a political animal was addressed not to natural rights, natural law, or an alleged prior compact which remains authoritative today, but rather to more conventional usage. It is the periodic appearance of this capacity across many cultures and time periods which evidences both its possibility and its necessity, as well as its rootedness in reason and rationality as a well-distributed human resource, which inspires such a claim in the face of Society's apolitical agenda for its citizens as members. The tension between reason and nature no longer allows us to make sufficient sense of present conditions to permit either term the sway it once had relative to the other. Institutions, on the other hand, as well as processes of institutionalization, remain no less significant than they were in the past, and no reference to their alleged functional rationality as a vehicle for formal meritocracy can modify this fact in any way. The main point relates instead to the capacity which an allegedly "objective" basis for legitimacy in legal-rational (meritocratic), rather than traditional and charismatic, authority has in underwriting public passivity and deference in ways more subtle, persuasive and consequential than were available to traditional and charismatic modes.[12]

I have gone further than simply citing Weber's three forms however, for it seems to me that there is a danger that the real reference of reason in the substructure, however much expressed by individuals, will be lost precisely because functionally rational and formally meritocratic institutions are traditionalizing, conventionalizing, even fetishizing, reason as a structural property coincident with an organizational and societal conception of collective order. With this fetishizing of institutions as rational rather than conventionally necessary goes a simultaneous downgrading of the individual and a reification of institutions. References to nature are disposed of by citing fallacies of logical reasoning and argumentation, as if it were even remotely possible to carry on discussions of a political and moral/ethical character without such terms and concepts playing a central role. The real issue, I would argue, is not whether such terms and concepts are employed, but whether those who inevitably utilize them for such discourse are willing to acknowledge it. Clarity and a mutual understanding and appreciation of these notions is one of the most important reasons for seeing the indispensability of politics both as process and display.

It is the way the claim of egoism and self-interest sanctions the prevailing conception of stability and order as organizationally produced which invalidates arguments against the possibility of political management based upon the fact that individuals are egoistic by nature. Ignored in all of this is not only the vested interest almost all of us have in the persistence of collective life and our continued membership in it, but the fact that self-interest has *always* had this collective reference. I emphasized earlier that the compact or contract, and its specific reference to natural rights based on laws of nature, is clearly an historical fiction intended to validate the individual, but at the price of his submission to Society, with its preference for an organizational conception of order and a legal-rational or meritocratic basis for legitimation. Self-interest may well be the best available hope for overcoming present passivity and deference, not in the narrow sense of a preoccupation with maximizing economic advantages, but as a consequence of the dawning realization that political management is essential in the form of process and display to the perpetuation and improvement of collective life in advanced industrial societies.

IV

Some of the other reasons advanced to show the impossibility of political management, not surprisingly, bear a striking similarity to the list put forward in chapter eight against the possibility of a responsible social science. In both instances, we are asked to indulge ourselves as members of the public in the well-established pastime of collective self-abasement. Alternatively, we can view ourselves, in the guise of writer and readers, as if *we* were an elite, in which case members of the "lay" public become a distinct group with a distinct problem rather than a clear opportunity to make the most of a crisis. Justice Holmes and John Dewey may have been required to confine their encomiums on behalf of the public to Holmes' famous "can't help" dictum, in which he argued that he couldn't help being for democracy and the sovereignty of the people even though he knew that elites were indispensable because the public could not, after all, govern itself.[13] I shall take up this elite theme further on in this and in the final chapter, but suffice it to say here that the idea of a split between the ideal and the actual situation fundamentally misconstrues the requirements of representation because it equates citizenship with membership and asserts that the former category or role must always be monopolized by agents.

Other major reasons, apart from the ones already cited, for turning aside arguments in support of political management include lack of ability, lack of interest as a result of preoccupation with other pursuits, or the desire to be governed based upon Fromm's "fear of freedom." These themes tend to dominate popular thinking, and serve to justify the prevailing approach to governance in advanced industrial societies based on democratic elitism and/or elite accommodation. Lack of ability, as I have pointed out on several occasions, presupposes that we "know" what we mean by the term, and that a particular set of properties can be isolated, either in advance of their required utilization, or *post hoc*, as a way of evaluating or justifying given decisions or actions. Such objectification is one of the least comforting trends of our age, functioning as it does as a way of downgrading the importance of process, deliberation and discussion. We do not have to look very far for the consequences of objectifying the notion of intelligence as a stable property either. It serves the ideology of rational domination by thoroughly undermining any appreciation of reason as a human property of the substructure which continues to be very well distributed in spite of unceasing efforts to invoke closure and status as a basis for the legitimation of organizational hierarchies and orders.[14]

Ability is employed, to be sure, more as a vehicle for getting the public to effectively disfranchise itself than as a way of validating politically-elected representatives in their "role" as agents. To the extent that this latter becomes a persistent feature of government in advanced industrial societies, it does so mainly in the manner that was discussed in chapter six. Politically elected officials need technical, functional or professional expertise in order to have the appropriate information on which to base policy decisions and choices. They necessarily depend as a consequence on bureaucrats, technocrats, lawyers, scientists, technologists and a wide range of professional and non-professional interest and lobby groups. I tried to make it clear that I have no criticism whatsoever of this requirement, but am mainly concerned with the way that professional and scientific authority, and the capacities and skills of special interests, are frequently permitted to become the sole basis for choices and lines of policy development about which the public is fundamentally ignorant. One is obliged to wonder whether the concern for stability and order has not manifested itself in these circumstances in a way designed to pacify the public by deflecting it into non-political roles and functions whose purpose is to affirm membership alone.

It is easy anough to extend this concern on the part of legal, professional and governmental agents by pointing to complexity, unpredictibility and the need for efficiency and dispatch in order to argue *against* anything as time-consuming as trying to "teach" the public about issues that are really beyond them, except in the most superficial sense. The same procedure holds for the organizational conception of collective order found throughout Society that holds for the asymmetrical and one-way approaches of the social, behavioural and managerial disciplines toward their subjects as objects. The public becomes a de facto "respondent" when it accepts the "efficiency and dispatch" argument as a basis for justifying the refusal of various elites and experts to discuss, deliberate and clarify the issues, no matter how complex. It is important not to be overly carried away by the argument from objective expertise and corollary public ignorance, for this argument functions in the main as a justification for non-democratic decision procedures *given* the *prior* commitment to an organizational, managerial, and technocratic conception of order, efficiency and effectiveness.[15]

The idea here is that the world as a politically, economically, and militarily sensitive patient really cannot afford more than periodic lip service to formalized representative mechanisms if we are to survive and prosper. Economics is pitted against politics and the political in this equation, since the idea is to argue, as I noted before, that process and display regarding public matters may well redound to our economic disadvantage. Japan, as well as other nations with an equally brief history of representative democracy and the rule of law, are cited as cases in point justifying vigorous efforts to turn national states either totally or sectorally into giant firms and workhouses in behalf of survival and growth in the emerging international economy. What is problematic beyond the requirement of organizational efficiency and effectiveness, and the effect this has on process and display, is the manner in which knowledge and expertise is defined in such a way as to *exclude* the political field and the substructure at one and the same time. In effect, the only kind of knowledge and expertise worth having is narrowly technical, functional and professional, because it alone is alleged to be sufficiently "objective" to be capable of operating speedily and on its own independent of context and of the public and its problems.

What I am saying here ties in directly to the problem of contemporary formulations of reason and rationality cited earlier. The least cumbersome form of reason is the most objective, therefore the best, because of the way it can be insulated from debate and discussion. These latter function mainly as a sop to get a reading on some inchoate "public opinion", so that governments or private interests can move ahead relatively undisturbed *and without the need of serious deliberation*. Thus polls are equally amenable to my earlier criticism of direct democracy not only because they short-circuit process and render display impossible, but because their purpose is to *avoid* the kind of discussion and deliberation which might release the public from its position on the receiving-end as respondents. Better to anticipate all possible developments, formulating policy proposals and taking decisions in order to avoid the loss of time and consequent loss of (organizational and managerial) effectiveness which goes hand in hand with representative democracy, supplemented by the emergence of the new public spaces which I have argued are essential for the proper functioning of mechanisms and processes as they exist in the present setting.

"Ability" and "capacity" is the rankest sort of ideology, then, because it takes advantage of the public by playing on its confidence in functional rationality, its belief in formal meritocracy, and its commitment to an organizational and managerial conception of stability and order. This in spite of the fact that claims on behalf of the superiority of technical, functional and professional modes of rationality only constitute a sensible basis for jettisoning display and process, debate and deliberation, if a thoroughly anti-political conception of effectiveness based on narrow criteria of efficiency is presumed to be indispensable. The interaction of time and complexity, coupled with the view of collective life as economy and membership through the ascription or acquisition of a panoply of passive roles and "functions," thoroughly justifies the incessant use of mass media and polls to shore up the anti-political bias of Society by allowing it to avoid everything that makes representation valuable when there is no viable direct democratic option available in place of it. Again it must be asked whether the purpose of representation is to maximize public participation while acknowledging the limits posed to its exercise, or to employ existing mechanisms and processes, along with public self-doubt, in order to avoid the constraints on efficiency and dispatch that it clearly involves.

Another set of overlapping concerns are encountered when we turn to the next argument against political management. Here it is less ability in a direct sense, and more the fact that members of the public are so preoccupied with other matters which are simply more important to them that they have no time and/or interest in matters political which is at issue. This readily shades into the trusteeship and delegation argument mounted most persuasively by Locke, for the idea is clearly that these activities are necessary requisites for the persistence of any collective. It is the configuration that the present permanent delegation has taken, however, which serves to underscore the fact that Society, as a culturally and historically specific form of collective life rather than a synonym for it, *needs to* redefine and modify representative, governmental and political mechanisms and processes so that they function vestigially and in a predominantly formal manner. That it suggests a link between Locke's conception of trusteeship or agency, and the need for stability and order in behalf of the emergence of Society as economy, should hardly come as a surprise. It is, after, all, central rather than peripheral to liberalism as a dominant ideology in modern democratic societies, for reasons that Wolin above all has made clear.[16]

From the standpoint of interest rather than time alone, the issue is not to cater to the public by giving it more information or access to information, since this redounds mainly or exclusively to the advantage of special interests. Without disputing the indispensable contribution such groups make to government and governance in advanced industrial societies, it must be clear that theirs is a necessary but not a sufficient condition for public policy formulation and implementation, something which is becoming more obvious with every passing year. The same or similar reasons can be cited in support of this position that were just cited in criticism of the idea of expertise and specialized knowledge as objective, efficient and independent of the substructure. Process, discussion and deliberation are *not* simply to be understood as formal or formalized rites of passage that agents and private interests "go through" or endure because the public needs to be pacified and given its "symbolic reassurance." They have *substantive* value for the same reason that thought and deliberation have always been known to be valuable, and it is only our present obsession with the organizationally and managerially efficient use of objective time ordained by Society as economy, and citizenship as membership, that blinds us to this fact.

Debate and deliberation, therefore time, is precisely what is and always has been necessary for the substructural capacity of commonsense rationality to surface and show its mettle. This in contrast to the *derivitive* resource held by a small portion of the people in their capacity as experts, members of one or another elite, and theorists, for in this case we are addressing a type of rationality whose alleged objectivity goes hand in hand with the independence it is seen to deserve because it is efficient and can be brought to bear on a problem rapidly and in a way which engenders *silence* rather than talk and discussion. The reason for not ignoring the resource held by all the people is therefore directly related to the present highly dangerous international situation, one which is almost completely a product of ignoring the people, whether for "traditional" or modern reasons justifying autocracy, or for contemporary ones focussed on time and the requirement of efficiency if Society is to be properly organized and managed. The point, however, is that the present ideology of rational domination has much more to answer for for assisting in the realization of this result than do alternative forms of regime in the second and third worlds. In effect, we have been persuaded that democracy must yield to societal and economic imperatives and priorities if it is to survive in any form whatsoever.

The question of the interest of the people, while not the same as one concerned with whether they do or do not have the time, clearly shades into the latter consideration when one realizes how closely linked the time to study and think about matters political is to the development of interest. In chapter seven I suggested that it is likely to be only immediate interests of a directly material nature which will move individuals heretofore apolitical to participate actively. A supplement to this, of course, has resulted from the emergence of new possibilities for the exercise and display of politics as a public activity. The form these activities has taken provides evidence of the role and significance of mass media as a device for circumventing established mechanisms and processes. In competition with what are alleged to constitute *other* forms of societal membership, citizenship has a difficult road to hoe. This is only reinforced by the fact that politics is viewed as down-time for everybody but politicians, experts and specialists. The public is persuaded that Society is first and foremost a division of labour where government and politics is a task best carried out by organizational, managerial and professional experts standing behind and effectively propping up public officials.

Interest in matters political, apart from instances in which one's material interest is seen to be directly affected, is often treated as bizarre and aberrant by other members of the public. Such individuals are understood to be busybodies or cranks in our highly conformist society, since if political activity is neither an immediate response to the direct impact of political decision-making on one's self, family or neighbourhood, nor someone's job in the societal division of labour, it is judged to be irrational in the ways noted.[17] The first "good reason" for such activity would be "rational" self-interest, while the second would point to functional rationality as the basis for the organizational conception of order, discipline and productivity central to the *societal* division of labour. Lack of interest, apart from its *suppression* by individuals who realize they cannot "justify" it on one or the other of these grounds, must be counted in large part a consequence of a socialization agenda which favours occupational function and career on the one hand and leisure, consumption and spectating as its "other side". A final point of some importance concerns the zero sum game that politically interested individuals are seen to be playing with their economic well-being in the absence of sufficient income. While such income is normally assumed, its absence is offered as proof of the essential irrationality of such individuals.

When interest is not immediate, by dint of either one's perceived self-interest or his functional role orientation to occupational performance, it is all-too-often judged to be non-existent or insignificant. I would continue with the position just articulated and argue that this fact necessitates not reversion to one or the other form of "rationality" presently acceptable in advanced industrial societies, but rather an attempt to overcome the demands of objective time with its bias towards a semi-permanent delegation to elites, experts and advisors. The idea that man's nature as a political animal necessitates this sort of special effort to allow it to flourish only

reaffirms my point about the conditions required for commonsense rationality as a substructural resource and human property to make its inimitable
and absolutely indispensable contribution to the sense and quality of politics. Just as representational processes and mechanisms are not mere symbolic forms lacking in substantive value for which we can readily substitute a
combination of narrow expertise, technocratic steering and direct democratic techniques and polls, so also with the capacities and power of the
people. That time is required for such capacities and powers to surface
should hardly count against them, but our present understanding of the
relation between politics, economics and collective life has led to just such a
conclusion in advanced industrial societies.

A final argument more categorically negative than any of those preceding it
is the claim that the people will accept anything short of the kind of tyranny
that produces the "objective conditions" for revolt and transcendence rather
than govern themselves. Erich Fromm called this phenomenon the "fear of
freedom," and Eric Hoffer subsequently labelled the individuals prone to
such a disposition as "true believers." The need to belong to and participate
in group or collective activity can be distorted into a- or anti-political channels and forms of expression, particularly where the history and traditions of
a people do not include democracy along-side the rule of law. For this
reason, one may appear warranted in dismissing these concerns as misplaced in countries with democratic traditions. Sinclair Lewis addressed this
point of view critically in his *It Can't Happen Here,* and it is a theme that
many others have concerned themselves with.[18] My argument for political
management stressed the imperative need for public participation in established representative and newly emergent public spaces not because I
feared tyranny or despotism as it is classically defined or understood. It was
rather the indispensability of such active and continuing participation to the
quality of public policy-making given present developments and trends that
I wanted to draw attention to.

The question for advanced industrial societies is how much longer we can
afford a system of government and politics based on functional rationality
and formal meritocracy as the essence of Society's organizational principle
in practice. Citizenship must no longer function as one amongst many passively ascribed or acquired roles expressive of societal membership. Fromm
and Hoffer were correct to point out the presence of a need to belong and
participate, but the form this need takes in an effort to realize itself must
change if wholesale alienation and anomie is to be avoided. Societal roles
can certainly provide a solid basis for membership, yet even here such "participation" can often be alienating or isolating because of the nature of what
nowadays passes for individuation. The fact that such a need exists therefore
talks as much to the desirability of alternate forms of collective life as it does

to the necessity for political display as distinct from *any* non-political forms of collective membership, societal or otherwise. Politics in the contemporary context must take shape as *both* representative process and personal display if human beings in advanced industrial societies are ever to achieve active individuation. If bourgeois negative individualism was an active but relatively unavailable form, post-bourgeois positive individualism is available but relatively passive in nature. Politics as process and display can realize a merger of activity and availability, and is therefore not only the best possible form individuation should take in advanced industrial societies, but one that is absolutely indispensable for the reasons indicated.

V

In this concluding section I want to focus on one particular line of research and study in political science and the social sciences. I have particularly in mind the concepts of democratic elitism and elite accommodation, and it is to the operative notion of democracy as much as the conception of elite that I shall direct my attention. Elite theory in general, as distinct from class analysis in the Marxian tradition, has sought to address the hierarchical nature of collective life, either in order to point out its inevitability as in the case of Mosca, Pareto and Michels, or as a means of addressing the need for an alternate basis for stratification premised on what are alleged to be the more "open criteria" of merit and meritocracy. Democratic elitism constitutes an attempt to respond to the hierarchy-inducing effects of industrialization while at the same time retaining representative forms and processes in the ways indicated. Few things are clearer than the gap between the ideals of liberal democracy and the demands and requirements of an urban industrial order based on commitment to the organizational conception of collective order so central to Society.

Elite accommodation, on the other hand, focusses on the necessity of adapting democratic systems in advanced industrial societies to the need for the "representation" of various regional, ethnic, racial, religious, linguistic and cultural groups. If democratic elitism has arisen as a response to the gap between the ideals of liberal democracy and the realities of life in urbanized and industrialized society in the United States, elite accommodation is generally viewed as a major requirement of countries whose democratic form is seen to be consociational rather than individualistic. Arendt Lipjhart's studies of Belgium, Holland, Switzerland and Austria inaugurated this approach, which has in recent years been somewhat modified, and Robert Presthus has argued that Canada provides overwhelming evidence of the presence of both elite accommodation and consociational democracy. Both democratic elitism and elite accommodation and consociational democracy have been employed to explain, and perhaps even to justify, the system's failure to move further in a truly democratic and participatory direction in the way I have argued is increasingly necessary. For this reason, such theories, concepts and frameworks require careful study as ways of *producing* particular results, rather than merely as a neutral means to their discovery.[19]

This matter becomes clearer when we realize that the neutrality of an elite focus only purchases this assessment either by turning on class analysis as an empirically dubious (rather than a morally unsatisfactory) approach to the study of stratification and social structure, or by addressing the naïvete of those who still realistically expect to produce a truly representative and participatory democratic order without losing the benefits of a stratification system based on functional rationality and formal meritocracy. It is much less popular to argue nowadays that elitism is simply inevitable, thus that we must accept and "accommodate" to it. Disciplines like political science and sociology are mobilized in order to provide good reasons why the concept of elite, as well as an elite focus and framework, constitute the best basis for studying in a value-neutral fashion the essential characteristics of advanced industrial societies. One thing these disciplines do is to quickly distinguish their allegedly neutral methods and approaches from those of class analysis. The Marxian reflex in this latter case is said to generate a persistent bias which is all-too- readily reflected in the failure of the concept of class to faithfully reproduce the present stratification order with fidelity.

This failure is seen to invalidate class analysis as a respectable and responsible social-scientific (or political-scientific) approach. An elite approach of one kind or another is infinitely to be preferred because it provides just enough framework but not too much. Besides, it is argued, an emphasis on elites has been employed to a number of different, even conflicting, intellectual and ideological ends, in contrast to the concept of class, which always endeavours to realize the same general objective. This characteristic of an elite focus is seen to demonstrate its neutrality as a tool which can be counted on to stand outside the battle zone between different ideologies and world views. An interesting case in point illustrative of this apparent difference is to be discovered in the work of the Canadian sociologist John Porter. Porter began his studies of stratification by addressing Canadian social structure using the concept of class. Only later did he switch to what has been called a "strategy of respectability" and employ an elite rather than a class-focussed approach. Indeed, Porter saw as a major objective of his pathbreaking study *The Vertical Mosaic* the obligation to actually employ an elite approach in order to invalidate an emphasis on class.

Class was not a truly empirical category in the final analysis any more than it could be employed in a neutral way to produce a wide range of research results. An elite focus, on the other hand, was not only neutral for the reasons cited, but provided a relatively faithful replication of the way advanced industrial societies actually were. Class tended on the whole to overestimate the role of conflict and confrontation, while an elite approach allowed those who used it in research to take account of either the presence of or the need for competition and circulation. If class tended to polarize, an elite approach focussed on either democratic elitism or elite accommodation showed the presence and significance of pluralism while at the same time admitting the inevitability of elites. The idea of emphasizing pluralism is to underscore how competition between and circulation of elites is actually not only compatible with but constitutes *the essence of* democracy in advanced industrial societies. The variegated substantive results of an emphasis on elites validate this approach to political and social research by pointing to the range of results as evidence of a lack of bias.

The point, however, is to realize that the scope of these studies may appear to be wide-ranging and comprehensive but that they are all of a piece in the sense that they not only exclude the results of a class-focussed approach but its basic animus as well. Porter's strategy of respectability becomes synonymous with what its subsequent users would call a responsible social science. This in contrast to my more radical understanding in chapter eight, one based on the proposition that the social, behavioural and managerial disciplines increasingly constitute the basis for an emerging, and in some cases an already established, *form* of social interaction, rather than being simply a neutral means of studying such interaction at a distance from it. The point about value-neutrality is that it is a *cultural artifact* whose purpose is to favour certain sorts of research and discourage others. If an elite focus can lend itself to a wide-range of substantive and value outcomes, then this should compel us to concern ourselves as much with what is *excluded* from its ambit as with what is included within it. Concepts, frameworks and approaches are therefore "neutral" only in this highly qualified sense, and it is as much the theorists' job to discover the motives behind the determination to use them *because* of the scope they provide as it is when their animus is more straightforward and confined.[20]

The operative notion of the "empirical" is directly related to this claim of neutrality. Together they constitute the ideological light infantry of politics and sociology as allegedly scientific disciplines. The empirical is said to be best reproduced through professional and scientific efforts to achieve distance and neutrality. My concern with the fact that it is in the main a convention or artifact is addressed less to a criticism of social-scientific research methods for its own sake, and more to the way these disciplines function in a normative or prescriptive way as prototypes favouring a particular mode or form of societal interaction. A microcosm of the public found in a functionally rational and formally meritocratic division of labour is all-too-often to be discovered in the status of the subjects-as-objects who constitute the respondents in and to social-scientific research. Though nowadays it is more chic to label respondents "participants," the essential asymmetry of the research situation and the role of respondents as objects rather than subjects is readily in evidence in the way individual biographies are pulled apart and the pieces aggregated to form a new collective no less expressive of the law of large numbers than Arendt's "public" in advanced industrial societies.

I want to concentrate, in what remains, on the way that social-scientific research employing an elite approach has been used to support the need for a new basis for elitism in place of those values which are alleged to be conventional and therefore obsolete and inferior. Both Porter and Presthus were anxious to use an elite framework to this end in their studies of Canadian society, while in the United States a similar focus on "strategic" and "policy" elites has arisen in an effort to show how dependent advanced industrial societies are on these groups as repositories of essential expertise and technocratic steering capacities. All of the criticisms I have levelled at earlier arguments regarding the impossibility of political management are appropriate to a critique of most of this social-scientific research in politics and sociology. At the same time, I want to make it clear once more that this is *not* something these disciplines can ever hope to remedy. They are the "sciences" of professional discipline and formally meritocratic control in a collective order premised on functional rationality. It is their mission to normalize what Durkheim called the abnormal division of labour, and a major assumption they make to this end is that rational domination is an objective basis for stratifying collective life and that politics as process and display threatens this goal unless kept on a very short leash.[21]

The determination to put an elite approach in the service of displacing an existing elite system with meritocracy appeals to everything that is thought to be good about advanced industrial societies, with their rationality, organizational, and role and status biases and preferences. Like St. Simon and Comte, election of officials and representation in general is considered a necessary evil like citizenship itself. As a role option for everyone not personally or materially affected by particular policies, or living off government and politics as an employment or career, it is seen as a holdover or residue from an earlier time which must be honoured, at least formally, in the interests of stability and order. The rule of law is a slightly different matter, as I noted in chapter three and off and on throughout the book. Hence the desire to achieve stability and order by producing a legal-rational and constitutional order as the basis for the claim to objective rational domination is irresistible. In addition, of course, there is the virtual indispensability of the rule of law in one or another form to the organizational principle as it takes shape in legal and judicial support for capitalism, and for the discipline that is required in order to maintain a ready work force at all levels of the formally meritocratic system.[22]

For the most part, those who promote a focus on elites as a research tool in politics and sociology argue that there will inevitably be elites and that the best possible outcome would be one in which their present "ascribed" and "traditional" bases of selection and authority were supplanted by more meritocratic ones. The ideology of merit and meritocracy is pointed to as evidence of the superior "openness" of a collective order premised on such an organizing principle, while other bases for membership are disputed because they are ascribed rather than achieved, and expressive of a closed and restrictive order. A strong case can be made for the claim that meritocracy in practice is no less (just differently) generative of a closed system, not so much because of its restriction to a small stratum of the population, but rather because its values are so homogeneous as a consequence of secondary socialization in appropriate modes of thought and behaviour. This is not to argue that there is no element of restriction present, just to suggest that its basis is as different as are the scope and nature of its effects. People are exluded from the possibility of becoming a member of the meritocracy by dint of background and prior socialization, to be sure, but this is not the same thing as the automatic exclusion of ascription where this can be discovered.

As it turns out, however, it is rare to find ascription the sort of basis for exclusion that takes no account whatever of the need for "new blood" and circulation. Where this has happened, the elite in question has not been able to perpetuate itself. Thus ascription is not so polar a notion in practice as those who revile it in the name of achievement usually assume. On the other hand, what is true of ascription turns out to be true of achievement, looking at the distinction from the other side as it were. Apart from the way that achievement or performance is effectively conditioned by factors of an ascriptive nature like race, gender, ethnicity and class, from the standpoint not only of initial exclusion but subsequent employment, advancement and general recognition, there is the unavoidable gap between the meritocratic ideal and meritocracy in practice readily discoverable in modern work organizations. What happened to the ideal when it was formalized in organizational structures, first of the civil service and thereafter in public education, was that it began to function as a device for exclusion, security and closure as against objective competence and performance, in much the same way that Michels described in his classic study of a social democratic political party in Continental Europe after the turn of the century.[23]

Chapter 11

Formalization means not only that concerns for job security and tenure must follow fast on the initial meritocratic preference in order to protect civil servants from dismissal for partisan reasons. It also means that its alliance with openness, so persuasive when it was battling already defeated elites and other retrograde elements standing in defense of pre-bourgeois landed values, is effectively sundered by the way that competence and performance are assessed, if at all. Initial screening is the major barrier to meritocratic employment, and the capacity to secure a probationary position generally requires the presence of a supportive labour market in the relevant skills and interests coupled with proper secondary socialization in the correct values and appropriate modes of behaviour. Once the probationary period has been surmounted, ascribed factors like seniority coupled with tenure tend to take over. The result is a version of the Peter Principle in practice, as individuals are *assumed* to be competent *because* they occupy a given position in an organizational hierarchy as a full time employee. A more insidious upshot of the dispersion of this mode of employment throughout Society is to be discovered in the way people are presumed to be expert and competent *because* they are scheduled or appointed rather than elected.

The effects of formalization include the failure to really impose meritocratic criteria throughout such employment situations in order to dismiss the incompetent and keep the jobs open for "new blood." Meritocracy in practice does not aid either the circulation of elites nor competition between them, and anyone seriously expecting merit to prevail over meritocracy probably needs to reconsider the claim to neutrality and objectivity central to this ideology of rational domination. The point, of course, is that the meritocratic ideal is thoroughly unworkable in practice, no less than the idealized understanding of value-neutrality in the study of political and social phenomena. Michael Young pointed out many years ago just how unmanageable a real meritocratic order would be from the standpoint of regularity and predictibility. There is also the question of who does the evaluating and rating and whether they themselves are subject to such assessment and if so then by whom? I simply want to argue that this "model at sea" functions in a radically different way than its supporters intend or are willing to admit to, and that this shows how ideological and self-serving meritocratic values can be when they are seen to be formalized and effectively in place in order to guarantee rational domination.[24]

In an earlier book I argued that the problem for a culture glutted with formal meritocracies as vehicles for secure employment and the promise of consumption and leisure almost without regard for output functions is the same as that described by Karl Mannheim in his critique of functional rationality in its relation to matters involving judgment. As a major vehicle for reaffirming societal membership, with all that this has come to mean, the new elite may indeed be too large to be called either an elite *per se,* or an elite as a fragment of some dominant class. The problem of rational domination is precisely the way it offers a ready alternative, at least for now, to individuation through display and participation in political process. Meritocratic status hierarchies are the leading edge of what is a decidedly a or anti-political approach to collective life as a whole in advanced industrial societies. Lack of openness toward evaluating the merit of employees beyond initial probation produces a climate in which the fear of display and concern for matters political, underwritten by constraints on political participation for civil servants, generates and underwrites a corollary fear of responsibility and risk. This is an unavoidable outcome of the view already cited which sees rationality mainly, if not exclusively, as a property of structures rather than of individuals.[25]

The need for political management is further underscored by an understanding of the role played by political science and the social, behavioural and managerial disciplines in promoting formal meritocracy and functional rationality through their research and policy recommendations. I have argued that there is no real option to this because of the nature of these disciplines and their unavoidable bias in favour of Society as a synonym for collective life rather than a culturally and historically produced form of it. As things now stand, the possibility of overcoming the present socialization of the public in its own incompetence and unworthiness appears dim in the absence of the objective conditions which we would naturally like to avoid. Representation as a function and as a system appears increasingly beleaguered by the ever greater power of the pressure and interest group system, by the growth of new opportunities for political display which I have argued must remain in a supplementary position relative to established processes but may not, and finally by the rise of direct techniques of sampling and polling, as well as proposals to end-run process altogether in order to allow the public to "vote" on practically everything. The issue is joined as well by the radically different conditions which must emerge if the indispensable substructural resource in the hands of the public is to even begin to make the needed difference.

Expertise and specialized knowledge is no less superstructural in a collective sense than it is for those individual practitioners who have no choice but to reaffirm their membership in the substructure at every turn. To have organized and stratified such knowledge and knowledge-claims in and through formal meritocracy and functional rationality is to have forgotten how dependent we are as members on our concerns and commitments as citizens. The present non representative structures in advanced industrial societies are not just a- or anti-political, and therefore problematic for abstract moral and ethical reasons. I would even argue that ethics and morality bear a far closer resemblance in the contemporary setting to socialization for membership and, like sociability and gregariousness, are a necessary but not a sufficient condition for collective life and living. These structures can no longer carry the load which they have had to undertake as a surrogate for the representative system in the absence of citizen commitment to process and display. Government's role as a distributor of social welfare, a guarantor of technical progress, and a technocratic steering arm for the national-state as a "firm" competing with other states in the international market, such as it is, may seem complete and sufficient unto itself, but its widening ambit, arm-in-arm with large corporations and financial institutions, is a house of cards built on an increasingly shaky foundation.

References

1 John Stuart Mill, *Representative Government* (NY: Everyman edition, 1953), p. 205.
2 C. B. Macpherson, *Democratic Theory* (London: Oxford University Press, 1973), pp. 3–76.
3 Charles Lindblom, *Politics and Markets* (NY: Basic Books, 1977); Wilson, "Science, Technology and Innovation: the Role of Commonsense Capacities", *op cit.*
4 Plato, *The Republic,* translated with an introduction by H. D. P. Lee (Harmondsworth: Penguin, 1955), books 3–5; and J. S. Findlay, *The Discipline of the Cave* (London: Allen and Unwin, 1966).
5 Paolo Freire, *Pedagogy of the Oppressed* (NY: Herder & Herder, 1971), Chapter 2; Georg Lukács, *History and Class Consciousness,* (London: Merlin Press, 1971), pp. 295–342.
6 See my "Values: On the Possibility of a Convergence between Economic and Non-Economic Decision-Making," in *Management under Differing Value Systems,* edited by Gunther Dlugos and Klaus Weiermeir (Berlin: Walter de Gruyter, 1981), pp. 37–71.
7 Thomas Schelling, "On the Ecology of Micromotives," *The Public Interest,* No. 25 (Fall, 1971), pp. 59–98.
8 See Peter Wiles, "The Necessity and Impossibility of Political Economy," *History and Theory,* Volume 11 (1972), pp. 3–14, and my response in "Capitalism, Science and the Possibility of Political Economy" (forthcoming).
9 See John Locke, David Hume, and J. J. Rousseau, *Social Contract,* with an introduction by Ernest Barker (London: Oxford, 1960).
10 *Ibid.* pp. 169–307 at pp. 185–186, 190–220.
11 A. V. Miller, *Hegel's Concept of Nature* (Oxford: Basil Blackwell, 1970). Compare to Alfred Schmidt, *The Concept of Nature in Marx* (London: New Left Books, 1971).
12 Max Weber, *Theory of Social and Economic Organization* (Glencoe: Free Press, 1947), pp. 327–333.

13 See generally Peter Bachrach, *The Theory of Democratic Elitism* (Boston: Little, Brown, 1965).

14 Erich Fromm, *Escape from Freedom* (NY: Holt, Rinehart and Winston, 1941). On intelligence as an allegedly stable property, Herbert Blumer, *Symbolic Interaction* (Englewood Cliffs, N. J.: Prentice Hall, 1969), p. 175; and Stephen Jay Gould, *The Mismeasure of Man* (NY: W. W. Norton, 1971).

15 See my "Technocracy and Late Capitalist Society," *op cit;* and "Elites, Meritocracy and Technocracy: Some Implications for Political Leadership," *op cit.*

16 Sheldon Wolin, *Politics and Vision* (Boston: Little Brown, 1960), chapter on liberalism and the rise of Society and the social. John Locke, *Second Treatise of Government* in Locke, Hume, and Rousseau, *op cit,* pp. 1–143.

17 See this study, Chapter Seven "Is a Practical Science of Politics Possible?."

18 Sinclair Lewis, *It Can't Happen Here* (NY: New American Library, 1976, 1938).

19 Bachrach, *op cit* Arendt Lijphart, "Consociational Democracy," *World Politics,* Volume 21, No. 2 (1969), pp. 207–225; Lijphart, *The Politics of Accommodation* (Berkeley: University of California Press, 1968, 1975); Robert Presthus, *Elite Accommodation in Canadian Politics* (London: Cambridge University Press, 1973); Presthus, *Elites in the Policy Process* (London: Cambridge University Press, 1974); Presthus, "Evolution and Canadian Political Culture: the Politics of Accommodation," paper read to the Conference on Revolution and Evolution, Duke University, October 12–14, 1976). Note, particularly in light of my earlier references to Presthus' work, that he is mainly addressing the role of interest group activity in his research. Also see the discussion in *Consociational Democracy,* edited by J. D. MacRae (Toronto: McClelland and Stewart, 1974). Compare the preceding to Lijphart's, *Democracy in Plural Societies* (New Haven: Yale University Press, 1977), where he seems to modify his original position on the appropriateness of "consociationalism" as a *description* of the four countries he originally studied – the Netherlands, Belgium, Austria and Switzerland.

20 Wilson, "Elites, Meritocracy and Technocracy," *op cit,* addressing the thesis and general argument of John Porter, *The Vertical Mosaic* (Toronto: University of Toronto Press, 1965).

21 Durkheim, *The Division of Labour in Society,* pp. 353–395 at pp. 353–373; Wilson, *The American Ideology,* Chapters 1, 2, 5, 8 & 9; Wilson, *Tradition and Innovation,* Chapters 2–4.

22 See Michel Foucault, *Discipline and Punish* (NY: Random House, 1978); and, of course, Karl Marx, *Capital,* Volume 1, parts 3, 6 & 7.

23 Robert Michels, *Political Parties: A Sociological Study of the Oligarchical Tendencies of Modern Democracy* (NY: Collier Books, 1962).

24 Michael Young, *The Rise of the Meritocracy, 1858–2033* (Harmondsworth: Penquin, 1958). The reference to the model at sea is to Lord Halifax (George Savile), *A Rough Draught of a New Model at Sea,* an essay first written about 1686.

25 Wilson, *The American Ideology,* Chapter 9; "Elites, Meritocracy and Technocracy," *op cit;* David Lebedoff, *The New Elite: the Death of Democracy* (Chicago: Contemporary Books, 1983).

Chapter 12
The Privilege of Experience

I

If those who argue that experience is the best teacher are right, then it is little wonder that political management seems such a utopian notion to most of us. Occupational life and its "other side" – consumption, leisure and spectating – appear to have coopted the field so that anyone unable to show either an immediate personal interest or commitment to an occupation or career is suspect when they engage in the political and governmental process through activity and display. Time is money and time off from work is for the passive roles that reaffirm societal membership while they extend the requirements for conformity on into "private" life. So long as citizenship is seen to constitute nothing more than one among many potentially or actually available role options in advanced industrial societies, the idea that it is a way of affirming membership which is based on ascription rather than on individuation in and through display remains virtually unchallengeable. I am not arguing that the legal conception of citizenship which distinguishes natural born from naturalized citizenship is no longer relevant or necessary, just that it is not sufficient, and that it nowadays functions in a way which underwrites the idea that citizenship is an ascribed and permanent status.

The point about all this concern on my part relates only tangentially to any moral or ethical issues which arise for me as a consequence of the gap between the ideal and the reality of representative democracy. My real concern has already been expressed. It acquires moral or ethical significance because this gap raises serious *practical* problems for our present form of collective life. It is important *not* to view my argument regarding the urgent need for public participation, display and full utilization of established governmental and political mechanisms and processes as a mere gesture of exaggeration, an attempt to invest an "ought" with practical urgency. The reason there is a strong tendency to do this is clear once we consider the notion of practice and the practical presently operative in advanced industrial societies. Practice is nowadays almost always equated with the technical, methodical and strategic or tactical, which is to say that the Aristotelian understanding of practice as ethically informed activity based on reflection has been broken down into its constituent parts in a way which renders not only activity in the world but reflection and ethical and moral considerations incomplete and without essential direction. Ethics as a consequence is treated as if it were a subject for thought divorced from activity, while activity in the public sphere in turn loses any point of reference apart from the instrumental.[1]

Action in the world is affected in a practical sense not only by the absence of ethical considerations, but also by the absence of reflection and prior contemplation. The essential unity of thought and action in practice and the practical is sundered in a way which not only has consequences for elected representatives and non elected officials, but for the public as well. Indeed, the very idea of representation as agency and delegation paves the way for its eventual recognition as a permanent feature of the social division of labour under norms of functional rationality in a *formally* meritocratic structure. Once representatives and non elected officials are viewed as agents or delegates, where agency or delegation is equated with a fixed job or function in the occupational sphere, the basis for an organizational and managerial approach premised on hierarchy, status and closure is firmly in place. I am not saying that the present system is so totally unsatisfactory that it ought to be jettisoned. On the contrary. I am simply suggesting that as it presently stands the system is dangerously incomplete without sustained public interest and participation through process as well as display, and that this is clearly why present institutions can no longer handle the load.

Again, however, I want to stress that this is not just a response to the exponential enlargement of government functions which has arisen as a result of the growth of public and civil administration, regulation, social services, and the role of foreign and defense policy. Governmental and political institutions were *never* intended to carry the load that has arisen out of the static conception of representation as a fixed division of labour between agents and members. And no attempt to circumvent this fact by generating an alternative to it in the form of legal status alone can possibly suffice. To be sure, the exponential enlargement of functions has aggravated aspects of the initial problem by further distancing the public from government and politics. But this has been largely the result of the emergence of a virtual light industry in public sector employment for scheduled and appointed officials and personnel. Thus these cadres at one and the same time constitute a permanent standing bureaucracy (and technocracy) engaged in policy formulating and implementing functions, often involving considerable discretion, while being formally excluded from the public sphere as real citizens as a consequence of legislation protecting "merit" through tenure, but with the requirement of political neutrality.[2]

A fixed hierarchical system can therefore be understood not only to distinguish agents from members, but agents from one another where most are non-elected. The fact that work, labour and occupational and career structures are organized in much the same way in the public sector that they are in private sector organizations would seem to compensate for the fixity and rigidity of the system to some extent, if only because one can comprehend government and politics as no less organizational and managerial in nature than commerce, finance, business and industry. To the apathy, indifference and deference which exists alongside the passive notion of citizenship as an ascribed status expressive of societal membership is added the fact that an increasing number of adults are excluded from real participation as citizens as a result of being public sector employees. This is problematic enough as it stands, to be sure, but becomes an even more serious matter if one considers the non-democratic, but often very effective, alternatives available to these officials and personnel through the exercise of unconfined and unstructured discretion. This point, I would argue, probably constitutes the best reason for *not* accepting the arguments put forward by supporters of the theory and practice of bureaucratic representation discussed in Chapters five and six.

The failure of representative institutions to maintain their essential (and very necessary) dynamism in the ways indicated also has a great deal to do with the distinction between the Greek conception of wealth and the Judaeo-Christian notion of property. If the first liberated its possessor from worldly cares so that he could participate actively and in a fairly sustained way in public matters, the second tied him to his possessions by requiring careful stewardship and management. Politics and government became the appropriate field of action for representatives of propertied interests who were viewed as agents or delegates in a manner not very different from what Locke had recommended. The purpose of politics was to reflect the dominant economic forces of a society, a conception invented neither by Marx, nor Ricardo, nor Smith, nor even by Locke or Harrington, but by Plato but particularly by Aristotle. Politics as superstructure has been a dominant theme of modern Western societies since at least the seventeenth century, and its effect has been to firm up a fixed hierarchical, and subsequently organizational model of governance which has militated against citizenship of the sort I believe to be increasingly necessary today. Stewardship and delegation will no longer suffice, nor will the static conception of citizenship which it favours for the public and for private "members."

Experience can only teach and encourage display and full utilization of process where its properties are fully understood. By experience I do not mean "raw" experience, nor do I have in mind thought and reflection on its own. Experience which fulfills the requirements of practice in the Aristotelian sense possesses a contemplative and an ethical aspect, but integrates action, thought and concern into an ongoing exercise as well. Neither is experience to be understood as a phenomenon isolated from collective life which takes the form of negative individuation, as if the individual were in some zero-sum relationship to Society. Individuation only has meaning in a collective setting, not only because it is collectively produced and sustained but because it requires the presence of others to make itself known. So far this characterization could apply to all forms of individuation, particularly Society's present pre-eminent form – through occupations and careers. The problem with all non-political forms of individuation is that they are not required to integrate action, thought and concern into an ongoing process of self-description, the *sine qua non* of lived experience. Theirs is a "one-dimensional" enterprise in which the person simply allows one role or role set to function as a static proxy for experience. Secondary group roles effectively define the person as an individual everywhere in collective life.[3]

This becomes all the more obvious when the relation between individuation, experience as I have defined it, and citizenship in the active and dynamic sense is recalled. The very idea of the individual as an aggregate or a bundle of roles and functions organized hierarchically according to their relative importance for significant others reveals the consequences of fetishizing Society the way we have. It is only by equating Society with collective life that we can sustain the idea of citizenship as nothing more than one among many role options. It can only offer a basis for "positive" individuation of the contemporary one-dimensional variety to the extent that one or the other of the two conditions already cited are perceived to be present. In the absence of a pressing personal or material interest, or the demands and requirements of a job or career, individuation is withheld by members as well as agents, who view such activity as suspect. One of the more acceptable ways of dealing with it on the relatively rare occasions when it arises is to "understand" the needs of the poor neurotic engaged in it, thereby reducing the objective content and value of the activity to the behaviour of a marginal or deviant person.

Individuation of the sort counselled by (and expressive of) political management thus possesses integrative properties which produce and sustain the person as a part of collective life while elevating him, however temporarily, beyond the constraints of the present collective form – Society – with its anti-political bias. This is what Hannah Arendt means by power in *The Human Condition,* and it is something to which I shall return in a later section of this chapter. Arendt shows how experience is truncated and one-dimensionalized as a consequence of our acquiescence in the organizational principle, the division of labour, and functional rationality as bases for defining the only acceptable notion of citizenship. Its unmistakeable *societal* auspices are evident from its fixed and ascribed nature, one among many role options whose job is simply to affirm membership. Aristotle's "solution" to the problem arising out of the difference between the production of good men and good citizens has never really been challenged in any effective

way. The line of least resistance, underwritten by the conformity and behavioural requirements of liberalism and the law of large numbers, is to opt
for a static *societal ethics* of the sort counselled by Durkheim, and thereafter
to equate one with the other, thereby denuding citizenship of its dynamism,
and, in the final analysis, its meaning.

We have come to a crossroad in Western development where it is becoming
prohibitively expensive to continue sustaining the passivity and ascription
on which the apparently self-sustaining cycle of production and consumption of late capitalist society so clearly depends. Macpherson is right when
he points out that there is no viable option to our recognizing this, and
recognizing it fast, for we have already found it necessary to extend the
zero-sum game globally in a way which is making mincemeat of development choices for Third World countries. The experts cannot do this with
their expertise, nor the planners and managers with their narrow and truncated visions, hostaged as they are to functional rationality, formal meritocracy and a *status*-based form of collective life which exhibits ever greater
closure. The source for change is the commonsense rationality of the people, yet there is no way to provide a strategy or method by which they can be
led to take back collective life from what presently sustains it, for reasons
that Friere has made apparent. On the other hand, the idea that we can
simply wait for "objective conditions" to assert themselves no longer holds,
if it ever did. There may not be enough time between recognition of the
problem and its resolution. Indeed, its very recognition may signify that this
is the case.[4]

II

Still, it is necessary to proceed sensibly on the assumption that such projec-
tions are overly pessimistic and that we in fact do have time. The timebind
approach to configuring a problem of this magnitude arises as a consequence of our very obsession with time, speed and narrow concepts of
efficiency and effectiveness, in ways that have been discussed by Ellul, Bateson, and Schelling, among others. Thus our concern that "time is running
out" causes us to employ the same problem-solution notion that get us into
the problem, with the likely result that the solution will be problem-gener-
ative. Indeed, strategies and techniques addressed to politics can serve to
underscore the anti-political nature of such remedies by creating problems
in the process of "resolving" them. In effect, our methods of resolution are
themselves a part of the problem *precisely because* they make sense as a
basis for resolution *within* a given problem-solution fix. The problem, con-

figured more widely and comprehensively, becomes the way we formulate problems so that available lines of resolution are built into them virtually by definition. The "solution", once the problem is viewed in this way, is to turn away from a strategic or technical approach, if only because the production of means has outpaced the number of sensible ends for which an instrumental orientation might be proximately useful.[5]

The matter comes to rest all too often in a situation where the surplus of means, or their ready availability and capacity to be generated, defines the parameters of what are thought to constitute meaningful problem-solution sets. Political management is seen to be hopeless and/or futile because there are so many factors to be considered, so many demands on time, so many things to be organized, managed or mastered in other ways. We sincerely believe, as I noted earlier, that the economy will collapse if we do not put the societal division of labour, with its present role and status configurations, first, and view citizenship as one way of affirming membership. The old chestnut of stability and order, and the terror of its loss, now takes on specific material and "standard of living" properties that would make even Hobbes blush.[6] We literally persuade ourselves that the argument for the priority of commonsense rationality as a well-distributed substructural resource possessed by people as a consequence of simply being human is no less a sop than the claim that political management is needed for urgent practical, rather than only distended ethical or moral, reasons.

The problem is with the people, not their governors, and no system of representation or democracy can possibly be accorded full recognition as such if it fails to resolve it. Indeed, it is important to stress not only that agents are first and foremost members, and that they do not lose this pre-eminent status by being agents, but that neither status is necessarily to be confused with citizenship in the active and dynamic sense that I believe to be so imperative. True, agents frequently can and do function in a citizenly way in this capacity, but there is no guarantee whatsoever that this will happen and it should never be assumed. It is an all-too-characteristic result of viewing competence in a formally meritocratic way. Thus, agents *must be* prototypical citizens because, after all, they are agents, and who in our complex societal division of labour is better able to perform this function? I have already explained why I find this notion not only unsatisfactory but potentially and actually dangerous as well. Functionally rational conceptions of citizenship equate its good exercise with the most pre-eminently visible societal members – our agents – then argue that since these latter are in the best position to exercise the citizenly function, no one else needs to concern themselves with it in the absence of an immediate and direct perception of self-interest, usually defined in material terms.[7]

This has been further complicated, as noted, by the qualitative and quantitative extension of governments in advanced industrial societies, particularly as *employers*. Substantial numbers of exemplary functions and occupations have been formally meritocratized, and thereby taken out of the sphere of responsible politics altogether. Though conceptions of political neutrality toward civil and public servants in all areas of the public sector, as well as private persons in privileged association with governments, appear to be changing somewhat, it is still too early to tell what the long-term effects of such developments will be. As things stand now, government and politics are under the gun to submit to increasing rationalization of their functions and the conduct of their operatives. This clearly has the effect of *de-politicizing,* even by reference to earlier versions of the same society. Role-taking and an obsession with status supplant any hope that the sense of display, alongside responsible use of process, will achieve fullscale public recognition. Meantime, the effect of rationalization in the "public sector" is to further underwrite its status as an apolitical *civil* sector where those that fall between the stools are even more readily treated as irrational given the pre-eminence of functionally rational predefinitions.[8]

Success in a career is no longer simply an option available to a restricted number of members who choose to function in an almost totally apolitical way. It is increasingly the *only* road to success for the large mass of persons whose goal is to acquire sufficient secondary socialization to get into a formal meritocratic structure of one kind or another, then solidify their position by the eventual ascription of a status which effectively defines them in an occupationally individualistic way as "persons." Outside the responsible public sphere in ways not only more direct but more compulsory than regular citizen-members, their sole way of compensating for the absence of this power is through the exercise of subtle forms of decisional discretion often far reaching in their individual and aggregate consequences. These individuals increasingly constitute a model for the manifestation and exercise of occupational individualism in ways not available to private sector managers and executives. "Social responsibility" dictates and directives have yet to be sufficiently factored into the secondary socialization process to obviate the blame placed upon private enterprise for system failures and excesses, whether economic, institutional, environmental, consumerist or legal in nature.[9]

The difficulty with the relationship, ideal and real, between the public and some form of needed political management can be configured in ways which draw upon the notion of experience just discussed. My purpose is to suggest that it is the way in which practice, theory and disciplined observation interact and are linked to one another in advanced industrial societies that best helps us to delineate the situation we face in trying to persuade the public of the urgency of its participation through process and display, while

yet being unable to offer a strategy, method or technique which will guarantee results. In a certain sense, it is wrong to make too much of the
distinction between process and results. Results are certainly not by this
reckoning unimportant, but a fixation on them produces attitudes toward
process which not only sees it as a means or instrument, but fails fundamentally to take into account unanticipated and unintended consequences. Process in the public sphere is very often its own justification, particularly when
its legal predefinition allows for participation and display in practice. The
argument against prevailing problem-solution fixes is really to be discovered
in the presumption they make about the possibility and desirability of final
solutions. In collective life there are no final solutions, nor should we wish
there to be.

I have argued elsewhere that the greatest problem facing us in our efforts to
encourage political management as a public activity uniting reflection, concern and action in an integrated and moving continuum is the way we rigidly
separate practice, its disciplined (and undisciplined) observation and theory
and distinguish them from one another as *empirical* properties of our human
world. Indeed, it is to our quite understandable failure to see empiricism as
a convention or cultural artifact that we must turn in order to make sense of
the way we invest pivotal dichotomies and distinctions with a fixed and one
dimensional empirical status as facts in the world. Instead of constituting
approaches to reality, they become descriptions of it, just as Max Weber's
ideal types did when they ceased to function heuristically as representations
of a reality allegedly too complex for them to appropriate. The empirical
convention in practice denudes collective life of its dynamism by carving up
the world into parts which are allegedly more concrete than the whole that
alone gives them meaning. The result of such a convention in operation on
its own is fully conducive to the development of causilinear reasoning, itself
essential to the generation of present-day notions of problem and solution.
Nowadays, to be sure, the very "complexity" of Society has generated a
preference for structural-functional and system notions as overlays on the
earlier causilinear focus, but this has been mainly reflected in the tendency
to see rationality as a property of structures rather than of people.

A major consequence of the coupling of the empirical convention with
structural-functional and systems overlays has been to disembody an observation function essential to human life from both practice and theory. Its
pre-eminence in disembodied form relative to both practice and theory is
precisely what requires it to become progressively more disciplined to compensate for this lack. Prototypes for this development are readily discoverable in the key institutions about which Max Weber was so preoccupied,
namely, capitalism, science, and the rule of law and modern bureaucratic
organization. In every case the standard for successful or competent indiv-

idual performance is how well one can exercise a thoroughly disciplined observation, whether to achieve comparative advantage in the marketplace, experimental success in the laboratory through "catching nature at work," or competent categorization and classification of clients. Disembodiment in the new equation becomes tantamount to discipline, as the latter's compensatory function takes on a self-generative quality conducive to the reconstitution of practice and the annihilation of reflection. With the full-scale emergence of an organizational order predicated on functional rationality and formal meritocracy, the status concerns of those anxious to secure occupational and organizational membership come to constitute a reflection of membership in collective life as presently constituted.[10]

So long as we find it impossible to overcome or transcend this separation and distinction, its consequences will rob us of any possibility that display can supplant mutual-role taking, that allegedly "natural" phenomenon that sociology chronicles when it implies that Society is the only available (and desirable) form of collective life, or a synonym for it. The starting point for this reconstruction and reformulation must clearly be reflection. Practice and the practical has by now become subject to so many predefinitions as an expression of proper secondary socialization that there is little sense in pointing to either a utopian or nostalgic conception of practice as a beginning. Fortunately reason is a human property and capacity which is well-distributed, and includes the capacity to contemplate and reflect. Everyone is and/or could be a theorist in the sense that the difference between the present small stratum and "everyone else" is more likely to be that the latter have never bothered to reflect on their theoretical presuppositions, not that they are incapable of doing so. To say and even recommend this is not to encourage idle speculation "for its own sake," any more than I argued that political management is an urgent necessity just to be "sincere." Reflection is the only way presently available for the people to break through the rigid and fixed mode of apprehending the world that increasingly constitutes a self-fulfilling prophecy.

None of this seeks to do anything more than *restore* the observation function to a more sensible role *vis a vis* practice and theoretical reflection. This function is absolutely necessary for both theorizing and practical conduct in everyday life, and has only become problematic as a result of its distending and disembodiment. Those institutions which have come together as models for defining and prosecuting certains norms of rationality in advanced industrial societies have created this problem individually or in the aggregate precisely because collective life is always more than any of its institutions, however preeminent. More to the point is the fact that even an aggregate of institutions like the three or four cited only speaks to the specific cultural and historical form that collective life has taken on as a consequence of developments, patterns and interests. In the contemporary setting, the problem of functionally rationalized meritocracies and managerial and professional cadres and groups is precisely the way that their own claim to autonomy as disembodied disciplined observers supports the notion of an autonomous discipline, now viewed more as a static moral property relevant to status, power, and claims to a right of autonomy than it is to technical proficiency, and the quality of institutional and personal delivery systems.[11]

III

Any attempt to elucidate the conception of experience which I believe to be so central to political management cannot avoid beginning with those aspects of the present situation which have played a major role in separating and distinguishing practice, theoretical reflection, and the observation function. The idea of experience itself also presupposes a context for its possible exercise, a space of potential display as well as established process. No approach to politics premised solely on display is realistic in the present circumstances any more than the emerging new spaces for its exercise can ever hope to circumvent these processes without consequence. Reference to the notion of space, while not only metaphorical, does address an *environment* (umwelt) for the exercise of politics and the political which presumes anchorage in the collective properties of sociability and gregariousness as well as self interest. Thus ethical and moral concerns which only make sense because they can be collectively comprehended as an essential aspect of membership must always be the starting point, a necessary but not a sufficient condition. Politics, whether in the form of display within or outside of established institutional processes, is therefore a qualitatively different activity which unites reflection, concern and action at a higher level.

This is not to dispute the idea of reason as a well-distributed substructural resource normally characteristic of human beings as such. It only underscores the well distributed nature of display in particular to say of its authors that they can and do come from all walks of life. Without in any way offering this fact as a defense of the present distribution of status, power and remuneration in advanced industrial societies, or the criteria on which this distribution is based, it must be clear that the sense of such a claim lies in the lack of permanence of its possession by *anyone,* no matter where they are found in Society. When Arendt refers to this as power, she is not just addressing its possessor as a subject of the action, but its environment or context as well. What makes politics as display a form of power is its transcendence, however temporary, of the fact of membership *which it nevertheless presupposes.* Just as the individual or individuals exhibiting this power rise above their membership, so also do those who actively participate in this unification and synthesis of thought, concern and action. They express individually and collectively the capacity to produce politics and the political over and above Society, with its decidedly anti-political bias and its determination to coopt and absorb such activity.[12]

By environment or context of experience I therefore do not necessarily mean a particular location or place in social or political space *per se,* but rather given events viewed as opportunities rather than constraints. These events, whatever they are, may or may not occur in legal, judicial, governmental or political space. When they do we should regard the action as either part of established processes or a response to them. Display outside of established processes may take shape in one or another of the new public spaces presently emerging, but this need not be the case either. Rising above the constraints and limitations posed by Society's equation of citizenship with membership can happen anywhere, and its most constant feature is its lack of permanence rather than the location or place where we may expect to find it. Indeed, a strong argument could be made against an overly defined sense of place on the grounds that it rigidifies the more fluid sense of *space* by guaranteeing its apparent permanence in one particular section of the societal division of labour. The specific roles or functions in hierarchical systems that are then pointed to with confidence often show how much is lost by and through such an exercise.

The desire for permanence in the political field ignores the beneficent aspects of power's very lack of permanence. This lack is precisely what makes it possible for it to constantly be recreated anew, an endless resource potentially present in all of us as human beings. Though it may appear to us as little more than speech or talk, which is then alleged to constitute a deed in its own right, this approach poses difficulties. It is too negatively individuating and too isolating, as if the only way to overcome Society would require its possessor to fall back into a position of moral superiority and distance based on an alienated vision like that of Max Weber in his more pessimistic moments. Arendt often falls prey to this tendency, which, however, is given further aid and comfort by her tendency to fetishize the Greek (Athenian) experience. As it happens, this approach has much in common with those who accede to the rationality of Society, then argue for irrationality in the face of this reality. Society becomes the arbiter of what is possible, and pessimism leads those with such an approach to turn away from the people as if their present status were irredeemable, particularly when the exercise that is called for is collective self-redemption.[13]

But this is precisely the point. There always remains the possibility of seeing through and locating Society as that particular form of collective life which tries to persuade its members that it and collective life are one and the same. And this possibility, no matter to what extent it may appear to be the repository of individuals, is by this very admission a collective reality whose very lack of permanence speaks to our ability to rise above and transcend membership again and again. This is ultimately why the desire to control the space of power by formalizing its location in a given locus or place is likely to be unsuccessful when it seeks to coopt the activity by so doing. True, the result of this effort is absolutely necessary, even primary, for the exercise of politics in and through process. The danger arises when the act of participating in process as either an agent or a member carries with it requirements of outward and inward conformity to established anti-political norms in the name of "responsibility" to stability and order in a state understood to be coterminous with its societal division of labour. I would argue that this constraint of space to place probably goes further to explain public apathy and indifference in advanced industrial societies than is generally recognized.

The individual's political participation or display in a relevant collective setting can thus be understood to constitute a response to given events or occasions which cannot be expected to occur again. Arendt's concern about the regularizing and categorizing of events is therefore as well taken as her concern for the idea of individual display as *necessarily* impermanent and non-recurring. Her point is that politics cannot occur at all where individual roles and functions are either predefined or predictable in the regularity of their occurrence. The same can be said of the events and occasions which give rise to such display, for in both cases it is the sacrifice of space to place which leads to the sort of fixity conducive to a functionally rational and formally meritocratic *societal* division of labour rather than to politics. The fact that we normally define space by reference to or in terms of place suggests how dependent stability and order is seen to be on the fixity and rigidity of hierarchical roles which require behaviour rather than action.[14] The issue of rationality is almost moot in this reckoning, constituting as it does more a cultural artifact of advanced industrial societies than anything else. It is really the question of how necessary the eclipse or cooptation of politics is to Society, and what it will do to realize it.

Place locates, not only in physical space, but also socially, since it is a precondition for function and form in society. Social and physical space thereby become essentially coterminous from the standpoint of the disciplined observer. His vision is to complete Society as a cultural and historical project, and to this end he will seek to annihilate theoretical reflection while reconstituting practice in Society's image. This is thoroughly incompatible with politics as I understand it, something which should hardly come as a surprise. The disciplined observer is the archetypal individual found in a collective form where life is a series of roles and role sets framed around occupation, consumption, spectating and leisure. His conformity manifests itself in a preference for behaviour over action, and the most "active" mode this behaviour can take is to *reproduce* the societal division of labour in its ideal (or idealized) form as a hierarchy of disciplined observers. The social, behavioural and managerial disciplines may be the advance guard of Society in the sense that their mission is pre-eminently to preserve, extend, and complete it, most notably by persuading its members that Society is coterminous with collective life rather than constituting a culturally and historically specific form of it. But the institutional basis for the rise of these disciplines is to be found much earlier in the dependence of capitalism, science and the rule of law on disembodied disciplined observation.[15]

Nowadays the functionally rational function of these disciplines is mirrored in the nature of societal interaction itself. The social sciences and related disciplines have become the sciences of organic solidarity and occupational individualism in the sense that their concepts, biases and values have been sedimented into the role, status and functional requirements and expectations of advanced industrial societies. The hierarchy of disciplined observers prefigured in the work of St. Simon and Comte in particular is the essential property which all the institutions of contemporary rational domination share in common. The fixity and rigidity given in the reformulation of space as place accords perfectly with the kind of solidarity that Durkheim believed would normalize the societal division of labour that existed around 1900. This normalization was to be achieved by reconciling industrial capitalism and modern technology with a formally organized status order presumably expressive of late medieval values. Stability and order in countries with large populations under industrial discipline would require a rational hierarchy characterized by functional interdependence between persons whose individuality must reside in their occupational roles and statuses. This conception, so central to the vision and values of the social, behavioural and managerial disciplines, could scarcely be further removed from the idea of citizenship as active display and commitment to process which I have attempted to elucidate.[16]

The unity of thought, concern, speech and action which is so essential to citizenly display and its generalization into political management is precisely what the "abstract society" of roles, statuses and fixed functions militates against with its commitment to specialization as a basis for self-definition. The resulting reformulation of the concept of personality in industrial societies so that it accorded more closely with the commitment to occupational specialization necessitated a substantial increase in secondary socialization. The fluidity so central to display and activity required a less fixed ascription not only of the individual but of the idea of public or political space, as noted. Persuading members that citizenship was at best one among many options in the absence of immediate self-interest or occupational and career responsibilities demanded that space be located and fixed in a formalized way in and through time and place. This obviated the possibility that events might themselves be sufficiently unique and individuated to inspire the sort of unified and integrated deed that is the essence of citizenship. Secondary socialization as a regularized property of growing up in advanced industrial societies seeks to rationalize both the unpredictibility of events and their uniqueness and the similarly unorganized potential for uncontrolled individuation on the part of societal members.

Controlling the fluctuation of events and their impact on individuals, as well as the impact of individuals on events, necessitates a preference for convergence and homogeneity regarding the core values of a culture. When this culture is at the same time highly complex, specialized and organized on the basis of functional rationalization and formal meritocracy, the need to secure stability and order requires that such convergence and homogeneity be based on the indispensibility of established hierarchies of order, status, role and occupational function. The "abstractness" to which Zijderveld in particular has referred certainly is problematic when it generates conflict, confusion, ambiguity, dissatisfaction, and unhappiness. My point in drawing critical attention to this central aspect of social structure is to show first how the problem is configured and thereafter how it is solved, or proposed to be solved. The problem-solution fixes of the social, behavioural and managerial sciences, in effect, seek to reconcile value congruence with role heterogeneity because the latter is an unavoidable property of advanced industrial societies which no amount of concern about the naturalization and standardization of values can ever hope to reconcile with the living standard on which continued stability and order are seen to depend.[17]

The context or environment of experience must continue to address space, events and citizenly display outside the control of Society's socializing agenda, even at the price of appearing to offer nothing "concrete" to those anxious to tinker with and reform the system in good faith. At the same time, it must resist the blandishments of the sort of linguistically-oriented thinking that takes off from the idea of speech and communication as the essence of politics. Speech and communication may validly be said to constitute a deed in its own right, but this can confuse the issue when the relation between thought, speech, concern and action is ignored in favour of viewing speech as a deed which is understood to be self-contained and autonomous. Such a tendency plays directly into the hands of those who prefer fixity in statuses, roles and functions by pointing to the societal division of labour as the central resource which provides the basis for the sort of specialization that includes specialists in the production of speech as a deed. Physical and geographical mobility can provide but slim cover for the lack of real mobility in an order whose hierarchically organized occupants now have no choice but to equate reason and rationality with the faithful reproduction of internalized norms and values in a status order which has generalized Weber's "closed body of office-holders" from bureaucracy to civil society as a whole.

Context or environment can only be fully subordinated to the requirements of place, status and organizational order where events and individuals have been sufficiently standardized to permit of little or no unpredictability and variance. This has not yet occurred to such an extent as to thoroughly preclude the possibility of citizenly display and its generalization into political management. On the other hand, public acquiescence in its own ignorance and/or incapacity constitutes a serious barrier to the increasingly urgent need to rise above membership, with all that it has promised and come to expect of us. The orientational basis for affirming membership, in whatever status, role or function we find it, is disembodied disciplined observation, and it is the key vehicle for securing "comparative advantage" not only (or even mainly) in economic and material matters, but in a vast number of areas bearing on "success in a career" in advanced industrial societies. That it has spread into the so-called primary group was almost foreordained by the drive to occupational personhood and interdependence, for in every case it is the perceived *necessity of continuous,* rather than intermittent, mutual role taking, as well as the infamous rehearsal in imagination, that defines "comparative advantage" under conditions in which even roles, statuses and functions are subject to norms of exchange rather than use values.[18]

IV

Max Weber has argued that the Western drive to mastery is self-defined and essentially given in the sense that "this tremendous development" produces its own end from inside itself rather than as a result of external factors. There is in Weber's analysis a great similarity to Aristotle's concept of formal cause, since the point of Weber's analysis is not simply to address "elective affinities" linking sequences of events over time in a causal way, but rather to imply a sort of evolutionary foreordinance. It is important to realize just how significant this notion of formal cause is, not only to Weber's view of rationalization and de-enchantment as a Western "fate", but to the way we as Westerners view ourselves even in everyday life. The idea that

our development is best seen in evolutionary rather than adaptive and ac-
commodative terms has played more than a small part in fueling our negative and defeatist attitude toward politics and the need for political management. There are several forms this attitude has taken which are relevant to
the matters considered here.[19]

There is first the way we have acquiesced in what is really a regressive form
of collective life, one which favours a notion of stability and order which
equates it with non-or anti-political behaviour. Central to this, as noted, is
the gradual process by which structures have become the preferred repositories of reason and rationality rather than individuals. This would appear to
constitute nothing more than a reference to the integrating capacities of the
new form of collective life as it emerged in its fullness in the Twentieth
Century. While this study has been very critical of Society, and has been
determined as a consequence to locate it as a culturally and historically
specific collective form, it is always necessary to realize that all forms of
collective life have in common the fact that they can only confer membership, and with it only the basis for the possibility of citizenship, nothing
more. The rest is up to individuals, and collectively, the public, which is *not*
simply reducible to specific, organized publics with special interests as some
would like us to believe. The rationalization of behaviour, individuation,
even events, may tempt us to accept this claim as a fact, but it is something
we must resist.[20]

We must resist it because today we have opportunities available, however
much covered over and repressed they may be, to exercise political management as a generalization of the phenomenon of citizenly display to a
greater extent than ever before possible. In a sense, this may justifiably be
cited as a contemporary possible manifestation of the *polis,* so long as this
does not lead to a misplaced nostalgia for the Greek city-state. More to the
point is the fact that such a possibility very much resembles the sort of
development which one would have to use to "fill in" the period from the
"revolution" and the establishment of proletarian dictatorship to the final
communist stage in Marx's eschatology. Arendt wrongly charged Marx with
being anti-political when it seems clear that his intention was only to address
the "withering away" of *the state* as a necessity because it constituted the
"executive committee" of the ruling class. I would argue that in the long run
such an eventuality, however utopian it may seem to us today, is what really
makes politics as display fully possible, as against the established form of
governmental organization so central to the apparatus of the late capitalist
state.

Without wishing in any way to downgrade the role and even the function of
display, I would take issue with Marx's characterization mainly because of
its dependence on obejctive conditions and my skepticism about the feasi-

bility of waiting around for these conditions to "happen". Thus I have argued for making full use of existing representative institutions and processes while taking serious account of new spaces for the exercise of politics which are emerging. Display on its own simply makes no practical sense given the problems we face and the fact that the existing apparatus, though unable to bear the present load, must be our starting point. Indeed, a zero-sum emphasis on *either* display *or* process is all too often a reflection of a social division of labour whose academic and professional division of labour makes one choose either a "utopian" or a "realistic" approach to the problem. An emphasis on display, for instance in Arendt's *The Human Condition,* is all too readily teamed with a pessimistic prospect in real terms, as if such an alternative *must* be posed even though there is not the slightest possibility of its being realized. Arendt would appear to have equated an optimistic prospect with Marx, and his allegedly utopian ideas, in much the same way that Popper discredited such optimism because of what its alleged materialization had brought into being.[21]

Similarly, an emphasis on process has been adjudged hardheaded, the expected response of those who tolerate contemplation and reflection only when it can be guaranteed to produce "practical" results. The split between an emphasis on display and one on process certainly reproduces within the discipline of political science an interesting schism once again reminiscent of Aristotle. In this case, it was the difference between the Aristotle of the *Ethics* and the *Politics* on the one hand, and the Aristotle of *The Constitution of Athens* on the other. My point has been to argue that such a bifurcation is not only counterproductive in political science, but in collective life as a whole, because it makes it difficult if not impossible to even consider the prospect of bridging the gaps between contemplation, concern and activity in the world. I have tried to make a case for reinstating an Aristotelian conception of practice and the practical in order to overcome the present obsession with disembodied disciplined observation as the major reality-orienting and constructing device of our form of collective life. Its consequences for experience underwrite the idea of fragmentation given in the notion that thought, speech, concern and activity ought to be understood as *empirically distinct* properties of reality.

One point that needs to be made has only been hinted at in the preceding, and concerns the way that this zero-sum split between display and process has consigned the former view of politics and the political to the status of ethics and speech, or rather ethical speech. This view of politics has understandably been a detriment to the acceptance of the idea and possibility of political management, for reasons that must be apparent in the presently held notion of what the societal division of labour is and what it requires of those who wish to be counted members. The idea of either politics or ethics as speech distended from action is problematic precisely because it fits so well into the existing division of labour, and therefore can be counted on to make its contribution to what is believed to constitute a viable (because manageable) problem. This bears on my resistance to the idea of speech on its own as a deed, *even if it is!* Speech has frequently been presumed to encompass thought in its ambit, no less today with Chomsky and his contemporaries than when Descartes first threw it down as an implicit and taken for granted requirement of the modern consciousness.

But there is something which is even more problematic about such an understanding, because it subsumes the idea of ethics into speech as a deed and goes on to treat politics and the political as either a version of ethical speech – display – or of hardheaded and presumably unreflective activity – process. Here we see in slightly altered form the difficulty already alluded to, for the split between the (alleged) two kinds of politics is believed to comport with the distinction between the utopian and the realistic. Thus politics as display is seen to possess what is in the main an ethical or moral component, while politics as process is believed to be totally devoid of such considerations. Max Weber faced this same ambiguity and conflict, and opted for an ethics of responsibility, which he viewed as equivalent to process and "responsible leadership" and described as "a slow boring at hard boards." Weber's equation of politics with *both* ethics *and* the problem of responsibility constitutes a quintessential formulation of the problem I believe to be central to our present understanding of politics and the political.[22]

In addition to my criticism of any effort to equate ethics with speech distended from action, there is the corollary problem of "ethicizing" politics and the political. Politics and ethics are neither the same thing, nor even related to one another in an immediate sense. Obviously the capacity for citizenly display, either in and through established processes or outside and alongside them, presupposes the notion of collective membership on which ethics and morals is at any given time and place based. But this is hardly to argue that they are one and the same. Indeed, in the face of the present understanding which sees ethics and politics in the form of display as speech addressed to utopian and idealistic notions and possibilities, the equation of ethics with politics shores up an unrealistic view precisely because of the present attitude to the ethical in particular. On the other hand, there is the view of politics as instrumentally rational behaviour aimed at comparative advantage and self-interest – Weber's politics of responsibility in a putatively representative democracy. As things stand at present, political science all too readily reflects this clash between the ethical and moral and the strategic and instrumental in its own academic division of labour.

The thought/action distinction is a major basis of the modern tendency to empiricize dichotomies and distinctions, as I have noted elsewhere. It is nothing less than the key distinction, along with the dichotomies between man and nature and mind and body, of modernity as a culture and system of thought and values. The distinction between thought and action is absolutely central to the present view of the *sense* of citizenly display, and its generalization as political management, held by the public as well as its agents. Thought, speech, concern and activity are distended from one another because it is not yet clear how Society is able to guarantee control of any activity which does not fall under the rubric of disembodied disciplined observation. Society has been battling the public's commonsense rationality for a long time on this score. This is evident from the continuing tendency on the public's part to insist on the need for a synthesis and integration of thought, speech, concern, and activity in the very way they so often *fail* to behave! Still, the situation has gone far enough to warrant careful scrutiny, since the price of keeping all these functions and activities apart has now begun to accelerate and further aggravate governmental confusion and dysfunction.

The idea of integrating these various aspects of collective life, now as before, seems too much for elites who nonetheless are convinced of the need to support and underwrite all the forms of complexity which seem to define the contours of progress as it is presently understood. Social structure must be organized and ordered in a way which makes minimal demands on the apparatus of technological, applied scientific and industrial productivity and development. This demand that it be essentially unobtrusive has necessitated the present day support for the approved means for maintaining stability and order from mass populations through consumption, leisure and spectating roles. The other side of this societal order – occupational individualism under norms of functional rationality – reaffirms the "total systems" nature of the emerging status order in advanced industrial societies. Its attitude to politics and the political is implicit in its criticism of citizenly display and political management, because they threaten the essentially apolitical notion of consensus which is so central a property of Society's present and future agenda.

The boundary between the ethical and the political as I have defined it is certainly not rigid and fixed, and it must be clear that any such boundary is not and never can be predetermined, but is a function of events, and the individuation appropriate to them. To say that events define whether an action is ethical or political is not to give up the matter to chance and contingency. On the contrary. It simply affirms the idea of difference that is implicit in the distinction between the two terms, however similarly we may employ them and for whatever purpose. To refuse to allow the two notions to be merged is to recognize the difference that is given in the notion of event on which each is based. Event achieves the merger of individual and collective on which our entire rhetoric is premised, because the point about the emphasis on event is that it generates the possibility of rising above Society as the concept which envisions and determines the distinction. Marx had already pointed out the way that the distinction between the general and the special interest was reproduced and defended by one side of the dichotomy but not the other.[23]

The *need* to integrate thought, speech, concern and activity is implicit in the distinction I have made here and elsewhere between theory, disciplined observation and practice. In every case the problem lies in the role of experience and the importance with which it is invested. It seems to me that if we were serious about the root of any and all democratic mandates in the people we would seek out their views in and through process and in other ways. We would not employ social-scientific surrogates, which in any case are used mainly to persuade the people that see and hear the "report" on television that it is in fact an accurate picture of the way "they" think. This is really the basis of my refusal to endorse any zero-sum game which places display and process in a mutually contradictory relation. Display cannot be used in the present circumstances to front for process, but the point of all this is to argue for the fact that display can occur in and through process just as readily as alongside it. And the attempt to reaffirm the distinction simply serves to fuel the flames which support the rigid dichotomy of thought and action so central to ideological understandings of both in a collective governed by disembodied disciplined observation.

Politics is truly the art of the possible, as Lasswell has argued. The question then, is really what this promise of possibility means. It clearly cannot be allowed to operate as a proxy for democratic elitism in either its present or its proposed future forms. Instead this promise must stand for the idea of process and display together, not simply because display must occur largely in and through process, but because both are necessary to citizenship and its generalization in the form of political management. Most of the debate around the viability of the above conception of politics has focussed on the question of its *status* as a science rather than a utopian hope, which is to say that the tension between the idea of politics as a science and as an art is central to *its* status relative to "everything else" in advanced industrial society. Furthermore, politics as a "discipline" favours its status as a scientific and professional activity only because it has been discovered that its status as an art fails to produce the kind of results that recognition as a science and a profession can deliver. But the point is to underscore the fact the politics has to do with the possible and not worry about its status in the societal division of labour.[24]

V

The present situation may not warrant excessive optimism, but this alone is no reason to enforce the sort of pessimism which points to the requirement of objective conditions as the sole basis for revising present trends. If commonsense rationality is a substructural resource which people possess by dint of being human, if it is as well distributed as I have argued, and if it is really the foundation which all superstructural modes of reason presuppose and in which they come to rest, then we should clearly not allow ourselves to embrace statistical probabilities and deny possibility by so doing. We need to capture, or perhaps recapture, the fluidity and integrative character of experience as a dynamic continuum combining thought, concern, speech, situational analysis and assessment and action. This will require us to reembody and resituate disciplined observation relative to both theory and practice, thereby acknowledging the indispensability of the observation function, but only by reference to its ongoing interdependence with *both* theory and practice. This cannot help but restore reflection and contemplation as an essential property of practice along with observation, while it allows us to make better practical sense of our everyday life experience.

This has considerable significance for the unfortunate split presently honoured between an allegedly realistic politics of process and an apparently utopian politics of display. That this distinction imposes an empiricized form of the thought/action distinction on what are in fact two interrelated modes of citizenly activity shows how insensitive the empirical convention is to the role of events and conditions as central elements in the emergence and contraction of political and public spaces. Events are both produced and encountered by citizens engaged in the sort of integrated activity which allows them to rise, however temporarily, above the membership-offering roles, statuses and functions of Society in the ways suggested. The spaces, as noted, are no more permanent than the events because the individual and collective activity which creates and/or encounters them can never guarantee or predict this temporary elevation. On the other hand, the very absence of permanence in a fixed and predictable sense is precisely what allows for the possibility that this integrated interest and capability, rooted as it is in commonsense experience, can always recreate itself anew. Resisting the rationalization and standardization of events, and the corollary effort to control the creation of public spaces by subjecting then to a ficed location or place in the division of labour, becomes not simply a moral duty but a practical necessity.

What I have just said may appear to favour display over process, even though I have argued that they are two modes of activity *both* of which have potential and actual practical significance. The first point that needs to be

made in order to correct such an impression is that display as I have conceptualized it is at least as much a possibility and an actual (and very necessary) property of citizenly activity *within* established processes as it is
outside them. Thus there is no bias here in favour of display as a form of
citizenly activity which is in a zero-sum relation to governmental and political institutions as a basis for citizenhsip. The reasons for this have already
been discussed, and it must be evident that the either/or option regarding
display versus process is precisely what has generated the present narrowly
instrumental approach to practice which effectively consigns more expansive conceptions of possibility to the realm of the utopian. It is important to
also be clear on the fact that display in and through existing processes and
mechanisms is absolutely essential if we are to respond effectively to the
present serious situation. New public spaces where contextually innovative
forms of display can occur, while also needed, can in no wise be considered
any substitute for full utilization of established governmental and political
institutions.

It may be thought less innovative to operate in a citizenly way in and
through established processes than outside them, but this only makes sense
if we define as innovative the activity of citizens which creates events and
spaces rather than encountering and responding to them. Reflection shows
such a narrow conception of innovation to be unsatisfactory, because an
equally valid conception would give at least as much credit to citizens working within fixed and established spaces who are able to create new possibilities through full utilization of these processes and mechanisms. The requirement of *beginning* in a fixed locus or place as citizens does not rule out
the possibility of citizenly display and innovation, and may even make it
more significant when it happens. Thus citizens, like agents (who are also
potential citizens as well as real members), may fashion events and spaces
within fixed places and structures. The fact that the first is impermanent
while the second is not certainly cannot be held against citizens, because this
is also a major property of display outside established structures and processes. Place may predefine event and space-creating possibilities or it may
not. In any case citizens (and agents) who create spaces out of predefined
places, thereby freeing events from a rationalizing and standardizing imperative, rarely receive the credit and appreciation that their unrelenting efforts
entail.

Weber's pessimistic assessment of the possibility of integrating thought,
concern, speech, experience, situational analysis and assessment, and action
is not as atypical of the way many think as we might wish to believe. Worse
in a way than sitting around and awaiting the emergence of objective conditions, Weber's understanding of politics and the political combined an
ethics of responsibility with the view of politics as a "slow boring at hard

boards." At the same time, however, Weber's hardheaded approach focussed on the role of leadership in national states engaged in power politics far more than it did on citizenship. This can perhaps be explained by Weber's view of rationalization and corollary de-enchantment as the "fate of the West." Thus it might be possible for individuals alone or in groups to slow down the pace of this development but not to alter its direction or eventual result. Charisma for Weber is always a possibility, even within a collective form undergoing rationalization and de-enchantment, but this possibility decreases, both in terms of its likelihood and the contemplated scope of its effects, as the process advances to the perimeters of Society. The result is a "dead mechanism" or "iron cage" incapable of transcending itself, and the only alternative becomes a regression to pre-rational forms of domination based on "new leaders and heroes."[25]

Weber's notion of charisma is illustrative of the contemporary tendency to assume that existing structures expressive of an organizational conception of order are the major (if not the sole) repositories of rationality. Thus charisma is an "irrational" property which given leaders evoke in the people, and this property is the only thing that Weber can imagine which might stand in the way of rationalization and deenchantment as a culmination and a fate. Weber thereby acknowledges that this process or development and its major effect ultimately become one with reason, and that no alternative form can be expected to challenge it. Charisma is itself unstable and temporary, being limited to the lifespan of one person, and the process of routinization which occurs thereafter can be expected to create a settled, if not a thoroughly secular, bureaucratic structure. The process is circular for Weber inasmuch as rationalization and de-enchantment can only be challenged by charisma, which in turn is destined to be routinized. To the extent that charisma occurs mainly, or exclusively, as a *residual* property of legal-rational structures which are based on representation and the rule of law, its individual and aggregate effects can be expected to be of steadily decreasing significance, since in neither case are such occurrences able to do anything more than alter the pace of developments.[26]

It is Weber's fixed notion of event and occurrence which I find most difficult to acknowledge. For him the people are *already* "fellaheen" incapable of turning things around because they are inside the system, and matters have simply gone too far for them to do anything more than temporarily slow down developments. The people are in an irredeemable state because they are seen to be the *products* of a tremendous development which was essentially foreordained. The idea of a substructural resource which is well distributed and on which all superstructural modes of reason and rationality depend is acknowledged for heuristic and analytical purposes by Weber the sociologist, but denied as a basis for individual and collective action possibilities by Weber the pessimist. Negative individuation is the only type for Weber, something which becomes apparent when one looks carefully at his typology of social action and its relation to the typology of authority and domination. This form of individuation manifests itself not only at (or within) the system level in his analysis of charisma, but at the commonsense level where it functions as a rearguard attempt to preserve defeated and obsolete economic forms, even in the face of the inevitability of their supercession.

This is evident from the way that one of the four social action types – *wert rational* or principled action – fails to make the transition into the authority typology. Traditional behaviour is paralleled by traditional authority, and *zweck rational* or goal rational action by legal-rational authority. Affective or emotive behaviour is paralleled by charismatic authority to the extent that the "gift of grace" which individuals see in the leader is inspirational and consequently "irrational." To be sure, the leader's perception of his own mission may partake of principle because it is premised on an ethic of ultimate ends rather than one of responsibility. Politics under such a conception of authority is far less a "slow boring at hard boards" than an exercise in spirited (though legitimate) domination. Still, charismatic authority must be evaluated by reference to the feelings and emotions of the members or subjects rather than the principles of the leader, if only because a leader's legitimacy is a function of what MacIver has called the "myth of authority," and this myth is totally dependent on the willingness of the people to accept his commands as authoritative. Authority or domination is not, then, a one way imposition from above, but a reciprocal and collective activity and exercise. This really serves to *underscore* the possibility for citizenly display and political management which lies with the people in advanced industrial societies.

Weber's conception of principled action is "negative" in the sense that it is associated in his thinking with resistance to the process of rationalization and de-enchantment. There is in Weber's notion of resistance a form of individuation which wants to regress to an idealized model of entrepreneurial and market capitalism already in eclipse to bureaucracy and Society even at the time he was writing. In effect, Weber deposits the blame for rationalization and deenchantment not with the major institution which generates it, namely capitalism and subsequent capitalist industrialization, but rather with its major organizational effect – bureaucracy. This preserves capitalism as a lost and nostalgic ideal even though Weber knows that modern secular bureaucracy presupposes the existence of a full-fledged money economy. Principled action, which Weber is at pains to defend as *rational* rather than emotive or affective in nature, nevertheless is at the same time self-justifying rather than addressed to any ulterior objective like goal-rational action. Weber's assessment of the possibility of principled action under present conditions of widespread rationalization resolves itself mainly into a regressive and nostalgic negative individualism of the sort described, but also into a residual charisma progressively less able to even affect the pace of this ubiquitous process.

Weber's ambivalence on this score manifests itself in his two-faced assessment of the possibility of a continuing antagonism of values in Society as a whole. Even though the essence of rationalization is a movement in the direction of value congruence and homogeneity under conditions of role, status and functional heterogeneity, Weber addresses the possibility of value pluralism by generating a sociology which is required to combine a generalizing objective from the natural sciences with an individualizing method from history. While not necessarily an impossible mandate, the effect of this double requirement is essentially to make a productive sociology extremely difficult, to say the least. It is as if Weber wants to make sociology unproductive because he "knows" that its mission is to extend and complete Society as a culturally and historically specific form of collective life by "normalizing" its abnormal division of labour, just as Durkheim had argued. On the other hand, however, there is Weber the hardheaded sociologist *inside* his discipline, arguing that in the final analysis the pivotal tensions in his work between formal and substantive rationality must be resolved in favour of formal rationality, since the concept substantive is in a certain sense a "formal" concept of sociology, rather than constituting a basis for the generation and defense of autonomous and antagonistic values which are objective rather than simply subjective phenomena.[27]

I have focussed on Weber's wide-ranging research and scholarship here because I believe it constitutes, to use his own term, a type-case of the contemporary temper far more than we like to think. What I have particularly in mind here is the tension between functional rationality and "sense of function." In common with my refusal to cede reason and rationality to structures and to the rationalization process goes a determination to recapture function rather than acceding to its present understanding as functional rationality. Thus sense of function is contrasted to functional rationality by the fact that in the first case form follows function while in the second form dictates function. If sense of function can be equated with what Arendt calls cooperation, and Weber a corporate group *(Verband),* functional rationality implies structural and organizational predefinition. Over time the two are dynamically interrelated with one another, to be sure, something which Weber on the whole refuses to acknowledge. Capitalist industrial society is usefully understood by reference to the ongoing interrelation between the two, and Weber's pessimism is given in his refusal to see the possibility that sense of function can ever hope to survive functional rationality as it is embodied in the alleged process of rationalization and corollary de-enchant-ment.[28]

From the standpoint of politics and citizenship, the distinction has particular significance. Established processes and mechanisms, while not necessarily functionally rationalized, do constitute structures which effectively circum-scribe function with formal predefinitions. This is another way of addressing the emphasis on place or location and its relation to the societal division of labour as a fixed and predefined hierarchial allocation of spaces and events. Display, whether within such processes and mechanisms or outside them in new and emerging public spaces, speaks to the *need* to reassert sense of function against functional rationality whenever it is possible to create or utilize events to generate public spaces, and whether or not these spaces arise within or outside fixed places or locations in Society. Sense of function, or cooperation, whereby a collective group is "built up" out of the interests and concerns of individuals, creates a whole which is not necessarily more than or different from the sum of its parts, but rather distinguished by its fundamental lack of predefinition. True, the only way this lack can be pre-served is if sense of function remains impermanent as the collective form of citizenly display. When it is converted into a permanent structure, as often happens in other forms of collective life as well as Society, it becomes a very likely candidate for functional rationality.

Citizenship can also include the relatively non-discretionary utilization of process which partakes of little if any display. The fixed notion of space as place, and the corollary drive to the standardization of events, is accepted as a given by members, who exercise citizenship as a societal role. Clearly this is insufficient on its own, but can nevertheless constitute a basis for the sort of experience which can eventually produce that integrated citizenly activity which successfully combines the various components already discussed, and thereafter allows its authors to rise above membership through individual display.[29] The dynamic and ongoing relationship between sense of function and functional rationality can be seen in the way that "formal" acknow-ledgement and recognition of the first creates the basis for transforming it into the second. Sense of function is therefore not only to be counted a useful conception for understanding the course of the economic growth and development of capitalist industrial societies, but also helps us make sense of the hope and possibility of political development as well. Sense of func-tion is the collective form that citizenly display takes whenever it is possible to create public spaces, whether inside or outside of established institutional structures, processes and mechanisms. Sense of function is the form of in-dividuation which best expresses the spirit and practice of political manage-ment.

VI

Aristotle's emphasis in the *Ethics* and the *Politics* has been contrasted to his concerns in *The Constitution of Athens* in order to underscore the *complementary* nature of the two approaches to government and politics. Display and process are interwined in his joint treatment of the practical ideal state and the qualities required of its citizens on the one hand, and the role of political science as that discipline committed to improving these qualities through careful reflection and comparative analysis on the other. Its method must be appropriate to its subject matter, rather than constituting a superficial imitation of methods employed by the then newly emergent "science" of medicine. Aristotle's major difficulty was one that this complementary approach could not, however, resolve, for it involved the redefinition of public space resulting from the collapse of the self-governing city-state and the rise of imperium. What had prevailed over Persia could not prevail over Macedon, and thereafter Rome. The city-state was henceforth to be a mere *social* space, an urban configuration located within a territorial state, a place within a state whose system of government was in turn based on a fixed sense of place and fixed functions.

It is in the context of this problem, one which we have failed to resolve even to the present time, that Aristotle addresses the dilemma of how to reconcile politics and the political with the emergence of the territorial state environing urban social spaces. Unable to make a complete break with the *polis* while yet realizing that it had been eclipsed by events, Aristotle opts for reformulating citizenship as membership, and thereafter supports a scheme aimed at the production of good men rather than good citizens. The emphasis shifts from citizenly display for the leisured few to secondary socialization on the order of Plato's *Republic*. It is in his effort to mediate a commitment to "polity," or the mixed constitutional state, with the rise of territory and place coincident with the collapse of the *polis* and the rise of imperium that Aristotle turns away from politics toward ethics. Ethics becomes the collective foundation on which any system of secondary socialization must be built, the moreso where its purpose is to provide a realistic alternative to the polis under changed conditions. Here the paramount requirement is stability and order, and what is needed is a docile population willing to acquiesce in the equation of citizenship with membership.

The tension between politics and polity, and the bias in favour of the latter, makes Aristotle's problem our problem. The "delicate equipoise" which I cited between politics and polity in chapter two is nothing less than a balance between sense of function and functional rationality, and not so much an achieved balance as one which we need to realize if we are reconcile stability and order with our own political development as a culture and a collective

form. Institutionalization was cited as a fundamental human effect resulting
from the sedimentation of forms and processes in structures over time, and
the particular *type* of institutionalization appropriate to Society was addressed as problematic for the needed equipoise. Here I had in mind the
organizational approach to collective order which is prefigured in the work
of Maistre and Bonald, and thereafter St. Simon, Comte and Enfantin. Its
institutional basis is the belief that we have in hand, or are capable of
generating, objective criteria on which to construct a system of hierarchically allocated roles, functions and statuses premised on rational domination. This is Weber's supreme problem, as I noted, and it becomes increasingly problematic as rationalization extends itself toward the outer (and
inner) perimeter of Society and finds it progressively easier to functionally
rationalize individual and collective acts of display.

The organizational principle in practice generates mainly *the belief* in objective criteria, particularly where reason, rationality and function are concerned, and it therefore must be seen to constitute a cultural artifact, not
unlike empiricism as a convention for the pursuit of inquiry under the regimen of the mastery and domination of external nature. Virtually given in the
operation of the organizational principle as the major vehicle of institutionalization in Society is the view that rationality ought to be comprehended
mainly as a property of structures rather than individuals. This is politically
regressive for the same reason that failure to acknowledge the well-distributed substructural basis of superstructural modes of rationality is. In both
cases it substitutes the role and status reference of functional rationality as it
has been extended in and through long-term and all-pervasive modes of
secondary socialization, and the effect of this is to subvert the possibilities
for social and political, as well as scientific and technical, innovation by
youth and young adults. The organizational principle of rational domination
reconciles "merit" with tenure in a hierarchical setting in which most of the
meritocracy that is achieved is formal rather than substantive in character.
This underpins Society's anti-political preference for passive roles, and for
citizenship as one of many role options available to members.

The present day tension between the rule of law and representation is the
major form that the modern type of institutionalization has taken. Hence
politics and polity are to a considerable extent merged by the sheer interdependence between them. Thus a legal and judicial framework is very
necessary to the genesis and perpetuation of the rules and conventions that
effectively ground representative democratic processes. At the same time,
mere legalism on its own cannot ever hope to substitute for the existence
and utilization of those processes. In this latter case, the all-too-predictible
result is formal legalism at best and "political justice" at worst. Law and the
judiciary have been sorely tempted, even in representative democracies, to

substitute their own judgments, methods, and forms of reflection, deliberation and decision for those of the people, and to extend them far beyond the protection of individual and minority rights and liberties. Indeed, this constitutes one of the less perceptible and more subtle forms of cooptation of political responsibilities carried out by non-elected officials and personnel in advanced societies. We are far more likely to be both more aware of administrative and bureaucratic discretion, and to have relatively settled views on its necessity or undesirability, particularly in common law countries. In contrast, there is likely to be a greater awareness of judicial discretion in code law countries, for reasons which were discussed in chapter three.

My decision to extend use of the concept of discretion not only to legal and judicial personnel, but to politicians, certainly constitutes unconventional usage. My reason for doing this was so that I could address the problem of the representative function, and the role of agents *vis a vis* members, as the basis for all other subsidiary grants of discretionary authority. It is never enough simply to explain discretionary delegations of authority by elected to non-elected officials as being necessitated by the former's lack of time or expertise. This is particularly evident when it is remembered that an axiom of delegation in representative democracies is that authority may be delegated but not the responsibility for its exercise. This problem of institutional polity is a constant reminder of what *should be* the costs of such delegation but frequently are not. Thus the inability of elected officials to delegate responsibility for the exercise of the authority delegated, for whatever reason, should require of them a controlling care for both the drafting of precise legislation allowing for needed discretion, and the ongoing legislative or governmental supervision of administration to make sure that the exercise of this discretion is as confined and structured as possible. Yet even here the role of functional expertise has underwritten a division of labour which frequently gives the law-drafting function to non-elected bureaucrats and administrative personnel.

While this may in large part be unavoidable, especially in parliamentary systems, its effects can be and frequently are pernicious, particularly in the absence of the counterweight to institutional polity in the form of citizen interest and display which I have argued is absolutely essential for political development in advanced industrial societies. A poor attitude to carrying out the representative function may arise out of the very structural characteristics which demand party loyalty or discipline, and cannot really be laid at the door of the individual agent. It reflects the failure of agents to remember that they are first and foremost members, and that their agency is only a formal basis for the *possibility* of citizenly display rather than a guarantor of it. One of the worst features of the present equation of citizenship with a passive and ascribed role option which affirms membership alone is the way that members persuade themselves (at least as much as they are persuaded) that agents are *automatically* better citizens, or at least ideally should be. It is a fundamental misunderstanding of citizenship that fails to see it as a temporarily achieved rather than a passively ascribed status which is a fault here. Citizenship, when not a role option for members, becomes synonymous with the occupational rationality and self-interest of the careerist, who views government and politics as a part of the societal division of labour under the sway of an organizational conception of institutionalization and order.

The focus on the important, though supplementary, role of the newly emergent public spaces was not intended to equate these possible spaces with the places where they might be found, except in an immediate locational sense. Politics and citizenly display *take off* from locations and places, but this possibility normally requires that events not be standardized and the spaces not be predictable. Local politics has been stigmatized in the public mind for a whole host or reasons related to its preference for more distant jurisdictions, and the effect of this has been disastrous. The idea of a practical science of politics must mean something quite different from a repertoire of methods and techniques like those which Mannheim alluded to in *Ideology and Utopia* and formulated more precisely in *Man and Society in an Age of Reconstruction* and *Diagnosis of Our Time*. Otherwise the effect of such a "practical" science will be substantially at variance with the only conception of practice to which I can subscribe. In place of Aristotle's integrated continuum of thought, concern, speech, assessment, evaluation and action, we shall generate a prescribed technology or methodology of civic and civil behaviour on the order of a civil religion. This is thoroughly incompatible with the notion of citizenly display within or outside established structures and processes which I believe to be central to political management, and therefore in the interests of *our* political development.

The purpose of political science must be discovered in the conception of "scientific" analysis which Aristotle had argued was appropriate to the character of *its* subject matter, rather than constituting some superficially scientistic endeavour at best formally rather than substantively imitative of science. This is of the greatest significance for my proposal to make the social sciences more "responsible" in a practical and political sense by radicalizing and politicizing the postulate of adequacy found in Schutz' phenomenological social science. The present endeavours of the social sciences are an inverted version of the least democratic features of bureaucratic administration. This should hardly come as a surprise, given their commitment to the normalization of the *societal* division of labour and the extension and completion of Society as a culturally and historically specific project, which, however, is rarely acknowledged as such. Asymmetrical scientism and professionalism trade on a banking conception of knowledge, while going about the business of disaggregating the biographical integrity of respondents, then assembling the resulting chaos on the basis of variable analysis. The result is a patchwork quilt whose outstanding characteristic is its disembodied nature. Its bias is clearly societal, as is evident from its preference for a passive and ascribed role and status structure over the idea of a body-politic.

Another possible space for politics is to be discovered in the contemporary university *precisely because* it increasingly functions as an extension of the public school system in many advanced industrial societies. Here the problem is clearly the failure of the faculty to complete the "revolution" which had earlier allowed them to refashion universities as professional rather than conventional bureaucratic organizations with specialists rather than generalists in line positions. The organizational conception of membership, coupled with the students' relatively temporary presence, underwrites the view that the university is first and foremost a work organization in the civil sphere. Because students are not paid a salary or wage, they are effectively banned from membership and become little more than clients, or the dependents of clients. Their temporary status is also pointed to in order to explain their present level and type of participation in the most important areas of higher education. This device is so characteristic of the bureaucratic conception of expertise and its tie to occupations and careers that it has managed to thoroughly sunder the very faculty-student relationship which still continues to constitute the *raison d'etre* of higher education. The point about citizenly display *by students* in the university is precisely the *irrelevance* of the argument from lack of permanence for reasons that have already been spelled out.

Innovation of a political and social-cultural kind is neither merely incidental to economic, technical and scientific innovation, nor something that can be counted on to accompany it. Indeed, I have argued that we are regressing relative to the apparent "progress" in the latter areas, and thereby becoming progressively *less* politically developed relative to what we *need* given the inability of the system to carry the load without the serious consequences we are already beginning to experience. A major resource for all forms and types of innovation are youth and young adults, wherever we find them. My focus on the university was not intended to slight the potential of those young people who have gone directly into the work force, but rather to deal with a situation in which the *in loco parentis* function, complemented by tutelage, has made the potential and actual contribution of university students *more* difficult to realize precisely because they *alone* are in a position of extended dependence. Innovative actions may be *less* problematic for those in the work force than for those in university, for secondary socialization continues in the latter case well into the twenties, if not longer. Society may no longer be able to suffer the absence of the contribution that these young people can and must make, especially if the relationship between youth and innovation holds as strongly as we often assume.

For every constraint or barrier that can be cited as a reason against the possibility or sense of political management in the absence of objective conditions, a reformulation of such obstacles as opportunities rather than constraints presents itself as the essence of realism and practicality. Our narrow and truncated vision of practice and the practical, and our organizational conception of politics and citizenship as a part of the societal division of labour, are what keep us from recognizing the significance of human reason as a well-distributed resource on which all superstructural modes depend, and one which must be fully utilized, whether within our outside of established structures and processes. Political management is the collective self care for public things, along with the requirement of determining just what these things are from time to time. The rigid bifurcation of agents and members freezes citizenly display into one among many passively ascribed role options, while status is accorded to occupational location in the societal division of labour. It is always important to see in the need for a dynamic equipoise between politics and polity the interdependence between sense of function and functional rationality. The former honours institutionalization while yet resisting its equation with the organizational principle in practice, in clear contrast to the latter.

A final point concerns the superiority of process that I have argued for throughout this book. Process is not simply to be honoured as its own justification because it is superior to either direct techniques or "bureaucratic representation" from a procedural standpoint. While it is true that there is no substitute for process and procedure on practical as well as moral grounds, the reason this is so relates as much to the *quality* of the outcomes as to the idea that process and procedure should be honoured for their own sake. Public decision making, in concert with representatives, which refuses to accept the ordinance that time is money is usually objectively superior in terms of outcomes, as well as by reference to the methods used to reach the decision or result. This is important, for it underscores the element of urgency and objective *need* which I have tried to argue is not simply a ploy.[30] The frontispiece to the original edition of Hobbes' *Leviathan* showed the sovereign's body to be comprised of the people, rather than separate and distinct from them. The greatest of all modern political philosophers saw subjects surrendering their natural rights in order to contract into society under government and law. This assessment is no longer correct, if indeed it ever was. Political management is the proper response to the urgency of the present situation, one which presents the sovereign people with an indisputable opportunity which they alone can grasp.

As the institutional and organizational basis for the practice of representative democracy, the modern territorial state has presented us with a challenge of an epic kind, one fit for the "practical" thinking of individuals as diverse and distinct in their attitudes toward it as Aristotle, Machiavelli, Hobbes, Locke, Halifax and Madison. We only provisionally resolved the tension between space and place by levelling out the political so that citizenship might coincide with membership, the good citizen with the good man, and citizenly display with agency, whether carried out by elected or non-elected officials. The basic dilemma implicit in our need for and fear of citizenship and a politics of display as distinct from collective, now societal, membership remains to haunt and curse us, as if we too had been persuaded of the urgent need to contract out of the state of nature in the way Hobbes suggested. Tyrannicide is not a fit deed for any people, whether on their own or through the agency of leading members, so the objective, looked at negatively, is to avoid becoming a victim of events that blood the public and thereafter obviate its best interests. Looked at in a more affirmative vein, it is now time to grasp destiny by the forelock, not because the state of nature once existed, or ever could return. The people need their own inestimable and inimitable resource and need it urgently, and no prince can ever hope to provide anything more than a superficial and transitory substitute for it, as Machiavelli in particular knew.

Though Lippmann and Dewey addressed the hidden public mainly in terms of opinions and interests, they did so because they rightly saw the public as the key focus for the problems of politics and polity.[31] Resurrecting space, and making place serve it, even while admitting our need for place, is one sure way to dynamize the public sphere so that relations between politics and polity are less fixed and asymmetrical in nature. This will of course necessitate challenging the power of Society by addressing its socializing agenda as something other than "natural" and given in its own right. The question now is how we can avoid the consequences of waiting for objective conditions to materialize, when we suspect, with Hegel, that their very materialization may well indicate that the possibility of a remedy is past. Neither nostalgia nor pessimism and cynicism is appropriate food for thought in the circumstances. Rather we must hope that our very participation in these conditions will allow us to form or frame aspects of their contours in a way which conduces to a helpful and useful direction. The need for process in politics is absolute, and the fact that the objective and the moral and ethical reasons in defense of it come together in the way I have indicated remains the best hope for political management.

References

1 Compare Aristotle, *Ethics* 1097 b 22 – 1098 a 20, 1005 19 b – 1113 a 12 to Aristotle, *Politics,* 1179 b 20 – 1181 b 12–15, 1295 a 25 – 1297 a 7. See W. D. Ross, *Aristotle,* pp. 183–261. Also Wilson, *Tradition and Innovation,* Chapter 3.

2 See this study, Chapter Six, "Discretion in Politics, Administration and Law"; Schwartz and Wade, *Legal Control of Government;* Max Weber, *From Max Weber,* pp. 209–214 on the distinction between quantitative and qualitative effects of the growth of bureaucracy; and Wilson, *The American Ideology,* Chapter 7.

3 See Herbert Marcuse, *One Dimensional Man* (Boston: Beacon Pres, 1964); and Anton Zijderveld, *The Abstract Society* (Garden City, NY: Doubleday Anchor, 1970).

4 Freire, *Pedagogy of the Oppressed;* Freire, *Education for Critical Consciousness* (NY: Seabury, 1973); Macpherson, *Democratic Theory,* pp. 24–38.

5 Jacques Ellul, *The Technological Society* (NY: Vintage, 1964); Gregory Bateson, *Steps To an Ecology of Mind* (NY: Ballantine, 1975); Schelling, *op cit;* Wilson, "Values . . .," *op cit;* and Wilson, "Technology and/as/or the Future," *Philosophy of the Social Scienses,* Volume 14 (forthcoming).

6 Thomas Hobbes, *Leviathan,* edited with an introduction by C. B. Macpherson (Harmondsworth: Penguin, 1968); John O'Neill, "The Hobbesian Problem in Parsons and Marx," in O'Neill, *Sociology as a Skin Trade* (London: Heinemann, 1972), pp. 177–208. Sociology's concern for collective (societal) order shows it to be a decidedly *conservative* rather than "liberal" intellectual enterprise. But see how Wolin brings them together in *op cit,* Chapters 9 & 10.

7 John Stuart Mill, *Representative Government* (NY: Everyman's edition, 1953), p. 205 on the consequences of such a default, cited in the last headnote to this study.

8 See Michel Crozier, *The Bureaucratic Phenomenon* (Chicago: University of Chicago Press, 1964), pp. 164–165, 299–300 and compare to Victor Thompson, *Modern Organization* (NY: Alfred Knopf, 1961), Chapter 2. Also see Wilson, "Technocracy and Late Capitalist Society," *op cit,* concluding section.

9 If this seems strange, think about the way the public either accords extensions of the public sector *automatic* and virtually uncontested legitimacy, or views such extensions as something akin to a "visitation of nature" in Mill's sense.

10 Wilson, *Tradition and Innovation,* Chapter 3 on disembodiment and discipline; *The American Ideology;* "Technocracy and Late Capialist Society;" and "Elites, Meritocracy and Technocracy" on functional rationality and formal meritocracy and their consequences for the "open" Society.

11 Wilson, *Tradition and Innovation,* Chapters 2–5 (passim).

12 Arendt, *The Human Condition,* p. 200.

13 Both Hegel, in *The Philosophy of Right,* and Durkheim, in *The Division of Labour in Society* and *Professional Ethics and Civic Morals,* saw the possibility of the ethical life only within the confines of the state, understood in both cases (though for different reasons) to be coterminous with civil society.

14 See Edward Hall, *The Hidden Dimension* (Garden City, NY: Doubleday Anchor, 1966), for an interesting cross-cultural study of the meaning of space to different peoples.

15 Wilson, *Tradition and Innovation,* Chapter 3.

16 Durkheim, *The Division of Labour in Society,* conclusion and preface to the 2nd edition (1902).

17 Wilson, *The American Ideology,* pp. 183–184; Zijderveld, *op cit.*

18 Compare Mannheim, *Essays on the Sociology of Knowledge,* pp. 249–253, discussing "Success in a Career," to Christopher Lasch, *Haven in a Heartless World* (NY: Basic Books, 1977) on what precisely is required in order for there to be a perception of sufficient stability to organize one's life for the deferred status, power and remunerative benefits of a career. Also see Lasch, *The Culture of Narcissism* (NY: W. W. Norton, 1979).

19 Max Weber, *The Protestant Ethic and the Spirit of Capitalism* (NY: Charles Scribners, 1958), last 5–6 pages; Weber, "Science as a Vocation," in *From Max Weber,* pp,. 129–156 at pp. 137–141; Gabriel Kolko, "A Critique of Max Weber's Philosophy of History," *Ethics,* Volume 70, No. 1 (October, 1959), pp. 21–36; and Wilson, *Tradition and Innovation,* Chapter 5.

20 Nor can we allow ourselves to fall prey to the sociological notion, so central to the societal bias of these disciplines, which argues that we are so totally a *product* of Society that terms like autonomy and freedom have no significance, if they ever did. See B. F. Skinner, *Beyond Freedom and Dignity* (NY: Alfred Knopf, 1971), for this view from a behavioural psychologist.

21 Arendt, *The Human Condition,* pp. 79–135; Karl Popper, *The Poverty of Historicism* (London: Routledge and Kegan Paul, 1957); and my critique of each in *The American Ideology,* pp. 62–65, 171–174 (Arendt), and Chapters 1, 5, and 10 (Popper).

22 Weber, "Politics as a Vocation" in *From Max Weber,* pp. 77–128.

23 Karl Marx, *The Grundrisse: Complete English Edition,* translated with a foreword by Martin Nicolaus (Harmondsworth: Penguin, 1973), p. 156. Politics presupposes ethics just as citizenship presupposes membership. Politics and citizenship, however, is the key to *both* social and political innovation.

24 See *The American Ideology,* Chapter 10, and this study Chapter 7.

25 Weber, *The Protestant Ethic and the Spirit of Capitalism,* pp. 181–183.

26 But note Weber's two-faced endorsement of bureaucracy as superior to all other ways of administering, *given* modern Western civilization, and his view of it as the leading edge of a process of rationalization and de-enchantment from which there is no escape – "the fate of the West." On the two ways of generating bureaucracies and their differences, Helen Constas, "Max Weber's Two Concepts of Bureaucracy," *op cit.* Also see *The American Ideology,* Chapter 7.

27 Weber, *Theory of Social and Economic Organization,* pp. 185–186, 275–278; Wilson, "Max Weber's Pessimism," *International Journal of Contemporary Sociology,* Volume 8 (April, 1971), pp. 183–188; Wilson, "Reading Max Weber: The Limits of Sociology," *Sociology,* Volume 10, No. 2 (May, 1976), pp. 297–315.

28 Wilson, "Functional Rationality and 'Sense of Function': the Case of an Ideological Distortion," *International Yearbook of Organization Studies,* edited by Graeme Salaman and David Dunkerly (London: Routledge, 1981), pp. 37–61; Weber, *Theory of Social and Economic Organization,* pp. 145–153.

29 Gabriel Tarde, *Laws of Imitation* (NY: Henry Holt, 1903) provides an instructive

parallel to this distinction in his contrast between imitation, non-imitation, counter-imitation and their respective relation to invention and innovation. Also see my *Tradition and Innovation,* Chapter 2 "Imitation/Counter Imitation," and compare to the two preceding sections, where Durkheim's understanding of innovation is addressed.

30 Harold Wilensky, in *Organizational Intelligence* (NY: Basic Books, 1967), argues *against* excessive deliberation in political and economic decision making, but he is only making my point because his assessment is based on the assumption that the present system of representative democracy is given.

31 Walter Lippmann, *Public Opinion* (NY: Macmillan, 1961, 1922); Lippmann, *The Public Philosophy* (NY: Mentor/New American Library, 1956); John Dewey, *The Public and its Problems* (Denver: Alan Swallow, 1954, 1927).

Reprise

I have been acutely conscious of the need for this study to be viewed as a complement to, rather than a substitute for, other work I have done in the area of critical, as opposed to traditional theory. I believe political management to be necessary in part because of my already noted conclusions regarding the feasibility of waiting for the emergence of "objective conditions." Political regression, even *within* the present culturally, and historically specific collective form, only seems to be an unsedimented notion because the actual dynamic of Society cannot be satisfactorily specified. While I have elsewhere underscored the need, following Adorno, Horkheimer and Marcuse, to stay true to the tension between the critical theory of Society, and the commitment to various types of reforms within Society's many mediations[1], the specifically political concerns of this study reflect an immediate concern of considerable moment for me. While I remain aware of the fact of contradiction between observable phenomena and their essence, I have consciously opted for an analysis of existing political institutions and processes, as well as the possibilities lying latent within them for individuals and groups.

If this has required me to turn to sources from the ancient, medieval, and early modern teaching, most conspiciously Aristotle, this was deemed necessary in large part because of the unresolved problems I believe they have presented us with, even (or especially) in the contemporary circumstances of late capitalism. Some might argue that in carrying out this study I have sacrificed thought to immediacy, and have fetishized the individual too much in the process. I would respond by saying that the locus in the individual of what I believe to be significant, albeit largely undeveloped, possibilities has not taken shape in the absence of a recognition of the priority of the culturally and historically specific collective form of life of our age: Society. Thus, though I have been prone off and on throughout *Political Management* to stress the immediacy of the problem, seen from one vantage point, and the need to focus on the individual as a consequence, I have not lost sight of either thought and critique or the nature of the collective form in which the people find themselves in advanced industrial societies. My task as I saw it required such accentuation, and the reader is advised to see this study in the context of earlier books, monographs and articles, many of which have been cited in the references and bibliography.

This, then, is not to be construed as an exercise in "traditional" theory whose aim is to accommodate individuals to Society by accentuating isolated actor subjectivity and intense activity for its own sake. In the first case the subject becomes little more than an object, while in the second the probable effects of such frenetic behaviour would be either "effective" sublimation, or the unravelling of the present system without the parallel emergence of viable alternatives to it. Another point must be mentioned, however. I do not accept the view that political and governmental institutions can any longer be treated as mere "superstructure" relative to the mode and means of production, if only because governments are major employers and direct and indirect economic actors which participate actively and continuously in the complex, but still unmistakeable, commodity forms found throughout advanced industrial societies. This makes governments participants in the most fundamental aspects and properties of the whole, rather than merely a set of obsolete institutions functioning as effects of causal relations to be discovered elsewhere in "the economy." As a corollary, I must note once more my belief that present representative institutions cannot be improved, and ultimately transcended, until they have been fully utilized. Even the acknowledgement of new public spaces must yield, I think, to this fact. The very persistence of these institutions is precisely what gives the lie to the arguments of both the functionalists and the so-called "realists."

References

1 Wilson, "The Meaning and Significance of 'Empirical Method' for the Critical Theory of Society", *op cit.* Also see generally Russell Jacoby, *Social Amnesia* (Boston: Beacon Press, 1975).

Literature

Abraham, Henry: *The Judicial Process*. NY: Oxford University Press, 1962

Adcock, F. E.: *Roman Political Ideas and Practice*. Ann Arbor: University of Michigan, 1964

Adorno, Theodor W.: *Prisms*. London: Neville Spearman, 1967

–, "Society." *The Legacy of the German Refugee Intellectuals*. Ed. by Robert Boyers. NY: Schocken Books, 1969, pp. 144–153.

–, *Negative Dialectics*. NY: Seabury Press, 1973

–, and Max Horkheimer: *The Dialectic of Enlightment*. NY: Herder and Herder, 1972

Agard, Walter: *The Greek Mind*. Princeton, NJ: D. Van Nostrand Co., 1957

–, *What Democracy Meant to the Greeks*. Madison, Wisconsin: University of Wisconsin Press, 1965, 1942

Allen, J. W.: *History of Political Thought in the Sixteenth Century*. London: Methuen, 1928

Almond, Gabriel, and Sidney Verba: *The Civic Culture*. Boston: Little Brown, 1965

Althusius, Johannes: *Politica Methodice Digesta*. 1603, 1610. Engl. transl. ed. by Carl J. Friedrich. Cambridge, Mass.: Harvard University Press, 1932

Apel, Karl Otto: *Transformations of Philosophy*. London: Routledge, 1980

Arendt, Hannah: *The Human Condition*. Chicago: University of Chicago Press, 1958

–, *The Origins of Totalitarianism*. 2nd enlarged edition. NY: Meridian Books, 1960, 1951

–, *Between Past and Future*. NY: Viking Press, 1961

Aristotle: *Aristotle's Constitution of Athens*. Ed. by Sir John Sandys, 2nd rev. and enl. ed. London: Oxford University Press, 1912

Aristotle: *Politics*. Transl. with an introduction, notes and appendices by Ernest Barker. London: Oxford University Press, 1946

Aristotle: *The Politics of Aristotle*. Transl. by W. L. Newman, 4 Vol. Oxford: The Clarendon Press, 1902

Aristotle: *Prior and Posterior Analytics*. Introduction, text and commentary by W. D. Ross. Oxford: Blackwell, 1949

Arnold, Thurman: *The Folklore of Capitalism*. New Haven: Yale University Press, 1937

–, *The Symbols of Government*. New Haven: Yale University Press, 1935

Avineri, Shlomo: *Hegel's Theory of the Modern State*. London: Cambridge University Press, 1972

–, *The Social and Political Thought of Karl Marx*. London: Cambridge University Press, 1968, pp. 43–52

Ayres, Clarence: *The Theory of Economic Progress*. 3rd ed. Kalamazoo, Mich.: New Issues Press, 1978

–, *Toward a Reasonable Society*. Austin: University of Texas Press, 1961

Babbitt, Irving: *Democracy and Leadership*. Boston: Houghton Mifflin, 1924
Bachrach, Peter: *The Theory of Democratic Elitism*. Boston: Little, Brown, 1965
Bagehot, Walter: *The English Constitution*. London: Oxford University Press, 1958
Bakan, David: *On Method*. San Francisco: Jossey Bass, 1969
–, "A Plan for a College, with Commentary." *Canadian University and College*. (June, 1969), pp. 30–34, 42–43
Baritz, Loren: *The Servants of Power*. NY: John Wiley, 1960
Barker, Ernest: *Greek Political Theory*. London: Methuen, 1960
–, *The Political Thought of Plato and Aristotle*. London: Oxford University Press, 1906
Barnard, Chester: *The Functions of the Executive*. Cambridge: Harvard University Press, 1938
Barzun, Jacques: "Tomorrow's University: Back to the Middle Ages?". *Saturday Review*. Vol. 52 (November 15, 1969), pp. 23–25
Bateson, Gregory: *Steps to an Ecology of Mind*. N. Y.: Ballantine, 1975
Bateson, M. C.: *Our Own Metaphor*. NY: Alfred Knopf, 1972
Battershill, Charles: *Power-Knowledge in Theory and Society*. Masters thesis. Department of Sociology, York University, June 1983
Becker, Carl: *The Heavenly City of the Eighteenth Century Philosophers*. New Haven: Yale University Press, 1932
Becker, Howard: "On Methodology." *Sociological Work*. Chicago: Aldine Press, 1975
–, Whose Side are We on?." *Social Problems*. Vol. 14 (Winter, 1967), pp. 239–247
Bell, Daniel: *The End of Ideology*. NY: Macmillan/Free Press, 1960
Beneveniste, Guy: *The Politics of Expertise*. London: Croom Helm, 1973
Benjamin, Roger: *The Limits of Politics*. Chicago: University of Chicago Press, 1980
Benn, S. I., and R. S. Peters: *Principles of Political Thought*. NY: Macmillan/Free Press 1965, 1959
Bentley, Arthur: *The Process of Government*. Chicago: University of Chicago Press, 1908
Berger, Morroe: *Equality by Statute*. Rev. ed. Garden City, NY: Doubleday and Co., 1967, 1950
Berlin, Isaiah: *Two Concepts of Liberty*. Oxford: Clarendon Press, 1958
Bezold, Clement (Ed.): *Anticipatory Democracy: People in the Politics of the Future*. NY: Vintage, 1978
Bickel, Alexander: *The Morality of Consent*. New Haven: Yale University Press, 1975
Blackburn, Robin (Ed.): *Ideology in Social Science*. London: Fontana/Collins, 1972
Bledstein, Burton: *The Culture of Professionalism: The Middle Class and the Development of Higher Education in America*. NY: W. W. Norton, 1976
Blum, Alan: *Theorizing*. London: Heinemann, 1974
–, *Socrates: The Original and its Images*. London: Routledge and Kegan Paul, 1978

Blumer, Herbert: *Symbolic Interaction*. Englewood Cliffs, N. J.: Prentice Hall, 1969
Bluntschli, J. K.: *Theory of the State*. Oxford: Clarendon Press, 1892
Bodin, Jean: *Six Books of the Republic*. Latin ed. 1576; Engl. transl. (Knolles) 1606
Boguslaw, Robert: *The New Utopians*. NY: Spectrum, 1965
Bonner, Robert J.: *Aspects of Athenian Democracy*. NY: Russell and Russell, 1967, 1933
Bosanquet, Bernard: *The Philosophical Theory of the State*. London: Macmillan and Co., 1899
Braybrooke, David: *Three Tests for Democracy*. Personal rights, human welfare, collective preference. NY: Random House, 1968
–, and Charles Lindblom: *A Strategy of Decision: Policy Evaluation as a Social Process*. NY: Free Press of Glencoe, 1963
Brecht, Arnold: *Political Theory*. Princeton: Princeton University Press, 1959
Brutus, Stephen Junius (Pseudonym): *Vindiciae Contra Tyrannos*. (Fr. ed. 1581), Rep. as *A Defence of Liberty Against Tyrants*. With an introd. by H. J. Laski. London, 1924
Buchanan, James and Gordon Tullock: *The Calculus of Consent*. Ann Arbor: University of Michigan Press, 1962
Bury, J. B.: *The Idea of Progress*. NY: Macmillan, 1932

Carritt, E. F.: *Ethical and Political Thinking*. Oxford: Clarendon Press, 1947
Calhoun, John: "A Disquisition on Government". In Calhoun: *Basic Documents*. Ed. and introd. by John M. Anderson. State College, Pennsylvania: Bald Eagle Press, 1952
Cassirer, Ernst: *The Myth of the State*. Garden City, NY: Doubleday, 1955, 1946
Catlin, G. E. G.: *The Science and Method of Politics*. Hamden, Conn.: Archon Books, 1964
Charlesworth, James C. (Ed.): *The Limits of Behaviouralism in Political Science*. Philadelphia: Annals of the American Academy of Political and Social Science, 1963
–, *A Design for Political Science: Scope, Objectives and Methods*. Philadelphia: Annals of the American Academy of Political and Social Science, 1966
Churchman, C. West: *Challenge to Reason*. NY: McGraw Hill, 1968
Cohen, Felix: *Ethical Systems and Legal Ideals*. Westport, Conn.: Greenwood Press, 1970, 1933
Collins, Randall: *The Credential Society*. NY: Academic Press, 1979
Constas, Helen: "Max Weber's Two Concepts of Bureaucracy." *American Journal of Sociology* 52 (1958), pp. 400–409
Cornford, F. M.: *Plato's Theory of Knowledge*. London: Routledge and Kegan Paul, 1935
Cox, Harvey: *The Secular City*. New rev. ed. NY: Macmillan, 1975
Crane, Diana: *Invisible Colleges*. Chicago: University of Chicago Press, 1972
Crick, Bernard: *The American Science of Politics*. Berkeley: University of California Press, 1959
–, *In Defense of Politics*. Harmondsworth: Penguin, 1960

Croly, Herbert: *The Promise of American Life*. Hamden, Conn.: Archon Books, 1963, 1909
–, *Progessive Democracy*. NY: The Macmillan Co., 1947, 1914
Crosskey, W. W.: *Politics and the Constitution in the History of the United States*. Chicago: University of Chicago Press, 1953, 1980
Crozier, Michel: *The Bureaucratic Phenomenon*. Chicago: University of Chicago Press, 1964

Dahl, Robert: "The Behavioural Approach in Political Science: Epitaph for a Monument to a Successful Protest". *American Political Science Review* 55 (December, 1961), p. 763–772
–, *Modern Political Analysis*. Englewood Cliffs, N. J.: Prentice Hall, 1963
–, *Preface to Democratic Theory*. Chicago: University of Chicago Press, 1956
–, *Political Oppositions in Western Democracies*. New Haven: Yale University Press, 1966
–, *Polyarchy: Participation and Opposition*. New Haven: Yale University Press, 1971
–, and Charles Lindblom: *Politics, Economics and Welfare*. NY: Harper, 1963
Davis, Kenneth Culp: *Discretionary Justice*. Baton Rouge, Louisiana: Louisiana State University Press, 1969
DeGrazia, Sebastian: *Of Work, Time and Leisure*. Garden City, NY: Doubleday Anchor, 1966
–, *The Political Community: A Study in Anomie*. Chicago: University of Chicago Press, 1948
De Jouvenel, Bertrand: *On Power, its nature and the history of its growth*. Boston: Beacon Press, 1962, 1948
–, *Sovereignty*. Chicago: University of Chicago Press, 1957
De Riencourt, Amaury: *The Coming Caesars*. NY: Capricorn Books, 1964, 1957
De Ruggiero, Dante: *The History of European Liberalism*. Boston: Beacon Press, 1959, 1927
De Tocqueville, Alexis: *Democracy in America*. 2 Vols. NY: Alfred Knopf, 1945
Dewey, John: *The Public and its Problems*. Denver: Alan Swallow, 1954, 1927
Deutsch, Karl: *The Nerves of Government*. New Haven: Yale University Press, 1963
Dicey, A. V.: *The Law of the Constitution*. 10th ed. London: Macmillan, 1959, 1965
Dickinson, John: *Administrative Justice and the Supremacy of Law*. NY: Russell and Russell, 1959
Diesing, Paul: *Reason and Society*. Urbana, Ill.: University of Illinois Press, 1962
–, *Science and Ideology in the Policy Sciences*. Chicago: Aldine Press, 1981
Donzelot, Jacques: *The Policing of Families*. NY: Pantheon, 1979
Downs, Anthony: *An Economic Theory of Democracy*. NY: Harper and Row, 1957
–, "The Public Interest: its Meaning in a Democracy." *Social Research*. Vol. 29, No. 1 (Spring, 1962), pp. 1–36
–, *Inside Bureaucracy*. Boston: Little Brown, 1967
Dreitzel, H. P.: "Social Science and the Problem of Rationality: Notes on the So-

ciology of Technocrats." *Politics and Society*. Vol. 2, No. 2 (Winter 1971–1972), pp. 165–182
Durkheim, Emile: *The Division of Labour in Society*. NY: Macmillan, 1952
–, *Professional Ethics and Civic Morals*. London: Routledge and Kegan Paul, 1957
–, *Rules of Sociological Method*. NY: Macmillan, 1964
–, *Selections*. Ed. by George Simpson. NY: Thomas Crowell, 1963

Easton, David: *The Political System*. NY: Alfred Knopf, 1953
–, and Jack Dennis: *Children in the Political System: Origins of Political Legitimacy*. NY: McGraw Hill, 1969
Edelman, Murray: *The Symbolic Uses of Politics*. Urbana, Ill.: University of Illinois Press, 1964
Ehrenburg, Victor: *The Greek State*. Oxford: Basil Blackwell & Mott, 1960
Ehrenfeld, David: *The Arrogance of Humanism*. NY: Oxford University Press, 1978
Ellul, Jacques: *The Technological Society*. NY: Vintage, 1964
–, *The Technological System*. NY: Continuum Books, 1980
Etzioni, Amitai: *The Active Society*. NY: Macmillan, 1968
–, *Modern Organization*. Englewood Cliffs, N. J.: Prentice Hall, 1964
Eulau, Heinz: *The Behavioural Persuasion in Politics*. NY: Random House, 1963
Ewen, Stuart: *Captains of Consciousness*. NY: McGraw Hill, 1976
Eysenck, H. J.: *The Inequality of Man*. London: Temple Smith, 1973

Fagen, Richard R.: *Politics and Communication*. Boston: Little Brown, 1966
Findlay, J. S.: *The Discipline of the Cave*. London: Allen and Unwin, 1966
Flathman, Richard: *The Public Interest*. Chicago: University of Chicago Press, 1966
Follett, Mary P.: *The New State*. Group Organization the Solution of Popular Government. London: Longmans/Green, 1934, 1920
Foucault, Michel: *Discipline and Punish*. NY: Random House, 1978
Frank, Jerome: *Courts on Trial, Myth and Reality in American Justice*. Princeton: Princeton University Press, 1949
Frascona, Joseph: *Agency*. Englewood Cliffs, NJ: Prentice Hall, 1964
Freire, Paolo: *Pedagogy of the Oppressed*. NY: Herder & Herder, 1972
–, *Education for Critical Consciousness*. NY: Seabury Press, 1973
Freud, Sigmund: *Civilisation and its Discontents*. Garden City, NY: Doubleday Anchor, 1958
Freund, Ernst: "The Use of Indefinite Terms in Statutes." *Yale Law Journal*. Vol. 30, No. 5 (March, 1921), pp. 437–455
Friedrich, Carl J.: *Constitutional Government and Democracy*. Rev. ed. Boston: Little Brown, 1950, 1941
–, *Constitutional Reason of State*. Providence: Brown University Press, 1957
–, *The New Belief in the Common Man*. Boston: Little Brown, 1942
–, (Ed.): *The Public Interest*. Nomos V. NY: Atherton Press, 1962
–, (Ed.): *Responsibility*. Nomos III. NY: Liberal Arts Press, 1960

Friendly, Henry: "Judicial Control of Discretionary Administrative Action," *Journal of Legal Education*. 23 (1971), pp. 63–69
Fromm, Erich: *Escape from Freedom*. N. Y.: Holt, Rinehart and Winston, 1941

Garfinkel, Harold: "The Rational Properties of Scientific and Commonsense Activities". In Garfinkel: *Studies in Ethnomethodology*. Englewood Cliffs, N. J.: Prentice Hall, 1967, pp. 262–283
Gibson, Quentin: *The Logic of Social Enquiry*. London: Routledge & Kegan Paul, 1960
Giddens, Anthony: *The Class Structure of the Advanced Societies*. London: Hutchinson, 1973
–, *New Rules of Sociological Method*. NY: Basic Books, 1976
Gifford, Daniel: "Decisions, Decisional Referents & Administrative Justice." *Law and Contemporary Problems*. Vol. 37, No. 1 (Winter, 1972), pp. 3–48
Gilb, Corinne: *Hidden Hierarchies*. NY: Harper and Row, 1966
Gilmour, Robert and Robert Lamb: *Political Alienation in Contemporary America*. NY: St. Martins Press, 1975
Goffman, Erving: "Cooling the Mark out." *Psychiatry* 15 (November, 1952), pp. 451–463
Goldman, Eric: *Rendez-Vous with Destiny*. NY: Knopf, 1952
Gooch, G. P.: *The History of English Democratic Ideas in the Seventeenth Century*. 2nd ed. London: Cambridge University Press, 1927
Goodin, Robert, E.: *The Politics of Rational Man*. London: John Wiley, 1976
Gould, Stephen J.: *The Mismeasure of Man*. N. Y.: W. W. Norton, 1971
Gouldner, Alvin: "Anti-Minotaur: The Myth of a Value-Free Sociology." *Sociology on Trial*. Ed. by Maurice Stein and Arthur Vidich. Englewood Cliffs, NJ: Prentice Hall, 1963
–, *The Coming Crisis of Western Sociology*. NY: Basic Books, 1970
–, "Cosmopolitans and Locals". *Administrative Science Quarterly* 2 (1957–58), pp. 281–302, 444–480
–, *The Dialectic of Ideology and Technology*. NY: Seabury Press, 1976
–, *Enter Plato: Classical Greece and the Origins of Social Theory*. NY: Basic Books, 1965
–, "The Sociologist as Partisan: Sociology and the Welfare State." *The American Sociologist*. Vol. 3, No. 2 (May, 1968), pp. 103–116
–, *For Sociology: Research and Critique in Sociology Today*. London: Allen Lane, 1973
Grant, George: *Technology and Empire*. Toronto: Anansi, 1969
Green, Robert W.: *Protestantism, Capitalism and Social Science: The Weber Thesis Controversy*. Lexington, Mass: D. C. Heath, 1959
Greenstein, Fred: *Children and Politics*. New Haven: Yale University Press, 1965
Grotius, Hugo: *De Jure Belli ac Pacis*. 1625. Engl. transl. by Francis Kelsey et al. Oxford: Clarendon Press, 1925

Habermas, Jürgen: "Aspects of the Rationality of Action." *Rationality Today*. Ed. by Theodore Geraets. Ottawa: University of Ottawa Press, 1979, pp. 185–212
–, *Communication and the Evolution of Society*. Boston: Beacon Press, 1979
–, *Legitimation Crisis*. Boston: Beacon Press, 1975

–, "Technology & Science as Ideology." In Habermas: *Toward a Rational Society*. Boston: Beacon, 1968, pp. 81–122

–, "Toward a Theory of Communicative Competence." *Recent Sociology*. No. 2. Ed. by H. P. Dreitzel. NY: Macmillan, 1970

Hall, Edward: *The Hidden Dimension*. Garden City, NY: Doubleday Anchor, 1966

Hallowell, John H.: *The Decline of Liberalism as an Ideology, with Particular Reference to German Politico-Legal Thought*. NY: H. Fertig, 1971, 1943

Hamilton, Alexander, James Madison and John Jay: *Federalist Papers*. Orig. ed. 1787–1788. NY: New American Library, 1961

Harman, Lesley D.: *The Modern Stranger: On Language and Membership*. Acad. Diss., Dept. of Sociology, York University, Toronto, September 1983

Harrington, James: *The Commonwealth of Oceana*. (Engl. ed. London 1656). Ed. by S. B. Liljegren. Heidelberg, 1924

Harrison, Deborah: *The Limits of Liberalism*. Montreal: Black Rose, 1982

Hart, H. L. A.: *The Concept of Law*. London: Cambridge University Press, 1961

Hegel, G. W. F.: *The Phenomenology of Mind*. Transl. with an introduction and notes by J. B. Baillie. NY: Harper, 1967

–, *The Philosophy of Right*. Transl. with notes by T. M. Knox. London: Oxford University Press, 1967

Herring, Pendleton: *Public Administration and the Public Interest*. NY: Russell and Russell, 1967, 1936

Herrnstein, R. H.: *IQ in the Meritocracy*. London: Allen Lane, 1973

Hill, Melvin (Ed.), Hannah Arendt: *The Recovery of the Public World*. NY: St. Martins Press, 1979

Hobbes, Thomas: *Behemoth*. (The Long Parliament) ed. Molesworth. NY: B. Franklin, 1963

–, *De Cive*. (Of Man and Citizen) ed. Molesworth. NY: Appleton Century Crofts, 1949

–, *Elements of Law Natural and Politic*. Ed. by Ferdinand Tonnies. 1st ed. 1889, 2nd ed. 1928

–, *Leviathan*. Ed. with an introduction by C. B. Macpherson. Harmondsworth: Penguin, 1968

Hodder, Alfred: *The Adversaries of the Skeptic*. London: Swan Sonnenschein and Co. Ltd., 1901

Hodges, Donald: *The Bureaucratization of Socialism*. Amherst and Boston: University of Massachusetts Press, 1980

Hoffer, Eric: *The True Believer*. NY: Harper and Row, 1951

Holmes, Oliver W.: *The Common Law*. Cambridge, Mass: Belknap Press, 1963

Hood, Christopher C.: *The Limits of Administration*. London: John Wiley and Sons, 1976

Horkheimer, Max: *Critical Theory*. NY: Herder and Herder, 1972

–, *The Eclipse of Reason,* NY: Seabury Press, 1974

–, and Theodor W. Adorno: *The Dialectic of Enlightenment*. NY: Herder and Herder, 1972

Hume, David: *Treatise of Human Nature*. Orig. publ. 1739–40. Oxford: Clarendon Press, 1960

Innis, Harold: *The Bias of Communication*. Toronto: University of Toronto Press, 1951
–, *Empire and Communications*. Toronto: University of Toronto Press, 1950

Jacobs, Jane: *The Economy of Cities*. NY: Random House, 1969
Jacoby, Russel: *Social Amnesia*. Boston: Beacon Press, 1975
Jaeger, Werner: *Aristotle: Fundamentals of the History of His Development*. Transl. by Richard Robinson. Oxford: Clarendon Press, 1934
John of Salisbury: *Policraticus*. (The Statesman's Book). Ed.: C. C. J. Webb. Oxford: Clarendon Press, 1909

Kant, Immanuel: *Perpetual Peace*. NY: Liberal Arts Press, 1957
–, *Critique of Practical Reason*. NY: Liberal Arts Press, 1956
Kariel, Henry: *The Decline of American Pluralism*. Stanford: Stanford University Press, 1961
Kaufmann, Felix: *Methodology of the Social Sciences*. New Haven: Yale University Press, 1944
Keller, Suzanne: *Beyond the Ruling Class*. NY: Random House, 1963
Kenniston, Kenneth: "How Community Mental Health Stamped Out the Riots (1968–78)". *Trans-Action*. (July/August, 1968), pp. 21–29
Kirchheimer, Otto: *Political Justice*. Princeton: Princeton University Press, 1971
Knight, Everett: *The Objective Society*. NY: George Braziller, 1960
Kolko, Gabriel: "A Critique of Max Weber's Philosophy of History." *Ethics*. Vol. 70, No. 1 (October, 1959), pp. 21–36
Konvitz, Milton and Arthur Murphy (Eds.): *Essays in Political Theory*. Pres. to George H. Sabine on the occ. of his retirement. Ithaca, NY: Cornell University Press, 1948
Kornhauser, William: *The Politics of Mass Society*. NY: Macmillan/Free Press, 1959
Kotarbinski, Tadeusz: *Praxiology*. Oxford: Pergamon Press, 1965
Krabbe, H.: *The Modern Idea of the State*. Westport, Conn.: Hyperion Press, 1980, 1922
Kroeber, Alfred: *Configurations of Culture Growth*. Berkeley: University of California Press, 1944
–, *Style and Civilizations*. Ithaca, NY: Cornell University Press, 1957
Kuhn, Thomas: *The Structure of Scientific Revolutions*. 2nd ed. Chicago: University of Chicago Press, 1970

Lane, Robert: "The Decline of Politics and Ideology in a Knowledgeable Society." *American Sociological Review*. Vol. 31, No. 5 (October, 1966), pp. 647–662
–, *Political Life*. NY: Macmillan, 1959
–, *Political Ideology*. NY: Macmillan, 1962
Larsen, J. A. O.: "Cleisthenes and the Development of the Theory of Democracy at Athens." *Essays in Political Theory*. Ed. by Milton Konvitz and Arthur Murphy. Ithaca, NY: Cornell University Press, 1948, pp. 1–16
Lasch, Christopher: *The Culture of Narcissism*. N. Y.: W. W. Norton, 1979
–, *Haven in a Heartless World*. NY: Basic Books, 1977
–, "Life in the Therapeutic State." *New York Review of Books*. June 12, 1980, pp. 24–32

Laski, Harold: *Authority in the Modern State*. Hamden, Conn.: Archon Books, 1968, 1919
Lasswell, Harold: *Politics: Who Gets What, When, How*. NY: Meridian, 1958
Lebedoff, David: *The New Elite: The Death of Democracy*. Chicago: Contemporary Books, 1983
Leiserson, Avery: *Administrative Regulation*. Westport, Conn.: Greenwood Press, 1975, 1942
Lewis, Sinclair: *It Can't Happen Here*. N. Y.: New American Library, 1976, 1938
Leys, Wayne A. R.: "Ethics and Administrative Discretion." *Public Administration Review* 3 (Winter, 1943), pp. 10–23
–, *Ethics for Policy Decisions*. NY: Prentice Hall, 1952
–, and Charner M. Perry: *Philosophy and the Public Interest*. Chicago: Committee to Advance Original Work in Philosophy, 1959
Lijphart, Arendt: "Consociational Democracy." *World Politics*. Vol. 21, No. 2 (1969), pp. 207–225
–, *Democracy in Plural Societies*. New Haven: Yale University Press, 1977
–, *The Politics of Accommodation*. Berkeley: University of California Press, 1968, 1975
Lindberg, L. et al. (Eds.): *Stress and Contradiction in Modern Capitalism*. London: Lexington Books, 1975
Lindblom, Charles: *Politics and Markets*. NY: Basic Books, 1977
–, "The Science of Muddling Through." *Public Administration Review* 19 (Spring, 1959), pp. 79– 88
–, and David Cohen: *Usable Knowledge: Social Science and Social Problem Solving*. New Haven: Yale University Press, 1979
Lindsay, A. D.: *The Modern Democratic State*. NY: Oxford University Press, 1962, 1943
Lippman, Walter: *Public Opinion*. N. Y.: Macmillan: 1961, 1922
–, *The Public Philosophy*. N. Y.: Mentor/New American Library, 1956
Locke, John, David Hume, and J. J. Rousseau: *Social Contract*. With an introd. by Ernest Barker. London: Oxford, 1960
Long, Norton: "Bureaucracy and Constitutionalism." In Long: *The Polity*. Chicago: Rand McNally, 1962
Lord Halifax (George Savile): *A Rough Draught of a New Model at Sea*. An Essay first written about 1686
Lowi, Theodore: *The End of Liberalism*. NY: W. W. Norton, 1969
Lukács, Georg: *History and Class Consciousness*. London: Merlin Press, 1971
Lynd, Robert: *Knowledge for What?* Princeton: Princeton University Press, 1939
Lynd, Robert S.: "The Sience of Inhuman Relations." *The New Republic* (August 27, 1949)

Machiavelli, Niccolo: *The Prince*. London: Dent, 1935
–, *Discourses on the First Ten Books of Titus Livius*. London: Routledge and Kegan Paul, 1950
MacIver, R. M.: *The Modern State*. Oxford: Oxford University Press, 1926
–, *The Web of Government*. Glencoe: Free Press, 1947
MacIver, R. M.: *The Web of Government*. Glencoe: Free Press, 1947

Macpherson, C. B.: *Democratic Theory*. London: Oxford University Press, 1973
–, *The Life and Times of Liberal Democracy*, N. Y.: Oxford University Press, 1977
–, *The Political Theory of Possessive Individualism*. London: Oxford University Press, 1962
–, *The Real World of Democracy*. Toronto: CBC Publications, 1965
MacRae, J. D. (Ed.): *Consociational Democracy*. Toronto: McClelland and Stewart, 1974
Madison, James: "Federalist 10 & 51". *Federalist Papers*. NY: New American Library, 1961
Maine, Henry J. S.: *Ancient Law, its Connection with the Early History of Society and its Relation to Modern Ideas*. London: Dent, 1960, 1883
–, *Lectures on the Early History of Institutions*, 7th ed. Port Washington, NY: Kennikat Press, 1966, 1883
Maitland, Frederic W.: *The Constitutional History of England*. Cambridge: Cambridge University Press, 1963, 1908
–, *Equity, also the forms of action at common law*. Rev. ed. Cambridge: Cambridge University Press, 1969, 1909
–, and Frederick Pollock: *The History of English Law Before the Time of Edward I*. 2nd ed. Cambridge: Cambridge University Press, 1952, 1898
Mannheim, Karl: *Essays in the Sociology of Knowledge*. London: Routledge and Kegan Paul, 1952
–, *Ideology & Utopia*. Transl. and ed. by Lewis Wirth. London: Routledge, 1954
–, *Man and Society in an Age of Reconstruction*. London: Routledge and Kegan Paul, 1940
Marcuse, Herbert: *One Dimensional Man*. Boston: Beacon Press, 1964
–, Barrington Moore, and Robert P. Wolff: *A Critique of Pure Tolerance*. Boston: Beacon Press, 1965
Marsilius of Padua: *The Defender of Peace. (Defensor Pacis)*. Orig. ed. 1324, transl. with an introd. by Alan Gewirth. NY: Harper and Row, 1967
Martin, Roscoe: *Grass Roots: Rural Democracy in America*. NY: Harper & Row, 1965
Marx, Karl: *The Grundrisse*. Compl. Engl. Ed. Transl. with a foreword by Martin Nicolaus. Harmondsworth: Penguin, 1973
Mayo, Elton: *The Human Problems of an Industrial Civilization*. Cambridge, Mass: Harvard Business School, 1933
McConnell, Grant: *Private Power and American Democracy*. NY: Alfred Knopf, 1965
McCoy, Charles A., and John Playford (Eds.): *Apolitical Politics*. A critique of behaviouralism. NY: Thomas Crowell, 1967
McHugh, Peter, Stanley Raffel, Daniel Foss, and Alan Blum: *On the Beginning of Social Inquiry*. London: Routledge, 1974
McIlwain, Charles H.: *Constitutionalism and the Changing World*. Cambridge: Cambridge University Press, 1939
Merriam, Charles: *Political Power*. NY: MacGraw Hill, 1934
Merton, Robert: "Manifest & Latent Functions." In Merton: *Social Theory & Social Structure*. 2nd ed. NY: Macmillan, 1957, pp. 19–84

Meynaud, Jean: "The Executive in the Modern State." *International Social Science Bulletin.* Vol. 10, No. 2 (1958)
–, *Technocracy.* London: Faber & Faber, 1965
Michels, Robert: *Political Parties: A Sociological Study of the Oligarchical Tendencies of Modern Democracy.* NY: Collier Books, 1962
Midgely, Mary: *Beast and Man: the Roots of Human Nature.* London: Methuen, 1979
Milgram, Stanley: "Some Conditions of Obedience and Disobedience to Authority." *Human Relations* 18 (1965), pp. 57–76
–, *Obedience to Authority: An Experimental View.* NY: Harper & Row, 1974
Mill, John Stuart: *Representative Government.* NY: Everyman edition, 1953
Miller, A. V.: *Hegel's Concept of Nature.* Oxford: Basil Blackwell, 1970
Mills, C. Wright: *The Power Elite.* NY: Oxford University Press, 1956
–, *Power, Politics and People.* NY: Oxford University Press, 1963
–, *The Sociological Imagination.* NY: Grove Press, 1959
Montesquieu, C. L. de Secondat: *The Spirit of the Laws.* Fr. ed. 1748. NY: Hafner Publishing Co., 1959
Moore, Barrington: *Political Power and Social Theory.* Cambridge, Mass: Harvard University Press, 1958
–, *Reflections on the Causes of Human Misery.* Boston: Beacon Press, 1973
Moore, Dorathy: *Juvenile Justice.* Masters thesis in the Interdisciplinary Studies programme. York University, Toronto, April, 1981
Moore, G. E.: *Principia Ethica.* London: Cambridge University Press, 1903
Moore-Milroy, Beth: *Criticism and the Plausible Plan: Theory and Method.* Ph. D. diss. in the School of Community and Regional Planning. University of British Columbia, April, 1981
Morgan, Elaine: *Falling Apart. The Rise and Decline of Urban Civilization.* London: Abacus Books, 1978
Morgan, Gareth (Ed.): *Beyond Method: Strategies for Social Research.* Los Angeles: Russel/Sage, 1983
Morris, Van C.: *Deaning: Middle Management in Academe.* Urbana: University of Illinois Press, 1981
Müller, Claus: "Notes on the Repression of Communicative Behaviour." *Recent Sociology.* No. 2. Ed. by H. P. Dreitzel. NY: Macmillan, 1970, pp. 101–114 and pp. 115–148
–, *The Politics of Communication.* A study in the political sociology of language, socialization and legitimation. NY: Oxford University Press, 1973
Müller, Herbert: *The Uses of the Past: Profiles of Former Societies,* NY: Oxford University Press, 1957, 1952

Nelkin, Dorothy: *Technological Decisions and Democracy: European Experiments in Public Participation.* Beverly Hills, California: Russell Sage, 1977
Neumann, Franz: *Behemoth: The Structure and Practice of National Socialism, 1933–1944.* NY: Oxford University Press, 1944
–, *The Democratic and Authoritarian State.* NY: Macmillan, 1957
Nisbet, Robert: "Conservatism and Sociology." *American Journal of Sociology* 58 (1952), pp. 167–175

Niskanen, William: *Bureaucracy and Representative Government.* Chicago: Aldine Press, 1971
Noble, David: *America by Design.* NY: Oxford University Press, 1977

Oakeshott, Michael: *Rationalism in Politics.* London: Methuen, 1962
Olson, Mancur: *The Logic of Collective Action.* Cambridge, Mass: Harvard University Press, 1962
–, *The Rise and Decline of Nations.* New Haven: Yale University Press, 1982
O'Neill, John: "Defamilization and the Feminization of Law in Early and Late Capitalism." *International Journal of Law & Psychiatry.* Vol. 5, No. 3/4 (1983)
–, "The Hobbesian Problem in Parsons and Marx". In O'Neill: *Sociology as a Skin Trade.* London: Heinemann, 1972, pp. 177–208
–, "Scientism, Historicism and the Problem of Rationality." Introd. to *Modes of Individualism and Collectivism.* Ed. by John O'Neill. London: Heinemann, 1973
Ophuls, William: *Ecology and the Politics of Scarcity.* San Francisco: W. H. Freeman, 1977

Parsons, Talcott: *The Social System.* NY: Macmillan, 1951
Perrow, Charles: *Complex Organization.* NY: McGraw Hill, 1972
–, "A Framework for the Comparative Analysis of Organizations." *American Sociological Review* 32 (1967), pp. 194–208
Perry, Charner M. (Ed.): *The Philosophy of American Democracy.* Port Washington, NY: Kennikat Press, 1971, 1943
Peter, Laurence: *The Peter Principle.* NY: Morrow, 1969
Pieper, Josef: *The Four Cardinal Virtues.* Indianappolis: Notre Dame Press, 1966
Pitkin, Hanna F.: *The Concept of Representation.* Berkeley: University of California Press, 1967
–, "Obligation and Consent." *American Political Science Review* 59 (December, 1965), pp. 990–999 and 60 (March, 1966), pp. 39–52
–, *Wittgenstein and Justice.* Berkeley: University of California Press, 1972
Plamenatz, John P.: *Consent, Freedom and Political Obligation.* 2nd ed. London: Oxford University Press, 1968
–, *Democracy and Illusion:* An examination of certain aspects of modern democratic theory. London: Longmans, 1973
Plato: *The Laws.* Transl. with an introd. by Trevor J. Saunders. Harmondsworth: Penguin 1970
Plato: *The Republic.* Transl. with an introd. by H. D. P. Lee. Harmondsworth: Penguin, 1955
Plato: *The Statesman (Politicus).* Transl. by J. B. Skemp and ed. and introd. by M. Ostwald. NY: Liberal Arts Press, 1957
–, *Plato's Republic.* Transl. with an introd. by F. M. Cornford. London: Routledge and Kegan Paul, 1941
Podgorecki, Adam: *Practical Social Sciences.* London: Routledge, 1975
Polanyi, Michael: *The Logic of Liberty.* London: Routledge and Kegan Paul, 1951
–, "The Republic of Science." *Minerva* 1 (1962), pp. 54–73

Pollock, Frederick: *An Introduction to the History of the Science of Politics*. New rev. ed. London: Macmillan, 1912, 1922

Popper, Karl: *The Poverty of Historicism*. London: Routledge & Kegan Paul, 1957

Porter, John: *The Vertical Mosaic*. Toronto: University of Toronto Press, 1965

Pound, Roscoe: *The Spirit of the Common Law*. Boston: Beacon Press, 1963, 1921

Pressman, Jeffrey, and Aaron Wildavsky: *Implementation*. Berkeley: University of California Press, 1975

Presthus, Robert: *Behavioural Approaches to Public Administration*. University, Alabama: University of Alabama Press, 1968

–, *Elite Accommodation in Canadian Politics*. London: Cambridge University Press, 1973

–, *Elites in the Policy Process*. London: Cambridge University Press, 1974

–, *"Evolution and Canadian Political Culture: The Politics of Accommodation"*. Paper read to the Conference on Revolution and Evolution, Duke University, October 12–14, 1976

–, *The Organizational Society*. 2nd rev. ed. NY: St. Martins Press, 1978, 1962

Pufendorf, Samuel: *De Jure Naturae et Gentium*. 1672. Engl. transl. by Basil Kennet. London: n. p., 1710

Raffel, Stanley: *Matters of Fact*. London: Routledge, 1979

Reiss, Albert J.: "Research on Administrative Discretion and Justice." *Journal of Legal Education* 23, (1971), pp. 69–76

Revel, Jean Francois: *The Totalitarian Temptation*. Garden City, NY: Doubleday and Co., 1977

Riemer, Neal: *The Revival of Democratic Theory*. NY: Meredith Publishing Co., 1962

Ross, W. D.: *Aristotle: A Complete Exposition of his Works & Thought*. NY: Meridian, 1959

Rourke, Francis, Van C. Morris and Glenn Brooks: *The Managerial Revolution in Higher Education*. Baltimore: John Hopkins, 1966

Rousseau, Jean Jacques: *Discourse on the Origins and Foundation of Inequality*. NY: St. Martins Press, 1964

–, *Discourse on the Sciences and Arts*. NY: St. Martins Press, 1964

–, *The Political Writings of Jean Jacques Rousseau*. 2 Vols. Ed. by C. E. Vaughn. London: Cambridge University Press, 1915

Rule, James B.: *Insight and Social Betterment*. NY: Oxford University Press, 1978

Runciman, W. G.: *Relative Deprivation and Social Justice*. London: Routledge and Kegan Paul, 1966

–, *Social Science and Political Theory*. London: Cambridge University Press, 1965

Russell, Bertrand: *Human Society in Ethics and Politics*. NY: New American Library, 1962, 1952

–, *Power: A New Social Analysis*. NY: W. W. Norton, 1938

Sabine, George: *History of Political Theory*. NY: Henry Holt, 1937

Salomon, Albert: *The Tyranny of Progess: Reflections on the Origins of Sociology*. NY: Noonday Press, 1955

Sartori, Giovanni: *Democratic Theory*. NY: Frederick Praeger, 1965
Savile, George (Lord Halifax): *The Character of a Trimmer*. In Savile: *Complete Works*. Oxford: Clarendon Press, 1912
Schattschneider, E. E.: *The Semi-Sovereign People*. NY: Holt, Rinehart & Winston, 1960
Schelling, Thomas: "On the Ecology of Micromotives." *The Public Interest* 25 (Fall, 1971), pp. 59–98
Schmidt, Alfred: *The Concept of Nature in Marx*. London: New Left Books, 1971
Schubert, Glendon: *The Public Interest*. Glencoe: Free Press, 1959
Schumpeter, Joseph: *Capitalism, Socialism and Democracy*. NY: Harper and Row, 1942
Schur, Edwin: *The Awareness Trap: Self-Absorption instead of Social Change*. NY: Quadrangle Books, 1976
Schutz, Alfred: *Collected Papers*. 3 Vols. The Hague: Martinus Nijhoff, 1962, 1964, 1967
–, *Phenomenology of the Social World*. Evanston, Ill.: Northwestern University Press, 1967
–, "The Problem of Rationality in the Social World." *Collected Papers, Volume Two*. Ed. and introd. by Arvid Brodersen. The Hague: Martinus Nijhoff, 1964, pp. 64–88
Schwartz, Bernard: *The Code Napoleon and the Common Law World*. NY: New York University Press, 1956
–, and H. W. R. Wade: *The Legal Control of Governments*. Oxford: Clarendon Press, 1972
Schwayder, David: *The Stratification of Behaviour*. London: Routledge and Kegan Paul, 1965
Scott, Andrew M. (Ed.): *Political Thought in America*. NY: Holt, Rinehart and Winston, 1959
Sennett, Richard: *The Uses of Disorder*. Harmondsworth: Penguin, 1970
–, *The Fall of Public Man*. NY: Alfred Knopf, 1977
Simon, Herbert: *Administrative Behaviour*. 2nd ed. Glencoe: Free Press, 1957
Simon, Yves, R.: *Philosophy of Democratic Government*. Chicago: University of Chicago Press, 1951
Skinner, B. F.: *Beyond Freedom and Dignity*. NY: Alfred Knopf, 1971
Smelser, Neil: *Theory of Collective Behaviour*. NY: Free Press, 1962
Smiley, Donald V.: *Canada in Question*. Toronto: McGraw Hill/Ryerson, 1980
Smith, Adam: *The Theory of Moral Sentiments*. Engl. ed. 1759. NY: Augustus Kelley, 1966
Smith, Howard R.: *Democracy and the Public Interest*. Athens: University of Georgia Press, 1960
Social Research. Vol. 44, No. 1 (Spring 1977), "Hannah Arendt".
Somit, Albert, and Joseph Tannenhaus: *American Political Science: Profile of a Discipline*. NY: Atherton Press, 1964
–, *The Development of Political Science*. Boston: Allyn and Bacon, 1967
Sowell, Thomas: *Knowledge and Decisions*. NY: Basic Books, 1980
Stankiewicz, W. J. (Ed.): *In Defense of Sovereignty*. London: Oxford University Press, 1969

Steiner, Joseph: "Judicial Discretion." *Cambridge Law Journal*. Vol. 35, No. 1 (April 1976), pp 135–157

Stephen, Leslie: *Hobbes*. Ann Arbor: University of Michigan Press, 1961, 1904

Storing, Herbert (Ed.): *Essays on the Scientific Study of Politics*. NY: Holt, Rinehart and Winston, 1962

Strauss, Leo: *The Political Philosophy of Hobbes*. Chicago: University of Chicago Press, 1952

Subramaniam, V. A.: "Fact and Value in Decision-Making." *Public Administration Review* 23 (December 1963), pp. 232–237

–, "Representative Bureaucracy: A Reassessment." *American Political Science Review* 61 (1962), pp. 1010–1019

Swabey, Marie C.: *Theory of the Democratic State*. Cambridge, Mass: Harvard University Press, 1937

Tarde, Gabriel: *Laws of Imitation*. NY: Henry Holt, 1903

Taylor, Charles: *The Pattern of Politics*. Toronto: McClelland and Stewart, 1970

Taylor, Harold: *Students without Teachers*. NY: McGraw Hill, 1969

Thomas, Alan: "Audience, Market, Public: An Evaluation of Canadian Broadcasting." University of British Columbia, Dept. of University Extension, *Occasional Paper 7* (April, 1960)

Thompson, James: *Organizations in Action*. NY: McGraw Hill, 1968

Thompson, Victor: *Bureaucracy and Innovation*. University, Alabama: University of Alabama Press, 1968

–, *Modern Organization*. NY: Alfred Knopf, 1961

Thorson, Thomas Landon: *The Logic of Democracy*. NY: Holt, Rinehart and Winston, 1962

Tigar, Michael: *Law and the Rise of Capitalism*. NY: Monthly Review Press, 1977

Tiger, Lionel: *Optimism: The Biology of Hope*. London: Secker and Warburg, 1979

Toulmin, Stephen: *The Place of Reason in Ethics*. London: Cambridge University Press, 1961

Trudeau, P. E.: *Approaches to Politics,* Toronto: Oxford University Press, 1970

–, *Federalism and the French Canadians*. Toronto: Oxford University Press, 1961

–, "Technology, the Individual and the Party." *Living in the Seventies*. Ed. by Allen M. Linden. Toronto: Peter Martin Associates Ltd. 1970, pp. 1–7

Truman, David: *The Governmental Process*. NY: Alfred Knopf, 1951

Tussman, Joseph: *Obligation and the Body Politic*. NY: Oxford University Press, 1960

Tyndal, C. R.: *You and Your local Government*. Toronto: Ontario Municipal Management Development Board, 1982

Van Dyke, Vernon: *Political Science: A Philosophical Analysis*. Stanford: Stanford University Press, 1960

Van Loon, Richard, and Michael S. Whittington: *The Canadian Political System*. 3rd ed. Toronto: McGraw Hill/Ryerson, 1981

Veblen, Thorstein: *The Higher Learning in America*. Boston: Huebsch, 1918

Voegelin, Eric: *The New Science of Politics*. Chicago: University of Chicago Press, 1952
–, *Order and History*. Baton Rouge: Louisiana State University Press, 1956
–, *Science, Politics and Gnosticism: Two Essays*. Chicago: Henry Regnery Co., 1968
Vygotsky, Lev Semenovich: *Thought and Language*. Ed. and transl. by Eugenia Hoffmann and Gertude Vakar. Cambridge, Mass: MIT Press, 1962, 1937

Wasserstrom, Richard: *The Judicial Decision*. Stanford: Stanford University Press, 1961
Weber, Max: *The City*. NY: Free Press/Macmillan, 1958
–, *Law in Economy & Society*. Cambridge: Harvard University Press, 1954
–, "Politics as a Vocation". In: *From Max Weber*. Ed. by Hans Gerth and C. Wright Mills. NY: Oxford University Press, 1946, pp. 77–128
–, *The Protestant Ethic and the Spirit of Capitalism*. NY: Charles Scribners, 1958
–, *Theory of Social & Economic Organization*. Glencoe: Free Press, 1947
Weick, Karl: "Educational Organizations as Loosely Coupled Systems". *Administrative Science Quarterly* 21 (1976), pp. 1–19
Weldon, T. D.: *States and Morals*. NY: McGraw Hill, 1947
Wenglinsky, Martin: "Review of Milgram's Obedience to Authority." *Contemporary Sociology: A Review of Reviews*. (1975), pp. 613–617
Wheare, K. C.: *Federal Government*. London: Oxford University Press, 1958, 1946
Wilensky, Harold: *Organizational Intelligence*. NY: Basic Books, 1967
Wiles, Peter: "The Necessity and Impossibility of Political Economy." *History and Theory* 11 (1972), pp. 3–14
Wills, Garry: *Inventing America: Jefferson's Declaration of Independence*. Garden City, NY: Doubleday and Co., 1978
–, *Explaining America: the Federalist*. Garden City, NY: Doubleday and Co., 1981
Wilson, H. T.: "Academic Bureaucracy," *Queens Quarterly*. Vol. 78, No. 3 (Autumn 1971), pp. 343–352
–, *The Academy and its Clients: Conflicting Perspectives on the Contemporary University*. Report to the Commission on Relations between Universities and Governments. Ottawa, 1970
–, *The American Ideology*. London: Routledge, 1977
–, "Continentalism and Canadian Higher Education." *Canadian Review of American Studies*. Vol. 1, No. 2 (Fall, 1970), pp. 89–99
–, "Critical Theory's Critique of Social Science: Episodes in a Changing Problematic from Adorno to Habermas." *History of European Ideas*. (forthcoming)
–, "Discretion and Administrative Process." *Osgoode Hall Law Journal*. Vol. 10, No. 3 (Autumn, 1972), pp. 117–139
–, "Elites, Meritocracy and Technocracy: Some Implications for Political Leadership." *Political Leadership in Canada*. Ed. by Hector Massey. (forthcoming)
–, "Functional Rationality and 'Sense of Function': the Case of an Ideological Distortion". *International Yearbook of Organization Studies 1980*. Ed. by Graeme Salaman and David Dunkerly. London: Routledge, 1981, pp. 37–61
–, "Innovation: The Practical Uses of Theory". *Social Change, Innovation and Pol-*

itics in East Asia. Ed. by Y. S. Yim, H. T. Wilson, and R. W. Wilson. Hong Kong: Asian Research Centre, 1980, pp. 9–29

–, *Knowledge and Totality:* A Critical Analysis of the Causal Principle in Science and Life. (Unpubl. manuscript)

–, "Max Weber's Pessimism." *International Journal of Contemporary Sociology* 8 (April, 1971), pp. 183–188

–, "The Meaning and Significance of 'Empirical Method' for the Critical Theory of Society." *Canadian Journal of Political and Social Theory.* Vol. 3, No. 3 (Fall, 1979), pp. 57–68

–, "Notes on the Achievement of Communicative Behaviour and Related Difficulties." *Dialectical Anthropology.* (forthcoming)

–, "The Paradox of Liberalism." *Philosophy of the Social Sciences.* Vol. 10, No. 2 (June, 1980), pp. 215–226

–, "The Poverty of Sociology: "Society" as Concept and Object in Sociological Theory". *Philosophy of the Social Sciences.* Vol. 8, No. 1 (March, 1978), pp. 187–204

–, "The Problem of Discretion in Three Languages." Research document. Judiciary Project, University of Paris, March 1980

–, "Rationality & Decision in Administrative Science." *Canadian Journal of Political Science.* Vol. 6, No. 3 (June, 1973), pp. 271–294

–, "Reading Max Weber: The Limits of Sociology." *Sociology.* Vol. 10, No. 2 (May, 1976), pp. 297–315

–, *The Regulation of Standard Radio Broadcasting, 1934–1952: Defining the Public Interest Through Licensing Policies.* Ph. D. diss. in the Dept. of Political Science. Rutgers University, January 1968. Ann Arbor, Michigan: University Microfilms, 1968

–, "Science, Critique & Criticism: The 'Open Society' Revisited," *On Critical Theory.* Ed. by John O'Neill. NY: Seabury Press, 1976, pp. 205–230

–, "Science, Technology & Innovation: The Role of Commonsense Capacities." *Methodology and Science.* Vol. 15, No. 3 (Fall, 1982), pp. 167–200

–, "Social Science and Social Change." (Unpubl. research paper)

–, "The Sociology of Apocalypse: Jacques Ellul's Reformation of Reformation Thought". *Human Context* 8, (Fall, 1975). pp. 274–294

–, "Technocracy and Late Capitalist Society: Remarks on the Problem of Rationality and Social Organization," *The State, Class and the Recession.* Ed. by Stewart Clegg, Geoff Dow and Paul Boreham. London: Croom Helm, 1983, pp. 152–238

–, "Technological Politics: Some Canadian/American Dimensions". Paper presented to the Canadian Political Science Association. Montreal: June, 1972

–, "Technology and/as/or the Future." *Philosophy of the Social Sciences* 14. (forthcoming)

–, *Tradition & Innovation: The Idea of Civilization as Culture and its Significance.* London: Routledge & Kegan Paul, 1984

–, "Values: On the Possibility of a Convergence between Economic and Non-Economic Decision-Making," *Management under Differing Value Systems.* Ed. by Gunther Dlugos and Klaus Weiermair. Berlin: Walter de Gruyter, 1981, pp. 37–71

Wolff, Robert P.: *The Poverty of Liberalism*. Boston: Beacon Press, 1968
–, *The Ideal of the University*. Boston: Beacon Press, 1969
Wolin, Sheldon: *Politics & Vision*. Boston: Little Brown, 1960
Wormuth, Francis D.: "Aristotle on Law". *Essays in Political Theory*. Ed. by Milton
  Konvitz and Arthur Murphy. Ithaca: Cornell University Press, 1948, pp. 45–61

Young, Michael: *The Rise of the Meritocracy, 1858–2033*. Harmondsworth: Penguin,
  1958
Young, Roland (Ed.): *Approaches to the Study of Politics*. Evanston, Ill.: Northwestern University Press, 1958

Zijderveld, Anton: *The Abstract Society*. Garden City, NY: Doubleday Anchor,
  1970
Ziman, John: *Public Knowledge: An Essay Concerning the Social Dimension of
  Science*. London: Cambridge University, Press, 1968
Znaniecki, Florian: *The Social Role of the Man of Knowledge*. NY: Columbia Uni-

Name Index

Subject Index

Action, 7, 13, 83, 86, 146, 198, 200, 208, 209, 254, 255, 262–266, 270, 271, 273, 274, 276, 277, 282.

Agency (Agent), 21, 47, 53, 54, 60, 61, 71, 73, 90, 114, 117, 118, 139, 193–199, 201, 202, 204, 205, 207–209, 211, 214–216, 226, 237, 240, 254–256, 258, 264, 271, 274, 281, 284, 285.

Athens, 6, 14.

Behaviouralism, 58, 128–138.

Body Politic (Constitution), 11, 18, 53.

Bureaucracy, 35, 36, 38, 43, 46–48, 52, 55, 56, 60, 62, 64, 73, 75, 77, 79, 81–83, 86–88, 95, 96, 101, 104, 110, 115–118, 125, 131, 132, 136, 144, 148, 155, 167, 169, 170, 175, 178–180, 183, 188, 205, 227, 233, 237, 254, 260, 267, 275, 276, 281–283.

Bureaucratic Representation, 87, 88, 100, 103, 104, 111, 255, 284.

Capitalism, 27, 28, 29, 30, 32, 35, 36, 43, 70, 74–76, 79, 83, 90, 96, 99, 134, 170, 171, 203, 204, 206–208, 210–212, 224, 225, 233, 247, 257, 260, 265, 268, 276–278, 289.

Career, 32, 33, 34, 138, 167, 168, 182, 185, 224, 246, 253, 254, 256, 259, 266, 267, 282, 283.

Citizenship (Citizen), 1, 2, 3, 10, 11, 13, 14, 15–21, 25, 30, 31, 33, 36, 38, 39, 41, 43, 45, 59, 69, 71, 73, 80–82, 84, 86–90, 94, 95, 99, 105, 106, 108–110, 112–114, 118, 124, 128, 132, 137, 139, 149, 150, 154, 156, 161, 169, 184, 187, 189, 193–209, 211, 212, 214–219, 224, 225, 227, 229–231, 234, 237, 240–242, 246, 249, 250, 253–259,

263, 265–268, 270–272, 274–276, 278–285.

City, 18, 27, 32, 62, 83, 193, 217.

City State (Polis), 5, 8, 12, 14, 15–17, 18, 19, 21, 23, 41–43, 62, 69, 128, 193, 195, 234, 268, 279.

Class, 243, 244, 245, 249.

Consensus, 1, 2, 38, 108, 152, 195, 198, 271.

Consent, 42, 203.

Constituency, 45, 54, 105–107, 109, 193–194, 202, 213–219.

Constitutions, 55, 74, 96–98, 100, 117, 125, 216, 246.

Contract, 206, 233, 235, 236, 285.

Cooperation, 41, 64, 81, 197, 201, 277, 278.

Corporatism, 94–96.

Decision-Making, 1, 3, 78, 90, 114, 117, 124, 127, 129, 132, 133, 139, 178, 208, 224, 238, 239, 241, 284.

Delegation, 19, 60, 102, 103, 110–114, 117, 118, 195, 206, 210, 214–216, 227, 239, 241, 354, 255, 281.

Democracy, 1, 8, 9, 18, 20, 24, 53, 56, 70, 77, 80, 88, 89, 94, 95, 100, 101, 103, 109, 114, 116, 117, 124, 133, 139, 194, 196, 197, 207, 209, 214, 216–219, 224, 226, 228, 231, 236, 238–240, 242–245, 253, 255, 258, 270, 280–282, 285.

Democratic Elitism, 207, 237, 243–245, 272.

Disciplined Observation, 73–77, 79, 84, 127, 133, 135, 137, 143–145, 148, 152, 160, 229, 259–262, 264, 265, 267, 269, 272, 273.

Discretion, 54, 88, 89, 93, 94, 96, 98–106, 109–113, 115, 117, 119, 127, 183, 184, 210, 212–214, 223, 254, 255, 259, 278, 281.

Display, 17, 32, 59, 69, 73, 83, 85,

Organization-based Conception of
Membership, 179, 180.
Organizational Principle, 54, 75, 78,
79, 83, 86, 87, 125, 174, 184, 215,
242, 247, 256, 280, 284.

Participation, 2, 5, 11, 45, 49, 52,
58–61, 80, 88, 89, 90, 106, 109, 110,
112, 116, 118, 124, 126, 127, 128,
137, 139, 145, 146, 150, 155,
156–158, 174, 184, 186, 188, 189,
193, 205, 209, 214, 230, 239, 241,
242, 244, 249, 253–255, 259, 260,
263, 264, 283, 285, 290.
Peter Principle, 248.
Place, 264, 282.
Political Management, 1, 3, 5, 7, 25,
43, 63–65, 93, 94, 116, 139, 143,
144, 150, 156, 161, 165, 188–190,
225, 226, 231, 232, 236, 237, 239,
242, 246, 249, 253, 256, 258–262,
265, 267–269, 271, 272, 276, 278,
284, 285, 289.
Political Parties, 2, 41, 45, 54–56, 60,
77, 82, 88, 90, 99, 101, 104, 105,
106, 107, 108, 109, 110, 115, 116,
118, 119, 208, 210–216, 218, 219,
247, 281.
Political Science, 8, 11, 12, 14, 16, 20,
23, 42, 50–52, 57–60, 64, 71, 73, 85,
87, 88, 123, 124, 128, 129, 130, 131,
132, 133, 134, 135, 136, 137, 138,
139, 143, 154, 159, 199, 200, 202,
206, 208, 243, 244, 246, 247, 249,
269, 270, 279, 282.
Politics, 1, 2, 3, 5, 6, 7, 8, 12, 13, 14,
16, 17, 18, 27, 37–43, 46, 47, 49,
51–54, 56, 57, 59, 60, 63–65, 69, 73,
74, 77, 78, 81–86, 88, 89, 93, 94,
96, 99–101, 103–105, 108, 112, 113,
115–118, 123, 124, 126–129, 131,
132, 135–138, 143, 152, 154, 155,
159, 161, 165, 174, 176, 184, 185,
193–197, 200–202, 204, 206–211,
215, 216, 218, 219, 223–226, 229,
230, 233, 236–243, 249, 253–257,
259, 262–264, 266, 268–272,

274–276, 278–282, 284, 285, 289,
290.
Polity, 8–10, 13, 14, 15, 18, 19–21, 31,
40, 42, 55, 59, 69, 93, 96, 117, 143,
152, 154, 155, 156, 159, 161, 196,
219, 279, 281, 284, 285.
Popular Sovereignty, 50, 101, 207,
210, 219, 236, 284.
Possibility, 11, 14, 19, 50, 53, 65, 66,
70, 86, 88, 90, 134, 196, 201,
204–206, 208, 213, 214, 219, 230,
232, 235, 236, 241, 260, 261,
268–270, 272–277, 281, 282, 284,
285, 289.
Postulate of Adequacy, 145.
Practical, 6, 7, 16, 18, 24, 25, 39, 53,
58, 59, 123, 124, 129, 130, 132–135,
137, 138, 147, 168, 170, 171, 182, 189,
193, 199, 207, 229, 231, 253, 254, 258,
261, 269, 273, 279, 282, 284, 285.
Practice, 5, 11, 13, 14, 16, 17, 19, 25,
28, 37, 40, 52, 55, 59, 78, 102, 127,
128, 129, 130, 131, 132, 133, 135,
138, 144, 148, 149, 150, 151, 194,
195, 197, 215, 217, 231, 249,
253–255, 260–262, 264, 269,
272–274, 278, 282, 284.
Problem-solving, 3, 61, 229, 231, 257,
258, 260, 266.
Process, 1, 3, 9, 10, 13, 23–25, 36, 46,
53, 56, 69, 77–79, 82, 84, 87, 89,
90, 98, 108, 109, 111, 114, 115, 116,
117, 118, 119, 125, 134, 143, 149,
154, 196, 198, 199, 203, 208–210,
217–219, 223–230, 236–243, 246,
249, 250, 253, 254, 255, 259, 260,
262–265, 269, 270, 272–275,
277–280, 284, 285, 289.
Property (see Stewardship), 19.
Public Sector, 30, 31, 32, 37, 55, 82,
96, 115, 132, 154, 178, 255, 259.
Public Sphere, 1, 2, 3, 13, 18, 19, 36,
42, 88, 89, 90, 91, 139, 155, 254,
259, 260, 285.

Rational Domination, 76, 80, 84, 148,
149, 155–158, 160, 175, 197, 200,

de Gruyter Studies in Organization

An international series by internationally known authors presenting current research in organization.

Organizing and organizations are pre-requisites for the viability and future developments of society. Their study and comprehension are indispensable to the quality of human life. Therefore, this series aims to:
- present to the specialist subject matter and information on significant problems, research methods and research results;
- give interested individuals access to different subject areas;
- aid decision-making on contemporary problems;
- stimulate ideas for the future modes of behaviour and research.

The series will include monographs, collections of contributed papers, and handbooks.

The Japanese Industrial System
By *Charles J. McMillan*
1984. 15,5 × 23 cm. 356 pages. Cloth. DM 88,–
ISBN 3 11 008894 0

Forthcoming Titles:

Limits to Bureaucratic Growth
By *Marshall W. Meyer*
1984. 15,5 × 23 cm. Approx. 300 pages. Cloth approx. DM 88,–
ISBN 3 11 009865 2

Guidance, Control and Evaluation in the Public Sector
Edited by *F. X. Kaufmann, G. Majone, V. Ostrom*
1985. 15,5 × 23 cm. Approx. 840 pages. Cloth approx. DM 198,–
ISBN 3 11 009707 9

Management in China
By *Olivia Laaksonen*
1985. 15,5 × 23 cm. Approx. 290 pages. Cloth approx. DM 88,–
ISBN 3 11 009958 6

Prices are subject to change without notice

WALTER DE GRUYTER · BERLIN · NEW YORK

ORGANIZATION STUDIES

A quarterly supranational journal
now in its 5th year of publication

Editor-in-Chief: David J. Hickson, University of Bradford, England

Co-Editor: Alfred Kieser, University of Mannheim, West Germany

Editorial Board Members from Australia, Belgium, Britain, Canada, Denmark, France, Israel, Italy, Japan, The Netherlands, Norway, Sweden, U.S.A., West Germany.

Some recent papers: *Oiva Laaksonen* (Finland): The Management Structure of Chinese Enterprises during and after the Cultural Revolution, with Empirical Data Comparing Chinese and European Enterprises. *Yvan Allaire & Mihaela Firsirotu* (Canada): Theories of Organizational Culture. *Bilha Mannheim* (Israel): Managerial Orientations and Workers' Job Responses in Labour-Owned and Private Industrial Plants in Israel. *Gibson Burrell* (Britain): Sex in Organizational Analysis. *Gordon Redding and Michael Ng* (HongKong): The Role of 'Face' In the Organizational Perceptions of Chinese Managers. *Lex Donaldson* (Australia): Divisionalization and Size: A Theoretical and Empirical Critique. *Anna-Jutta Pietsch* (West Germany): Interactions Between the Educational and Employment Systems in the German Democratic Republic and the Soviet Union. *Stephen McNamee* (U.S.A.): Capital Accumulation and the Du Pont Company: An Historical Analysis. *Behlul Usdiken* (Turkey): Interorganizational Linkages Among Similar Organizations in Turkey. *Giuseppi Bonazzi* (Italy): Scapegoating in Complex Organizations: The Results of a Comparative Study of Symbolic Blame-Giving in Italian and French Public Administration. *Ad Teulings* (The Netherlands): Interlocking Interests and Collaboration With the Enemy: Corporate Behaviour in the Second World War.

Subscription rates 1985 Per volume of four issues. Libraries and institutions **DM 108,–**/approx. US $ 38.75. Individuals (except FRG and Switzerland) **DM 54,–**/ approx. US $ 19.25 (DM-Prices are definitive, $-prices are approximate and subject to fluctuations in the exchange rate).

Published in collaboration with the European Group for Organizational Studies (EGOS) and the Maison des Sciences de l'Homme, Paris by

WALTER DE GRUYTER · BERLIN · NEW YORK

Verlag Walter de Gruyter & Co., Genthiner Straße 13, D-1000 Berlin 30, Tel.: (0 30) 2 60 05-0
Walter de Gruyter, Inc., 200 Saw Mill River Road, Hawthorne, N. Y. 10532, Tel.: (914) 747-0110